WHO'S·WHO
IN·CLASSICAL
MYTHOLOGY

WHO'S·WHO
IN·CLASSICAL
MYTHOLOGY

ADRIAN ROOM

GRAMERCY BOOKS
NEW YORK

For Peter Gamble

Even greater caution is required in the application of *etymology* to this subject. If applied judiciously it will give most valuable results, and prove, in fact, to be the master-key of mythology; if under no guidance but that of caprice and fancy, it will become the parent of all sorts of monsters and *lusus naturae.*

(Thomas Keightley, *Classical Mythology*)

CONTENTS

INTRODUCTION

Many of the most familiar names of classical mythology have long been firmly rooted in our literary consciousness, where they usually rank on a popular par with Biblical figures (especially those of the Old Testament) and the more memorable characters in Shakespeare's plays. As such, they occur and re-occur fairly predictably in the more challenging word games and contests, in the crossword puzzles and acrostics of the more serious daily newspapers, and, on a more constructive basis, in such school subjects as English and classical studies.

We have all thus heard how Theseus killed the Minotaur, how Romulus and Remus were suckled by a wolf with Romulus going on to found Rome, how Hercules heroically tackled his twelve Labours (even if we should not care to enumerate them), and how Actaeon saw Diana bathing naked and was set upon by his hounds for such gross impropriety.

Many of the names have passed into the English language either as phrases or as ordinary words, so that we talk or read of someone's 'Achilles' heel', of falling 'between Scylla and Charybdis', of carrying out a 'Sisyphean labour' or a 'Herculean task' and of being (after such strenuous efforts) 'safe in the arms of Morpheus'. Among the many words that derive from the names of mythological characters, even though we may often forget this, are 'siren', 'tantalise', 'chaotic', 'erotic', 'python', 'aphrodisiac', 'atlas', 'titanic', 'saturnine', 'hectoring', 'stentorian' and 'floral', among others.

And the stories featuring these characters continue to live, of course. Apart from the original accounts, which are retold in various literary forms ranging from scholarly translations of the *Odyssey* or the *Iliad* to modern adaptations and 'prettified' re-hashes (intended for little children who are actually much more worldly-wise than the storytellers suspect), we have a wealth of derivative material in the many plays, operas, poems and novels that enshrine the names. We have Shakespeare's *A Midsummer Night's Dream* and Handel's *Acis and Galatea*, Keats's *Endymion* and James Joyce's *Ulysses*. Through these and countless other literary and musical

1

works, in many European languages, we have heard and read of King Oedipus, Helen of Troy, Philemon and Baucis, Orpheus and Eurydice, and Proserpine in the Underworld. In the world of art, too, we have seen and often admired and loved the characters portrayed in many sculptures, paintings and drawings, including the famous Elgin Marbles in the British Museum (with representations of Zeus, Athena, Aphrodite, Artemis, Heracles, Poseidon and Persephone, among others), *Laocoön* in the Vatican Museum, Michelangelo's *Dying Adonis*, Titian's *Bacchus and Ariadne*, Michael Ayrton's *Minotaur*, Bernini's *Apollo and Daphne*, the *Winged Victory of Samothrace* in the Louvre and the many glowing portraits by Sir Edward Burne-Jones and other Pre-Raphaelite painters. The centuries pass, but the interest and influence of the figures remain constant. In 1887 thousands of orders were placed by classically and romantically inclined Englishmen for framed photographs of the three bas-relief panels of Psyche executed that year by the sculptor Harry Bates, Britain's best answer to Rodin. A hundred years later the classical names still flourish, although in new and sometimes incongruous media: the advent of a militaristic and technological age has produced missiles, spacecraft and artificial satellites named 'Poseidon', 'Nike', 'Atlas', 'Apollo', 'Saturn', 'Titan' and 'Gemini', and a commercial and consumer society has promoted 'Ajax' kitchen cleansers, 'Mercury' automobiles, 'Hyperion' Press books, 'Hercules' chemicals, and 'Midas' mufflers. (O mighty Caesar! Dost thou lie so low?) The names have transferred also to centres of habitation. In the United States you can visit Achilles, Va., Apollo, Pa., Argo, Ala., Athena, Fla., Scylla and Charybdis, both also Fla., Juno, Tex., and Venus, W. Va. In London a taxi can take the classically inclined visitor to Juno Way (SE14), Neptune Street (SE16), Orpheus Street (SE5), Achilles Road (NW6), Ceres Road (SE18), Pegasus Place (SE11) and either or both of the two Endymion Roads (SE4 and N4). Even our farm animals and pets assume the ancient names, so that we find cows called Phoebe, cats called Alexander, and tortoises named Achilles. A learned Russian study of farm animal names in Kazakhstan cites a breeding establishment accommodating bulls named Mars, Neptune, Cupid, Bacchus and Zeus and a cow called Venus [G.F. Fel'de, 'Zoonyms of the Tyul'kulbas Region of the Chimkent District', in *The Ethnography of Names*, Moscow 1971].

Two of the most prominent areas to which classical names have long transferred are, of course, those of astronomy and our own personal names. Of the nine planets in the solar system, all except our own Earth have classical names (Mercury, Venus, Mars, Jupiter, Saturn, Uranus, Neptune, Pluto), and many of them have satellites ('moons') that in turn bear mythological names, such as Mars' Phobos and Deimos, Jupiter's Amalthea, Io, Ganymede, Callisto and Pasiphaë (among others), Saturn's Rhea, Titan, Hyperion and Phoebe (of its total of nine) and Neptune's Triton and Nereid. In outer space are the constellations of Perseus, Orion, Gemini, Hydra, Cassiopeia, Pegasus, Centaurus, Argo, Hercules, the Pleiades, and Andromeda, among others. We shall be considering the origin of such names again towards the end of this Introduction (page 11).

Among the thousand-plus classical names entered in this Dictionary, some familiar – and a few less familiar – personal names will be noted. More of them are girls' names than boys', and they include Alexander, Anna, Camilla, Chloë, Daphne, Diana, Doris, Evadne, Hector, Helen, Hermione, Irene, Iris, Jason, Lara, Lavinia, Linda, Pandora, Penelope, Phoebe, Phyllis and Victoria. By no means all of these originated from their mythological namesakes – Linda certainly did not. Even so, in the entries for these names an indication will almost always be given as to the link, direct or indirect, between the classical name and its modern counterpart.

All in all, it is perhaps surprising that not more of the familiar classical names have been adopted as personal names, as have many Biblical and Shakespearean names. Even if the precise story behind the name has been forgotten or ignored, many mythological names are sufficiently mellifluous and pronounceable to lend themselves to forename use. Perhaps some more adventurous parents may like to consider Argus, Midas, Orion, Priam, Remus or Troilus for their baby boy, or Cressida, Electra, Ianthe, Leda, Minerva ('Hey, Min, you coming?'), Pandia, Philomela, Scylla, Thisbe or Vesta for their little girl?

The mythological characters who bore these names, and many hundreds more, were remarkable people, to say the least. In their lives and deeds we see the widest possible range of human activities. Indeed, it is not only all human life that is there, but all super-human and sub-human life as well. On the one hand are the great heroic undertakings of Achilles, Jason, Odysseus, Perseus and Theseus, on the other the monstrous machinations of Cerberus, the Cyclopes, the Harpies, the Minotaur and the Sphinx. Noble and moving love stories, such as those of Philemon and Baucis, Cupid and Psyche, Orpheus and Eurydice, Perseus and Andromeda, Pygmalion and Galatea, Pyramus and Thisbe, to say nothing of the countless 'affairs' of Zeus and other gods, are counterbalanced by cruel and horrific incidents and descriptions, many of which, if not containing 'Freudian' undertones, fall into

3

the modern literary category of 'sexually explicit'. In a number of tales, key importance is attached to such acts as castration (Uranus by Cronos), maiming and mutilation (Procrustes), dismembering, both alive (Pentheus by Agave and her sisters) and dead (Apsyrtus by Medea), necrophilia (Achilles of Penthesilia), bestiality (Pasiphaë, Philyra), coitus interruptus (Hephaestus with Athena), phallicism, or more precisely ithyphallicism (Hermes, Priapus), trans-sexualism (Iphis), transvestism (Heracles, Achilles, Leucippus, Procris), incest (Jocasta), homosexuality and paedophilia (Narcissus, Hyacinthus, Hymen, Ganymede, Chrysippus: all on the receiving end), breast-removal (Amazons), eye-gouging (Polyphemus by Odysseus), tongue-extraction (Lara by Jupiter, Philomela by Tereus), head-axing (Zeus by Hephaestus), foot-piercing (Oedipus by Laïus), decapitation (Argus by Hermes, Medusa by Perseus), poisoning (Heracles by Deïanira), throttling (numerous victims by the Sphinx), crushing (Laocoön and his sons by snakes), vomiting and spewing (the baby Heracles of the Milky Way, Cronos of all Rhea's children except Zeus), urination (Orion), drunken orgies (Bacchus) and murders, sacrifices, rapes, abductions and abandonments ('exposures') at every turn.

Yet amid all these X-rated performances, there are still tales with light, poignant and humorous touches, so that we warm to Elpenor, who fell off a roof while sleeping off a hangover, Enalus and Phineïs, young lovers rescued at sea by dolphins, Leander, swimming nightly to his love Hero by the light of a lighthouse, Nausicaä, playing ball with her maids by the sea, and Argus, Odysseus's faithful old dog, who welcomes his long-gone master home with a wag of his tail, and then dies. And to offset the horrors of many of the stories, there are golden girls and handsome young men in plenty to inject a consistently wholesome dose of beauty, innocence, nobleness, purity, self-sacrifice, love and duty.

Over the years, indeed over the thousands of years since these marvellous characters first appeared, several attempts have been made to establish the meanings and origins of their names. Why is Ulysses called Ulysses? What does Agamemnon's name mean? Does the name of Saturn have any special significance? The ancient classical writers themselves were the first to ponder on the interpretation of the names of the men and women who peopled their stories. Very often they would include an explanation, as they saw it, when introducing a character or describing an incident in his or her life. Both Homer's *Iliad* and Virgil's *Aeneid* contain several, as do the *Odyssey*, Ovid's *Metamorphoses* and, in particular, Hesiod's *Theogony* ('Birth and genealogy of the gods'). If the explanation of a name involved a play on words, the Greek authors were particularly pleased, and in such a manner Sophocles related the name of Aias (better known as Ajax) to *aiazo*, 'to call "ah!"', Pindar linked the same name with *aietos*, 'eagle', and Euripides connected the name of Zethus with *zeteo*, 'to seek'. Ever since, efforts both persistent and sporadic, scholarly and amateur, have been made to put a meaning to the names.

This dictionary aims to summarise what has already been proposed and to move the study of classical name origins a step further forward. In recent years, and certainly in the present century, there has been little published in widely and popularly accessible form on the subject in English, and it is hoped that the book will fill an embarrassing gap. After all, there are a hundred and one books dealing with the meanings of Christian names, yet little on the mythological classical names that continue, as we have seen, to occupy a firm and prominent place in the world of names which we encounter daily.

All names originally had some meaning or specific derivation, and the more reliable 'boys' and girls' names' books will tell you that John comes from the Hebrew for 'the Lord is gracious', that Peter began as the Greek for 'rock', that Jennifer is of Celtic stock meaning 'fair and yielding' and that Nora is short for Latin *honoria* and so means 'honourable'. These quite common English names all evolved from a language other than English, so the fact that our classical names will also need translating is not an unusual feature in name interpretation. The two languages we shall mostly be concerned with, of course, are Greek and Latin – mainly the former, in fact, since Greek mythological names outnumber Roman ones by almost ten to one. This is because of historical and religious developments in both Greece and Rome: most of the Roman gods and goddesses were 'imported' from Greece, almost as and when required, and are thus virtually doubles of their Greek counterparts. Zeus, for example, became Jupiter, Athena was adopted as Minerva, Aphrodite was turned into Venus, and so on. (A list of the most important correspondences appears as Appendix VII, page 338).

Given this state of affairs, our task looks fairly simple. We set about translating the Greek names from Greek and the Roman names from Latin, then study the character in question to see how the name could apply to any aspect of his or her nature or life. Thus, we take the name Circe, deduce that it derived from Greek *circos*, meaning 'circle' or 'hawk', and then examine Circe's character and general *modus vivendi* and see if in some literal or metaphorical way circles or hawks can be said to feature in her life. Similarly, if Cleopatra has a name that means 'glory to her father',

5

from *cleos*, 'fame', 'glory' and *pater*, 'father', we read the stories about her to see how, exactly, she glorified her father, or possibly how she shared in or influenced her father's glory.

So far so good, and we can proceed quite happily in this manner for a while. But we soon encounter two sizeable obstacles. The first, as might be expected, is that some of the names do not readily or easily 'translate' from the Greek or Latin, and there is apparently no similar or even distorted word that offers itself as a possible origin. The second problem is that although we seem able to translate the name easily enough, we cannot find an obvious or suitable application of the name to its bearer. For example, we translate Hippodamia as 'horse tamer', from *hippos*, 'horse' and *damao*, 'to tame', but cannot find in the tales about her any reference to a taming of horses.

With regard to the first obstacle, the 'untranslatable' names, the answer usually is that the name is actually not Greek (or Latin) at all, but is either pre-Greek or, say, in some such language as Phoenician or Hebrew. And if some names are obviously not Greek, might it not be that some of the 'difficult' names in the second category are also really not Greek, but have simply come to resemble Greek? This very often is the case, we may be sure, although in many instances we lack a certain guide-line as to what the name should be if it is not Greek.

The cause of this problem lies with the Greeks themselves. In spite of their fine ideals and their lofty aspirations they were only human after all, and when they came up against a name that they could not understand, they adapted it, either consciously or unconsciously, to something that actually made sense. This was what happened with the names of Aias and Zethus mentioned above: Sophocles, Pindar and Euripides moulded an unfamiliar name into a meaningful one. And from there it is only one step towards the invention of a story that actually incorporated this meaning somehow into the myths that already existed concerning the character. It is as if we were to take the name of the Celtic giant Fingal (of 'Fingal's Cave' fame), interpret his name as meaning 'finger', and invent a new adventure for him in which he created a gigantic cavern out of fingers of basalt.

There is little doubt that far more of the even quite famous Greek names are actually non-Greek than we suspect or can establish. The Greeks themselves saw Achilles' name, for example, as deriving either from *a–*, 'not' and *cheile*, 'lips', and so meaning 'lipless', or from *achos*, meaning 'grief'. The latter can fairly easily be introduced as an element in most people's life and times, but 'liplessness' requires a good deal more ingenuity. In Achilles' case it is traditionally said to allude to the fact that he had never been suckled as a baby, that is, his lips had not touched a breast. But Achilles' name may well not be Greek at all. Similarly, Aphrodite (the Roman Venus) has a name that seems pure Greek, with its *aphros* meaning 'foam' and explaining the goddess's famous birth from the foamy sea. But in her case we have fairly certain evidence that her name originated as either a Philistine deity called Atargatis or a Hebrew goddess named Ashtoreth, and that one or other or even both of these names gradually evolved into the Greek-looking Aphrodite. (See her entry for more on this.)

The conscious or unconscious assimilation of unknown words and names to something more meaningful is not by any means an exclusively Greek phenomenon. We have long been doing it ourselves in the English-speaking world. If asked what the name 'Frank' meant, we would almost certainly say, 'Why, "frank", of course, "honest", "sincere".' Yet actually it means 'French', and has been smoothed by us to an English word. Similarly the girl's name Rose, although popularly associated with the flower, like a number of girls' names (May, Erica, Poppy, Violet, Iris), in fact originated as 'horse'! The same thing happened with surnames, so that Graves is not to do with tombs or undertakers but really means 'steward', Sidebottom is not an anatomical freak but was originally 'one who dwells in the wide valley', and Woolrich was not rich in wool but was 'wolf powerful'. (In Greek he would have been called Lycomenes.) This constant seeking to make a name mean something is technically known as 'folk etymology' or 'popular etymology', and is an important psycholinguistic factor in the evolution of names. It can also be seen at work in place-names, where we 'read' the name Aldershot as 'alder shoot', Edinburgh as the 'burgh' of one 'Edin', and Swansea as a seaside town where swans swim on the sea.

But of course the Greeks, and to a lesser degree the Romans, also invented names. In assimilating an existing mythology or mythologies, they created their own, and they devised names to give to the characters they had both adopted and created. The question of *how* exactly the mythological characters evolved is a much discussed and highly complex one, and to this day classicists are still divided as to whether the characters are personifications of natural forces and phenomena or of religious beliefs, idealisations of real persons (see **euhemerism** in Technical Terms, page 14), symbolisations of historical, political or ritualistic and cultic events, or a blend of these. However derived, the characters had to have names, and the type of name given to any one character varied according to a number of fairly well defined principles found in the naming systems of many countries apart from Greece. The main categories of name are as follows:

1 The name is virtually a standard word that defines the character. Names of this type particularly apply to abstract characters, such as Nyx (night), Erebus (darkness), Gaia (earth), Cupid (desire), Uranus (heaven). These are true 'word into name' instances.

2 The name is an epithet, describing a character's main role, function or nature. Examples are Creon and Creusa (both 'ruler'), Jupiter ('father sky'), Prometheus ('forethought') and Autolycus ('very wolf').

3 The name is descriptive, but more allusively, referring (sometimes indirectly) to a specialised characteristic, a physical property or even a possession of the character. Examples are names such as Aërope ('air-face'), Nereus ('wet one'), the Harpies ('snatchers') and Mercury ('god of commerce').

4 The name relates to a place associated with the character. There are very many such names, and for a number of well-known and less well-known places in Greece there seems to be a character of the same name. In several instances these are kings, who have given their names to the cities they rule. But there are many noted examples of other name identities, the most familiar, of course, being Athena and Athens. In such cases the question invariably arises: which came first, the place or the character? In other words, was Athens named for the goddess who protected it, or was Athena specifically 'invented' to be the city's special guardian goddess? The latter would seem the more logical and likely, yet the matter is by no means finally resolved, since Athena's name may well be pre-Greek (see her entry).

5 The name relates to a specific incident in the character's life (or to his or her birth or death). Obvious examples here are the names of the many characters who were metamorphosed into something else, usually a plant, a bird or an animal. Among them are Aedon ('nightingale'), Daphne ('laurel'), Myrmex ('ant') and, more indirectly, Acalanthis ('thistle', although she was actually turned into a goldfinch) and Myrmidon ('ant', as which Zeus was disguised when he deceived Myrmidon). Many of the incidents that gave a name to a character occurred not directly to that character but to a member of his or her family, so that Gorgophone ('Gorgon-killer') did not herself kill a Gorgon but was named for the beheading of Medusa by her father, Perseus. Other incidents

are more direct, such as Hippolytus ('horse-releaser'), Paris ('wallet') and Pelias ('bruised'). (See the entries for these names for the incidents.)

A very large number of names, however, do not fall into any of these categories – at least, as far as can be ascertained from what we know about the characters who bear them – and these are the many generally *propitious* names, as I have called them. These are the names that wish their bearer well: may he or she be rich, famous, brave, beautiful, powerful or whatever. A glance through the lists of elements in Appendix I, page 316, will show the sort of desirable attribute that a name, it is hoped, will confer. This 'name power' was by no means restricted to the Greeks – who, incidentally, used such a method when naming real flesh-and-blood children – but was also practised by the Germanic races, the Celts and the Slavs, among others. Several English names originated as propitious ones, designed to bring a desirable attribute to their bearers. Among them are names such as Godfrey ('peace of God'), Gertrude ('spear-enchanter'), Walter ('army-ruler'), Richard ('strong king') and Frederick ('peace ruler'). Among propitious Celtic names are Kevin ('comely birth'), Morag ('great') and Gwendolen ('white circle'), and among favourable Slavic names are Yaroslav ('strong glory'), Bogdan ('God-given') and the famous Good King Wenceslas ('great glory').

In every case where a character appears to have a purely propitious name, it is always worth considering carefully whether the name might not have a specific application, usually as an 'incident' name, and I have done this wherever feasible, discussing the possibilities. (See, for example, the entry for the name mentioned earlier in this connection – Cleopatra.) It may well be, in fact, that for some of the apparently propitious names (in a general sense) there once was a specific incident which has not come down to us, and that Hippodamia actually *did* tame a horse or horses. But we must be wary of falling back too readily on this assumption for a name that appears to have no precise application!

It is worth noting, however, that in more than a few instances names appear to link or repeat in families, and that one character 'inherits' the name of a parent or more remote forebear, or passes a name on to his offspring. Such occurrences are pointed out in their respective entries, among which are those for Euryale and Hippodamus, whose family had more than a few 'horsy' connections.

For the rest of the names, that do have or are thought to have particular origins, I have aimed to give as many relevant etymologies as possible, as proposed by the 'experts' even where they are very likely suspect or at least fanciful. I make no apologies for including explanations that professional classicists will doubtless deride; after all, if the etymologies are fanciful, so are the characters to whom they relate, and in mythology, as in love and war, all is fair. So here will be found the name origins offered by both classical authors and more recent writers. The former we have already mentioned in this Introduction as etymologists. Among the latter, whose works are listed in the Bibliography (page 340), special mention should be made of Dr William Smith and Thomas Keightley, writing and working in the nineteenth century, and Robert Graves, in the twentieth. These three specialists have offered name origins that are roughly in ascending order of reliability but equal order of informativeness, and I have derived much useful and interesting material from their writings. True, in the case of Dr Smith I am overlooking the many scholars (thirty-five in number) who contributed to his massive three-volume dictionary. But when it comes to this present dictionary, the names of Keightley and Graves appear more than once in the various entries, often where perhaps an origin is best left for future analysis (and even rejection) rather than blind acceptance. While disagreeing with a number of the interpretations of Robert Graves, and not being personally attracted to or convinced by his ritualistic, totemistic and cultic school of thought, with its 'sacred mushrooms', 'orgiastic nightmares' and the like, I greatly respect and appreciate his linguistic endeavours to interpret the meanings of the names, notably in his *The Greek Myths*.

Of course, the whole business of interpreting the names is made no easier by the fact that not only are the various accounts and stories told and retold by different authors, who vary them to suit their subject or style, but the characters themselves frequently feature in differing roles in these accounts. Characters, places, times and relationships are often intermixed and confused, and although a single standard version of a story with fixed roles usually emerges, there are contradictions and inconsistencies aplenty as we trace our way through the labyrinthine profusion of stories.

Such variances will almost certainly be reflected in this book, and will thus be a constant reminder of the unstable nature of its source material. However, the main aim of the book, as mentioned, is to explain and explore the names themselves, and many of the familiar tales will not be told here unless they are relevant to the name under consideration.

As said above, names frequently 'run in the family', and for this reason as well as for general ease of identification I have thought

10

it important to state the family relationship of almost all characters, and in particular his or her parentage. In cases where characters' names have transferred to heavenly bodies (and usually 'thereby hangs a tale'), I have included an account or a consideration of how that body, often a planet or a constellation, came to acquire its name. How the planets, constellations and other heavenly bodies actually acquired their names is a fascinating subject which demands a book in itself (and indeed has found two excellent ones in those by Allen and Karpenko, included in the Bibliography). Suffice it to say here, for our present purposes, that the Greeks were not the first to name the constellations and planets, but for the most part borrowed the names from the east – from the ancient Egyptians, Phoenicians, Assyrians and Babylonians – and then translated and adapted them as they did the names of many of the mythological characters. The Romans, in turn, then translated the Greek names. With regard to the planets, for example, we know that the Roman names of Mercury, Venus, Mars, Jupiter and Saturn, ancient though they are, were known by the Greeks in the time of Pythagoras (the sixth century BC) under different names. Mercury was Stilbon, Venus was both Hesperos and either Phosphoros or Eophoros, Mars was Pyroeis, Jupiter was Phaethon, and Saturn was Phainon. (See the five Roman names respectively for the meanings of these Greek names.) However, the Babylonians, who had known of the existence of the planets several centuries before this, had given them their own names, and when the Greeks learned of the Babylonian astronomers' discoveries and observations – chiefly through Egypt and also as a result of the expeditions of Alexander the Great – they renamed the planets using the names of their own gods. As a result of this, Mercury became Hermes, Mars became Ares, Jupiter became Zeus, and Saturn was renamed Cronos, while when the Greeks realised that Hesperos and Phosphoros were one and the same heavenly body, they named it Aphrodite. Aristotle, living in the third century BC, mentions all these names.

The dictionary contains entries not just for the names of individual mythological characters, but also for collective names, such as those of the various kinds of nymphs (Oceanids, Nereids, Naiads, Oreads, Dryads, and so on) and other well-known groups such as the Amazons, the Argonauts, the Centaurs, the Charites or Graces, the Dactyls, the Epigoni, the Fates, the Furies, the Gorgons, the Hours, the Lapiths, the Lotus-eaters, the Muses, the Myrmidons, the Lares and the Penates, the Sirens and the Telchines. Also entered are the Giants and the Nymphs themselves (as individual words). Of course, the names of individual members of these groups, for example, the nine Muses, will also have their own separate entries.

Having given considerable thought to the matter of the spelling of Greek names, I decided in the end to settle for the ones that are the simplest and most familiar, even if they are not strictly precise transliterations from the Greek. Broadly speaking, this means that many names will end in -us instead of -os, and that 'c' will be used instead of 'k' (and 'ch' instead of 'kh'). The reader will thus find Cerberus, not Kerberos, Cyclops, not Kyklops, and Chione, not Khione. (The single exception to this is Nike, who is more familiar in this spelling, if only from the American guided missile, and also to avoid the strange-looking 'Nice'.) I have also not indicated, as some works on Greek mythology do, the difference between a long vowel and a short, notably between short epsilon (ϵ) and long eta (η), which are both transliterated as just 'e', and between short omicron (o) and long omega (ω), which are both transliterated as 'o'. However I have used a diaeresis (¨) to show that the second of two vowels together is to be pronounced separately, as in Laocoön and Menelaüs. For the sake of consistency, I have extended this principle of transliteration to the Greek words that appear in almost every Greek name entry. I am aware that professional Greek scholars may well throw up their arms in horror at this, but I have the ordinary non-Greek-speaking reader to think of, and I am convinced that any loss of accuracy is greatly compensated for by simplicity and ease of recognition, especially when comparing a Greek word and the name that derives from it. So Cleopatra's name derives from *cleos* and *pater*, not *kleos* (with an epsilon) and *patēr* (with an eta).

Four of the seven Appendices (beginning on page 316) give extensive lists of some of the many by-names of, respectively, Aphrodite (Venus), Apollo, Athena (Minerva) and Zeus (Jupiter). These by-names – often known as epithets or even surnames, which can be misleading – were usually used together with the main name of the god or goddess, but could also be used on their own. Sometimes the former led to the latter (see **Pallas** in the dictionary).

Finally, I would like to express my sincere thanks to Elizabeth Fidlon, who searched London libraries and museums for suitable illustrations for the book, and to Jacqueline Holford, who most professionally and accurately typed out almost the whole of the typescript with its many unfamiliar names and words.

Petersfield, Hampshire   Adrian Room

TECHNICAL TERMS

This is a short explanatory list of some of the more specialised terms relating to the Greek language that are used in the dictionary. It also includes some words and phrases that are generally encountered with regard to Greek mythology, but which are not actual names and so do not have their own entries in the dictionary.

Aegis The shield of Zeus, often borrowed by Athena. Originally it was a thundercloud, later it seems to have been a goatskin, this dissimilarity doubtless caused by the resemblance of *aix, aigos*, 'goat' to *cataigis*, 'hurricane'. The word is used in the English phrase 'under the aegis of', meaning 'under the auspices or sponsorship of'.

Aeolic One of the five main dialects into which classical Greek was divided, the others being Achaean, Attic, Doric and Ionic. It was the dialect of Lesbos, Boeotia and Thessaly, and had little literary importance, being used mainly by Sappho and Alcaeus.

Attic One of the five main dialects of classical Greek (see **Aeolic**). It was predominantly spoken in Attica (the area round Athens), and was the chief literary dialect of the language. One of its chief distinctive features was that the long 'a' that occurred in other dialects changed to a long 'e', so that Doric *mater*, 'mother', for example, became Attic *meter*. It is sometimes regarded as a sub-dialect of Ionic.

Cretan A later dialect of Greek spoken on Crete and developing from the Doric dialect.

Doric One of the five main dialects of classical Greek (see **Aeolic**). It was spoken in the Peloponnesus, Locris, Phocis, and the Dorian colonies and islands in the east and west Mediterranean, including Crete. It was the dialect of Greek choral poetry, with Pindar one of its main writers.

13

Eleusinian Mysteries Secret cults held in honour of Demeter at Eleusis, a city near Athens, in the month Boedromion ('Running-to-aid' month), i.e. late September–early October. The cults were so secret that even today we know very little about the ceremonial.

Epic Greek A highly elaborate style of Greek, with a large number of traditional verbal formulas (such as 'grey-eyed' of a girl, or 'dark-prowed' of a ship), used by the oral poets, and especially Homer, to compose long narrative poems such as the *Iliad and the Odyssey*.

Euhemerism The theory that the Greek gods were originally kings and conquerors and other mere mortals, i.e. that they originated as real human beings. It was proposed by Euhemerus, a Greek mythographer of the fourth century BC. The idea was taken up at a popular level and was extended to all mythological characters so that, for example, the Cyclopes were originally a race of Sicilian savages, Atlas was an astronomer, and Pegasus was a fast-sailing pirate.

Golden Fleece The fleece of the ram that saved Phrixus (whom see in the Dictionary) from being sacrificed by his father, Athamas. The ram was the offspring of Poseidon and Theophane, and after it had been sacrificed by Phrixus, its golden fleece became the object of the voyage of the Argonauts, who sailed with Jason in search of it.

Ionic One of the five main dialects of classical Greek (see **Aeolic**). It was spoken mainly in the Ionic colonies of Asia Minor and was related to the Attic dialect. Ionic was the language of the earliest Greek writers, and in particular of Herodotus and Homer.

Knossos City in ancient Crete that was the capital of King Minos. The excavation of the Palace of Minos by Sir Arthur Evans between 1900 and 1930 was one of the most important achievements in the history of archaeology, since it revealed Crete as a mainspring of Aegean Culture, also known as Minoan Culture (after Minos) or Mycenaean Culture (after the other main centre, Mycenae, a Greek city in the north-east Peloponnesus on the plain of Argos). Aegean Culture itself was the Bronze Age civilisation of the area that flourished from approximately 3000 BC to 1000 BC. See also **Linear B tablets**.

Labours of Hercules These were the twelve superhuman tasks imposed on Heracles (Hercules) by Eurystheus, king of Tiryns, as atonement for murdering his own sons and nephews. They were (outcome in brackets): 1 The Nemean Lion (strangled), 2 The Hydra of Lerna (beheaded), 3 The Cerynitian Hind (captured), 4 The Erymanthian Boar (captured), 5 The Augean Stables (cleansed), 6 The Stymphalian Birds (shot), 7 The Cretan Bull (captured), 8 The Mares of Diomedes (captured), 9 The Amazon's Girdle (seized), 10 The Cattle of Geryon (captured), 11 The Golden Apples of the Hesperides (fetched), 12 The Descent to the Underworld for Cerberus (captured).

Labyrinth A mazelike building at **Knossos** (which see) built by Daedalus as a prison for the Minotaur. Theseus found his way in and out with the aid of Ariadne, although Daedalus was later imprisoned there with his son, Icarus.

Linear B tablets Unbaked clay tablets found at Knossos, Mycenae and elsewhere with the Greek syllabic script (i.e. with symbols representing syllables, not letters) Linear B. This was deciphered in 1952 by two English scholars: the architect Michael Ventris and the classicist John Chadwick. Linear A, an earlier script also found on tablets, has still not been deciphered. ('Linear' as the script uses lines, as distinct from earlier pictographic writings.)

Mycenaean The most ancient form of Greek ever discovered, written in **Linear B** (which see, above). It has been found on pots and jars at Mycenae (see **Knossos**) and elsewhere.

Old Man of the Sea A name given by the Greeks to Nereus, Proteus, and Phorcys (see these names).

Oracle A shrine where a god or goddess was consulted by a means of divination, such as casting lots or even making a direct enquiry of an inspired person who then replied orally. Oracles were dedicated to particular deities, the most famous being the one of Apollo at Delphi.

Phoenician A Semitic language spoken in ancient times on the coast of Syria and Palestine, from where it spread to colonies of Phoenicia such as the North African city of Carthage (where it became known as Punic). It is very close to Hebrew and dates from at least the thirteenth century BC.

15

Privative prefix In Greek, the prefix *a-* has the sense 'not', like the English 'un-', and is thus technically called 'privative' since it denotes the loss or absence (as it were, 'deprivation') of the basic sense of the word. For example, *sophos* means 'wise', *asophos* means 'unwise'. A number of English words have the same prefix, as 'amoral'.

Seven Against Thebes The seven champions of Argos who besieged Thebes: Adrastus, Amphiaraüs, Capaneus, Hippomedon, Parthenopaeüs, Polynices, Tydeus. There was also a tragedy by Aeschylus called *Seven Against Thebes* describing their exploits.

Siege of Troy An alternative name for the **Trojan War** (see below).

Sown Men Men born in Thebes from the teeth of the dragon (Ares' sacred serpent) sown in the ground by Cadmus after he had killed it. Originally a whole company of men, only five remained after the majority had been killed in an instant battle. These were Chthonius, Echion, Hyperenor, Pelorus and Udaeüs. The Greek name for them is *Spartoi*.

Trojan War The legendary war waged by an alliance of Greek cities against the Phrygian city of Troy (traditionally dated 1194–1184 BC). In popular mythology, the cause of the war was Helen ('of Troy'), whose face 'launched a thousand ships', i.e. started the war, when she eloped there with Paris.

Underworld The gloomy, sunless region otherwise known as Hades (whose name see) to which the souls of the dead were ferried across the river Styx. It was closer to the Hebrew *Sheol* than the Christian Hell or Purgatory.

Wooden Horse The large statue in which the Greeks entered Troy undetected at the end of the Trojan War, thus capturing the city and sacking it. The building of the large hollow horse was advised by Odysseus and the construction of it was carried out by Epeius. The Trojans allowed it inside their walls because they believed, mistakenly, that the Greeks wished to offer it to Athena.

DICTIONARY

Abas was the name of at least three people. The best known were Abas, King of Troy, the son of Lynceus and Hypermestra, Abas the son of Melampus and Lycippe, and Abas the son of Celeüs and Metanira. This last Abas once saw Demeter gulping down barley water in the heat, and on asking her why she drank so greedily was changed by her into a lizard, for which the Greek is *ascalabos*, a word whose last four letters could give his name. To be changed into a lizard is not such a terrible fate, since lizards can live in hot places for a long time without water. (See also **Ascalabus**.)

Abderus was the son of Hermes and was loved by Heracles who made him his armour bearer. He had the misfortune to be torn to pieces by the man-eating mares of Diomedes, which Heracles had given him to guard. The Greek *deris*, 'battle', may lie behind his name.

Acacallis was the daughter of Minos and Pasiphaë, and bore Apollo a son, Amphithemis – and possibly also Miletus. Her name may have the root *ace*, 'point', 'edge', which with the privative prefix *a-* could be taken to mean 'unwalled'. The reference would be to the west Cretan unwalled city of Tarrha which was captured by the Hellenes, with all the inhabitants fleeing to Libya. This historical event may lie behind the myth in which Acacallis was banished to Libya by Minos as a punishment for being seduced by Apollo. (She was his first love.)

Academus is a name that gave the English 'academy' (and similar words in other languages). It was that of an Arcadian invited to Attica by Theseus. Academus came to acquire an estate near Athens where philosophers met – hence 'academy'. Arcadia was a peaceful pastoral (and mountainous) area in southern Greece, so the name Academus could mean 'of a silent district', from *aca*, 'softly', 'silently', and *demos*, 'country district'.

Acalanthis was one of the Pierides, that is, one of the nine daughters of Pierus, king of Macedonia. When she and her sisters defied the Muses to sing as well as they could, the Muses changed all the girls into birds, with Acalanthis being turned into a goldfinch. Her name thus derives from *acantha*, 'thistle', a weed that goldfinches like to eat. (The connection between goldfinches and thistles is even closer in French, where *chardon* is 'thistle' and *chardonneret* 'goldfinch'.)

Acamas was the son of Theseus and Phaedra, whose other son was Demophon. Acamas loved Laodice, and although he eventually married Phyllis, his name, *acamas*, 'untiring', may reflect his initial constancy.

Acanthis was the only daughter (with four brothers) of Autonoös and Hippodamia, and she was sometimes known as Acanthyllis. The family as a whole owned extensive but barren lands, full of thistles (*acantha*) and rushes (*schoinos*). After the death of Acanthis' brother Anthus (he was killed by some mares who did not wish to leave their pastures) all the family were grief-stricken, so that Apollo pitied them and changed them into different types of birds, for example Autonoös became a bittern and Hippodamia a crested lark. Acanthis, however, became a goldfinch, a fitting name for one whose property was closely associated with thistles. (See also the similar story of **Acalanthis**.)

Acarnan was the son of Alcmaeon and Callirrhoë. His name would appear to be linked to 'thistle' (*acantha*), as are Acalanthis and Acanthis, but there is no story to support this.

Acastus, who became a king of Iolcus, was the son of Pelias and Anaxibia. He seems to have been unreliable in some way, for his name may derive from *acatastatos*, 'unstable', with the privative prefix *a-* and *cathistemi* meaning 'to be set'. Acastus was one of the Argonauts.

Acesidas was the fifth Dactyl, that is the 'little finger' of the group. In his name can be seen the abode of the Dactyls, Mount Ida in Phrygia, and if the first part of his name derives from *acestor*, 'saviour', then his whole name means something like 'rescuer from Mount Ida'.

Acestes was the son of the river god Crimissus and a Trojan woman named Aegesta. His name also occurs as Aegestes, so there is an obvious link with the name of his mother. The word for 'goat', *aix, aigos,* may lie behind both names, with some ritual or sacrificial reference.

Achaeus, son of Xuthus and Creusa, gave his name to the Achaeans, the word used by Homer for the Greek people generally. His name could be seen as prophetic if its basis is *achos,* 'grief'. This same Greek word is related to English 'ache', which also closely resembles the Greek name.

Achates was the famous close friend and armour-bearer of Aeneas, *Fidus Achates,* 'faithful Achates', as Virgil called him in the *Aeneid.* The name is actually the Greek word for 'agate', and was also that of the river in Sicily where agate was first found. But although Achates may have been a 'precious stone' as far as Aeneas was concerned, his name seems much more closely connected with that of the river.

Acheloüs was a river god, the son of Oceanus and Tethys, and himself the father of several sea nymphs, including Callirrhoë (who married Alcmaeon) and the Sirens. With all this water about, we might expect some influence of Latin *aqua* in his name, but perhaps it is better to go straight to Greek and from *acheo,* 'to mourn' and *louo* or *louso,* 'to wash away' derive a propitious sense on the lines of 'he who banishes care'.

Acheron is one of the better-known man-into-river metamorphoses in mythology. He was originally, although according to a fairly late tradition, the son of Helios and Gaia (or perhaps Demeter), that is, the offspring of the sun and the earth. He was then changed into the river of hell or the Underworld, so that his name came to be used by Virgil and Cicero to denote the Underworld itself. His name is usually said to mean 'river of sorrows' or something similar, from the phrase *o achea rheon,* 'the river of woe'. Certainly hell and woe make a suitable match, and we may well find the same root in the name, *achos,* 'pain', 'grief', that we saw in Achaeus.

Achilles is, of course, one of the most famous of all mythological names – yet its origin is anything but straightforward. According to Apollodorus, the renowned son of Peleus and Thetis was so named by Chiron because the young child had never been suckled, or put his lips to a breast. This is the standard explanation, with the Greek being the privative *a-* and *cheile,* 'lips'. So 'lipless' was

Achilles slays Penthesilea. Achilles had been grieving for Patroclus, killed by Hector in the Trojan War. Now he in turn kills Penthesilea, Queen of the Amazons, and after her death was to grieve over her body. Both his name and hers could contain the root of 'grief'.

the hero's name. This could be quite satisfactory, since we can take the name literally and also metaphorically, for a great hero who needed no lips but 'spoke' through his valiant deeds instead. *Facta non verba*, 'deeds not words', as the Latin tag goes. But on the other hand, we may well see in his name the same 'grief' root, *achos*, as in Achaeus and Acheron, and indeed the central theme of the *Iliad*, in which he is the chief hero, is that of the pain and distress caused by the wrath of Achilles. (Yes, handsome and brave he may have been, but think of all those battles and the killing of Hector!) In fact the word *achos* occurs in several passages of the *Iliad*, for example in Book 16 we read: *toion gar achos bebiecen Achaious*, 'for such a grief had beset the Achaeans'. 'Grief' seems more personally relevant than 'liplessness', as well as being more probable linguistically. In one of his tales, Apollodorus mentions that a previous name of Achilles had been Ligyron, 'clear-voiced' (from *ligys*, 'clear-toned').

Acidusa was the wife of Scamander, who named a spring in Boeotia after her. Was she catty? Maybe we can see *ancistron*, 'fish-hook' in her name, or simply the basic word *ancos*, 'bend' from which the fish-hook comes. Such a derivation could denote a 'barbed' or sharp-tongued person. The second half of her name is *ousia*, 'a being'.

Acis loved Galatea, as everyone knows, even if rather from Handel's opera than the story of Ovid. But Polyphemus the Cyclops loved Galatea, too, and when she spurned him, preferring her Sicilian shepherd, took his revenge on his rival by crushing him to death with a rock while he was in his loved one's arms. Hapless Galatea, unable to bring her beloved Acis back to life, changed his blood as it gushed out beneath the rock into a river – the river Acis in Sicily. So what shall we try for the origin of his name? As with Acheloüs, Latin *aqua* springs to mind for one who became a river god, but perhaps instead we should think in terms of *acis*, 'point', 'barb' for some literal or metaphorical reference. (The river Acis is in fact at the foot of Mount Etna, a 'point' of some note.) But most likely the real origin is pre-Greek in the river name itself.

Acmon was one of the two Cercopes, with his brother Passalus the other. The word is direct Greek for 'anvil', maybe a suitable name for a dwarf who plagued Heracles (actually daring to steal his armour) and whose general behaviour, like that of his brother, was rumbustious. It is tempting to see a link with the thunderbolts of Zeus, who changed Acmon and Passalus into monkeys for their capricious behaviour, but perhaps we should resist such a tenuous connection.

Acontius was a youth from the island of Ceos who loved Cydippe, an Athenian girl. Perhaps he was an accomplished javelin-thrower, for *acontion* means 'dart', 'javelin'.

Acrisius was the name of two kings of note. The first, king of Argos, was the son of Abas and Aglaia, and the twin brother of Proëtus. He became the father of Danaë, having married Eurydice. The second, king of Cephallenia, was the father of Laërtes. Both names seem to derive from *acrisia*, 'want of judgment', and it is certainly true that the first Acrisius mentioned here was killed by a lack of judgment: Perseus had thrown a discus at Polydectes' funeral games and it accidentally struck him. It may be no coincidence, too, since name origins run in any direction, that the Argive king was buried after this mishap on a height (*acron*) – the town of Larissa Cremaste ('Larissa the Suspended') that is located high up on Mount Othrys. There seems to be no specific ill-judgment in the life (or death) of the other Acrisius.

Actaeon is famed for being the hunter who was torn to pieces by his own fifty hounds (see Appendix VI, page 336) having been turned into a stag by Artemis, whom he had seen bathing naked. Taking his name literally, we get *acteon* meaning 'one must lead', no doubt a suitable name for a superior huntsman, the proud son of Aristaeüs (with his own 'aristocratic' name!) and Autonoë. But perhaps we should settle for the root *acte*, 'sea shore', for his birthplace or native district, even though nowhere in Greece is all that far from the sea.

Actaeus was the earliest king of Attica and the father of Agraulus (the Agraulus who married Cecrops). We may well be able to see *acte*, 'beach', 'shore' here, as possibly for Actaeon, since Attica, being a peninsula (on which Athens is situated), is surrounded on three sides by the sea coast.

Actis was an astronomer, the son of Helios and Rhode. He killed his brother, however, and for this crime of fratricide was banished from Rhodes and fled to Egypt where he founded Heliopolis in honour of his father. Helios was the sun, of course, so it seems reasonable to see *actis*, 'ray', 'beam' as precisely what it is.

Actor was a common name for several mythological characters, including a king of Phthia, as one, the son of Deïon, king of Phocis, as another, the brother of Augeas, as a third, and the son of Phorbas as yet another. The name common to all four is related to the 'doer' that the English 'actor' is, but it does not come directly from this word (which is Latin *actor*) but rather from the Greek *actor* meaning 'chief', 'leader', from *ago*, 'to lead'. As such it is simply a propitious name of a non-specific nature.

Admete, 'untamed', 'unmarried' – a somehow appropriate name for the daughter of Eurystheus for whom Heracles undertook his Ninth Labour: to fetch the golden girdle of Ares worn by the Amazonian queen Hippolyta. And was not Hippolyta 'untamed', like all the dauntless Amazons? (This is not, of course, what her name actually means!)

Admetus has a name of the same meaning as Admete, 'untamed', or even 'untamable'. Not 'unmarried', however, for this king of Pherae married Alcestis, although not before he was obliged to win her hand by coming to her in a chariot drawn by lions and boars. 'Untamable' he himself may have been, but he certainly tamed these beasts.

Adonis, the beautiful boy, has a name whose meaning is clear beyond any doubt: 'lord'. It is not so much a pure Greek name as a Semitic or Greek-Hebrew one. Ancient Hebrew *adon* means 'lord' and was translated thus to refer to God in the Old Testament by the English writers of the Authorised Version of the Bible. If Adonis impressed by his handsomeness, then it is hardly surprising (on the 'like attracts like' principle) that Aphrodite, the paragon of female beauty, should become infatuated by him. Fortunately, the attraction turned out to be mutual. See also **Cinyras**.

Adrastea was a Cretan nymph who nursed the baby Zeus and fed him on the milk of the goat Amalthea. Adrastea was also one of the by-names of Nemesis, with whom the Cretan nymph was identified locally. This by-name ostensibly derived from Adrastus, who had erected an altar to Nemesis, but from the very nature of Nemesis (she was the goddess of retribution) the name came to be interpreted as meaning 'inescapable', from the privative prefix *a*- and *didrasco*, 'to escape'. Compare the name of **Adrastus** himself.

Adrastus, we have just seen, means 'inescapable'. In the case of Adrastus, son of Talaüs and Lysimache, and leader of the Argive forces in the war of the Seven Against Thebes, however, it means more 'he who does not run away', 'he who flees from nothing', which as the *Oxford Classical Dictionary* points out is a suitable name for a warrior prince. Indeed, at the conclusion of the war Adrastus was the only one to survive, by escaping on his horse Arion. Escaping, thus, but himself inescapable, however paradoxical this may appear. The fact that he alone survived has also prompted an interpretation of his name to mean 'he who does nothing', 'Do-Nothing', from *a-*, 'not' and *drao*, 'to do'. But this seems an unsatisfactory and negative way of looking at things. A third possibility could be the meaning 'fruitful', from *adros*, 'full-grown', or *adrosyne*, 'ripeness'. This is a good propitious name, but somehow not quite on target for Adrastus. Let us settle for *adrastos*, 'not running away'. (There was another Adrastus who was the son of Merops and a Trojan. We must make him 'inescapable' too, for want of any more specific interpretation.)

Adymnus, the son of Cephalus and Eos, was stolen as a child by Aphrodite to keep watch by night over her most sacred shrines. From this office we can thus get 'not setting' (that is, alert through the night), from the privative *a-* and *dysomenos*, 'setting'. Significantly, Adymnus is frequently identified with Phaëthon, which of course was the name of the son of the sun, Helios.

Aeacus may have a name that is the same as Aeas, the name of a river. He was the son of Zeus and the river-nymph Aegina. In turn he was the father of Peleus and Telamon by Endeïs and of Phocus by Psamathe. Perhaps *aia*, the poetic form of *gaia*, 'earth' lies behind his name, that is, 'earth-born' as distinct from a supernatural origin. A river is very much a thing of the earth.

Aeanes, the son of Amphidamas, seems to have a name that means 'everlasting', from *aianes*. But this seems unsuitable, for Aeanes is also identified with Cleitonymus, who was killed by Patroclus and so therefore anything but 'everlasting'. Perhaps we should consider one of the more general meanings of *aianes* as more appropriate, such as 'wearisome' or 'horrible'. To be killed as the result of a quarrel over a game of dice is indeed a dismal fate. That was what happened to Cleitonymus, alias Aeanes.

Aechmagoras seems to have a name that is a combination of *aichme*, 'war' and *agora*, 'market place'. So this son of Phialo may have had simply a part-factual, part-propitious name, meaning 'one with a warlike spirit from the crowd'.

Aedon was the daughter of Pandareüs, and she married Zethus, king of Thebes. She was the victim of a tragedy, for jealous of Niobe, the wife of her brother Amphion, who had six sons and six daughters, she attempted to kill Niobe's eldest son at night while he was asleep, but mistook the bed and instead killed her own son Itylus, who was sharing the bedroom. Zeus assuaged her grief by turning her into a nightingale, for which the Greek is . . . *aedon.*

Aeëtes, the son of Helios and the Oceanid Perse, was a cruel, ruthless man – and also the father of Medea. Perhaps his name, like that of Aias, derives from *aetos*, 'eagle', a powerful but predatory bird. The eagle in mythology, too, commonly represents the sun, and this is appropriate for Aeëtes' father Helios. On the other hand, there could be another link with the sun if we derive the name of this cruel king of Colchis from *aitho*, 'to light up', 'burn', thus making him 'fiery' as befits the son of Helios. Both derivations are suitable.

Aegaeon is the name used by Homer in the *Iliad* for Briareüs, and it appears to derive, as perhaps does Aegeus, from *aix*, 'goat'. Perhaps the monster was somehow connected with a goat god or goddess.

Aegeus has a name that immediately calls to mind that of the Aegean Sea, and in the famous story of how he, the father of Theseus, threw himself into the sea on seeing Theseus' black sail instead of the white one he had promised to display as a sign of his safe return from Crete, it was in fact the Aegean that received him. But there could also be a connection with *aix*, 'goat' (genitive *aigos*), since this was a popular if poetic term for the waves (much like our 'white horses'). Again, his name may have an echo of *aisso*, 'to move quickly', with or without reference to the rushing of the waves, the leaping of goats, or his own speedy fall into the sea. This last Greek word lies behind the word for 'seashore', too, *aigialos*, which also suggests the name of Aegeus.

Aegialia must surely have a name that is connected with *aigialos*, 'seashore' (see **Aegeus**). She was the daughter of Adrastus and Amphithea, and the wife of Diomedes. She was induced by Nauplius, a 'sea' man if ever there was one, to commit adultery with Cometes, the son of Diomedes' friend Sthenelus.

Aegimius was a king of Doris who called for the aid of Heracles in driving out the Lapiths from his lands. As with other names

27

starting *Aeg-*, it is tempting to suggest a 'goat' connection here as well, especially since he was on the side of the Centaurs against the Lapiths. Before they became famous as 'horse-men' the Centaurs were depicted as goat-men.

Aegisthus, as a baby and the son of Thyestes and his daughter (sic) Pelopia, was abandoned or 'exposed', as mythologists like to say, in a wood. There he was found by a shepherd and nourished, or rather suckled, by a goat. So here we seem able to say 'goat strength' quite readily, from *aix, aigos* 'goat' and *sthenos*, 'strength'.

Aegle was the name of several minor mythological characters, including a girl, the daughter of Panopeus, with whom Theseus fell in love after he had left Ariadne. Another Aegle was one of the Hesperides. For her certainly, and doubtless for many of the others as a generally propitious name, Aegle means 'brightness', 'lustre', 'sunlight' – *aigle*. A 'bright' name like this is suitable for any girl, especially a goddess. The names of all the Hesperides refer to the sun and its light as it sets in the west.

Aegleïs, too, has a name that like that of Aegle means 'bright'. She was one of the four daughters of Hyacinthus, and was sacrificed by the Athenians to Persephone on the grave of the Cyclops Geraestus to rid them of earthquakes.

Aegyptus, the story goes, was sent by his father Belus to rule Arabia. There he conquered the land of the Melampodes ('black feet') and named his kingdom Egypt after himself. But that does not explain his own name, which may again refer to 'goat', from *aix, aigos*. (Possibly 'crouching goat', with the latter half of his name from *ptosso*, 'to cower'?).

Aellopus was a Harpy, who with another Harpy, Ocypete, plagued Phineus. (She was driven off by the sons of Boreas – Calaïs and Zetes.) For such a pest, her name may well derive from *aella*, 'storm', 'whirlwind' and *pos*, 'foot', otherwise 'Stormfoot', a highly apt name for the bird-like blustering creature.

Aeneas, the hero of the *Aeneid* and the son of Anchises and Aphrodite, has simply a pleasantly propitious name – 'praiseworthy', from *aineo*, 'to praise', 'to approve'. Aeneas married Lavinia.

Aeolus was the name of three characters of note. The first was the son of Hippotes, and the king of the (floating) island of Aeolia.

This was the famous controller of the winds. The second was the son of Hellen and Orseïs. He married Enarete and she bore him a good many children, including Sisyphus. He is often confused with the first Aeolus, for example in Ovid's account of the story of Alcyone. (And if the great Greek classical authors confused their heroes, who can blame us if we mere twentieth-century mortals sometimes muddle them up?) The third Aeolus was the son of Poseidon and Melanippe – who was the daughter of Aeolus No. 2 just mentioned! Thinking first and foremost of the wind controller (he was a mortal, not a god), we may find it easy to accept the derivation offered by the seventeenth-century French philologist Samuel Bochart, who claims that Homer got the name from the Phoenician *aol*, 'whirlwind', 'tempest'. Or, looking directly at Greek, perhaps we can consider *aia*, the poetic form of *gaia*, 'earth' and *luo*, 'to destroy', in other words 'earth destroyer'. Or of course, and even more directly, we can go straight to *aella*, 'whirlwind' – the classical Greek equivalent to Bochart's Phoenician word. Yet another possibility, and one that could apply to any Aeolus, is *aiolus*, 'cunning'. It is significant, perhaps, that Hesiod calls Sisyphus *aiolometis*, 'full of various wiles'. In short, the whole matter of identifying and interpreting the various Aeoluses is rather complex, and is not helped by the classical authors' confusion over them. (Diodorus also had problems sorting them out.)

Aërope was the daughter of Catreus, king of Crete. She was bought and married by Atreus, but committed adultery with his brother Thyestes. However, this infidelity does not seem to have a bearing on her name, which would appear to be a propitious one, literally 'air face', from *aer*, 'air' (originally 'mist', i.e. the lower, thicker air as opposed to *aither*, the pure upper air) and *ops*, 'face'. Or if 'air face' sounds somewhat odd, let us rephrase it poetically: 'She with the face of white mist'.

Aesacus fell in love with the nymph Hesperia, and on one occasion while he was pursuing her she was stung by a snake and died. In his grief, Aesacus threw himself into the sea, although he was saved by Thetis who changed him into a diver bird (which constantly plunges into the sea from a height). Perhaps we can see *aisa*, 'fate', 'destiny' behind the name. Aesacus was the son of king Priam and Alexirrhoë (at any rate, according to Ovid's *Metamorphoses*).

Aesculapius is the Latin spelling of the Greek Asclepius. Either way he was the god of healing, and in the Greek accounts was the son of Apollo and Coronis. The Romans 'acquired' him, it seems, in 293 BC when they needed a god to heal a pestilence. Robert Graves has a gallant go at deriving the Latin form of the name from *ex aesculeo apiens*, 'hanging from an esculent oak', with 'esculent' meaning 'fit for food'. In other words, he sees it as mistletoe, the all-healer! For the various possibilities of the Greek spelling, see **Asclepius**.

Aeson was the father of Jason, whose own name seems to echo his father's. Aeson's name may be a propitious one meaning 'ruler', from *aisymnao*, 'to rule over'. If this was the case, its propitiousness was not fulfilled, since he did not become king of Iolcus, as his father Cretheus had been. (He *should* have inherited the throne, but it was usurped by Pelias.)

Aethion or Aethiops was the name of one of the four horses that drew the chariot of Helios. Appropriately, his name means 'fiery', 'burning', from *aithos*, 'burnt', 'fire-coloured'. Taking the second variant of the name, however, we can get either 'fiery face' or 'burnt face', with the latter perhaps meaning 'black'. One still popular version of the origin of the geographical name Ethiopia maintains that it is so called since the inhabitants, the Ethiopians, have black faces!

Aethra was the mother of Theseus by Aegeus. Her name simply seems to mean 'bright sky', from *aithre* (later *aithra*), 'clear sky', 'fair weather'. Another name of good omen, therefore.

Aethylla was the sister of Priam and made her mark by setting fire to the ships of Protesilaüs after she and others had been captured by him. (Normally, of course, one burns one's own boats.) Fittingly, her name means just that: 'one who kindles timber', from *aitho*, 'to light up', 'kindle' (as mentioned when considering Aeëtes) and *hyle*, 'timber'.

Aetolus, the son of Endymion and one of a number of women, accidentally killed Apis by running him over in his chariot at the funeral games held in honour of Azan (the son of Arcas and Erato). We may well be justified, therefore, in seeing a name of ill omen here: perhaps 'cause of destruction', from *aitia*, 'cause' and *olethros*, 'destruction'.

Agamede was a witch, and the daughter of Augeas. Homer says she 'knew all the drugs that grow on earth' (*Iliad*, Book 11), so may we not see 'very cunning' as her name? This would come from *agan*, 'very' and *medea*, 'cunning'. See also **Medea**.

Agamedes has a name that must surely mean the same as Agamede, that is, 'very cunning'. With Trophonius he was the son of Erginus, king of Orchomenus. He was also a clever architect and builder, as was his brother, and both of them displayed considerable cunning in their construction of a treasure-house for Hyrieus (or for Augeas, depending which version of the account one reads). They arranged for one of the stones to be a removable slab, so that thereafter they could gain entry to the treasures unnoticed. This they did, paying several profitable visits, until the king (Hyrieus or Augeas) set traps on discovering that his precious stores were diminishing while the locks remained intact. One such trap ensnared Agamedes, who was entering ahead of his brother on a routine haul, and Trophonius, seeing he was caught fast, cut off his head to conceal Agamedes' identity and also to save him from the agony of the trap. (He himself subsequently, although not immediately, was swallowed up by a hole in the ground.) Cunning indeed, therefore – but at a price.

Agamemnon was the famous (or notorious) husband of Clytemnestra, and himself the son of Atreus (or of Atreus' son Pleisthenes) and Anaxibia. His name borders on a title, since it means 'very resolute', 'he who stands very fast', from *agan*, 'very' and *menos*, 'resolve'. This steadfastness seems to relate not to his numerous violent deeds (such as killing Tantalus and his young child so that he could marry Clytemnestra) but to the 'long stand' of his army before the siege of Troy. Even the sixteenth-century English historian and antiquary William Camden interpreted the name thus in his *Remains Concerning Britain*, where in his chapter 'Christian Names' he writes: 'Agamemnon signified he should linger long before Troy . . . because *Agan menon* . . . implieth such accident'. And twentieth-century scholarship, seeing the name as possibly Mycenaean *Aga-men-mon*, gives it exactly the same sense.

Aganippe is the first 'horse' name in our alphabetical list; 'horse' for the element *hippos* (which, since Aganippe was the wife of Acrisius and the mother of Danaë, we should more exactly render as 'mare'). The first half of her name seems to mean 'gentle' from *aganos*, 'kind'. She was thus 'the gentle mare', which we can take as a generally favourable or propitious name.

Aganus, like Aganippe, also has a name that presumably was intended to be propitious and that also means 'gentle'. Alas, this baby son of Paris and Helen was killed with his two brothers by a roof collapse in Troy . . .

Agapenor was the son of Ancaeüs and grew up to become king of Tegea. His name must mean exactly what it says, 'manly', 'loving manliness', from *agapenor* (itself a compound of *agapao*, 'to be fond of' and *aner*, 'man'). So simply a 'good' name.

Agathyrsus, with Gelonus and Scythes, was one of the triplet sons of Heracles and the woman-serpent monster Echidna. For the offspring of such fearsome parents, it seems reasonable to expect a name that means 'much raging', from *agan*, 'very', 'much' and *thyo*, 'to storm', 'to rage'.

Agave was the daughter of Cadmus and Harmonia, and the wife of Echion. Her name seems to be the straightforward propitious epithet *agauos*, 'illustrious' (a by-name, incidentally, of Persephone among others). Or if we allow greater flexibility in the name, we can derive it from *eugenes*, 'well-born'. But both meanings are similar. We can compromise by choosing a word of classical origin and call her 'Agave the August'. Her son Pentheus indeed was illustrious, since he became a king of Thebes.

Agelaüs was the name of several personages, but perhaps we should consider three of them: one of the three sons (with Lamus and Laomedon) of Heracles and Omphale, a son of Damastor who was one of the suitors of Penelope, and Priam's chief herdsman who adopted Paris, the baby son of Hecabe (whom he was in fact told to put to death). For the last of these three we can straight away see *agele*, 'herd' as being the obvious word. Such an origin is not so appropriate for the first two, since there is no evidence that they were herdsmen (or indeed that they were not), so perhaps we can extend the 'herd' concept and see *agelaios*, 'common' (i.e. one of the common herd) as a possibility for them.

Agenor, 'very manly', from *agan*, 'very', and *aner*, 'man' – this is the meaning of the favourable name borne by a number of people, including the son of Poseidon and Libya who became king of Phoenicia, and the son of Antenor who fought in the Trojan War.

Aglaia was one of the three Graces, and the wife of Hephaestes, Homer tells us in the *Iliad*. And her name is a suitably 'graceful' one, since *aglaia* means 'splendour', 'beauty', 'brightness'.

Aglaurus or **Agraulus** was the name of two Athenian women who need distinguishing as carefully as the confusing alternative spellings of their name. The first was the daughter of Actaeus, the first king of Athens. She married Cecrops. The second was the daughter of this same Cecrops and the first Aglaurus, and the mother of Alcippe by Ares. We therefore have two similar names to interpret and two close relationships to consider. Aglaurus we can take to mean 'bright one', from *aglaos*, 'beautiful', 'bright' (compare Aglaia in the previous entry), related to *aigle*, 'sunlight'; Agraulus can be derived from the exact word *agraulos*, 'dwelling in the fields' (*agros* is 'field'), so 'rural', 'rustic'. Both names are either generally descriptive or simply favourable. The first Aglaurus had three daughters (the Aglaurides) whose names are similarly rustic. One of them, of course, was Aglaurus No. 2, which is straightforward enough – like mother, like daughter. The other two were Herse and Pandrosus. It seems that the original spelling was Agraulos. Both variants were also used as by-names for Athena (see Appendix IV, page 327).

Aglaüs was one of the three sons of Thyestes and a Naiad, his two brothers being Callileon and Orchomenus. In spite of his grisly fate (he was killed by his uncle Atreus, together with both his brothers, and served up to his father Thyestes as a tasty dish) his name simply means 'splendid', 'beautiful', *aglaos* (compare **Aglaurus** in the previous entry).

Agrius was the name of the son of Odysseus and Circe, it was the name of the son of Porthaon and Euryte, and it was the name of a giant, among others. They all come from the common adjective *agrios*, 'wild' – in the sense 'rustic' (compare Agraulus, under **Aglaurus**).

Aias, see **Ajax**.

Ajax is the Roman version (and to us the familiar one) of the name that to the Greeks was *Aias*. In fact there were two great warriors of the name. The better-known one, second only to Achilles in the *Iliad* as a powerful Greek warrior, was the son of Telamon of Salamis and Periboea. Traditionally, his name derives from *aietos*, 'eagle', from the one seen by his father when, before his birth, Heracles prayed to Zeus to give his friend a brave son. The second Ajax, sometimes known as the Lesser Ajax, was the son of Oïleus, king of the Locrians, and Eriopis. He was a suitor for Helen, and, although he often fought on the same side as the

Achilles and Ajax. Both men are great warriors, both great friends. Here they relax together over a board game. Note each man's armour behind him, with Ajax' helmet on top of his.

'Great' Ajax, was different from him in a number of ways. 'Great' Ajax was tall and slow; 'Little' Ajax was short and fleet of foot. The Lesser Ajax, too, was arrogant and conceited, unlike his better-known namesake. For him we can perhaps suggest the other derivation for the name sometimes favoured – 'of the earth', from *aia*, the poetic form of *gaia*, 'earth'. Though of course there is no reason why this interpretation should not be applied to Telamon's son, or indeed either derivation to either. Sophocles related the name to *aiazo*, 'to wail', 'cry ah' (Greeks exclaimed *aiai* to mourn or wail, rather like the English 'alas!'), and indeed both heroes came to a grievous end: 'Great' Ajax killed himself with his sword, the gift of Hector, when filled with remorse for planning an attack on his own allies; the Lesser Ajax, having swum to safety on a rock when his ship sank, was drowned when Poseidon blasted the rock to pieces with a thunderbolt. So we have here a choice of three possible origins.

Alalcomeneus was a hero who founded the town of Alalcomenae, in Boeotia, where Athena was said to have been born. His name appears to mean 'guardian', from *alalcein*, 'to defend' and *menos*, 'strength'. It is no coincidence that his name is the masculine form of one of Athena's by-names (as guardian goddess of Boeotia).

Alastor was the son of Neleus and Chloris and married Harpalyce. His name means 'avenger' (*alastor*, from *a*-, 'not' and ultimately *lanthanomai*, 'to forget'), but there is no record of vengeance in any of the stories about him (chiefly those of Apollodorus). Perhaps a lost story had an account of Alastor being the victim of some sacrifice. According to Hesychius and the *Etymologicum Magnum*, Alastor was also one of the many by-names of Zeus.

Alcaeüs, whether the son of Perseus and Andromeda who was the grandfather of Heracles, or the son of Androgeüs and grandson of Minos, has a name that means 'the mighty one', from *alce*, 'bodily strength', 'force'. Such a name is highly apt for the grandfather of the mighty Heracles, and in fact according to Diodorus it was actually the original name of Heracles. See also **Alcon**.

Alcathoüs, like Alcaeüs, has a name based on 'force'. He was the son of Pelops and Hippodamia, and he won the kingdom of Megara by an appropriately 'forceful' act – he killed a lion (thus also obtaining Euaechme, daughter of the king of Megara, Megareus, for his wife). The second half of his name must come

35

from *thoos*, 'quick', 'ready', so his whole name means something like 'impetuous prowess'.

Alcestis also has a 'strong' name, from *alce*, 'force', with the second half of her name deriving from *estia*, 'home'. So she was the 'power of the home', the 'force of the family'. She was the daughter of Pelias, king of Iolcus, and Anaxibia, and she married Admetus. Her heroic self-sacrifice (she volunteered to die for Admetus on the promise of Apollo that Admetus would never die if someone else could be found to die in his place) is the subject of Euripides' play with her name as its title, and also of Gluck's opera *Alceste* based on this play.

Alcides see **Heracles**.

Alcidice was the daughter of Aleüs and the first wife of Salmoneus, king of Salmonia, to whom she bore Tyro. Her name means 'mighty justice', from *alce*, 'force', 'mighty' and *dice*, 'right', 'justice'. There is little in the stories about her that indicates any specific rendering of justice (in fact she died young, and Salmoneus married Sidero), so her name must simply be propitious.

Alcimede also has a propitious name: 'mighty cunning', from *alce*, 'force' and *medea*, 'schemes', 'cunning'. She was the mother of Jason by Aeson, and the daughter of Phylacus, king of Phylace. See also **Alcon**.

Alcimedes has a name that means exactly the same as that of Alcimede: 'mighty cunning'. Moreover his name reflects that of his mother, Medea. His father was Jason. Alcimedes and his five brothers were all seized and put to death by the Corinthians, who were incensed by the murder of Glauce and Creon. With a male, incidentally, we must always consider the possibility that the '-mede' or '-medes' element in a name could also mean 'genitals', another sense of Greek *medea*. Compare **Ganymede**.

Alcimedon was the father of Phillo, an Arcadian girl who was seduced by Heracles. He himself was a minor Arcadian hero, but not a king in spite of his name which means 'mighty ruler', from *alce*, 'power' and *medon*, 'ruler', 'guardian'. The name is merely a favourable one.

Alcinoüs has a name that means 'mighty mind', from the familiar element *alce*, 'might' and *noos* or *nous*, 'mind', 'resolve' (the English 'nous' popularly used to mean more 'gumption'). He was the son of Nausithoüs and a grandson of Poseidon, and himself the father of Nausicaä and five sons. His name is particularly famous in the *Odyssey*, since it was to him that Odysseus related the tale of his wanderings. Perhaps his 'mighty mind' made him the right person for this honour!

Alcippe is the name of two girls of note, and of a number of others in various authors. The two best known are the daughter of Ares and Aglaurus who was raped in Athens by Halirrothius (he was slain by Ares for this crime), and a girl who was (unwittingly) similarly violated by her brother Astraeüs. In spite of these subjections, the name is simply a 'good and noble' one, meaning 'mighty mare', from *alce*, 'might' and *hippos*, 'horse', 'mare'. See also **Alcon**.

Alcis, the daughter of Antipoenus, together with her sister Androclea, gave her life 'for the common good' in place of her father, whose obligation this act of self-sacrifice really was. She thus lived up to her rather understated name which simply means 'might', 'prowess', from the now all-familiar *alce*.

Alcithoë (sometimes spelt Alcathoë) was one of the daughters of Minyas. Her name means exactly the same as that of Alcathoüs – 'impetuous might'. In spite of this purely propitious name, all three daughters (the other two were Arsippe and Leucippe, both 'mare' names) were turned into bats.

Alcmaeon was the son of Amphiaraüs and Eriphyle, the brother of Amphilocus, and one of the heroes of the saga of the Seven Against Thebes, although not one of the Seven himself (his father was). Appropriately, the name of the man who led the Seven and captured Thebes means 'mighty endeavour', from *alce* and *maiomai*, 'to endeavour', 'strive'.

Alcmene was the daughter of Electryon and Anaxo, and the wife of her uncle Amphitryon. Even more importantly, she was the mother of Heracles. (After the death of Amphitryon she married Rhadamanthys.) Her name could mean 'mighty wrath', with the second element *menis*, 'wrath', 'anger', or even 'might of the moon', from *men*, 'month', 'moon'. Her 'might' can be seen in her refusal to grant Amphitryon his conjugal rights until he had avenged the death of her brothers who had been killed when trying to protect Electryon's cattle in a raid by men from the Taphian islands.

37

(Amphitryon got the cattle back but in the process accidentally killed Electryon.) See also **Alcon**.

Alcon was a Cretan archer, famous for shooting the snake that had seized his sleeping child (without harming the child). In this deed he justified his name which, like those immediately before it here, means 'mighty'. The popular name-word *alce* can range from 'bodily strength' and 'might' through 'defence' and 'aid' to 'battle', 'fight' in its meanings, so we can choose, for each of the above-listed characters from Alcaeüs on, whichever shade of meaning seems the most fitting.

Alcyone is a name shared by more than one character. The best known is probably the Alcyone who was the daughter of Aeolus, king of Thessaly, and Enarete (or maybe Aegiale). She was the wife of Ceÿx, and the two were so happy that they presumptuously called themselves 'Zeus' and 'Hera', for which sacrilege they were turned into birds – Ceÿx into a gannet and Alcyone into a king-fisher, for which the Greek is *alcyone* (compare the English word 'halcyon'). According to another story, however, Ceÿx was drowned at sea while going in search of an oracle, and Alcyone, overcome by grief, later found his body washed up on the seashore. Taking pity on them, the gods turned *both* of them into kingfishers. Kingfishers nest every winter, and to enable them to do this Aeolus, commander of the winds, sends calm weather; sailors called such weather the 'halcyon days' – hence the English expression. How-ever, the 'kingfisher' explanation is not the only one for the name. Also proposed have been 'sea-dog', from *hals*, 'sea' and *cyon*, 'dog', 'bitch' and (predictably) 'strength', 'might', from *alce*, perhaps in the meaning 'defence' (see **Alcon**). Another well-known Alcyone was the daughter of Atlas and Pleïone, and the name was also one of the by-names of Cleopatra, the daughter of Idas and Mar-pessa and wife of Meleager.

Alcyoneus was a giant who fought Heracles (and lost). One would expect a 'mighty' name for him, and so here we can use *alce*, 'might', with confidence. The latter half of his name may have no special significance, although it could derive from *onus*, 'ass', with some reference to the wild asses that lived in the deserted areas of the isthmus of Corinth where Alcyoneus held sway.

Alecto was one of the Furies, and the name of one of these female spirits of vengeance appropriately means 'unceasing', from the privative *a-*, 'not' and *lego*, 'to lie down', thus 'never-ending', 'not easing up'.

Aletes was the name of both the son of Hippotas and the son of Aegisthus and Clytemnestra. We can see as the origin either *aletes*, 'wanderer', 'rover' or *alethes*, 'true', 'sincere'. The only wandering undertaken by either was the journey of Hippotas' son to Corinth disguised as a beggar in order to learn, by being given a 'token' of a lump of earth, whether he would become king of Corinth. (He was given the earth and became king.) The second interpretation is just a vaguely commendatory one.

Aleüs has a name that means 'grinder', from *aleo*, 'to grind', 'pound'. Quite what grinding or pounding this king of Arcadia did is not clear. Perhaps the name has a metaphorical sense, indicating a kind of rough or dogged persistence. Aleüs married Neaera who bore him four children.

Alexander is the name preferred by Homer for Paris. Either way (and it is unusual to have such a prominent character featuring under two different names) he was the son of Priam, king of Troy, and Hecabe. Any book of boys' names will (or should) tell you that this still-common first name means 'protector of men'. At birth Alexander was given to a shepherd, Agelaüs, to abandon in the open. Agelaüs did so, but on checking his fate found that the child had been suckled by a she-bear. He was unable to bring himself to kill the boy, so adopted him. The child grew into a strong, handsome and brave lad, and, the story goes, Agelaüs, or all the shepherds, named him Alexander *apo tou alexein tous andras*, 'from the defending of men'. The two elements of the name are thus *alexo*, 'to ward off', 'repel', hence 'defend' and *aner*, genitive *andros*, 'man'. In Homer's account of the siege of Troy, Alexander (Paris) does not show marked aggressiveness or valour, in fact, and in the battle against the Trojans fought only one duel face-to-face, which was with Menelaüs. It was Paris (Alexander), however, who finally killed Achilles. See also **Paris**.

Alexiares was one son of Heracles and Hebe, the other being Anicetus. For the son of such a hero he has a fittingly belligerent name: 'one who wards off war', from *alexo*, 'to ward off' and *ares* (see **Ares**), 'war'.

Alexirrhoë was the wife of Dionysus and mother of Carmanor. Her name seems to have the somewhat curious sense of 'repelling

39

the flowing', from *alexo*, 'to ward off' and *rrhoe*, 'flow' (as in 'dia-rrhoea' if one may quote some medical Greek). She is mentioned in Ovid's *Metamorphoses* as being a daughter of the river Granicus, so here may be the origin of the 'flowing', or lack of it. However she may have had the power to prevent the flowing of something undesirable, as of blood, or an enemy force.

Alöeus, the son of Uranus and Gaia, has an agricultural name, 'of the threshing floor', from *aloao*, 'to thresh'. He married Iphi-media first, and then Eriboea, who interestingly also has an agri-cultural name.

Alope was the daughter of Cercyon, and was dearly loved by Poseidon – by whom she had Hippothoüs. Her name seems to be based on *alopex*, 'fox'. Perhaps in some way she was a cunning little vixen.

Alpheius was a river god, the son of Oceanus and Tethys. His name simply seems to be a propitious one, since *alphano* means 'to yield', 'to acquire'. The nymph Arethusa bathed in his river, and Alpheius fell for her and married her.

Alphesiboea, the daughter of king Phegeus, married Alcmaeon, and she is alternatively known as Arsinoë. As Alphesiboea, her name means 'bringing in oxen', from *alphano*, 'to bring in', and *bous*, 'ox'. Such a title was not meant literally – she was not a cattlehand or cowgirl. What it implied was that the girl's parents would be given many presents of oxen from those who sought to marry her, so perhaps we can regard the name as nearer 'much-wooed'. Perhaps Alcmaeon's oxen, if he brought them, were rather special. (We do know that he gave his new wife two rather unusual presents: the necklace and wedding dress of Harmonia, which originally Cadmus had given to her as *her* wedding presents.)

Althaea has a name that apparently derives from *althomai*, 'to heal'. She was the mother of Meleager by her uncle Oeneus. There was a story that at the birth of Meleager Althaea had been told by the Fates that when a log burning in the fire was quite burnt out her son would die. She quickly snatched it out and kept it in a chest. In keeping the log 'whole' like this, we may have a hint at the significance of her name. Later, however, when Meleager killed her brothers Toxeus and Plexippus during the famous Calydonian boar-hunt, she angrily put the log back on the fire. It burnt through and Meleager died. There may be another link in the Greek word for 'marshmallow', *althaia*, a plant thought to have healing properties.

Althaemenes was hardly a pleasant person. This son of Catreus, king of Crete, kicked his sister Apemosyne to death when he heard she was pregnant as a result of being raped by Hermes, then killed his father. In the end, however, he repented of these terrible deeds and either died from grief or, depending on the story, was swallowed up in the earth. Perhaps the root of his name is also *althomai*, 'to become whole', 'heal', as in the end he prayed to the gods for forgiveness and Diodorus even tells how the Rhodians came to regard him as a hero.

Amalthea was a she-goat, or the nymph who owned it. In many stories she was the goat who suckled the baby Zeus (see **Adrastea**). The goat's horns flowed with nectar and ambrosia. According to Ovid, one of them broke off and the nymphs filled it with fruit for Zeus – hence the Latin term *cornu copiae*, 'horn of plenty' that gives the English 'cornucopia'. Eventually Amalthea was turned into the constellation Capricorn, that is (Latin again), *capri cornu*, 'goat's horn'. But what of the name Amalthea itself? There are several theories as to the origin, many of them having *amalos*, 'soft', 'tender' as the basis. (*Amale thea* would mean 'tender goddess'.) On the other hand a popular explanation would certainly be apt. Hesychius sees the origin in *amaltheuein*, 'to nourish', 'enrich', and others again suggest *amalthactos*, 'hard', 'unsoftened' (presumably a reference to the horns) – but this is almost the exact opposite of the 'tender' theory. And the French philologist Bochart, whom we quoted on Aeolus, says the name derives from the Phoenician *amantha*, 'nurse'! In short, as Dr Smith says in his *Dictionary* (see Bibliography, page 341): 'The ancients themselves appear to have been as uncertain about the etymology of the name as about the real nature of Amalthea.'

Amazons present almost as much difficulty as Amalthea when it comes to the origin of their name. They were, of course, the famed race of warrior women who came not from the region of the river Amazon (which was named allusively after them, in reference to some tribal women here who impressed the early explorers) but from somewhere in or near the Caucasus. The popular origin of their name, but one that the *Oxford Classical Dictionary* calls 'fanciful', is in *a-*, 'not' 'without', and *mazos* 'breast', that is, 'breastless'. According to the traditional tales, the girl children of the race were trained in the usual skills of war as well as riding, hunting,

An Amazon in battle. The name could mean 'warrior' in some ancient language. Here the Amazon does not have her right breast bared, as in many depictions of the women.

and land cultivation, but each of them had her right breast cut off, allegedly to enable her to shoot more accurately with the bow when hunting or fighting. (The boys, meanwhile, were either ignominiously sent away to the Gargareans, a race with whom the Amazons coupled once a year in the mountains in order to propagate their kind, or put to death.) Such a derivation is, one might say, not only 'fanciful', but anatomically hardly justifiable. Indeed, it would make more sense to interpret the idea as meaning 'not brought up by the breast', or even to regard the prefix a- not as a privative but as an intensive, thus giving a sense 'with strong breasts'. A more reasonable theory is to propose a-, 'not' and *maza*, 'barley', 'barley-cake', since being hunters the women were meat-eaters, not domestic stay-at-home breadmakers. Not 'breastless', therefore, but 'breadless'. But perhaps the most likely derivation is in some old word actually meaning 'warrior', probably Iranian in origin. The French philologist Émile Boisacq, in his *Dictionnaire étymologique de la langue grecque*, claims that there may have been an Old Persian word *hamazan* meaning just this. Not as colourful, of course, but truth is not always stranger than fiction, at any rate in etymology.

Ameinias was a young admirer of Narcissus, and his most persistent suitor. When Narcissus sent him a sword, however, his lover killed himself with it on the very threshold of Narcissus' house, so that – says one story – Narcissus took his own life in remorse. (For more about this, see **Narcissus**.) Ameinias seems to have a name that means 'not tarrying', 'unpausing', from a-, 'not' and *meno*, 'to stay behind', 'tarry'. This would be an appropriate name for an ernest suitor.

Amor is the Roman equivalent of Eros, the god of love, and the word is simply a translation of the Greek name. He was alternatively known, of course, as Cupid. He had no independent place in Roman mythology, since the Romans knew of him and told of him only what they had learned from the Greeks.

Ampelus was a beautiful boy loved by Dionysus. Alas, a wild bull gored him and so Dionysus turned him into a vine (*ampelos*). A vine is rather a satisfactory memorial for one you have loved – both attractive and pleasure-giving.

Amphiaraüs was the son of Oïcles and Hypermestra, and a seer. He married Eriphyle, the sister of Adrastus, and was the father of Alcmaeon and Amphilocus. The element *amphi-* has a number of meanings, and we must consider whichever is fitting in each case. Its basic meaning is 'on both sides' or 'around' (as in 'amphitheatre'), but it can also mean 'for', 'near' and 'by means of'. We would do best to try the 'double' or 'around' sense first for this name and those that follow. Here perhaps we have the meaning 'doubly cursed', with the second half of the name *araios*, 'cursed'. As a seer, he could (of course) foresee the future, and so knew that the expedition of the Seven Against Thebes was bound to fail. Eriphyle, however, insisted that he should go. Thus he was doubly cursed: whether he went on the expedition or not, it was doomed to fail. (In fact he was not killed during the battles: just as he was about to be speared in the back, Zeus opened up a hole in the ground which swallowed Amphiaraüs up, together with his chariot and horses.) If we see 'Ares' in the latter half of his name, however, we get a similar sense – 'twice Ares-like'. Ares was the god of war, and Amphiaraüs was a great warrior; at the same time he was a prophet, so had an additional or second 'strength'. This would make him 'doubly Ares'. A third possibility would be to read the second element of his name as *ieros*, 'holy', so that his complete name would mean 'twice sacred'. This could be to emphasise that he was a real man, as the Greeks did not use *ieros* of a god. It is in fact still doubtful whether Amphiaraüs was actually a god or a mortal.

Amphictyon was a king of Athens, and the son of Deucalion and Pyrrha. If the first half of his name means more 'around' than 'double' we get 'one who lives round', or (using one of the other senses of *amphi*- mentioned above under **Amphiaraüs**) 'one who lives near'. In this sense he could perhaps personify the people who 'lived roundabout' Thermopylae, and some accounts say he was the founder of the so-called Amphictionic League of Thermopylae, this being an association of people who were connected with the local temple and maintained a cult there. There were several such leagues, but the one at Thermopylae was the most important. His name passed into the language – the English language as well (see the *Concise Oxford Dictionary*, for example, or *Collins English Dictionary*).

Amphidamas was one of the Argonauts, together with his brother Cepheus. He was the son of Aleüs. Another Amphidamas, sometimes confused with him, was the son of Lycurgus and the father of Melanion and Antimache. Whether one or two persons, the name means 'taming all about him', from *amphi*-, 'around' and *damazo*, 'to tame'. This would be a generally propitious name for a child growing up in a land of battles to be won and obstacles to be overcome.

Amphilocus was also the name of two men, this time uncle and nephew. The uncle was the younger son of Amphiaraüs and Eriphyle, and one of the Epigoni who made war on Thebes ten years after the attack of the Seven. His name is clearly and practically warlike, since it means either 'double ambush' or 'ambush all round', with the second half of the name coming from the word for 'ambush', *lochos*. Amphilocus the nephew was the son of Alcmaeon and Manto, and fought in the Trojan War.

Amphimarus was sometimes said to be the father of Linus by Urania. He was also a musician, as whom we can interpret his name as 'ambidextrous', since *amphi-* means 'double' and *mare* is an alternative word for *cheir*, 'hand'.

Amphinomus was a suitor of Penelope in the *Odyssey*, and was killed by Telemachus. With *amphi-* giving 'about', the second half of his name seems to mean 'pasture', 'feeding' or 'division' (*nome*). Perhaps the last of these is suitable, since he sought to dissuade all the other suitors from killing Telemachus on his return from Sparta, that is, he 'divided all round'.

Amphion was the son of Zeus and Antiope, and with his twin Zethus ruled Thebes. Here we seem to have 'one from both lands', from *amphi-*, 'both' and *onos*, 'land'. This is very appropriate for Amphion, since he was a citizen of both Thebes and Sicyon. Of course, in view of Zethus we could extend the sense to 'double land', that is, 'a district ruled by two'.

Amphissa was the daughter of Macareus and Canace, and she was loved by Apollo. Her name appears to mean 'double strength', from the familiar *amphi-*, 'double', and *is*, 'strength', and would simply be a favourable name: 'may this child have the strength of two'.

Amphissus, the son of Apollo and Dryope, has the name of precisely the same meaning as Amphissa: 'double strength', or using another sense of *amphi-*, 'strength on both sides'. This is a good propitious name.

Amphitrite was a sea goddess, the daughter of Nereus and Doris, or according to another version, of Oceanus and Tethys. She

45

married Poseidon, and one of the children she bore him was Triton. There are plenty of maritime connections here, but it is not so easy to find an appropriate sense for the name, especially the second half of it. Assuming *amphi-* is the usual 'round' or 'on both sides', what can we propose for *-trite*? Of course, 'Triton' immediately suggests itself, and we know one of her children was so named. This is helpful, but still does not tell us the exact sense – and it is not certain that Triton had a name that is Greek in any case (see this name). Greek *tritos* means 'third', but what would 'third around' mean? Robert Graves settles for this interpretation (more precisely, 'the third one who encircles'), ingeniously seeing the sea as the third of the four ancient elements: it is cast about the earth, which is the first element, and above it rises the air, the second element. But if we take *-trite* (and also perhaps the name Triton) to be based on *tryo*, 'to wear out', 'consume', then we have the overall sense of Amphitrite's name to mean something like 'corroder', 'she who wears away all round'. Perhaps this is the version we should prefer for the goddess of the sea.

Amphitryon, son of Alcaeüs and grandson of Perseus, married his cousin Alcmene (Electryon's daughter). His mother was Astydamia. His name could well mean what we proposed finally for Amphitrite, that is, 'one who wears away on both sides', in the sense of 'all-round harasser'. Amphitryon certainly caused a good deal of harassment: he accidentally killed his father-in-law Electryon (as mentioned under Alcmene), killed Comaetho who had fallen in love with him, and threatened to kill the whole family of Heracles. His name seems appropriate, therefore!

Amyclas was the son of Lacedaemon and Sparte, and father of Hyacinthus by Diomede. We are told little about him, and certainly not enough to justify interpreting his name (perhaps) as 'very lustful', with *a-* here the intensive prefix ('very') and *machlos* meaning 'lewd', 'lustful'. This sense therefore can only be a conjecture.

Amycus was a barbarous and belligerent man who used to challenge all newcomers in Bithynia, where he was a king, to a boxing match. He always won and killed them, until he met his match in Polydeuces who beat him easily and killed *him*. In view of this violent career, we may see his name as based on the intensive prefix *a-*, 'very', 'much' and *mycoamai*, 'to bellow'. This son of Poseidon and Melia, therefore, was a 'loud bellower'.

Amymone was one of the fifty daughters of Danaüs, and she bore Poseidon a son, the famous sailor Nauplius. Her name simply seems to be a generally propitious one, from *amymon*, 'blameless', 'excellent'.

Amyntor, son of Ormenus, has a name that means exactly 'defender', 'avenger' (*amyntor*). Not only was he king of Ormenium, a city that he did indeed defend, but was killed by Heracles when refusing him the hand of his daughter, Astydamia. Amyntor's wife was Cleobule, who also bore him a son, Phoenix.

Amythaon was the son of Cretheus and Tyro. He married Idomene, who bore him Melampus and Bias. His name means 'great speaker', from the intensive prefix *a-*, 'much' and *mythos*, 'speech', 'talk', 'tale'. This is a suitable name for a man who not only had a great seer as his son (Melampus) but also whose wife's name means 'seer', 'one who knows' (from *eido*, see **Idmon**).

Anax was the giant king of Anactoria, and the son of Uranus and Gaia. His name simply means 'king', which is perfectly adequate, if commonplace. (Even the name of his kingdom, Anactoria, means 'kingdom'! Later, so the story goes, the Cretan Miletus conquered the land and changed its name to . . . Miletus.)

Anaxagoras has a rather agreeable name, meaning 'king of the market place', from *anax*, 'king' and *agora*, 'place of assembly', 'market place' (hence 'agoraphobia' as a medical term for the fear of public places or open spaces). He was indeed a king, of Argos, and his name is really little more than a title for one who rules over a populated place.

Anaxarete was a Cypriot princess loved despairingly by Iphis, who finally hanged himself when she would not respond to his continued entreaties of love and lamentations. In spite of her callous indifference (which maybe had some justification, for all we know), her name is a fair one, not a foul: 'excellent princess', from *anassa*, 'princess' (the feminine of *anax*, 'lord', 'king') and *arete*, 'excellence'.

Anaxibia was a name borne by at least two mythological ladies. One of them was the daughter of Bias and Iphianassa, who married Pelias; the other was a daughter of Pleisthenes and a sister of Agamemnon and Menelaüs. Although not apparently princesses

47

or queens, both women have 'royal' names, in a propitious sense: 'queenly strength', from *anassa*, 'queen', and *bia*, 'strength', 'might'.

Anaxo was the sister of Amphitryon (who married her daughter Alcmene). She married her uncle, Electryon, brother of her father Alcaeüs. Her name simply means 'queen' (*anassa*, feminine of *anax*, 'king'). The sense is generally commendatory, not actual.

Ancaeüs could be one person or two, depending which story about him one takes. One Ancaeüs could have been the son of Lycurgus and Creophile (or Eurynome); the other was perhaps the son of Poseidon and Astydamia. Either way, Ancaeüs was an Argonaut who was killed by a boar, either (Ancaeüs One) in the Calydonian boar-hunt or (Ancaeüs Two) in his own vineyard. There is no reference to the sea or a boar in the name, however, which would appear to derive from *ancon*, 'bend', 'anything in the shape of a bend'. But perhaps the 'bend' was that of the boar's fatal tusks?

Anchiale was a nymph noted for throwing dust in the cave in Crete where Zeus was reared, the dust becoming the Dactyls of Mount Ida. Her name means 'near the sea', from *anchi*, 'near' and *hals*, 'sea', a rather vague descriptive name which could be appropriate for anyone associated with a smallish sea-girt island like Crete.

Anchinoë, the wife of Belus, was a river nymph. Her name, *anchinoia*, 'ready wit', 'shrewdness', is either descriptive or simply favourable.

Anchises was the father of Aeneas by Aphrodite, no less, so a person of some importance. It is possible to see in his name the sense 'near to Isis', from *anchi*, 'near' and the name of the great Egyptian goddess. Why Isis? We know that this goddess had a widespread cult that extended to Greece, where she was identified with Demeter. Possibly Anchises' name thus shows that Aphrodite could also be identified with Isis. Both, for example, were originally important as goddesses of fertility. But on the other hand Aphrodite's Asiatic equivalent is usually thought of as Ishtar, not Isis, and unless the latter half of Anchises' name is in fact 'Ishtar', this explanation seems very uncertain. Geoffrey Grigson points out that Anchises could be a form of Agdistis, the other name of Cybele.

Ancius was a Centaur, and together with Agrius one of the first to assail Heracles when he was on his way to his Fourth Labour (The Erymanthian Boar). Perhaps he came from a bend of the river, or a dell (*ancon*).

Androclea was the daughter of Antipoenus. Together with her sister Alcis she gave her life in place of her father, whose duty this really should have been. Her name means 'glory of men' (*aner, andros*, 'man' and *cleos*, 'fame', 'glory') – perhaps an unintentional reflection of the patriarchal society of the time!

Androgenea was the mother of Asterius and several other children by Minos. Her name seems apt for her basic role, what we know of it, as a progenitrix, for it merely means 'mother of men', 'man begetter', from *aner, andros*, 'man' and *genea*, 'birth' (compare English 'generation' and similar words).

Androgeüs was one of the sons of Minos and Pasiphaë, with the somewhat basic name meaning 'man of the earth': *aner, andros*, 'man' and *ge*, 'earth'. The name almost hints at someone who is 'down-to-earth', just another one in the same mould.

Andromache has something of an Amazonian name – 'she who fights against men', from *aner, andros*, 'man' and *mache*, 'battle', 'fight'. She was the daughter of Eëtion and wife of Hector, later becoming the war bride of Achilles' son, Neoptolemus, who gave her three sons (Molossus, Pergamus and Peilus), and after that becoming the wife of Helenus, to whom she bore one son, Cestrinus. Virtually her whole life was a 'battle against men', since her father and seven brothers were put to the sword by Achilles, as was her first husband Hector, with her baby son by him, Astyanax, being thrown off the walls of Troy, and her second husband Neoptolemus being killed at Delphi. From her touching scenes in the *Iliad*, Andromache came to stand for all women who suffer in war.

Andromeda, whose name is as familiar from the constellation (and science fiction stories) as from the paintings of the girl chained to a rock at the foot of a cliff (where she was rescued by Perseus), was a 'ruler of men', according to her name which is composed of *aner, andros*, 'man' and *medon*, 'ruler', 'guardian' (compare **Medusa**). She was the daughter of Cepheus, king of Joppa, and Cassiopea, and although promised to Phineus became the wife of her deliverer, Perseus. She herself was not a ruler in the accepted sense, but of course she was of royal stock and Perseus later became

49

king of Argos, as his grandfather Acrisius had been before him. Her name, therefore, is a blend of part-factual, part-favourable. The constellation name is so ancient that we must wonder which came first, the stars or the girl of mythology.

Andron, the son of Anius and Dorippe, was king of Andros, and was taught augury by Apollo. His name actually means 'man's apartment', *andron*, perhaps emphasising his kingly role.

Anicetus was the son of Heracles and Hebe, and brother of Alexiares. As befits the son of such a great hero, his name is a belligerently favourable one: 'invincible', from *anicetos* (*a-*, 'not' and *nicao*, 'to conquer').

Anippe was the daughter of the river Nile and was the mother of Busiris (although some accounts say Lysianassa was) by Poseidon. As simply a compliment, her name means 'queenly mare', from *anassa*, 'queen' and *hippos*, 'horse', 'mare'.

Anius was the son of Apollo and Rhoeo. He became king of the island of Delos and married Dorippe, who bore him Andron, Elaïs, Oeno and Spermo. His name means 'troublous', from *anios*, a shortening of *aniaros*, 'grievous', 'distressing'. According to the classical accounts, Rhoeo, mother of Anius, had been locked in a chest by her father Apollo when he discovered she was pregnant, and the chest had been set adrift at sea. Washed ashore on the coast of Euboea, Rhoeo escaped from the chest and gave birth to a boy whom she named Anius 'because of the trouble she had suffered on his account'.

Anna, a name still popular today, was the sister of queen Dido of Carthage and Pygmalion, and the daughter of Belus. (She is sometimes referred to as Anna Perenna, since she was worshipped as the nymph of the river Numicius under this name, allegedly, if naively, because she lay in a 'perennial' river.) Her name, of course, means whatever Ann(e) means, and it is generally held to be of Semitic origin, having the sense 'the gracious one'. (Compare the Biblical Hannah, whose name means this, in the opening chapters of I Samuel.) But perhaps of greater interest to us are the classical interpretations of the name. One is given by Ovid in his *Fasti* (the title means roughly 'A Poetical Calendar'), where he writes of Anna being the name of the moon, *quia mensibus impleat annum* – 'because by its months it fills up the year'. Another Roman writer, Macrobius, states in his *Saturnalia* that Anna's festival on

15 March (the Ides of March!) was celebrated by the Romans with great joy and merriment, the people praying *ut annare perennareque commode liceat* – 'that it might be permitted them in proper measure for the year and throughout the year'. A suitable prayer, naturally, at the return of spring. In short, the 'ancients' equated her name with Latin *annus*, 'year'.

Antaeüs was a giant, the son of Poseidon and Gaia. His name seems to be based on *anti*, 'opposite', in some way, but the exact allusion is not very clear. The Greek word *antaios*, which is close to his name, means both 'set over against' and 'besought with prayers'. Perhaps this latter sense is applicable to him somehow. Or perhaps he was 'opposite' in the sense that people came face to face with him, that they met him suddenly (an awesome experience, surely). The Greek verb *antao* means 'to come opposite to', 'meet face-to-face'. Or again maybe he was 'opposite' as an opponent. This seems very suitable, since he fought all strangers and killed all of them until he was himself beaten by Heracles. There may furthermore be a historical reference here to the opposition shown the Greeks when they settled in Libya. It is certainly clear that Antaeüs was more 'anti' than 'pro'.

Antagoras seems something of an aggressive name. It literally means 'facing the market place', from *anti*, 'against', 'opposite' and *agora*, 'market place', 'common assembly'. Fittingly, Antagoras was a shepherd who wrestled with Heracles on the island of Cos. The fight became a general brawl and, uncharacteristically, Heracles had to flee to the house of a 'stout Thracian matron' and disguise himself in her clothes. The name may allude to this and similar incidents – or it may simply mean 'man who comes from a house by the market'.

Antenor, the son of Aesyetes and Cleomestra, has an unusual name, which appears to mean 'anti-man', 'instead of a man', from *anti*, 'in opposition to', 'instead of' and *aner*, 'man'. He was one of the elders who sat with Priam and was the husband of Theano. Perhaps the correct sense of the first half of his name is more 'anti', since although a Trojan he was very friendly towards the Greeks (they were enemies, of course) and just before the taking of Troy was so amicable towards them that he was a near-traitor to his own people, an 'anti-man'.

Anteros, with Eros, was the son of Ares and Aphrodite. His name not only matches that of Eros – 'anti-Eros' – but suggests an

Heracles wrestles Antaeüs. The giant Antaeüs had killed many opponents by outwrestling them. Here Heracles squeezes Antaeüs to death by lifting him off the ground. Antaeüs, always 'anti', has met his match. This famous vase painting is signed by the artist: the lettering between the girls reads EUPHRONIOS EGRAPHSEN, 'Euphronius painter'.

answering love in reply to an original one, in other words he personifies mutual love.

Anthas was the son of Poseidon and Alcyone, and the father of king Aëtius. His name, 'flowery' (*anthos*, 'flower'), is not a descriptive one but simply a name of good omen for one who should bloom and flourish.

Antheïs was one of the daughters of Hyacinthus. Her name, 'flowery' (see **Anthas**), is both an allusion to the name of her father and a propitious name for one who should bloom and be bright. Alas, she was sacrificed on the grave of the Cyclops Geraestus in Athens in the hope that this offering would bring an end to a series of earthquakes, so was cut down in the flower of her youth.

Antheus is yet another 'flowery' name (see last two entries). Like Antheïs, this young son of Antenor was also cut down when he had not even reached the bloom of youth: he was accidentally killed by Paris with a toy sword.

Antia (sometimes spelt Anteia) is a name used by Homer for Stheneboea, the wife of Proëtus. The basis of the name, as for Antaeüs, is *anti*, 'against' or *antao*, 'to meet face to face'. What was Stheneboea against, or whom did she meet? She was certainly hostile to Bellerophon, trying to bring about his death when she failed to seduce him. Perhaps this is the motive for the name. Stheneboea's own name (which see) sheds no light on the sense of *anti*.

Anticlea was the name of more than one person. The best known was the daughter of Autolycus who became the wife of Laërtes and mother of Odysseus. She was also seduced by Sisyphus. Her name could refer to a specific incident, since it appears to mean 'false key' or 'instead of glory', from the versatile *anti*, 'against', 'instead of' and even 'equal to', and either *cleis*, 'key' or *cleos*, 'glory'. Whatever the exact sense, the reference seems to be to Odysseus, so perhaps we can consider something on the lines of 'meeting the famous one', or of her being the 'corresponding key' by which Odysseus entered the world. Another Anticlea was the wife of Machaon, the great healer, to whom she bore three children, Alexanor (whose name means the same as that of Alexander), Gorgasus and Nicomachus.

Antigone was one of the most poignant figures in mythology, the daughter of Oedipus and Jocasta, the mother of Oedipus. Her birth was thus an incestuous one, and is reflected in her name which means 'contrary birth', 'against motherhood', from *anti*, 'contrary', 'against' and *gonos*, 'child', 'birth', 'that which is begotten'. In spite of this ill-omened start in life, she was a noble and faithful daughter to Oedipus, and when he put his eyes out in despair at the fate that had driven him to murder his father (Laïus), she accompanied him to Attica and remained with him until he died. Her own fate was tragic: she was buried alive in the same tomb as the body of her brother, Polynices. Or so the account of Apollodorus goes. (According to Sophocles, she was immured in a cave, where she committed suicide.)

Antileon was one of the twin sons (with Hippeus) of Heracles and Procris. In spite of the fact that *anti* usually seems to mean 'against' in classical names, here it appears to have its virtually opposite sense of 'equal to', so that *antileon* means 'lion-like', and is a commendatory name. (The 'equal' sense of *anti* here is not actually a contradictory one to the usual 'against' meaning, it simply indicates 'the other half' regarded differently.)

Antilochus was the eldest son of Nestor, king of Pylos, and was a suitor of Helen. His name means 'one who is in ambush against', from *anti*, 'against', and *lochos*, 'ambush'. Antilochus must have been involved in several ambushes during the Trojan War. He was killed by Memnon when he went to his father's rescue after Paris had shot one of Nestor's chariot horses.

Antinoüs was the leading suitor of Penelope in the *Odyssey* – and the first to be killed by Odysseus upon his return. His name literally means 'contrary mind', from *anti*, 'against' and *noos* or *nous* 'mind'. Whether this means specifically 'hostile thought' or more generally 'contradictory' is hard to tell. It certainly does not seem to be a name of very good omen. Antinoüs, too, seems to have been an unpleasant and insolent person.

Antiochus was the son of Heracles and Meda, the daughter of Phylas. He was said to have been the founder of the Athenian deme or township that bears his name. The second half of his name appears to be based on *ocheo*, 'to drive', 'ride'. With its *anti* first half the name as a whole thus means 'one who drives against', a belligerent (or conquering) name.

54

Antiope was the name of two noted women. The first was the daughter of Nycteus. She was captured by Lycus who gave her to his wife Dirce as a slave. This Antiope was also loved by Zeus. The second one was either a sister of Hippolyta, queen of the Amazons, or else the name was a by-name for Hippolyta herself. In any event, she bore Theseus a son, whose name was Hippolytus. Her name means 'with face opposite' or 'beholder', depending whether we take *ops* to mean 'face' or 'eye'. Either of these senses will do for the first Antiope, perhaps to refer to her encounter with Zeus. If we modify the sense of 'face opposite' to mean 'one who opposes', then perhaps we have more the second Antiope, who led her female warriors against Athens (but was defeated). At one point Apollodorus calls the first Antiope *euopis*, 'fair-eyed' or 'fair of face'.

Antiphas was, with Thymbraeüs, a twin son of Laocoön. His name means 'speaking against' or 'speaking instead of', from *anti*, 'against', 'for' and *phas*, 'speaking' (the present participle of *phemi*, 'to speak'). This seems to suggest some sort of prophetic power, whether actual or wished for. The two boys were crushed to death by two huge serpents together with their father.

Antiphus was the name of a son of Priam and Hecuba, and also of a friend of Odysseus who during his Odyssey was eaten by the Cyclops Polyphemus. The name perhaps means 'contrary man', with *anti*, 'against' and *phos*, 'man' (a poetic word for *aner*, *andros*). In what sense the two were 'contrary' is not clear: they were certainly both killed (the first by Achilles).

Antipoenus was the father of Androclea and Alcis, who both died in his place when the oracle had promised Heracles victory against the Minyans if the noblest person in Thebes took his own life. It was expected that Antipoenus, a descendant of the Sown Men, would make the offer, but it was his daughters who carried out the self-sacrifice. Hence Antipoenus' name, which means 'penalty instead of', from *anti*, 'in place of' and *poine*, 'penalty'. The daughters' act was after all a vicarious one.

Apemosyne was a sister of Althaemenes and daughter of Catreus, the son of Minos. Her name seems to mean 'out of memory', 'unremembered', from *apo*, 'from', 'away from', 'far from' and *mnemosyne*, 'memory'. The wretched girl had been kicked to death by her brother after returning home and reporting ruefully to him that she had been tricked into being raped by Hermes. Possibly

Althaemenes wanted to erase the misadventure from his memory, or from the family's record.

Apesantus, the son of Acrisius, was killed by the Nemean Lion in the First Labour of Heracles. His name may mean 'he who lets loose', from *apoluo*, 'to loose from', but the sense and derivation are not really clear.

Aphareus was a king of Messenia, and a son of Perieres and Gorgophone. He married his half-sister, Arene. Behind his name may be *phao*, 'to shine', with the first letter being the intensive prefix *a-*, 'much'. This would make it a kind of propitious name – 'may he shine much'.

Aphidamas was one of the offspring of Aleüs and Neaera, together with Auge, Cepheus and Lycurgus. His name may be a form of *amphidamas*, in which case he is the 'all-round tamer', just as the Argonaut **Amphidamas** is.

Aphidaus was a friend of Theseus. He guarded the 12-year-old Helen for him in Aphidnae when Theseus had won lots for her against Pirithoüs. Later Aphidaus became the adoptive father of the Dioscuri when Aphidnae fell. He was thus a kind and helpful person, and we might expect to see a reflection of this in his name, if only propitiously. His name is difficult, however. We might try dividing it not as Aphi/daus but as Aph/idaus to get a version of *apo*, 'from', 'away from' and *idnoo*, 'to bend'. This would make him 'one who bends away from', or a reluctant or hesitant or timid person. Such a person could still be kindly.

Aphrodite has a famous name that has always traditionally been derived from *aphros*, 'foam', since she was born from the foam of the sea, as depicted in Botticelli's well-known painting (sometimes familiarly known as 'Venus on the Half-Shell'). This 'foam' birth of the goddess of love is narrated only in Hesiod, however, where the foam is not so much that of the sea but that engendered by the severed genitals of Uranus, when flung into the sea by his son Cronos. According to Homer, who tells quite a different story, Aphrodite was the daughter of Zeus and Dione, and the wife of Hephaestus. Her name looks Greek enough, but if *aphros* is the first half, what is the *-dite*? Can we perhaps see it as the familiar '-ite' suffix we have in English (as in 'Israelite') to mean 'one descended from or connected with'? In other words was she a 'Foamite'? This is not impossible, since this suffix had its Greek equivalent in *-ites*, and the 'd' could have been inserted for ease of pronunciation. Or perhaps the latter half of her name derives from *eimi*, 'to go', so that she is a 'foam-walker'. William Camden, the English sixteenth-century antiquary who made a special study of names, reminds us of another possibility in his *Remains Concerning Britain*, where he says: 'In Greek Venus was called Aphrodite, not from the foam of the Sea, but, as Euripides saith, from Aphrosune, that is, Mad folly.' The truth of the matter, as with many other apparently 'Greek' names, is very likely that her name is either pre-Greek or not Greek at all. Geoffrey Grigson, studying the origins of the great and beautiful goddess, says that in Cyprus the Philistines called her Atargatis, for whom the Hebrew name was Ashtoreth. Subsequently the Greeks in Cyprus gradually turned this name via Astoreth or Ashtoreth (and Attorethe and Aphthorethe) into Aphrodite. But this is not to belittle the poetical, if fanciful, origins of the name offered by the ancient writers. (See also, of course, **Venus**, her Roman name, and for many of her by-names, Appendix II, page 319.)

Apis was a son of Phoroneus, the founder of Argos, and the nymph Teledice. His name could be derived from *apios*, 'pear-tree', perhaps referring to some folk ritual, or else *apios*, 'far away', 'long ago' – a term that might with some justification be applied to any mythological character. Apius was killed by Aetolus. For a somewhat similar name, see **Priapus**.

Apollo, the greatest god of both the Greeks and the Romans, has a name that most sources derive from *apollymi* or *apolluo*, 'to destroy', 'to kill'. Apollo the Destroyer, therefore. This negative aspect of the god who was a great healer and prophet and who inspired the arts can be seen in the plagues that he sent (and admittedly also dispelled). Or as he was also a sun god, perhaps his destruction was the work of his fierce rays? Whatever Greek sources have been proposed, it is almost certain that, as with Aphrodite, his name is not of Greek origin. Perhaps he is somehow connected with the Hittite god Apulunas. Or maybe his name is based on an Indo-European route *apel-* meaning 'to excite', 'promote', 'procreate'. (This would certainly be appropriate for the god of sun and light.) Or possibly the name derives from the Laconian verb *apellazo*, 'to hold', 'summon' (the standard Greek equivalent of this is *ecclesiazo*, giving English 'ecclesiastic'). We do know that early on his name was recorded as Apellon. Whatever the truth, it is interesting that the Romans, who 'adopted' him some time before 450 BC for his powers of healing, did not give him a new name or

Apollo as Sun God. Here Apollo appears under his by-names of Hyperion ('going over') and Phoebus ('bright', 'splendid') as he rides his chariot across the sky at sunrise.

even latinise the name. See Appendix III, page 323, for many of his by-names.

Apriate was a heroine of Lesbos who was loved by Trambelus, the son of Telamon. She did not reciprocate his love, however, so he seized her and threw her into the sea where she drowned. (Or, according to another version, she threw herself in.) This highly-charged fate may be reflected in her name, since *apriaten* means 'without price', 'without ransom' (from *apriatos*, 'unbought'). Compare the name of **Priam**.

Apsyrtus was the son of Aeëtes, king of Colchis, and also the brother of Medea. In Ovid's story about him, Medea took him when a child with her on the *Argo* as a hostage in the flight of the Argonauts with the Golden Fleece and when the pursuing fleet of Aeëtes was close, killed Apsyrtus, cut up his body into small pieces, and threw the pieces overboard as a delaying tactic so that Aeëtes would have to stop to retrieve each piece and bury it. This grisly incident can be seen in his name if we derive it from *apo*, 'down', 'away', and *syro*, 'to draw', 'sweep away', referring to the sweeping away in the current of his cut-up body. But the 'true' name of Apsyrtus is also said to be Aegialeus, since 'Apsyrtus' merely records what happened to his dismembered body. If this is the case, his name could mean 'seashore', appropriately enough. Compare **Aegialïa**.

Arachne was the daughter of Idmon of Colophon, who was a famous dyer in purple. Arachne herself was an expert weaver, and even challenged Athena to compete with her. Arachne's work was so perfect that Athena tore it to pieces – and in despair Arachne hanged herself. Athena thereupon changed the rope from which she hung into a cobweb and Arachne herself into a spider (*arachne*). This was not an act of kindness on Athena's part, for Athena hated spiders!

Arcas, the son of Zeus and Callisto, became king of Arcadia and gave his name to it, as was the tradition. His name seems to be derived from *arctos*, 'bear', and in fact Artemis had turned Callisto into this animal.

Archemoros has a forbidding name that means 'beginning of doom' or 'forerunner of death', from *arche*, 'beginning' and *moros*, 'fate', 'doom', 'death'. In fact it was his second name. This baby son of Lycurgus and Eurydice was originally named Opheltes.

When the Seven Against Thebes stopped at Lycurgus' house to ask for water, Opheltes' nurse Hypsipyle showed them where they could obtain some, but in so doing was obliged to abandon her charge for a while. In her absence the baby was killed by a snake. The Seven killed the snake, buried the child, and Amphiaraüs, the seer, announced that the event was prophetic of their own doom and so renamed the baby Archemoros.

Archippe, the daughter of Pelops and Hippodamïa, and mother of Eurystheus and Alcyone, has a name that is both propitious and reflects her mother's own name. It means 'supreme mare', from *arche*, 'first', 'excellent' and *hippos*, 'horse', 'mare'.

Arcisius was the father of Laërtes and grandfather of Odysseus. In one story, his mother was a she-bear (*arctos*), which may explain his own name.

Arene was the half-sister and wife of Aphareus, to whom she bore Idas and Lynceus. Her name (not related to Irene) seems to mean 'manly', from *aner*, with the consonants transposed, as sometimes happened. If this is so, the name is intended to be a complimentary one, not a perverse one.

Ares was the famed god of war, with Mars his Roman equivalent. He was the only son of Zeus and Hera. He had no wife but several 'affairs', especially (and understandably) with Aphrodite, who bore him Harmonia and the twins Phobos ('Panic') and Deimos ('Fear'). His name can be linked with a number of suitable words to match his martial character, such as *aner*, 'man', *arren*, 'male', *arete*, 'manhood', 'prowess', 'excellence', and even *era*, 'earth' and *eris*, 'strife'. Maybe the 'masculine' interpretation is the one to prefer, especially since Mars (which see) may have had a similar origin. The two satellites of the planet Mars, which were discovered in 1877, have the names of Ares' twins, Phobos and Deimos.

Aresthanas was a goatherd who became involved in something of a mystic experience. When once on Mount Titthion looking for stray goats, he came upon the baby son of Coronis, Asclepius, being suckled by them. He went to lift the baby up, but a bright light around it deterred him and he piously turned away, reluctant to meddle in any divine mystery. The baby was thus left to the protection of its father, Apollo. A reflection of this religious happening (which even has Biblical echoes) can be seen in his name: 'strength of prayer', from *are*, 'prayer' and *sthenos*, 'strength'.

60

Arete was the wife of Alcinoüs and mother of Nausicaä. We can give her either a favourable or a decidedly unfavourable name. If the former, we can take it direct from *arete*, 'goodness', 'excellence' (see **Ares**); if the latter, we can perhaps base it on *arretos*, 'unsaid', 'mysterious', 'what should not be told', 'horrible'. So therefore Arete the Excellent or Arete the Unspeakable – with little in her doings to justify the latter, incidentally, although she *did* secretly arrange for Jason and Medea to meet in a cave and legally consummate their marriage there.

Arethusa was a wood nymph who bathed in the river Alpheius. She was the daughter of Oceanus and was turned into the spring Arethusa on the island of Ortygia. Perhaps as for Ares and Arete we can see *arete*, 'excellence', 'virtue' in her name. In view of her associations and fate, however, it might be more appropriate to settle for *ardousa*, 'waterer'. It must be said, incidentally, that there were several springs or fountains named Arethusa, the most famous being at Syracuse. (The root for the 'waterer' origin is the verb *ardo*, 'to water' – as in watering cattle – 'to drink'.)

Arge was one of two Hyperborean girls (the other was Opis) who came to Delos with Leto, Apollo and Artemis and died there. Her name is simply an agreeable one, meaning 'brightness' (*argos*, 'shining', 'bright'; see **Argos**).

Argia has a similar name to Arge – 'bright'. She was the daughter of Adrastus, king of Argos (significantly, in her case), and the wife of Polynices.

Argiope means either 'bright face' or 'white face', both intended as favourable names, from *argos*, 'bright' or *arges*, 'white' and *ops*, 'face'. One Argiope was the daughter of Teuthras who married Telephus. Another was a nymph who bore Thamyris to Philammon.

Argo was the name of the ship in which Jason went to seek the Golden Fleece together with the Argonauts. The popular derivation of the name is that the ship was said to have been built by one Argus on the orders of Jason, and that Athena aided him in this unique task. As a rival popular explanation there is the story that the ship was built at Argos. Cicero favoured the story that it was so called because it carried Argives (i.e. Greeks), and Ptolemy apparently liked the idea of Heracles building the ship and calling it Argo after Jason's son, who was so named. (The Argus who

61

built the ship was also one of the Argonauts on board her.) But why should we not settle in favour of the ordinary word *argos*, which not only meant 'shining', 'bright' (see the preceding three names) but also 'swift'? Such a name is perfectly apt for a fine ship, much as modern warships are given names like 'Valiant', 'Intrepid' and 'Illustrious'. It is not impossible, too, that there may even be a connection with 'ark', and with a stretch of the imagination one may see certain parallels between Jason's journey in the Argo and Noah's voyage in the Ark. For further considerations of the name, see **Argus**.

Argonauts was the collective name for the men who sailed with Jason in search of the Golden Fleece. The name simply means 'Argo sailors', from *Argo* and *nautes* (Latin *nauta*), 'sailor', 'seaman'. The term must have influenced more modern words such as 'aeronaut' (a 'sailor' in another element) and, through this, recent 'astronaut' and 'cosmonaut'.

Argus is perhaps best known for being the name of the monster that had eyes all over its body. It was also the name of several other mythological characters, including Argus the son of Zeus and Niobe (who inherited Niobe's father's kingdom and renamed it Argos); Argus the eldest son of Phrixus and Chalciope, who sailed with his brothers in the Argo to Greece with Jason and Medea; and of course Argus the legendary builder of the ship, whose parentage is uncertain, but who we do know was one of the Argonauts. For all these we can accept 'bright' (*argos*) as appropriate, including the shining eyes of the monster. It is interesting that Argus (or Argos) was also a standard name for a dog with the sense 'swift', 'because', as Liddell and Scott explain it, 'rapid motion is accompanied by a kind of flickering light'. Odysseus' faithful dog was called Argus, as was one of the hounds of Actaeon (see Appendix VI, page 336). Neither Argus nor Argo, incidentally, seems to be related to the word 'argosy', in spite of this word being a poetic term for a fleet of ships. An 'argosy' was originally probably a ship from Ragusa in Italy. Both Argo and Argos, doubtless because of their classical associations, have become quite popular as trade names. (The gas called argon derives its name from the other meaning of Greek *argos*, 'not working', i.e. 'inert', from *a-*, 'not' and *ergon*, 'work'.)

Argyra was a sea nymph who loved, then tired of, Selemnus (who died of a broken heart after such inconstancy). Her name may come from *argyros*, 'silver', a word related to Latin *argentum* and

62

itself based on *arges*, 'white' (i.e. a white metal). This is a common epithet of rivers or water in general. Compare the name of Argentina, where the 'silver' is both for the metal and the country's great rivers.

Ariadne, the daughter of Minos, king of Crete, and Pasiphaë, was the girl who fell in love with the Minotaur but who actually married Dionysus. Most sources agree that her name appears to mean 'very pure', from *ari-*, 'very' and *hagnos*, 'pure', 'chaste', although the second part of the name could be derived from *handano*, 'to please', 'delight'. Either way, she has a highly complimentary name.

Arion was the name of the son of Cyclos who was a poet and musician, and also that of the horse that was the offspring of Demeter and Poseidon. (The first Arion is not fully mythological, since there appears to have been a historical character so named in the seventh century BC.) The name may derive from *argos* in its sense of 'swift', particularly with regard to the steed, or even a combination of *ari-*, 'very' and *argos*. But we could also consider *rheo*, 'to flow', 'stream' for the second half of the name. This could be symbolic of a 'spring' that was the offspring of the earth (Demeter) and the sea (Poseidon). Interestingly, the name of Pegasus is popularly thought to be associated with a spring (see his name).

Arisbe was the daughter of Merops, king of Percote. She married Priam and was the mother of Aesacus. Perhaps her name contains some kind of blend of *aristos*, 'best' and *bia*, 'life', this being a propitious name.

Aristaeüs clearly has an 'aristocratic name' and is a kind of 'best man'. He was the son of Apollo and the nymph Cyrene. He married Autonoë, the daughter of Cadmus, and was the father by her of Actaeon. All these names are commendatory or 'good status' names, to a greater or lesser degree, especially those of Apollo and the two women.

Aristippe, sometimes known as Arsippe, was one of the three daughters of Minyas, the other two being Alcithoë and Leucippe. Her name is a favourable one and means 'best of mares', from *aristos*, 'best' and *hippos*, 'horse', 'mare'. Notice the 'mare' name of one of her sisters as well.

Aristomenes was a commander in the war of the Messenians against the Spartans, and was given a good deal of trouble by the Dioscuri. In spite of (or perhaps to equip him for) such challenges, his name means 'best strength', from *aristos*, 'best' and *menos*, 'strength', 'force' (also 'wish').

Armenus was a companion of Jason on the Argo and a Thessalian from Lake Boebe who, it is said, settled in Armenia, a land that took its name from his. Strabo the Greek geographer who lived in the early years of the Christian era pointed out that Armenians still wore Thessalian dress. Of course, all this is highly tentative, as would be an attempt to link his name with that of Harmonia to mean 'unison'. It must be said, however, that the actual origin of the name of Armenia (now a Soviet state) is still uncertain, and that Armenians themselves talk of a mythical founder named Armenak.

Arnacia was said by some classical authors, Apollodorus among them, to be the name of Penelope before the ducks saved her after she had been thrown in the sea by Nauplius (on the order of her father, Icarius). The only Greek word like this name is *arnacis*, 'sheepskin', but that is not necessarily an unsuitable name for a woman who was renowned for her weaving. See also **Arnaea**.

Arnaea was, like Arnacia, a former name of Penelope, and it contains the basis for both names, *arnos*, 'sheep'. See also **Arne**.

Arne was the name of Poseidon's nurse in Arcadia. She was a Thracian woman who betrayed her native island country of Siphnos to Minos for gold and was consequently turned into a jackdaw. The name is the exact word for 'ewe-lamb', although one would expect some other name for the traitress.

Arrhippe was the 'chaste attendant' of Artemis, and a noted huntress. Her propitious name, meaning 'best of mares' (see **Aristippe**), fits her well in this role but grates with her violent end (having been raped by Tmolis on a couch in her mistress's temple, she hanged herself).

Arsinoë is an alternative name for Alphesiboea (which see). It appears to mean 'male minded', from *arsen*, 'male' (the Ionic and Attic form of the later *arren* that we mentioned for Ares) and *noos*, 'mind'. The implication is not, of course, 'thinking about men' but 'one who has the mind of a man'!

Arsippe, as mentioned, is an alternative name for Aristippe. It was also the name of one of the daughters of Minyas, who was turned into a bat. It may well be identical in meaning to Aristippe and Arrhippe, in other words be 'the best of mares'.

Artemis was a famous versatile and even apparently self-contradictory goddess, since not only was she the goddess of hunting but also was a defender of wild animals. Although, as in so many cases, her name is probably really *not* Greek, there have been several gallant attempts to find a suitable meaning in such origins as *artao*, 'to fasten to', 'be fitted', *ardo*, 'to water' (so 'to nourish'), *temno*, 'to cut up' (as a huntress?) and of course primarily *artemes*, 'safe and sound'. This last could be a generally propitious name or specifically refer to the 'safeness' (purity) and 'soundness' (health) of her virginity. Another theory is the one that sees the origin in *ari-Themis*, that is, 'very like Themis' (*ari-*, 'very', was a 'strengthening' prefix). Themis, the Titaness who was the goddess of order, was obviously a suitable person for her to resemble. Some sources see a link between the name of Artemis and that of Arethusa. We have less complexity with the name of her Roman equivalent, Diana.

Ascalabus is identifiable as being the third Abas we mentioned (see this name), which explains why his name derives from *ascalabos*, 'lizard'. As Ascalabus, the name of his mother is usually given as Misme.

Ascalaphus was the name of the son of Ares who was killed by Deïphobus, and of the son of the river Acheron and the nymph Orphne (or Gorgyra). This latter Ascalaphus 'split' on Persephone when she was in the Underworld by revealing to Pluto that she had eaten part of a pomegranate when, as a condition for returning to the upper world, she had been charged to eat nothing. As a result Demeter (or according to another account, Persephone herself) turned him into a short-eared owl, *ascalaphos* – a bird of ill omen.

Ascanius was the son of Aeneas and his first wife Creusa. His name would seem to denote some kind of poverty or exile, for it could be derived from *a-*, 'not' and *scene*, 'tent' (related to English 'scene'), in other words, 'tentless'. There are no specific accounts of this, though he certainly did a good deal of travelling: as a start he sailed with his father on his long voyage to find a home in Italy for those who had survived the Trojan War. But perhaps his name means that he did not actually need a tent when travelling.

Asius was the name of two Trojan warriors. One was the younger brother of Hecabe, the other was a son of Hyrtacus and Arisbe. The name means 'slimy', 'miry' (*asios*), which is hardly complimentary.

Asclepius was the god of healing known to the Romans as Aesculapius (which also see). He was the son of Apollo and Coronis, married Epione (or Lampetia), had two sons Machaon and Podalirius, and one daughter (Hygea) or possibly three (Aegle, Panacea and Iaso). (Hygea was the goddess of health, and even the other three girls have 'healthy' names meaning respectively 'brightness', 'all-healing' and 'healthy'!) Can we not find a suitably 'healing' origin for Asclepius? It is in fact a difficult name to interpret. Perhaps it derives from *scallo*, 'to stir up', originally 'to cut' (compare Greek *scalme*, 'knife' and English 'scalpel'). This is certainly an apt name for a surgeon. Or perhaps it somehow connects with the verb *scalapazo*, 'to turn round and round'. This would incidentally help to explain the snake that winds round the staff that he holds in traditional depictions of him. Unfortunately, we cannot be more precise than this.

Asopus was the god of two rivers so called, who are in fact often confused. (One flows into the Gulf of Corinth, the other into the Aegean.) It is tempting to see the name originating in a combination of *asios*, 'slimy' and *pelos*, 'mud', 'clay'. The trouble is that most names of Greek rivers or their gods seems to be 'good' ones referring to their brightness or rapidity.

Assaracus, the Trojan leader, was the son of Tros and Callirrhoë. If his name derives from *asarcos* then he was 'lean', 'without flesh' in some way.

Astacus, the father of Melanippus, has a name that may be linked with *astactos*, 'not trickling' (that is, doing the reverse – gushing in streams), or *asticos*, 'townsman' (as opposed to a countryman). Either possibility would make a reasonable name, the first being propitious, the second descriptive.

Asteria was a Titaness, the daughter of Coeüs and Phoebe. She married Perses and bore him the goddess Hecate. She leaped into the sea as a quail and turned into Ortygia, 'Quail Island' (*ortyx*, *ortygos*, 'quail'), which was later renamed Delos. Her name, however, clearly has a 'starry' connection, as do the next four names, from *aster* (Latin *astrum*), 'star'. So she was a 'starry goddess'. The name is suitable for a Titaness. Possibly the story about the quail was an attempt to explain the name of the island: there may have been a local belief that the island was formed when a 'falling star' or meteorite fell into the sea.

Asterius (or in some stories Asterion) was the name of several mythological characters, the most famous being that of the Minotaur. (Many people are surprised to discover that the Minotaur actually *had* a name.) Apart from him it was also the name of a king of Crete, the son of Tectamus, who married Europa and adopted the three sons she had borne to Zeus (Minos, Rhadamanthys and Sarpedon). The name is simply the masculine form of Asteria, so means the same: 'starry'. One hardly thinks of the Minotaur as this, but propitious names simply wish for excellence or success of some kind, and do not actually provide it.

Asterodea was the wife of Aeëtes and the mother of Medea and Apsyrtos (or Phaëton). Her name, a favourable one, means 'star-goddess', from *aster*, 'star' and *dia*, 'the godlike one' (compare Diana).

Asterope, often called Sterope, was the daughter of Atlas and Pleïone, and so one of the Pleiades. She was the mother of Oenomaüs by Ares (or according to another account, his wife). Her name means 'star-face', from *aster*, 'star' and *ops*, 'face' – or alternatively 'starry eyes', since *ops* also means 'eye'. A 'star' name is of course very fitting for one of the Pleiades.

Astraeüs was the son of the Titan Crius and Titaness Eurybia, and he was the father of the winds Boreas, Zephyrus and Notus and (rather extravagantly but impressively) all the stars of heaven, his wife for this feat being Eos, the goddess of the dawn. The name could hardly be more fitting ('starry').

Astyanax was the name, almost more a nickname, of the little son of Hector and Andromache. All the Trojans called him so in the hope that he might prove as effective a defender of their city as his father was. His name means literally 'city king', understood as 'lord of the city' or even 'bulwark of the city', deriving from *asty*, 'town', 'city' and *anax*, 'king', 'lord'. His 'real' name was Scamandrius, which perhaps had the same meaning as Scamander (which see).

Astydamia was the daughter of Cretheus (or Pelops or Amyntor) and the wife of Acastus, king of Iolcus. She fell in love with Peleus, who later killed her. Her name really means 'city killer', from *asty*, 'city' and *damao*, 'to tame', 'subdue', 'kill'. The name was perhaps a propitious one that was not fulfilled.

Astyoche was the name of at least three married ladies: the daughter of the river Simoïs who married Erichthonius and bore him Tros, the daughter of Priam who married Telephus, and the daughter of Phylas, king of Thesprotia, who bore Tlepolemus to Heracles. Her powerful name means 'possessor of the city', from *asty*, 'city' and *ochos*, 'that which holds'. Either the son or father of all three respectively 'possessed' a city as a king.

Astypalaea, the daughter of Agenor or his son Phoenix, was said to have borne Poseidon the Argonauts Ancaeüs and Eurypylus. Her somewhat venerable name means 'ancient city', from *asty*, 'city' and *palai*, 'of old', 'long ago'.

Atalanta, the great huntress, appears in two main accounts, one by Hesiod, the other by Apollodorus. Hesiod says her father was Schoenus; Apollodorus says he was Iasus; both writers say her mother was Clymene. But whichever account is followed, these points agree: she was a huntress who took part in the Calydonian Boar-hunt, she was loved by Meleager, she finally married Melanion (or Hippomenes), and she was the mother of Parthenopaeüs. Her name seems to mean something like 'equal in weight', 'equivalent to', from *atalantos* (from *talanton*, 'balance', 'something weighed'), with *a-* not a privative prefix but a so-called copulative or 'joining' one. But if the *a-* actually does mean 'not', as it often does, then the base of her name could be *talanteros*, the superlative of *talas*, 'suffering', so that her name means 'not one who suffers much' – in other words 'most joyful one'! This means that she is either 'balanced' or 'not suffering'. The different possibilities give her name something of a link with that of Atlas, although not directly.

Ate was the eldest daughter of Zeus, and came to personify blind folly. Her mother was Eris, who personified strife. From this it is not surprising that her own name means 'distraction', 'folly', 'delusion' (*ate*).

68

Athamas was the son of Aeolus, king of Thessaly. He married first the nymph Nephele, then Ino. If we take the *a-* to mean 'not' then the best we can get for the rest of the name is something like *thameios*, 'crowded' (from *thama*, 'in crowds', 'thick'), which hardly makes sense. Perhaps it is best to segment the name as Ath/amas and get something like the root *ath*, meaning 'spike', 'peak', 'high' (as in Mount Athos), and *amao*, 'to reap', 'to mow', suggesting an abundant harvest.

Athena, the goddess of war and of many crafts and skills, has a name that is inextricably linked with that of Athens, and the usual explanations of her name simply say that it means 'of Athens'. She would thus be first and foremost an Athenian goddess. But her name is actually very ancient, and could well predate that of the city, and so be pre-Hellenic. On the famous Linear B tablets at Knossos her name appears as *a-ta-na*, this *-na* suffix being a non-Greek one. Of course, we can consider, as with Athamas, the root *ath*, 'spike', 'point', this here denoting that her spear is lightning. Or with 'pure' Greek we can be tempted by *athanatos*, 'immortal', 'not subject to death' (*a-*, 'not', *thanatos*, 'death'). But the meaning of the Mycenaean name on the Knossos tablet could be 'protectress', and perhaps we should leave her as such. See also **Minerva**, her Roman counterpart, and for many of her by-names see Appendix IV, page 327.

Atlas was a Titan, the son of Iapetus and Clymene, who changed into the mountain of the same name, where he was still what he had traditionally been before – a giant who supported the sky. So his name is perhaps based on *tlao*, 'to endure', 'bear', with the initial *a-* simply for euphony or as an intensive ('very'). Atlas is thus 'he who bears', 'he who endures'. His name came to be used for the book of maps that we now call an atlas because sixteenth-century collections of maps included a drawing of Atlas holding up the sky.

Atreus was a son of Pelops and Hippodamia. He became king of Mycenae, and was the father of Agamemnon and Menelaüs. The best bet for his name, and one attested in the Linear B tablets of Knossos, is 'fearless', 'not running away', from *a-*, 'not' and an old element *tres* that gives the Greek verb *treo*, 'to tremble', 'run away', 'flee'. There have been other attempts to derive the name from such words as *hadros*, 'stout', 'strong', or *adeo*, 'to satiate', or *ate*, 'ruin', 'devastation' (compare **Ate**), but the Mycenaean origin seems the most promising.

Atropos was one of the Fates, and has the appropriate name *atropos*, 'not turning', 'unchangeable', so 'inevitable'. What the Fates decreed was something you could not avoid.

Atthis was the daughter of Cranaüs, king of Attica, and Pedias. Attica, which before had been called Actaea, was said to have derived its name from her. And her own name? The interpretation is difficult, but perhaps the second half of her name is *thea*, 'goddess', with the first half being related in some way to Athena or Athens. But see also **Cranaë** (and also **Attis**).

Attis was a handsome youth who was loved by the Phrygian goddess Cybele. His name may be close to that of Atthis (whose own name is sometimes spelt Attis), but more likely it is a non-Greek word. Pierre Grimal proposes either Lydian *attis*, 'handsome boy' (which certainly makes sense) or a Phrygian word *attagus*, 'he-goat', this being the goat that suckled him.

Atymnius was the son of Zeus and Cassiopea, and another beautiful boy, this time one who was loved by Sarpedon. Perhaps we can even see a connection with the *attis* proposed for Attis. The latter part of his name seems to suggest *hymnos*, 'hymn', 'festive song', which might make the whole 'handsome boy whose praises must be sung'. Failing that, we can try *atos* for the first element of the name, this meaning 'insatiate'. That would make Atymnius 'one who is never satisfied with songs of praise', 'one whose praises cannot be too highly sung'. Whatever the sense, he seems to do well out of it.

Auge has a nice straightforward name. She was the daughter of Aleüs and his niece Neaera. She was seduced by Heracles, to whom she bore Telephus. Her name simply means 'bright light', *auge*. (Let us be more poetic and call her 'The Radiant One'.)

Augeas is a name that is identical to that of Auge, so he too is 'bright' or 'radiant'. He was the king of Elis whose stables Heracles cleaned out as his Fifth Labour (The Augean Stables). Significantly, he was the son of Helios, who is very much 'bright' and 'radiant'.

Aurora is the Roman equivalent of Eos, goddess of the dawn, and 'Dawn' is what her Latin name means. In fact both versions of the name, Aurora and Eos, are linguistically linked.

Autolycus was notorious for his cunning and for being a thief (notably a cattle-stealer) and a liar. With his great reputation as a robber, it is not surprising that his name is popularly derived from *autos*, 'self', 'the very' and *lycos*, 'wolf', so he is 'a very wolf', 'a real dog' (as we might say). But it is interesting that the names of the various mothers who are said to have borne him (Chione, Stilbe and Telauge) all denote some kind of brightness or radiance (see the respective names), so that perhaps originally the root of the latter half of his name may not have been 'wolf' but *lyce*, 'light'. This would then have been a propitious, family-based name which was not realised. The father of Autolycus is usually given as either Hermes or Daedalion. According to the *Odyssey*, Autolycus named his grandson Odysseus when he was visiting Ithaca.

Automedon was the charioteer of Achilles. After Achilles' death, he became the companion of his son Neoptolemus. His name is a 'good omen' one meaning 'independent ruler', 'one who rules himself', from *autos*, 'alone', 'ideal' and *medon*, 'ruler', 'lord'.

Automedusa was the daughter of Alcathoüs and Euaechme. She married Iphicles and bore him Iolaüs. Her name means 'cunning itself', 'a real ruler', and is really the feminine equivalent of Automedon. Compare **Medusa**.

Autonoë was the daughter of Cadmus and Harmonia, the wife of Aristaeüs, and the mother of Actaeon and Macris. Her name is more propitious than descriptive, and means 'thinking for herself', 'with a mind of her own', from *autos*, 'self', 'on one's own' and *noos*, 'mind', 'resolve'.

Auxo was, with Hegemone, one of the two Charites or Graces worshipped by the Athenians. Her name means 'growth', 'increase' (*auxe*), so she was the goddess of growth and of the spring.

Axion was a son of Priam killed by Eurypylus. His name is simply a complimentary one, as *axios* means 'worthy', 'estimable'.

Bacche was a nymph on Mount Nysa who with other nymphs (Bromië, Erato, Macris, Nysa) nursed the baby Dionysus in a cave. For this service, Zeus turned all the nymphs into the Hyades. Her name, like that of the famous Bacchus, means 'shouting for joy', 'raging', a name often associated with mountains which often evoke a wildness of spirit or a kind of heady joy.

71

Bacchus, the god of wine, has a name that is really the Latin rendering of the Lydian name Bakis, which was both the epithet for Dionysus, his Greek equivalent, and also the original of the Greek mystic name for the god, Bacchos. It is an unusual name, in that it has no real meaning. Instead, it is more an expression of joy made by shouting such random phrases as *euoi saboi*: Bacchus was, after all, a god who symbolised ecstatic liberation, realised through the effects of drinking wine together with elaborate ceremonial. At the same time, we can see more immediately behind the name the verb *iacho*, 'to cry', 'to shout' (which, correctly or not, suggests the 'hooch' that is the joyous cry of Scottish dancers). If we have to put a more concrete interpretation on the name, then it must be expressed in a term such as 'raging', 'shouting ecstatically'. Bacchus was the son of Zeus and Semele.

Balius was one of Achilles' immortal horses, together with Xanthus. His name is a purely descriptive one – 'piebald', 'dappled', from *ballo*, 'to throw', 'dash'. A dappled horse has spots or patches 'dashed' over him. Compare the name of **Xanthus**.

Batia was the name of the daughter of Teucer, first king of Troy. She married Dardanus, to whom she bore Erichthonius, the father of Tros. Batia was also the name of a Naiad who bore Icarius to king Oebalus of Sparta. Her name appears to come from *batia* or *batos*, 'bush', 'bramble', which would perhaps be more appropriate for a Naiad, as a water or fountain nymph (where brambles grow), than for a king's daughter.

Baton, sometimes known as Elato, was the charioteer of Amphiaraü, with whom he perished after the battle of Thebes. (Both were swallowed up in the ground at the point where Zeus had thrown a thunderbolt.) His name, like that of Batia, means 'bramble', which perhaps had a special significance of some kind apart from its association with water. Robert Graves points to a widespread taboo on eating blackberries in Europe, as the fruit (for its colour?) was associated with death.

Battus is the name of two characters of note. The first was the founder of Cyrene in Libya. His name was really a nickname meaning 'stammerer' (*battos*, a word formed from the sound of a stammer), and his real name was Aristoteles, the son of Polymnestus, a noble Theran, and Phronime, the daughter of a Cretan king, Etearchus. (The story goes that Battus lost his stammer when he met a lion in the country outside Cyrene; he shouted at it, it fled, and he then found he could speak freely!) The second Battus was an old man who spotted Hermes driving away some cattle of Apollo that he had stolen. To stop him revealing what he had seen, Hermes turned Battus into a stone. This fate would presumably have made him quite tongue-tied.

Baubo was Demophon's old dry-nurse (his wet-nurse was Demeter). Her name may derive from *bauzo*, 'to mutter', 'reproach', or *prauno*, 'to soothe', 'calm'. Either epithet is suitable for an old nurse.

Baucis was the elderly wife of Philemon, and the elderly couple featured in a well-known story where they gave Zeus and Hermes hospitality in their little humble peasant cottage without realising who they were, thus 'entertaining gods unawares'. Perhaps Baucis has a name that is similar in origin to that of Baubo, in which case we may prefer the *prauno* ('soothing') interpretation to the *bauzo* ('muttering') one. Philemon has an appropriately attractive name.

Bellerophon was the son of Glaucus, king of Corinth (or else the son of Poseidon), and Euronyme. His great feat was taming Pegasus. Traditionally, his name is regarded as a nickname or epithet, since he had earlier killed a tyrant (according to some versions, his brother) named Bellerus. He was thus 'slayer of Bellerus', with the last part of his name from *phone*, 'murder', 'slaughter'. Since this was a nickname, his real name was actually Hipponoüs or, some say, Chrysaor (see these names). The interpretation of the name is tantalising, since it is not really clear what 'Bellerus' is supposed to represent. Perhaps he was just one man. Perhaps on the other hand he symbolises some power of evil or darkness, so that Bellerophon is a 'monster-killer' in general. There are similar names. Hermes, for example, after he had killed Argus was given the by-name of Argeiphontes, and of course there was Gorgophone, the daughter of Perseus who had killed the Gorgon Medusa, and Persephone, who presided over the death of mankind (although her name is by no means straightforward). Robert Graves suggests quite a different origin: 'bearing darts', from *belos*, 'dart' and *phoreo*, 'to bear', 'carry'.

Bellona was the Roman goddess, the equivalent of Enyo, who personified war. She is sometimes regarded as the sister or wife of Mars, but she has no real mythology. Her name is simply a form of Latin *bellum*, 'war'.

Belus, king of Egypt, was the son of Poseidon and Libya and the twin brother of Agenor. He married Anchinoë, daughter of the river Nile, and had two sons by her, Danaüs and Aegyptus. His name is almost certainly a graecised form of the Semitic *Baal*, 'lord' (compare the Baal of the Old Testament and the Bel of the Apocrypha).

Benthesicyme was the daughter of Poseidon and Amphitrite, and the foster-mother of Eumolpus. Her parents, of course, have strong 'sea' associations, so it is to be expected that her own name should be similar. It means 'deep wave', or more lyrically, perhaps, 'she who dwells in the depths of the waves', from *benthos*, a poetic form of *bathos*, 'deep' and *cyma*, 'wave'.

Beroë was the old nurse of Semele. Hera disguised herself as Beroë when she wished to suggest to Semele that Zeus might not really be Semele's lover, as he claimed to be, and thus that her child might not be his. (This was pure jealousy on Hera's part, since it had indeed been Zeus and the child was Dionysus.) Beroë has rather a difficult name. Robert Graves ingeniously suggests 'bringer of eggs', from *phero*, 'to bring' and *oon*, 'egg'. This would suit a nursemaid.

Bia, the son of the Titan Pallas and the river Styx, had a sister Nike. He also had a brother Cratos, and the two names are usually associated, since together they were given the task of forcibly chaining down Prometheus to the rock of Caucasus as a punishment for giving the gift of fire to mankind. Their names for undertaking this are appropriate, with Bia meaning 'force' and Cratos meaning 'might'. (The Greek words are the same as their names.)

Biadice was the wife of Cretheus who fell in love with Phrixus. When he did not return her love she accused him in front of his father, Athamas. An echo of this may be found in her name which means 'forceful justice', 'law by force', from *bia*, 'force' and *dice*, 'law', 'justice'.

Bias was the son of Amythaon and the brother of the seer Melampus. He married Pero, whose father Neleus had refused to give to anyone unless the would-be suitor brought him the oxen of Iphiclus. By his courage and skill (and force?) Bias managed this, hence perhaps his name 'force' (*bia*).

Biton and Cleobis were two young brothers of Argos, famed for pulling their mother, who was a priestess of Hera at Argos, to the temple in an ox-cart as the oxen were late. Biton's name means 'wild ox', from *bous*, 'ox' (related to the English word 'bison').

Boeotus was the son of Poseidon and Melanippe, and the brother of Aeolus (not the wind controller). He was said to have given his name to Boeotia. His name itself means merely 'herdsman', from *boutes* (in turn from *bous*, 'ox').

Bona Dea was a Roman goddess, usually identified with Fauna, whose name is simply a title, 'the good goddess'. It is possible that her name may be a literal translation of the Greek goddess Agathe Theos, related to Hygea, and that her worship was brought to Rome in the third century BC. Bona Dea was worshipped exclusively by women.

Boreas was the god of the north wind, and the son of Astraeüs and Eos (i.e. of the stars and the dawn). His name may derive from *boros*, 'devouring', or possibly from *oros*, 'mountain', since it was from the mountains that the harsh north wind blew.

Branchus was the son either of Apollo or of Smicrus, and he was the founder of an oracle at Didyma, near Miletus, of which his descendants, the Branchidae, were the priests. His name means 'hoarse' (*branchos*), which perhaps via 'grunting' suggests an association with pigs or a pig cult, especially as his son's name was Cercyon (see this name).

Briareüs was a giant monster with (traditionally) a hundred arms, the offspring of Uranus and Gaia. His normal duty was to guard the Titans imprisoned in Tartarus, but he also performed several other deeds involving a greater or lesser degree of force. His name must be related to *briao*, 'to strengthen', or *brithos*, 'weight'. He was also called Aegaeon (see **Aegeus**), and jointly with his brothers Cottus and Gyes formed the giant group called the Hecatoncheires ('hundred-armed'). See **Cottus** for a special 'natural phenomena' interpretation of the names of all three.

Briseïs was the daughter of Briseus, a priest at Lyrnessus, near Troy. She was captured by Achilles, who killed her family and her husband Mynes. Her name, deriving from *britho*, 'to be heavy', 'outweigh', means 'she who prevails' – even though ultimately she did not. By a rather tortuous process her name also became that

Boreas abducts Orithyia. The names of both could contain the word for 'mountain', *oros*. Boreas, the North Wind, blew from the mountains; Orithyia raged on them.

of Cressida (which see). She is sometimes alternatively named as Hippodamia. Of course, her name is also simply that of her father.

Britomartis was a Cretan goddess similar to Artemis. She was the daughter of Zeus and Carme. Her name is usually interpreted as 'good maid', 'sweet maiden', from *britys*, 'sweet', 'blessing' and *martis*, a form of *marna*, 'maiden', both these being Cretan words. (For the latter word, compare Greek *parthenos*, 'maid, 'virgin'.) This is obviously a highly desirable name for a goddess to have, since it epitomises the Greek ideal.

Bromië was a nymph who tended Dionysus on Mount Nysa with Bacche (which name see) and her other sisters. Her name is a suitable 'mountain' name, since it derives from *bromos*, 'roaring', from *bremo*, 'to roar', 'clamour', thus giving the sound that matches Bacche's fury.

Bronte was one of the four horses that drew the chariot of Helios. His name means 'thunder' (*bronte*). Compare the similarly apt names of his companions: Eos, Aethion (or Aethiops) and Asterope (or Sterope).

Brontes, together with Arges and Steropes, was one of the three original Cyclopes. His name, like that of the steed Bronte, means 'thunder'. The names of all three appeared quite late. (Arges' name means 'bright', see **Arge**; Steropes' name means 'lightning', see **Sterope**.)

Broteas was the son of Tantalus, king of Phrygia. He was a worshipper of Cybele, but refused to acknowledge the majesty of Artemis, who for this crime drove him mad. In this deranged state he threw himself into the fire, thinking he would be immune from the flames, but was instead burnt to death. This was a bloody end, and his name reflects it: from *brotos*, 'gore'.

Budeia (or Buzyge) was a Boeotian princess, the mother of Erginus. Her name is purely propitious, meaning 'goddess of oxen', from *bous*, 'ox' and *dea*, Doric for *thea*, 'goddess'. See also **Buzyge**.

Bunomus also has a propitious name, although, alas, it proved quite ineffective, since he and his two brothers Aganus and Idaeüs were killed at Troy by a roof collapse when they were still babies. The three were the sons of Paris and Helen. His name means 'ox-grazing', from *bous*, 'ox' and *nemo*, 'to graze'.

Busiris was a king of Egypt, and the son of Poseidon and Lysianassa. He wrestled with Heracles, who slew him. His name seems clearly to contain the name Osiris (or perhaps Isis), with the Bu- perhaps meaning 'house' or 'place', so that the whole means 'house of Osiris'. Diodorus claimed the name meant 'grave of Osiris'.

Butes was the name of a son of Boreas who conspired against his half-brother, Lycurgus, and also the name of one of the Argonauts, the son of Poseidon (or Pandion) and Zeuxippe. It simply means 'herdsman' from *boutes*, 'cowherd', 'herdsman'. Compare **Boeotus**.

Buzyge is an alternative name for Budeia, the mother of Erginus. It also relates to oxen and means 'ox-yoker', from *bous*, 'ox' and *zygon*, 'yoke'. The name expresses the wish that she may have many oxen to yoke. Compare **Zeuxippe**, who was a 'horse-yoker'.

Cabiri (or Cabeiri) were early fertility gods, sometimes called the children of Hephaestus or of Uranus (while on Samothrace they were regarded as the sons of Zeus and Calliope). Their name is of doubtful origin, perhaps deriving from a Phoenician word *qabirim*, 'mighty'. Their Greek title was 'great gods' (*megaloi theoi*). They seem at times to be confused with the Curetes and Corybantes, who were also confused with each other and not clearly distinguished anyway. (See these names.)

Cacus was a fire-breathing monster and the son of Vulcan. He stole some of the fine herds of Heracles, when the latter was driving them (he had himself stolen them from Geryon) back to Greece. As an evil, dangerous and belligerent monster who fed on human flesh and littered his cave with skulls and bones, it is hardly surprising that his name is Greek *cacos*, 'bad', 'evil'. However, the German nineteenth-century philologist Johann Hartung suggests in his *Die Religion der Römer* ('The Religion of the Romans') that Cacus and his sister Caca (who exists in some accounts) were really Roman *penates* or household gods, and he connects their names with Greek *caio*, 'to kindle a fire', Latin *caleo*, 'to be hot' and Latin *coquo*, 'to cook', 'to fry'. All these 'hot' names are quite apt, of course, but perhaps *cacos* is the most likely source of the name. It has not been proved that he is connected with Caeculus (which see), who also had to do with fire.

Cadmus was the son of Agenor, king of Tyre, and Telephassa, and the brother of Europa, Phoenix and Cilix. He was the founder of Thebes, originally called Cadmeia. Most authorities agree that his name, a pre-Greek one, means 'east', from the same word that gave the name of the Saracens. (Compare also the name of his sister **Europa**.) Attempts have also been made to derive his name from *cazo*, 'to adorn', 'order', linking this in turn with *caio*, 'to burn' (see **Cacus**), with such 'burning' being a metaphor for 'illustriousness'. It has also been suggested that his name echoes *cosmos*, the ordered universe. If Cadmus came from Tyre, of course (this is the Biblical 'Tyre and Sidon' now in Lebanon), he would indeed have come from the east.

Caeculus was the founder of the Italian city of Praeneste (now Palestrina, and the birthplace of the famous composer), about 23 miles from Rome. He is said to have been conceived when his mother was sitting on the site of this future city by a fire and a spark flew out into her lap. As a result of this, his father was therefore alleged to be Vulcan. The mother abandoned her baby, who was found by some girls lying near the fire which was kept burning in a shrine. They named him Caeculus because he appeared to have been turned blind (Latin *caecus*) by the light of the fire.

Caeneus, originally Caenis, was the daughter of Elatus, a king of Thessaly. Upon Poseidon raping her she changed into a man, Caeneus, but later reconverted to Caenis. After such a convenient expedient we can easily see that her name derives from *cainos*, 'new', to denote the new person that she became. (As the man Caeneus she was quite active, killing six drunken Centaurs at the wedding of Pirithoüs. It was when the rest of them attacked that she was driven underground and became Caenis again.)

Caenis was the feminine *alter ego* of **Caeneus**, which name see.

Calaïs and Zetus were the twin sons of Boreas and Orithyia. Both of them have 'windy' names, as might be expected for the sons of the north wind, with Calaïs' name probably deriving from *caio*, 'to burn', 'dry up', related to *celeos*, 'burning', *celas*, 'windy' and *calon*, 'firewood'. Calaïs is thus a hot wind, not a cold one. Ancient philologists felt that Calaïs' name implied 'he who blows gently', while Zetus' name was 'he who blows hard'. Yet in spite of such reasoning, there is a much more obvious word: *calais*, 'topaz', 'chrysolite'. But perhaps after all there is a link between the changing hues of the topaz and the flickering heat of the hot wind.

Calamus was a son of the river god Maeander. He loved another young man, Carpus, who was the son of Zephyr and one of the Hours. Both were bathing one day in the Maeander and Calamus tried to outswim his friend, but Carpus died in this contest. Filled with remorse, Calamus pined away and became a reed (*calamos*).

Calchas was a noted seer of the Greek army in the Trojan War. His name seems to mean either 'brazen', from *chalceos*, or be somehow associated with *calche*, 'murex', 'purple limpet' (from which a dye was obtained). Liddell and Scott say his name originally meant 'searcher', which certainly seems fitting for a famous soothsayer.

Cale was, with Pasithea, one of the two Charites mentioned by Homer. Her name is simply 'beautiful', *calos*. Robert Graves thinks that the two names of the goddesses could be wrongly divided, and that they could be *Pasi thea cale*, meaning 'the goddess who is beautiful to all men' (literally 'to all goddess beautiful'). In other words, perhaps there was originally only one goddess.

Callidice was queen of Thesprotia in Epirus. Odysseus married her (returning to Penelope after her death) and she bore him Polypoetes. Her name means 'fair justice', from *calli-*, 'beautiful' and *dice*, 'justice'. This was a good name for a queen.

Calliope was the Muse of epic poetry, and a daughter of Zeus and Mnemosyne. With all names ending in '-ope' or '-ops' we always have the problem of wondering which is the more apt, 'voice' or 'face', since *ops* has both meanings. We must certainly give Calliope a 'beautiful voice', since otherwise we cannot hear any of her poetry, but why cannot we give her a 'fair face' as well? The first half of her name, as of the next few here, is *calli-*, 'beautiful' (as in 'calligraphy', 'beautiful writing'). The voice of the modern calliope is not necessarily beautiful to all ears – but then maybe nor was epic poetry.

Callipolis was one of the sons of Alcathoüs and Evaechme. He was killed by his father as the result of a sad misunderstanding: he pulled the logs off the fire where his father was sacrificing to Apollo on the grounds that his brother Ischepolis had just been killed, and it would have been inauspicious to sacrifice at such a moment. In spite of this fate, his name is a propitious one, 'fair city' (from *calli-*, 'beautiful' and *polis*, 'city'), perhaps given in the hope that he would one day be a king or capture a city.

Callirrhoë was the daughter of the river god Acheloüs and the wife of Alcmaeon. She unwittingly sent her husband to his death when she devised a trick by which he could obtain the bridal gifts (originally the necklace and wedding dress of Harmonia) that he had given to Arsinoë, his first wife, whom he had deserted in a fit of madness. There was another Callirrhoë who was loved by Coresus but who did not return his love. On Coresus stabbing himself, she was filled with remorse and killed herself as well. In spite of all these dreary deaths, Callirrhoë's name means 'fair flowing', from *calli-*, 'beautiful' and *rheo*, 'to flow'. In the case of the second Callirrhoë, this could refer to the spring where she stabbed herself. The first Callirrhoë, of course, had a 'fair-flowing' river for her father.

Callisto had a somewhat uncertain parentage. Her father was either Lycaon, king of Arcadia, or perhaps Nycteus or Ceteus. Callisto herself may have been a nymph. Whatever she was, she was 'most beautiful', *callistos* (the superlative of *calos*, 'beautiful'). She dedicated herself to Artemis, but was loved and pursued by Zeus – to whom she bore Arcas, which means 'bear' (see this name). Callisto was then turned into a bear.

Calybe was a nymph and shepherdess who bore twins to Laomedon (without being his wife, who was Strymo). Her name means 'cabin' (*calybe*) and maybe this was the hut where she bore her two children or conceived them?

Calyce was a nymph who was the daughter of Aeolus and Enarete. She married Aethlius and became the mother of Endymion either by him or by Zeus. Her name seems a purely decorative one, since it means either 'flower-bud' or 'ornament' (in particular one shaped like a bud). The Greek word for both is *calyx*. Such a name is rather attractive for a nymph, one in a 'rosebud garden of girls', as Tennyson put it.

Calypso, with her curiously modern name, was the daughter of Atlas, and she was either a goddess or a nymph. Her name means 'concealer', 'hider', for she lived on Ogygia and when Odysseus was on his way home from Troy she concealed (*ecalypse*) him here for seven years. (The basic verb 'to cover', 'conceal' is *calypto*.) Of course, the 'concealment' could be understood differently, and Alexander Pope saw it thus, suggesting that 'this wise man Atlas called his daughter by a name that signified a *secret*' – which conjures up the 'little secret' of a forthcoming birth. In classical

81

times, Pliny proposed that Homer had so called the goddess to denote the 'hidden' phenomena of the natural world. Calypso's name is seen in the English word 'apocalypse', literally 'uncovering', especially the Apocalypse or Revelation made in the last book of the Bible, but exactly how the popular West Indian song came to be called a calypso is still something of a mystery. (The only likely link seems to be between Calypso's island of Ogygia and one of the islands of the West Indies.)

Cameira was one of the daughters of Danaüs, her name apparently meaning 'sharer out', from *catamerizo*, 'to distribute'. This virtually identifies her with Lachesis, one of the three Fates (see this name).

Camilla, in Roman mythology, was the daughter of Metabus, king of the Volsci, and Casmila. She was loved and protected by Diana, and fought Amazon-style with one breast bared to give her bow arm greater freedom. She was killed by a spear from Aruns. The origin of her name is uncertain. Maybe she was created by Virgil, since he is the only author in whose writings she is to be found. Her name is very close to that of her mother, of course, and Virgil's own explanation of the name is that her father took his wife's name and 'drowned one hissing letter in a softer sound' to produce Camilla. There may be some association with a sacrificial rite, since the boy and girl attendants of priests at such ceremonies (where the priests had no children of their own) were called respectively *camilli* and *camillae*. Ultimately, her name is probably of Etruscan origin. The popularity, such as it is, of the modern-day girl's name Camilla really originated with this Roman heroine.

Campe was an old woman-gaoler of Tartarus. She was killed by Zeus in order to release the Cyclopes and Hecatoncheires who were imprisoned there. Very aptly, her name means 'crooked', from *campe*, 'bending', 'winding', referring perhaps not so much to her crabbed self as to the winding passages of Tartarus.

Canace was a daughter of Aeolus who had incestuous relations with her brother Macareus and either committed suicide or was put to death by her father, who threw the child she had by her brother to the dogs. (Macareus killed himself.) Her name seems to come from *canasso*, 'to make a gurgling sound' (or any ringing, tramping, gnashing or clashing sound when in the noun form *canache*). Could this refer to the barking of the dogs? One hesitates to apply it to anything else in this grim catalogue. The modern

82

name Candice appears to be based on this, but perhaps it more directly comes from the traditional name of the Ethiopian queens (see Acts 8:27) than that of the wretched Greek girl.

Canthus was one of the Argonauts, coming from Euboea. He was killed by the shepherd Caphaurus, whose flocks he was in the process of driving away. His name may come from *canthos*, 'pack-ass', whose function in a way he may have performed as a shepherd (especially if carrying sheep on his back).

Capaneus was one of the Seven Against Thebes. He was the son of Hipponoüs and Astynome, and married Evadne, who bore him Sthenelus. Perhaps we can look to *capnos*, 'smoke', for the origin of his name: when he swore while setting a ladder up against the walls of Thebes, Zeus punished him by striking him with a thunderbolt!

Caphaurus was the son of Amphithemis (also known as Garamas) of Libya, and he killed two Argonauts. *Caphaura* means 'camphor', and presumably this was meant to indicate his somewhat exotic African origin. It is unfortunate that camphor does not actually grow in Libya – it is found mainly in China and Japan.

Capys was the name of two Trojans. The first was the Trojan who suspected that the famous wooden horse was a trick (and how right he was). The second was a ruler of Troy, the son of Assaracus and father of Anchises by Hieromneme. He was, moreover, the grandfather of Aeneas, and was said to have founded Capua. It is in this last name, of course, that we can see an echo of the Trojan's own name, which seems to derive from *capto*, 'to gulp down', or perhaps *capyros*, 'dried'. Neither of these seems particularly relevant to either man – although the first Capys proposed that the wooden horse should be thrown into the water, and so perhaps 'gulped down' by it.

Carcinus was a crab who lived in the marshes of Lerna. In the fight of Heracles against the Hydra, Carcinus nipped him on his heel, whereupon Heracles angrily crushed it. Hera, however, rewarded Carcinus for his pincer movement and put him in the sky as the constellation of Cancer, otherwise the Crab. *Carcinos* is the Greek for 'crab', *cancer* is the Latin.

Cardea was a Roman goddess similar to Artemis, that is, a virgin goddess of the hunt. Her name derives from the Latin for 'hinge', *cardo*, from the fact that Janus (also a 'door' god) gave her the power over doorways, in other words, over family life. (The story goes that Janus granted her this favour for yielding to his embraces. Janus' traditional two-facedness obviously enabled him to score here.)

Carmenta was a nymph from Arcadia who bore Evander to Hermes. She was also a noted prophetess. Her original name was said to have been Nicostrate (which see), but she was renamed Carmenta for delivering oracles in verse – which prompts the obvious conclusion that her name derives from Latin *carmen*, 'song', 'oracle'. But this was more the Roman explanation of the name, from the fact that she had commanded Evander to find a new home in Italy, giving him letters of the Roman alphabet duly adapted from Greek to fit the Roman tongue. (The Greeks identified her with Themis.) But if not *carmen*, then what is the origin of her name? Could it be, as one source suggests, from Latin *carens mente*, 'being without a mind', 'mindless', with reference to her inspired frenzies? Almost certainly not. But perhaps we can see the 'mind' root added to the goddess named Car or **Carya** (which see) who gave her name to Caria (and whose nut-nymphs are called Caryatids). In this case her name means 'Car the intelligent'.

Carpus was a handsome young man loved by Calamus (which name see). He lost a swimming race against him and perished. Calamus withered away and became a reed. Carpus, meanwhile, had become the 'fruit of the fields' (*carpos*, 'fruit') which dies and is reborn every year.

Carya we mentioned when considering Carmenta. She was the daughter of a king of Laconia and was loved by Dionysus. When she died suddenly at Caryae, he changed her into a walnut tree. Artemis brought the news of this to the Laconians who built a temple to 'Artemis Caryatis', from which comes the name of the Caryatids, originally nut-nymphs but now the term for female statues used as supporting columns. To know that *caryon* means 'nut' is enough to complete the picture.

Cassandra (also known as Alexandra, a version of this name) was the noted prophetess who was the daughter of Priam, king of Troy, and Hecabe. Her name means 'entangler of men', 'man-snarer', from *cassyo*, 'to concoct a plot' and *aner*, *andros*, 'man'. She was certainly involved with a number of men, including Othryoneus and Coroebus, two would-be suitors who were killed in the Trojan

War, Apollo, who courted her but was refused his attentions, Aias, who sacrilegiously raped her in the temple of Athena where she had sought refuge, and Agamemnon, to whom she bore Teledamus and Pelops. William Camden, in his seventeenth-century *Remains Concerning Britain*, says her name means 'inflaming men with love', which is perhaps rather overstating the case. In fact her 'mensnaring' could also refer to her gift of prophecy, since she foretold the harm that Paris would do to Sparta (her warnings went unheeded by the Trojans), and foresaw the doom that would overtake Agamemnon as well as the rest of his family.

Cassiopea was the wife of Cepheus, king of Joppa, and daughter of Hermes' son Arabus. She was the mother of Andromeda, so was like her also a constellation name. The ending of her name seems not to be the usual *ops*, 'face', 'voice', but to be *opos*, 'juice', so that he whole name means 'cassia juice'. Cassia was a rather inferior type of cinnamon (today sometimes called 'Chinese cinnamon') that mostly came (and comes) from China but which the Greeks thought came from the 'exotic' east, that is, the east Mediterranean lands. No doubt Cassiopea was given the name to indicate her oriental connections, with her father having an 'Arabic' name and her husband being king there. In this respect she has a name like Caphaurus (which see). Of course, her name even slightly resembles that of her husband, and attempts have been made to link both Cassiopea and Cepheus (which see) with *caio*, 'to burn'.

Castor and Pollux were, of course, the 'Heavenly Twins', known jointly as the Dioscuri. Castor was thus a son of Tyndareus, king of Sparta, and Leda, and a brother of Helen and Clytemnestra. His name traditionally means 'beaver', which in both Greek and Latin is *castor*. But why? It may be an oblique reference to the story in which Nemesis changed into a beaver (or an otter) in order to pursue fish, with the roles then being reversed, this symbolising the female in pursuit of the male (Nemesis after Zeus) and the converse of this. But this is a ritualistic interpretation, and does not bear directly on Castor, although it is true that in one version of his story he and his brother were the sons of Zeus. Perhaps we can derive his name from *cosmeo*, 'to arrange', 'adorn' (hence our 'cosmetic'), so that he is 'the adorner'. This would be to give the brothers' names symbolic meanings, so that Castor is the day, whose light 'adorns', and Pollux would be the night. Pursuing this idea, we can even see Castor and Pollux respectively as the sun and the moon, with Castor's name related to *aster*, 'star' – and Pollux, with his Greek name of Polydeuces, as really 'Polyleuces', that is, having 'much light' (*polys*, 'much' and *leucos*, 'light', 'bright')! That was the theory proposed, somewhat over-ingeniously, by Thomas Keightley, who also resorted to his favourite *caio*, 'to burn' for a name that is also that of a star. Returning, however, to the 'beaver' theory: it is possible, one must admit, that things happened the other way round, and that the beaver (*castor*) was named for the god or the star. The French philologist Émile Boisacq thought that, his own original explanation being that beavers secrete a pungent, oily substance used in medicine and perfumery, and Castor was a 'noted preserver of women'! Be all this as it may, modern research into the origins of the Greek language simply suggests that his name means 'one who excels', with the *Cas-* element being that also found in Nausicaä, and this *cas-* root meaning 'excel'. Perhaps we may leave him there – but see also **Pollux**.

Catreus was the son of Minos and Pasiphaë. He had four children: a son Althaemenes, and three daughters Aërope, Clymene and Apemosyne. An oracle told him that one of his children would cause his death, so he arranged to 'dispose' of them, with his son and Apemosyne emigrating to Rhodes, and the other two girls sold into slavery. If his name is taken to be a contraction of *catarrhoos*, we get a 'down-flowing', or a 'sweeping away' of his children.

Cecrops was the name of a 'snake-man' (what the Greeks called a *gegenes*, an 'earthling'), having a man's body and a snake's tail. He was the first (or maybe the second) mythical king of Attica, and his wife was Aglauros – who significantly bore him children all of whom have names connected with agriculture, as befits such a father. (Their names were Erysichthon, Aglaurus or Agraulus, Pandrosus, and Herse. See all these names.) His name, therefore, may be a blend of *cercos*, 'tail' and *ops*, 'face', in other words a 'tail-face'.

Cedalion was the boy servant of Hephaestus, given by him as a guide to Orion on the latter's route to Lemnos. We can see the 'guide' or 'guardian' element in his name in *cedo*, 'to be concerned for', and if we combine this with *haliadia*, 'seamen', we get something like 'he who guides sailors'. Orion, after all, had the power either to walk over the waves or to wade through the sea. Cedalion, during his guiding, rode on Orion's shoulders, which presumably served as a kind of crow's nest to the 'ship's boy'.

Celaeno, according to Virgil, was the 'eldest of the Harpies'. She

86

was also one of the seven Pleiades, and the mother of Lycus by Poseidon. The name of both comes from *celainos*, 'black', 'dark', 'murky'. Perhaps this is a reference to the 'murky' nature of the Harpies, or the darkness of the sky or sea.

Celeüs was a king of Eleusis in Attica. He was married to Metanira, and was the father of Demophon. With a rather short name like this, we are left with a number of options. Perhaps we can turn again to the familiar *caio*, 'to burn', with reference to the story about how Demeter used to put Celeüs' son Demophon on the fire at night 'to destroy his mortal parts'. (Robert Graves points to grim rituals where young boys were burnt to death as a kind of vicarious sacrifice for a new king.) Or perhaps we can go for *celeo*, 'to charm', 'bewitch', meaning that Celeüs was a sorcerer. Or after all perhaps we can decide in favour of *celeos sitte*, 'woodpecker', as a suitable name for a king who ruled over forest lands.

Centaurs were creatures with the body and legs of a horse and the torso, head and arms of a man. They were the offspring of Centaurus, a son of Apollo and Stilbe. A popular explanation for their name is to derive it from *cento*, 'to prick', 'goad', 'wound', seeing them as horsemen with lances or simply goaders or drivers. There were tales of Centaurs doing all kinds of brutal and lascivious things (except Chiron, who was wise and gentle). More than one source says that Centaurs originated from men on horseback rounding up wild bulls, and that their appearance in the distance (doubtless Wild West-style, outlined against the horizon) gave rise to the 'men-horses'. (Xenophon called them Hippocentaurs, thus emphasising their 'horsiness'.) Of course, their name may somehow link up with Latin *centum*, 'hundred', especially as they went in war bands of some size. One of the more novel explanations derives their name from *centein ten aeran* 'piercers of the air'. This, too, alludes to the lancers. But we must not forget that the actual word for a bull, *tauros*, supports the 'bull-punching' theory quite strongly.

Cephalus seems to be the name of two people: of the son of Deïon, king of Phocis, and Diomedes, and of the son of Hermes and Herse. Ovid's romantic tale of Cephalus and Procris in the *Metamorphoses* may be a blend of both. Either way, his name derives from *cephale*, 'head', presumably for his handsome appearance. There was thus rivalry for his 'handsome head' between Procris and Eos. However, in view of the fact that Cephalus was carried off by Eos (the Dawn), it is tempting to see his name connected with *cnephas*, 'darkness', 'dusk', 'twilight', since it is the morning twilight that is 'carried away' by the dawn.

Cepheus, king of Joppa, was the father of Andromeda by Cassiopea. There were others of the name, too, of which one of the better known was the Cepheus who was the husband of Neaera. When considering Cassiopea, we mentioned the possibility of a link with *caio*, 'to burn', since Cepheus is also the name of a constellation, as are Cassiopea and Andromeda. This seems more satisfactory than the other derivation proposed for his name, from *ceporos*, 'gardener'.

Cephissus was a river, the father of Narcissus, borne to him by the nymph Liriope. The resemblance between the names of father and son (-issus) has a significance that is more linguistic than meaningful, since it represents the pre-Greek *-inth* suffix found also in Hyacinthus, 'Corinth' and 'labyrinth'. We should look for some riverine or rural word for the first part of his name, however, and perhaps here it is (unlike with Cepheus) *cepos*, 'garden', 'plantation'.

Cerambus was a shepherd of Othrys in Thessaly. During the so-called 'Deucalion's Flood', sent by Zeus against the impious sons of Lycaon, he took refuge in the mountains and there the nymphs gave him wings and turned him into a stag-beetle, *carabos*, from which his name is said to derive (compare English 'scarab' for a type of beetle).

Cerberus was the watchdog of the Underworld, the brother of Hydra and Chimaera. His number of heads varied according to his authors: Hesiod gave him three (or fifty), Horace gave him a hundred. His name probably is not Greek at all, but may be related to that of another mythical dog, Karbaras, who in Asian mythology was one of the two dogs of Yama, the Hindu god of death. If we seek a Greek origin, however, we can perhaps consider *Ker berethrou*, 'evil of the pit' (see **Ker**; *berethron*, 'pit', is the Epic and Ionic form of *barathron*), or recall one of his by-names, *Creoboros* 'flesh-devouring', from *creas*, 'flesh', 'meat' and *boros*, 'devouring'. (Another of his by-names was *Creophages*, meaning much the same, from *creas* and *phagein*, 'to eat'.) Is it possible that ultimately his name is simply a representation of a bark or snap? (The initial C is pronounced hard in his name.)

Cercopes were a pair of mischievous dwarfs who plagued Heracles, in particular robbing him while he was asleep. Their names are usually either Acmon and Passalus or Olus and Eurybatus. They were changed into monkeys by Zeus for having deceived him as well, and this probably explains their name which derives, as does that of Cecrops and Cercyon, from *cercos*, 'tail'. In fact, they may be exactly the same as Cecrops, that is, 'faces with tails', *cercos* and *opes*, 'faces'.

Cercyon, a king of Eleusis, was notorious for forcing all passers-by to stop and wrestle with him. He killed all of them, either during the contest or afterwards. His parentage is given differently in different sources: he was either the son of Poseidon, or of Hephaistus and a daughter of Amphitryon, or of Branchus and the nymph Argia. If the latter, we can translate his name as 'tail' (*cercos*), since he was the son of Branchus whose own name suggests the grunting of pigs (see his name). Or, seen from another angle, perhaps the 'tail' was that of a snake, referring to the coils round his victim when he wrestled with him. Another character with a similar name associated with snakes is Cychreus (see his name also).

Cercysera was the 'cover name' under which Achilles was disguised as a girl by his mother Thetis when he lived under the care of Lycomedes, king of Scyros, in the latter's palace. Although similar to the name of Cercyon, this name probably derives from *cercis*, 'shuttle', a name that suggests the feminine occupation of wielding the distaff.

Cerdo was the wife of Phoroneus, king of Argos. Unfortunately, we know little about her, and not quite enough to explain why she should be called 'the wily one' (*cerdo*) – if that is the true origin of her name. Although she was not the mother of Phoroneus' children Apis and Niobe, it is possible she may have borne him Car, who became king of Megara. (The two names are similar, of course.) Car, we know, instituted the worship of Demeter locally, and two by-names of Demeter were 'Weasel' and 'Vixen', both of which are 'wily ones'. This is very tentative, however, since we have so little to go on.

Ceres was the Roman goddess of corn and the harvest, the counterpart of Demeter. Her name may well derive from the root of *creare*, 'to create', 'produce', 'beget', which is most suitable for such a 'productive' goddess. (Compare English 'cereal', which, via Latin, derives from her name.) The cult of Ceres seems to have been introduced to the Romans around 500 BC.

Ceryx means 'herald' (*ceryx*). It was the name of one of the two sons of Hermes and Herse (the other son was Cephalus) who was indeed a herald – the first herald of the so-called Eleusinian Mysteries (the secret cult practised by initiates at Eleusis in honour of Demeter). Another Ceryx was the younger son of Eumolpus, who succeeded his father as a priest, also at the Eleusinian Mysteries. (In some accounts these two are one and the same person.)

Ceto was the monster-daughter of Pontus (the sea) and Gaia (the land). She married her brother Phorcys and bore him the Graiae and the Gorgons. Her name means 'whale', 'sea-monster', from *cetos*, although another theory points to *ceimai*, 'to lie', 'be situated' as a possible source, referring to the sunken rocks in the sea that lie in wait like monsters.

Ceuthonymus was the father of Menoetes, who was a herdsman who had wrestled with Heracles in the latter's Tenth Labour (The Cattle of Geryon) and had his ribs broken in the attempt. All we know about Ceuthonymus is that he was the father of Menoetes: his remaining activities are a mystery. Hence, no doubt, his name which means 'hidden name', from *ceutho*, 'to conceal' and *onoma*, 'name'! ('Ceuthonymous' would be a handy word in English on the lines of 'anonymous' or 'pseudonymous' to describe someone who has a name but chooses not to reveal it.)

Ceÿx was the son of Eosphorus (the 'dawn-bringing' morning star) and the father of Alcyone. He was also father-in-law to Cycnus. Ceÿx and Alcyone (see her name) were the boastful couple who dared to call themselves 'Zeus' and 'Hera' and were punished by being turned respectively into a gannet and a kingfisher. (The story is that told by Apollodorus.) *Ceyx* means 'seagull' (or some similar sea bird). Note also that his son-in-law's name is that of another bird (see **Cycnus**).

Chalciope was the daughter of Aeëtes, king of Colchis, and the Oceanid Idyia. She married Phrixus and bore him four sons, Argus, Phrontis, Melas and Cytissorus. Her name means 'bronze face' or 'brazen face', from *chalcos*, 'brass' (later, 'bronze') and *ops*, 'face'. This is probably intended as a complimentary name, rather than one of disapproval. See also **Chalcodon**.

Chalcodon was the son of Abas and the father of Elephenor. He became king of Euboea and was killed by Amphitryon. His name could mean either 'brazen path' or 'bronze tooth', depending whether we take *odos*, 'path' or *odous*, 'tooth' for the latter half of his name. As with Chalciope, his name either way would be regarded as a propitious one. Chalcodon also had a daughter named Chalciope (not the same as the above) who married Aegeas as his second wife. (His first wife was Meta; his third, the best known, was Medea.)

Chaos was really where, at any rate according to Hesiod and his *Theogony*, it all started. Chaos was the void from which sprang Gaia, Tartarus, Erebus and Nyx (and possibly also Eros), and is scarcely personified in mythology. The name does not really mean 'empty space', and still less the 'confusion' that it means to us today. It means more 'to yawn', 'gape', 'open wide', *chaino*.

Charis was one of the Graces. This was the name Homer used for Hesiod's Aglaia (which see). Charis means, simply, 'grace', *charis*. (English 'charity' derives rather from Latin than this Greek word. See next entry.)

Charites is the Greek name for the three Graces, known in Latin as *Gratiae*. Their name comes from Greek *charis*, *charitos*, 'grace', with Latin *caritas*, in turn from *carus*, 'dear', giving English 'charity'. The three Graces were Aglaia, Euphrosyne and Thalia, the daughters of Zeus and Euronyme. 'From the glancing of their lidded eyes bewildering love distils; there is beauty in their glance, from beneath brows', wrote Hesiod of them in his *Theogony*. (In certain other authors they have different parents, and occasionally different names. See, for example, **Cale**.)

Charon was the son of Erebus and Nyx, and the famous ferryman of the dead over the river Styx (or according to some Acheron) into the Underworld. He was so named for his bright eyes, *chara*, 'joy', 'delight' and *ops*, 'eye'. Or perhaps we should say for his fierce bright eyes, since *charopos* meant more 'bright-eyed', 'fierce-eyed' than simply 'glad-eyed'. No doubt he revelled in his work.

Charybdis was the name of the whirlpool at the north end of the Strait of Messina, regarded as a female monster, the daughter of Poseidon and Gaia. She was the terror of sailors, since three times a day she sucked down the waters round about her, and later belched them out again. Mariners would try to avoid her, but in steering away from her ran the risk of falling victim to Scylla, her opposite number, so to speak, who lived in a cave on the cliff opposite the whirlpool (see her name). Charybdis must surely derive from *roibdeo*, 'to swallow greedily down', from *roibdos*, 'rushing', although here we have lost the initial *Cha-*. Perhaps there is an influence of the Hebrew root *kharab*, 'to dry up' (hence, perhaps, the name of Arabia), referring to a violent current that now flooded, now exposed the land in a series of tides.

Cheimarrhus was the leader of a band of pirates who were beaten off by Iobates. He had a ship with a lion figurehead and a serpent-shaped stern. He also had a fiery nature. But it seems that these two elements were introduced into the story in which he figures (Bellerophon destroying the Chimaera) by some euhemerist (see Technical Terms, page 14) to explain away the Chimaera itself, with its front-part lion, snake's tail and fiery breath. But the Chimaera did have a goat's middle, and the name of Cheimarrhus – and of the Chimaera (which see) – is close to *chimaros*, 'he-goat'. Alternatively, we can consider *cheimarroos*, literally 'winter-flowing'. This could refer to the lead that Bellerophon forced into the Chimaera's mouth: it melted in her fiery breath and trickled down her throat, thus causing her demise. (In fairness, Hesiod does not tell us how Bellerophon killed the Chimaera, but other authors mention the molten lead method.)

Chiade was one of the daughters of Amphion, king of Thebes, and Niobe. Maybe we can consider the name of her mother here and arrive at a subtle distinction: Chiade's name comes from *chion*, 'fallen snow'; Niobe's name derives from *niphas*, 'fall*ing* snow'. Falling snow, after all, results in fall*en* snow. See also **Niobe**.

Chimaera was one of a rather grisly brood produced by Typhon and Echidna, themselves hardly fountains of delight. The whole family, in fact, consisted of monsters, with the Chimaera's siblings including the Hydra, Cerberus and Orthus. The Chimaera was a dragon-like fire-breathing monster. She did not resemble a dragon, however, but had the front part of a lion, the middle part of a goat, and the rear quarters and tail of a snake. She also had (most accounts say) three heads, and she was finally disposed of by Bellerophon. (See **Cheimarrhus** for this and more about her.) Her name is the word *chimaera* for 'she-goat', with reference to her central section. This was technically in Greek the word for a one-year-old goat, one that had passed one winter (*cheima*, 'winter'). Her name is thus by an indirect but certain linguistic link related to that of the Himalayas, whose name comes from Sanskrit *hima*, 'snow' (the Greek *cheima*) and *alaya*, 'residence'.

Chione was the name of the daughter of Daedalion and also that of the daughter of Boreas and Orithyia. For both girls the originating word is *chion*, 'snow', either referring to their beauty (such as Snow White had), or in the case of Boreas' daughter with allusion to her father, the north wind (bringer of snow). Daedalion's daughter was a proper Snow Maiden: she was raped by Hermes on snowy Mount Parnassus (this before Apollo had a chance) and as a result bore him Autolycus.

Chiron (also spelt Cheiron) was a Centaur. He was not descended from Ixion or his son Centaurus, like the others, but was the son of Cronos and Philyra. Unlike the others, too, he was less lascivious, more considerate (see **Centaurs**). In fact, he had considerable skill as a surgeon (*cheirourgos*), who of course needs a practised and steady hand (*cheir*).

Chlidanope was a Naiad. She became the wife of Hypseus, king of the Lapiths, and the mother of Cyrene. Her name rather charmingly means 'delicate face', from *chlidanos*, 'delicate' and *ops*, 'face'. That is a very nice name for a Naiad.

Chloë was the girl traditionally loved by Daphnis in the Greek pastoral romances of the second century AD (which is quite late compared to most of the other personages here). As Liddell and Scott attractively define it, *chloe* is 'the tender shoot of plants in spring, the blade of young corn or grass'. In short, Chloë the Green Shoot. The name was also a by-name of Demeter. Note how Chloë's leafy name matches that of her lover. See **Daphnis**.

Chloris was either the daughter of Niobe or the daughter of Amphion (the son of Iasus). Her name comes from *chloros*, 'green' (compare **Chloë**), since she was one of the very few of Niobe's many children to survive, after the others – because of Niobe's boast to Leto that her children were superior – were killed by Leto's children, Apollo and Artemis. In other words, Chloris survived the destruction of winter, and the snow with which Niobe is closely associated, and appeared alive in the green spring.

Chrysaor has a name that means 'golden sword' (*chrysos*, 'gold' and *aor*, 'sword'). This was a fairly common by-name among the gods: how did this son of Poseidon and Medusa and brother of

Pegasus come by it? Both Chrysaor and Pegasus sprang from the blood that flowed from Medusa, when Perseus had cut off her head. Perhaps Perseus used a golden sword for this? Or perhaps it simply alludes to one who gives light and lustre, as it is when used as a by-name (*Chrysaoros*) of Demeter and Apollo. We are told at any rate that at his moment of birth Chrysaor was brandishing a golden sword.

Chryse was the daughter of Almus, king of the Almones. By Ares she became the mother of Phlegyas. Her name is simply a propitious one, 'golden', from *chrysos*, 'gold'.

Chryseïs was the daughter of Chryses, who was a priest of Apollo at his shrine on the island of Chryse, near Troy. According to some accounts, her real name was Astynome ('city protector'). One tale says that Chryseïs bore a son to Agamemnon, calling him Chryses after his grandfather and passing him off as Apollo. There are enough references to gold (*chrysos*) here to emphasise the origin and value of her name. Traditionally, too, Chryseïs was fair-haired, slender and dainty ('blonde, mince et petite', as Pierre Grimal puts it) and nineteen years old – the idealised Greek golden girl.

Chryses was the name of the priest of Apollo who was the father of Chryseïs (whose name see), and also that of the son of Agamemnon and this same Chryseïs. There is no doubt as to the import of the name. Gold was as significant to the Greeks as it still is today: not for nothing did Jason and the Argonauts seek to recover the priceless Golden Fleece (in Greek called *to panchryson deras*, literally 'the all-gold hide').

Chrysippus was a handsome young man (no doubt golden-haired) who was the son of Pelops and a nymph. He was kidnapped by Laius, king of Thebes. His name implies both wealth and status: 'he of the golden horse', from *chrysos*, 'gold' and *hippos*, 'horse'.

Chrysothemis was the daughter of Agamemnon and Clytemnestra, and the sister of Orestes, Iphigenia and Electra. Among such illustrious company, it is fitting that she should have a shining name: 'golden order', from *chrysos*, 'gold' and *themis*, 'law', 'order'. See **Themis**.

Chthonia was one of the daughters of Erechtheus, king of Athens, and Praxithea, a Naiad. Her name means 'she of the soil', or 'earth girl' (*chthon*, 'earth', 'ground'). Her name echoes that of her father who, Homer tells us, sprang straight from the ground without any human parents.

Chthonius has a similar name to that of Chthonia. He was one of the Sown Men, and as befits one of the warriors who sprang from the dragon's teeth sowed in the ground by Cadmus, has a name that means 'earth man', 'he of the soil'.

Cilix was one of the sons of Agenor, king of Sidon. He was the brother of Cadmus, among others, and his sister was Europa. When the latter was abducted by Zeus (disguised as a handsome white bull), Cilix and his brothers set off to trace her. He halted in a land to which he gave his name, Cilicia. In view of Zeus the Bull, we can perhaps see in his name a blend of *ceras*, 'horn' and *helix*, 'twisted', or even a link with *cyllos*, 'crooked', all these with reference to the abductor's horns which, we are told, 'were like a crescent moon'.

Cilla was one of the daughters of Laomedon and Strymo, and thus a sister of Priam. When Hecabe was pregnant with Paris, the seer Aesacus declared that mother and child must be put to death in order to avert a great calamity that he foresaw. Priam, however, referred this prophecy to Cilla and her son (by Thyometus) Menippus, who therefore perished in place of Hecabe and Paris. Cilla's name seems to derive from *cillos*, 'ass', and this could be a reference to the seer's prophecy and her own fate, since dice made from an ass's bone were traditionally used for divination. The modern girl's name Cilla is not derived from this, but more likely is a pet form of a name such as Priscilla.

Cinyras was a king of Cyprus, either the son of Poseidon and Paphos, or else of Eurymedon and a nymph. According to one tale, Cinyras had a daughter Myrrha (or Smyrna) who had a passion for him and by an incestuous relationship bore him Adonis, herself being changed for this crime into a myrrh tree. Adonis has been identified with the Babylonian fertility god Tammuz mentioned in Ezekiel. Both gods underwent an annual death and resurrection (a symbolic reference to the death of crops in the winter and their rebirth in the spring) and both were mourned until they reappeared. Ezekiel (8:14) talks of 'women weeping for Tammuz' and Milton, in his *Paradise Lost*, refers to the identity of both gods:

95

> Thammuz came next behind,
> Whose annual wound in Lebanon allur'd
> The Syrian damsels to lament his fate
> In amorous ditties all a summer's day,
> While smooth Adonis from his native rock
> Ran purple to the sea.

This lamenting seems to lie behind the name of Cinyras, from the Hebrew word *kinnor* that gives Greek *cinyros*, 'wailing' (in turn apparently related to the Irish 'keening').

Circe was the daughter of Helios and Perse, an Oceanid. She was the sister of Aeëtes, king of Colchis. Above all, she was a powerful witch, with perhaps her *tour de force* being the transformation of several of Odysseus' companions into a herd of pigs when they were visiting her island of Aeaea. Her name is usually derived from *circos*, 'hawk' or from this same word meaning 'circle' (hawks wheel in circles when they fly). Hawks are fearsome, destructive birds, possessing the powers that Circe did: Homer describes Circe as living in the middle of a wood, while round her house prowled lions and wolves, the drugged victims of her witchcraft. (Hawks live in trees and prey on small mammals.) The 'circle' derivation could apply to Circe's island, her witch's territory. On the other hand, she has been identified with the Egyptian goddess Isis, possibly from the circle or 'halo' often shown above her head in drawings of her. Some mythologists have seen Circe as a personification of the moon, hence the hawk and its circular flight and the circle itself of the moon's daily orbit. Circe was the consort of Odysseus, and after his death married Telemachus.

Cisseus, according to Euripides and Virgil, was the father of either Theano or Hecabe. Otherwise, this was the name of the son of Melampus, and a companion of Heracles in his Labours. His name derives from *cissos*, 'ivy', or *cisseus*, 'crowned with ivy', this being a by-name of Theano in honour of Athena whose chief festival fell in the 'ivy month' (starting on 30 September).

Cleisithyra was the daughter of Idomeneus and Meda. She was murdered, together with Meda, by Nauplius in the temple where they had taken refuge. This attempt to hide seems to be shown in her name of Cleisithyra, which means 'door locker', from *cleis*, 'key', 'bar' and *thyra*, 'door'.

Cleitonymus (sometimes known as Aeanes) was the son of Amphidamas. He was killed by Patroclus in a quarrel over a game of dice. His name means nothing more than 'famous name', from *cleitos*, 'renowned', 'famous' and *onoma*, 'name' (in its Aeolian form *onyma*). This is a rather generalised propitious name, even an unoriginal one!

Cleobis was the brother of Biton, who both pulled their mother to the temple in Argos in an ox-cart (see **Biton**). Cleobis simply means 'famous life', from *cleo* 'to be famous' and *bios*, 'life'. This is just a generally propitious name: may he have a praiseworthy life.

Cleobule was the mother of Phoenix by Amyntor. Her name, like most of those starting 'Cleo-', is also simply a favourable one. In her case it means 'famous counsel', from *cleo*, 'to be famous' and *boule*, 'counsel'.

Cleodaeus is another 'praiseworthy' name, meaning 'famous warrior', from *cleo*, 'to be famous' and *daios*, 'hostile'. Cleodaeus was the father of Aristomachus and himself the son of Hyllus and Iole. Hyllus had made an unsuccessful attempt to invade the Peloponnese; Cleodaeus also made an attempt but was equally unsuccessful. He did not therefore live up to his name.

Cleodice was the sister of Himertus, son of Lacedaemon and Taÿgete. She was raped by him (unwittingly) in a night revel arranged by Aphrodite. Her name does not reflect this, however, since it is merely favourable: 'famous justice', from *cleo*, 'to be famous', and *dice*, 'order', 'right'.

Cleola was the wife of Atreus. She died after giving birth to Pleisthenes, and Atreus married Aërope. Her name like the other 'Cleo' ones is a propitious one, expressing the wish that she will be 'wholly famous', from *cleos*, 'fame' and *holos*, 'whole'.

Cleopatra is a very common name in both mythology and history, with probably the best known being the Egyptian queen who lived first with Julius Caesar in Rome and later with Mark Anthony. (This was the Cleopatra who committed suicide by putting a poisonous asp to her bosom.) Among the many mythological Cleopatras we have the wife of Meleager and the wife of Phineus, the former being the daughter of Idas and Marpessa, and the latter that of Boreas and Orithyia. Whichever Cleopatra we consider, her name will always mean the same: 'fame of her father', from *cleos*, 'fame' and *pater*, 'father'. Of course, the interpretation can be made in two ways: either wishfully ('May she be the fame of her father') or actually ('She is famed for her father'). In fact most of the Cleopatrine fathers were not particularly famous, and even the Egyptian queen was the daughter of just one of a number of Ptolemies. According to Apollodorus, the real name of the daughter of Idas and Marpessa was **Alcyone** (which name see).

Cleothera was the daughter of Pandareüs and the sister of Merope. She was brought up by Aphrodite, Hera and Athena, but was abducted by the Harpies and enslaved by the Furies. Despite this fate, her name is just a propitious one, meaning 'famous hunting' or 'famous huntress', from *cleos*, 'fame' and *thera*, 'hunting'. (One could also interpret the second half of her name as *ther*, 'wild beast', which would make her a 'famous animal' or a kind of wild beauty.) To some extent she lived up to her name, inasmuch as Hera endowed her with beauty and superhuman wisdom.

Clio was the name of the Muse of history. Fittingly, her name simply means 'fame', 'renown'. She is thus a proclaimer of deeds of renown.

Clite was the daughter of Merops, king of Percote, and she became the wife of Cyzicus, king of the Doliones. Something of a royal lady, therefore, as we might expect anyway from her name which means 'famous' (*clytos*).

Clitus was the son – beautiful, we are told – of Mantius. He was carried off by Eos to live with the gods. Like Clite, he is 'famous' (*clytos*).

Clotho was one of the Fates. She spun the thread of life, and her name comes from *clotho*, 'to spin'. There does not seem to be any evidence that her name is directly linked with the English 'cloth'.

Clymene was the name of several ladies, among them the daughter of Catreus who married Nauplius, the nymph who bore Phaëthon to Helios, the daughter of Minyas and wife of Cephalus, and the daughter of Oceanus who bore Atlas, Menoetius, Prometheus and Epimetheus to Iapetus. Apart from the second of these, where the connection is more obvious, the name is merely a favourable one: 'famous strength', from *clytos*, 'famous', 'glorious', and *menos*, 'strength', 'might'.

Clymenus has a name that is identical to that of Clymene: 'famous strength'. The best known of the name were the king of Argos who was the father of Harpalyce, and the grandson of Phrixus who became king of Orchomenus in Boeotia.

Clytemnestra has a name almost as impressive as those of her family or her terrible deeds (she plotted with her lover to kill her father, among other things). She was the daughter of Tyndareüs, king of Sparta, and of Leda, and she was the sister of Helen and of Castor and Pollux. She first married Tantalus, who was killed by Agamemnon, then Agamemnon himself, to whom she bore Iphigenia, Electra, Chrysothemis and Orestes. Her lover was Tantalus' brother Aegisthus. He killed Agamemnon, with Clytemnestra's connivance, and she then killed Cassandra, whom Agamemnon had brought back from Troy as his concubine . . . But hold, enough: what does her name mean? It means either 'famous bride', from *clytos*, 'famous' and *mnesteira*, 'bride', or in a more general way 'praiseworthy wooing', with the latter half of her name from *mnesteuo*, 'to woo'. Wooer she may have been; 'praiseworthy' is another matter.

Clytia was a nymph who was spurned by her former lover Helios. Forlorn and inconsolable, she wasted away to become a heliotrope. She was destined for better things, for her name means 'famous' (*clytos*). Note, however, that the name of the flower she became means 'turning to the sun' – a touching memorial to her lover.

Clytius has the same origin for his name as Clytia, 'famous'. None of the characters of this name were particularly famous, however. Among the best known are the Argonaut who was killed by Aeëtes, the Trojan elder who was the son of Laomedon and brother of Priam, and the giant killed by Hecate in the 'Gigantomachia', the war between the gods and the giants.

Cocalus was a king of Camicus in Sicily. Daedalus took refuge in his court from Minos after escaping (or being released) from the Labyrinth. Minos went on a grand tour visiting all the palaces of western rulers and presenting each with the same problem: how to thread a spiral shell. When he challenged Cocalus with this the shell was returned to him threaded and he was then sure that he was harbouring Daedalus for, as he assumed, no one else (without knowledge of the Labyrinth) would be able to perform such an exacting task. (Daedalus is said to have bored a hole in the top of the shell and hitched the thread to an ant, which found its tortuous

99

way out.) All this is reflected in the name of the king, since *coclea* in Latin (and *cochlias* in Greek) means 'snail'. Compare English 'cockle'.

Coeüs was a Titan, the son of Uranus and Gaia. He was the father of Leto and Asteria by his sister (sic) Phoebe. His name is so short we can suggest a number of suitable derivations for it, from *caio* 'to burn' (so 'the lucid one') and *coeo*, 'to mark', 'perceive' (thus 'the intelligent one') to a shortened form of *coiranos*, 'ruler', 'leader'. Each of these is as likely (or unlikely) as the other.

Comaetho was the name of a priestess of Artemis at Patrae, who sacrilegiously conducted affairs with her lover Melanippus in the temple itself and as a result was sacrificed. It was also the name of the daughter of Pterelaüs who pulled out the single gold hair of her father's head that otherwise ensured his immortality (or that his city would not be taken). For both women the name is suitable, since it means 'bright hair', from *come*, 'hair' and *aitho*, 'to light up', 'burn'. The former girl may have had bright hair (she also perhaps ultimately had her hair burnt); the latter removed a vital golden hair causing the death of her father and the fall of his city.

Cometes was the son of Sthenelus who seduced Diomedes' wife Aegialia. His name means 'long-haired' (*cometes*). This was not necessarily a compliment, since it was a sign of immaturity: Greek boys had long hair, and this was ritually cut short when they reached the age of maturity and manhood at eighteen. (The word *cometes*, incidentally, gives the English 'comet' which was originally observed to have a long tail of 'hair' trailing behind it.)

Connidas was the teacher or pedagogue of Theseus in Troezen. His name is apt for one who is learned: 'knowing man from Mount Ida', from *conneo*, 'to know' and *Ida*, 'Ida'.

Consus was a Roman god of rather vague speciality. He seems to have been connected with horses and mules, but perhaps he was really the god of 'counsel', *consilium*. On the other hand, he may well have been the god of harvest and the granary, in which case his name may come from *condere*, 'to store'.

Copreus was the son of Pelops and the herald of his nephew, king Eurystheus of Mycenae. More importantly, he informed Heracles what his Fifth Labour was: the cleaning of the Augean Stables (see **Augeas**). Hence he has the positively functional name of 'dung man', from *copros*, 'dung', 'manure'. Of course, this in another context might have denoted some peaceful agricultural occupation as a 'manurer'. But we have a specific 'muck out' link for Copreus.

Core was a later name of Persephone (the Roman Proserpine). The name simply means 'girl', 'maiden', and is probably the origin of the modern girl's name Cora.

Corinthus may have been a son of Zeus. In any event, he had a daughter Sylea (although no sons) and he gave his name to Corinth. So the tales go, but in actual fact the name of Corinth is almost certainly pre-Greek, even though it has been linked with *corys*, *corythos*, 'helmet', that is, the top of a mountain.

Coroebus was the son of Mygdon, a Phrygian king, and he fought on the side of the Trojans in the Trojan War. He wanted to marry Cassandra but was killed by either Diomedes or Neoptolemus. His name seems to denote 'feaster on ox', from *coros*, 'satiety' and *bous*, 'ox'. Perhaps this is a suitable name for a big, burly warrior.

Coronis was the name of at least three women. The first was the daughter of Phlegyas, king of Orchomenus, who became the mother of Asclepius by Apollo (although while still carrying Asclepius she actually married Ischys). The second was a follower of Dionysus. She was raped by Butes, the son of Boreas. The third was the daughter of one Coroneus who was pursued by Poseidon who was in love with her. The common link for all these, and certainly the first and third, is 'crow', *corone*. When Apollo heard that the first Coronis had married Ischys, he angrily turned the crow from its former white colour to black. The third Coronis was turned into a crow by her protectress Athena, to save her from the pursuits of Poseidon. The second Coronis does not seem to have had any definite crow-connection, but this may simply be because whatever it was has not come down to us. (We must, however, be wary of using this handy explanation too frequently for a name that is difficult to interpret!)

Coronus was the son of Caeneus, and he reigned over the Lapiths in the time of Heracles. He was also an Argonaut. His name, like Coronis, also means 'crow', but we are not given any precise justification for this. The bird symbolised discord and strife, and doubtless Coronus was involved in his fair share of this before he was killed by the Dorian king Aegimius, to whose aid he had come.

101

Corybantes were male followers of Cybele who celebrated her rites by a kind of orgiastic dance brandishing weapons and the like. They were often identified (or at least confused) with the Curetes, who followed Zeus. Their name is of uncertain origin. It may be a Phrygian word meaning something like 'whirlers'.

Corythus was the name of a son of Zeus who became king of Lydia and the father of Dardanus and Iasion by Electra. It was also the name of a son of Paris and the nymph Oenone who was killed by his father (out of jealousy for Helen's love of Corythus). The name may mean 'helmet', from *corys, corythos* (see also **Corinthus**) since Dardanus, the son of the first Corythus mentioned here, had founded the city of Corythus in memory of his father and also, apparently, because he had lost his helmet. (He later recovered it.)

Cottus was one of the Hecatoncheires, the 'Hundred-handed Giants', who were the offspring of Uranus and Gaia. His name may mean 'striker', 'smiter', from *capto*, 'to smite'. One theory maintains that Cottus represents hail (which 'smites'), while Briareüs represents snow and Gyes rain (see the names of these two).

Cotytto was an orgiastic goddess worshipped in Thrace whose festivals resembled those of Cybele. Her name is almost certainly non-Greek, and also of uncertain meaning. Robert Graves suggests that Cottus (whom see) may have a name based on hers.

Cranaë was the daughter of Cranaüs and Pedias and the sister of Atthis. Her name seems to derive from *cranaos*, 'rocky'. This may be a reference to some sacrificial ritual (in which the victim was thrown from rocks into the sea?) or, more ingeniously, we can interpret the name of Atthis as *actes thea*, 'goddess of the seashore' and get our rocks from there.

Cranaechme was, with Atthis, another sister of Cranaë. If we interpret her name as 'rocky point', from *cranaos*, 'rocky' and *acme*, 'point', we are left with such speculative origins as were proposed for Cranaë and Atthis.

Cranaüs was the third mythological king of Athens, the husband of Pedias. He sprang from the soil as his predecessor Cecrops had done. Here we can with some justification see his name as 'rocky' (*cranaos*).

Cratos was the son of the Titan Pallas and the river Styx, and the brother of Bia and Zelus. His sister was Nike. He was obviously strong: he and his brother Bia chained Prometheus and nailed him down to the rock of Caucasus as a punishment for his gift of fire to mankind. *Cratos* means 'strength', 'might'.

Creon means 'ruler', and as such is hardly more than a title for any king who bore the name. Among those who did were the son of Menoeceus, who was a ruler of Thebes, and the son of Lycaethus, who was a king of Corinth.

Cresphontes was a descendant of Heracles. He was a son of Aristomachus and king of Messenia. His propitious name means 'stronger slayer', from *creisson*, 'stronger', and *phoneus*, 'slayer', 'murderer'. He was strong enough to conquer the Peloponnese (with the help of his brother Temenus and his nephews), but not quite strong enough to avoid being killed by rich Messenians who regarded him as too lenient towards the commoners.

Cressida is the heroine of Shakespeare's *Troilus and Cressida*, which has no basis in classical mythology. Since, however, Troilus *is* a classical name, and since Cressida is usually regarded as at least originating from the classical tales, we can accommodate her here. Shakespeare took the name from the *Roman de Troie* ('Tale of Troy') written by Benoît de Sainte-Maure, a twelfth-century French poet. This tale was itself based on supposed records of Dares Phrygius (who features in Homer's *Iliad* as a priest of Hephaestus among the Trojans) and one Dictys Cretensis, allegedly a Cretan from Knossos who accompanied Idomeneus to the Trojan War. These stories, which were the basis of medieval tales about Troy and the Trojan Wars, were also used before Shakespeare by, respectively, Guido da Colonna, a thirteenth-century Sicilian writer (who also borrowed from Benoît de Sainte-Maure), Boccaccio, the great fourteenth-century Italian writer and humanist, and Chaucer in England. For his heroine, Colonna took the name Briseida, based on Homer's Briseïs (which see), making her the daughter of Calchas, with Troilus and Diomedes her successive lovers. Boccaccio changed Briseida to Griseida, and Chaucer changed the name to Cryseyde for his *Troylus and Cryseyde*. This last version produced the name Cressida. In fact there are several *Iliad* characters in Shakespeare's play. Cressida itself is usually interpreted as 'golden' and derived from *chryseos* meaning this.

Crete was the daughter of Asterius, king of Crete, and she is said to have given her name to the kingdom. Her name may well derive from *cratos*, 'strength', 'might', a suitable name for the goddess daughter of a ruler.

Cretheus was the son of Aeolus and Enarete. He was also the founder of Iolcus in Thessaly and its first king. For him the origin of 'ruler', from *cratos*, 'power', seems just right.

Creüsa was the younger daughter of Erechtheus, king of Athens. Creüsa was also the name of the daughter of Priam, king of Troy, and Hecabe. In fact, there were several of the name, which is really the feminine of Creon, so means 'ruler', 'princess', 'queen'. All Creüsas seem to have been either married to a king or born into a royal family.

Crius was a Titan, the father of Astraeüs, Pallas and Perses by Eurybia. The precise origin of his name is not very clear. Perhaps it somehow derives from *crino*, 'to separate'. Or perhaps we should look for some 'powerful' name in view of Crius' gigantic nature and the name of his wife, which means 'wide force'. In this case we can consider *crios*, 'ram' (both the sheep and the battering-device).

Cronos, the son of Uranus and Gaia, king of the Titans and Titanesses, has a name that has long wrongly been held to be associated with *chronos*, 'time'. For this reason he has been depicted as an old man with a scythe, the original 'Father Time'. (He did, after all, castrate Uranus: hence the scythe.) In support of this 'time' theory it has been pointed out that he was the son of Uranus (i.e. heaven) whose sun and moon measure time; that he was married to Rhea whose name means 'flowing', and time 'flows'; that he devoured his own children and time destroys what it has brought into existence! But if it does not mean 'time', then what does his name mean? Robert Graves thinks it may derive from *corone*, 'crow', since he is often pictured in the company of one and the crow was an 'oracle'. Leonard Ashley settles for 'rocky', from *cranaos* (as we considered for Cranaë, Cranaechme and Cranaüs). Jane Harrison cites an ancient theory that his name may be linked with *craino*, 'to accomplish', since Cronos 'accomplishes' the full circle of the year, that is, he is really a 'year god'. But the truth is probably that his name is not Greek at all. See, however, his Roman equivalent, **Saturn**.

Croton gave his name to Croton (now Crotone), southern Italy.

He was accidentally killed when Lacinius tried to steal Heracles' cattle. His name seems to derive from *croton*, 'tick'. Could this be connected with the cattle?

Crotopus was a king, the father of Psamathe, a princess of Argos. Psamathe's son Linus was murdered by Crotopus, and this may explain his name if we derive it from *croteo*, 'to strike', 'knock' and *pous*, 'foot' – in other words 'thumping foot'! Pliny approved this theory, saying that Linus (which see) means 'flax' and therefore Crotopus, in murdering him, represented the mallets that pound the flax. Moreover, flax grows in sandy soil, and Psamathe's name means 'sandy'.

Cteatus was one of the Moliones, the sons of Actor and Molione. He and Eurytus are sometimes regarded as Siamese twins. His name derives from *ctaomai*, 'to gain', 'procure', so that he was an 'acquirer'. One theory suggests that the twins were symbols of foreign trade. See **Eurytus**, whose name could support this.

Ctessipus was the son of Heracles and Deïanira (or Astydamia). His name seems to be a propitious one, meaning 'possessor of horses', from *ctesios*, 'of one's property' and *hippos*, 'horse'.

Cupid, of course, was the Roman god of love, also known more abstractly as Amor. (His Greek equivalent is Eros.) His name means 'desire', from Latin *cupido*. Compare the English word 'cupidity', meaning 'greed for gain'.

Curetes were minor Cretan gods who protected the baby Zeus. According to some they were the sons of the Dactyls. Their name means 'young men', from *couros*, 'young man', either because they resembled groups of Cretan youths performing ritual dances, or (more obviously) because they attended Zeus in his youth. They were often confused with the Corybantes.

Cyamites was an Arcadian rewarded (in rather vague circumstances) by Demeter with all kinds of grain but forbidden by her (also rather mysteriously) to sow beans. He did, however – hence his name, from *cyamos*, 'bean'.

Cyane was a Sicilian nymph who gave her name to a fountain and a pool. It was also the name of the wife of Aeolus. For the first Cyane, at least, the origin of the name is descriptive, since it means 'blue', from *cyanos*, a dark blue substance, perhaps blue steel, used by the Greeks to decorate metalwork.

Cyathus was a wretched cupbearer struck (with one finger only) by an angry Heracles and killed, since the great man did not drink. His name denotes his office: *cyathos* means 'wine-cup'. Another young cupbearer who suffered an identical fate was Eunomus.

Cybele was originally a Phrygian goddess. She is usually identified with Rhea, the mother of Zeus, and like her personified the earth ('Mother Earth'). We can try relating her name to *come*, 'hair' and *copa*, 'axe', but these are not very convincing, unless they indicate some ritual. Perhaps her name is linked with the cymbals (*cymbos, cymbala*) that were used in her worship?

Cychreus was the first king of Salamis. In many stories he is associated with a snake. In this respect, his name could link up with that of Cercyon, for whom we considered *cercos*, 'tail' as appropriate for the coil of a snake. The only other word that closely resembles his name in Greek is *cichora*, 'chicory'.

Cyclops was really the generic name (plural Cyclopes) for one of a number of one-eyed giants, with the best-known probably Polyphemus. The name means 'round eye', from *cyclos*, 'round', 'circle' and *ops*, 'eye', although admittedly the word could also mean 'round face', since *ops* also means 'face'. In his *Theogony*, Hesiod explains their name thus: 'Cyclopes was the name given them, by reason of the single circular eye that was set in their foreheads.' The French philologist Samuel Bochart regarded the name as of Phoenician origin, perhaps in some such form as Chek-lub or Chek-lelub. This, he says, was the name of 'men living round the promontory of Lilybaeum (now Marsala) in Sicily', and the word was transformed by process of popular etymology to Cyclops by the Greeks. There has been much dispute regarding the significance of their round eye: what does it represent? Is it allegorical, symbolising the human hatred or passion which 'focuses' on a single object? Or perhaps it relates to some folk cult involving a whirling, dervish-type dance? In this latter respect, it is interesting that several of the Cyclopes have 'whirling' or at any rate fairly dynamic names, such as Brontes ('thunder'), Steropes ('lightning') and Arges ('brightness', 'swiftness').

Cycnus was the son of Ares, and was killed by Heracles in a fight. Another Cycnus was the son of Poseidon and Calyce. A third one of the name was a king of the Ligurians in Italy, and yet another Cycnus was a son of Apollo and Hyrië. The name means 'swan' (*cycnos*) into which, for one reason or another, most of them were turned, usually when they died or were killed. The swan was sacred to Apollo, and Plato quotes the well-known belief that a swan's song was heard only when it knew that its death was near.

Cylarabes was the son of Sthenelus who succeeded Cyanippus as king of Argos. His rather unusual name may be a form of 'Cyclarabes', in which case it might mean 'rattling wheels', from *cyclos*, 'round', 'wheel' and *arabeo*, 'to rattle'. These would presumably be chariot wheels, suggesting a grand-style presence or arrival.

Cyllene was the nymph by whom Pelasgus became the father of Lycaon. The name seems to be based on *cyllos*, 'crooked', 'lame'. Perhaps this refers to Mount Cyllene, on which Hermes was born (with one of his by-names Cyllenios). A nymph would not normally be crooked or lame.

Cynortas was a king of Sparta, the father of Oebalus. He himself was the son of Amyclas and Diomede. His name appears to mean 'dog rouser', from *cyne*, 'dog' and *orso*, 'to arouse'. There is nothing in the tales about him (mainly in Pausanias) to indicate what this might signify. Perhaps it is a reference to some sacrificial ceremony.

Cyparissus was the son of Telephus, and was a beautiful boy loved by Apollo. The boy had a pet stag which he accidentally killed as it lay resting in the shade, one summer's day. Overcome with grief, Cyparissus wished to die also, and asked the gods to make him weep eternally. In answer, the gods (in particular Apollo) turned him into a cypress (*cyparissos*), a tree that is a symbol of mourning. Apollo also loved another handsome boy, Hyacinthus (whose name see), and it has been pointed out that these young men were really doubles of himself, as indeed also were the girls he loved.

Cyrene was a nymph, the daughter of Hypseus, king of the Lapiths, and the Naiad Creüsa, and she was carried off by Apollo to Africa in his chariot. Her name may hint at her royal parenthood and her abduction, for it means 'mistress of the bridle', from *cyria*, 'mistress', 'lady' and *henia*, 'bridle', 'rein'. Note also the queenly name of Cyrene's mother.

Cytissorus was one of the sons of Phrixus, his brothers being

107

Argos and Melas and his sister Phrontis. His name could derive from 'clover', *cytisos*, perhaps in reference to some ritual or custom.

Cyzicus was the son of Aeneas and Aenete. He became king of the Doliones and married Clite. His name is difficult to interpret. Robert Graves sees it as deriving from *auxo*, 'to exalt' (perfect tense *euxeca*, 'exalted'). This is reasonable for a king, but is rather far removed from his actual name.

Dactyls were somewhat obscure Cretan spirits born on Mount Ida. They were said to be the sons of either Anchiale or Rhea. Originally there are believed to have been ten of them, but in practice there seem to be only five, at any rate with names, which are: Heracles (not *the* Heracles, of course), Epimedes, Idas (or Acesidas), Paeonius and Iasus. The fact that they are said to have been ten in number (or five) springs probably from their name, which means 'fingers' (*dactylos*, 'finger'). Rhea, who may have given birth to them, also bore Zeus, and in one account she is said to have pressed her fingers into the soil when in labour: hence the Dactyls.

Daedalus was a craftsman, the son of either Eupalamus ('clever-handed') or Metion ('knowledgeable') and Alcippe, or Merope, or even Iphinoë. He it was who designed and built the Labyrinth. He also manufactured the bronze cow in which Pasiphaë hid to gratify her lust for a bull (the result, of course, was the Minotaur). In short, he had considerable practical skill, and this is shown in his name, which means 'ingenious' or 'cunning worker', from *daidalos*, 'curiously wrought', in turn perhaps related to *daio*, 'to kindle', 'burn', 'cut' or *dao*, 'to teach', 'learn'. Daedalus' cleverness is also seen in the name of his father (one or the other). His name is preserved in the French *dédale*, used for a maze of streets (like the Labyrinth) or any intricate thing, and also in the rareish but rather impressive English word 'logodaedalus', meaning 'one who is cunning in words' (*Shorter Oxford Dictionary*). It is strange that with all his cunning (for another example of it, see **Cocalus**) Daedalus was unable to devise for his son Icarus wings that were sufficiently heat-resistant when they both flew near the sun. The result was that the wax on Icarus' wings melted causing him to plummet into the sea and drown.

Damascus was the name of the hero who founded the city of Damascus, in Syria. He was either the son of Hermes and the nymph Halimede, or else a companion of Dionysus in his conquest of India. But the city name may well have come from another hero called Damas, also a companion of Dionysus, who erected a tent (*scene*) on the site of the future town, which was thus *Dama scene*, 'Damas' tent'. (The real name of Damascus is at least three thousand years old, and probably derives from some Semitic language meaning 'business', 'commerce', though even this is disputable.)

Damastes see **Procrustes**.

Danaë was the daughter of Acrisius, king of Argos, and Eurydice. She was the mother of Perseus by Zeus. Her name means 'she who judges', not from a Greek word but from the Hebrew that gives the name of the Biblical Dinah (the daughter of Jacob avenged by Simeon and Levi in Genesis 34). There is however, no noticeable act of judgment in the story of Danaë, unless it be in the fate that befell Polydectes who wanted to marry her: Perseus turned him into stone by means of Medusa's head. Her name could also derive, however, from *danos*, 'burnt', 'dried', perhaps referring to the notoriously dry or parched land of Argos.

Danaüs, with Aegyptus, was the twin son of king Belus and Anchinoë. As with Danaë, his name seems to mean 'judge'. (Compare the Biblical name Daniel, meaning 'God is judge', and also that of Dan, one of the Tribes of Israel; remember, too, the famous words from *The Merchant of Venice* that speak of 'a Daniel come to judgment'.) Also as with Danaë, the name may denote the dryness of the land of Argos. Homer and Hesiod used the name Danai (sometimes called the Danaans) as a general name for the Greeks. The use of a name for a race like this is a special feature of Danaüs and his family, for if he was the 'father' of the Danai or Greeks, then his brother Aegyptus founded the Egyptians, his brother-in-law Phoenix the Phoenicians, and his grandmother Libya the Libyans. In actual fact, as Thomas Keightley points out, 'the names of nations have never, except among nomadic tribes, been derived from persons; they always come from the character of the people or that of the soil'. (The statement is rather a broad generalisation, but the principle holds good.)

Daphne was a nymph, the daughter of the river Peneius in Thessaly. Like Artemis, she was a huntress; like many young people, she was loved by Apollo. Apollo, in fact, pursued her through the woods until on the banks of her father's river he very nearly caught her. Here she prayed urgently to the river god to save her, and he changed her into a laurel tree (*daphne*). Robert

109

Graves, seeking a more ritualistic explanation for the name, offers *daphoinos*, 'blood-red', as its origin, referring to some kind of orgy.

Daphnis was the son of a nymph, with Hermes either his father or lover or friend. His name, like that of Daphne, means 'laurel', either because he was born in a laurel grove or because his mother abandoned ('exposed') him on Mount Hera in such a grove at his birth. (Robert Graves again prefers the 'blood-red' derivation, as for Daphne.) It was only later that Daphnis fell in love with Chloë (whose name see): in the classical stories he loved a nymph called Pimplea or Thalia.

Dardanus was the son of Zeus and Electra, the daughter of Atlas (or possibly of Corythus and Electra). He married Batia, the daughter of king Teucer of Phrygia, and his son Erïchthonius was the father of Tros. He is said to have founded the Dardanelles, the strait between the Aegean Sea and the Sea of Marmara that was formerly the Hellespont (see **Helle**). He also built a city on the slopes of Mount Ida and called it Dardania. His name may perhaps derive from *daio*, meaning either 'to burn' or 'to divide'. Perhaps, in view of his foundations, the latter sense is more appropriate.

Dascylus was a king of the Mariandyni, a people who inhabited Bithynia. He was also the father of Lycus. His name suggests *dactylos*, 'finger' (see **Dactyls**), but in what sense is not clear. Perhaps in some way he was a 'pointer'.

Daunus was a king of Ardea in Latium, the son of Pilumnus and Danaë. There was also a Daunus who was the son of Lycaon and who led an Illyrian army. Either way, the name seems to mean something like that of Danaë (the mother of the first Daunus), and so perhaps we should think in terms of 'judge' or 'dry land'.

Deïanira had what would appear to be a highly unpropitious name. She was the daughter of Oeneus and Althaea, and the second wife of Heracles. On the face of it, her name seems to mean 'man's enemy', from *deios*, 'hostile' and *aner*, 'man'. Or perhaps the link is with the related verb *deioo*, 'to slay', 'ravage'. Her story seems to support such hostility and destruction, since she featured in several violent scenes involving men, among them Heracles, who won a wrestling match against Acheloüs to gain her and later shot the Centaur Nessus who was trying to rape her. Deïanira took some of Nessus' blood from his wound and later, learning that Heracles had acquired Iole as a mistress, sent him a tunic

110

with the Centaur's blood which he put on. It burnt him to death and Deïanira killed herself.

Deïdamia was the daughter of king Lycomedes of the island of Scyros. As a boy, Achilles was entrusted to her father by Thetis so that he could escape the fate of fighting and dying at Troy. Lycomedes dressed him in girl's clothes and called him Pyrrha, placing him in the women's quarters. Achilles took advantage of the situation to sleep with Deïdamia, who subsequently bore him Neoptolemus. It may be to this episode that her name relates, since it means 'forcer of enemies', 'one who ravages a hostile one', from *deios*, 'hostile', and *damao*, 'to tame', 'force', 'subdue'. If there is not specific reference, then her name can perhaps be seen as a propitious one: may she ravage her enemies.

Deïleon was the brother of Autolycus (not the famous robber, but the son of Deïmachus). Both men together with their other brother Phlogius joined Heracles in his expedition against the Amazons. Deïleon's name may refer to this expedition, or to his warlike nature in general, since it means 'ravaging lion', from *deioo*, 'to treat as an enemy', 'to ravage' and *leon*, 'lion'.

Deïmachus was the name of at least two people. One was the father of Enarete, another was the father of Autolycus (the brother of Deïleon and Phlogius). The name is one of good omen for a warrior, meaning 'battle ravager', from *deioo*, 'to ravage' and *mache*, 'battle', 'fight'.

Deimos, with Phobos, was the son of Ares and Aphrodite. His name means 'fear' (*deimos*). With his brother he was a personification of terror on the battlefield, where he accompanied his father. See also **Ares** and **Phobos**.

Deino was one of the Graiae, one of the three weird sisters of the Gorgons. Her name, suitably, means 'terrible', 'fearful' (*deinos*). Compare the names of her two terrible sisters, **Enyo** and **Pemphredo**.

Deinus was one of the four stallions kept by Diomedes and fed the flesh of unsuspecting guests. They occur in the story of Heracles' Eighth Labour, where they were originally mares ('The Mares of Diomedes'). His name means 'terrible', as it does for Deino. The names of the other three stallions were Lampon, Podargus and Xanthus.

111

Deïon was a king of Phocis, and the father of Cephalus and Phylacus. His name means 'ravager', from *deioo*, 'to lay waste', 'ravage'. Once again, it is a name intended to bestow strength and ruthlessness in battle.

Deïoneus was a son of Eurytus, and the father of Dia. As with the names above, the base meaning is 'young ravager', from *deioo*, 'to ravage', and *neos*, 'new', 'young'.

Deïphobus is a name that is yet another variation on the 'ravaging' theme. It was that of the son of Priam and Hecabe. Deïphobus was the brother, therefore, of Hector. The name means 'one who scares the ravager', from *deioo*, 'to ravage' and *phobos*, 'terror', 'fear'.

Deïpyle was the daughter of Adrastus and Amphithea. She became the wife of Tydeus and the mother of Diomedes. Her rather forbidding name means 'hostile gate' from *deios*, 'hostile' and *pyle*, 'gate'. The reference is to the gate of a city, not the gate of a house.

Delphinus was a messenger sent after Amphitrite by Poseidon to arrange a marriage with her. Delphinus succeeded, and in gratitude Poseidon set his image among the stars as the constellation of Delphinus, the Dolphin. This is thus the meaning of his name. The Greeks seem to have been impressed by dolphins, since they frequently occur in their writings, usually as a child's mount or as the rescuer of someone at sea. Amphitrite was a Nereid, of course, so like Poseidon is very much sea-based.

Delphyne is a name that has a certain connection with dolphins. It was that of a monster woman with the body and tail of a snake who guarded Zeus' sinews for Typhon when he cut them out in his attack on the gods. Her name means 'womb' (*delphys*), this being the link with the dolphin which, one theory says, is so called either because it has a womb (unlike most sea creatures) or because it resembles one. Delphyne does not, in spite of her name, seem to have given birth to any kind of offspring. Her story is sometimes half-confused with that of Python.

Demeter was the great earth goddess, the mother of Persephone. Her name is usually interpreted as 'earth mother', with *de* given as a form of *ge*, 'earth' and *meter* being 'mother'. It is difficult to see, however, how *ge* could have become *de*, and there seems to be no evidence for such a change of spelling. Perhaps the first part of her name is Cretan *deai*, 'barley'. This makes good sense, and is appropriate for her, but the trouble is that Demeter is not really connected with Crete. If we change her name to 'Dameter' we can get something like 'mother Da' (whoever or whatever Da was). Eric Partridge sticks his neck out and plumps for 'mother of the gods', with the first element in her name being *dio-*, which in composite words means 'the gods'. He says his theory is 'at least as probable as the others'. If truth be known, we could take almost *any* suitable Greek word beginning with *d-* (such as *dais*, 'meat', 'food') and propose it for the first part of her name. Her Roman equivalent, Ceres (which see), is more clear-cut.

Demonassa was the daughter of Amphiaraüs. She married Thersander and bore him Tisamenus. Her name is a 'royal wish' name: 'queen of the people', from *demos*, 'the people' and *anassa*, 'queen', 'lady'.

Demonice was either the mother of Thestius by Ares or the sister of Thestius. She was the daughter of Agenor and Epicaste. Her name means 'one who conquers her people', from *demos*, 'people' and *nice*, 'victory', 'conquest'.

Demophon (or Demophoön) was the name of the son of Theseus and Phaedra who became king of Athens, and also of the baby son of Metanira, entrusted to Demeter. There was a third Demophon who was king of Elaeus and a notorious sacrificer of virgins. The name can be interpreted in two ways, either as 'voice of the people', from *demos*, 'people' and *phone*, 'voice', or as 'light of the people', from *demos* and *phos* (Epic Greek *phoos*), 'light'. Either name is agreeably propitious and the 'light' origin certainly suits the son of Metanira since Demeter placed the baby in the fire at night to 'burn the mortal part out of him' and thus make him immortal. We could in fact also interpret his name a third way, as 'slayer of the people', with the second half of his name deriving from *phone*, 'murder', 'slaughter' (as in Bellerophon). This would be a fitting origin for the king of Elaeus.

Desmontes was a childless woman who adopted Arne (who was originally named Melanippe) for Aeolus. As soon as Arne was old enough, Poseidon seduced her, and Desmontes, seeing Arne was pregnant, blinded her and immured her in an empty tomb with bread and water. This deed may be indicated in her name, if we derive it from *desmoo* or *desmeno*, 'to fetter', 'put in chains', that is, imprison. It could be, however, that Desmontes evolved by an error. She occurs in the writings of a Roman author of the second century AD, Hyginus, whose knowledge of Greek was somewhat shaky. In summarising Euripides' 'Melanippe Enchained' (*Melanippe he desmotis*) he seems to have thought that 'desmotis' was a name.

Despoina was the daughter of Poseidon and Demeter. Her name simply means 'mistress', 'lady' (*despoina*, the feminine of *despotes*), so is little more than a title. It was, in fact, often joined on to the names of goddesses.

Deucalion was the son of Prometheus and Pronoia, who married Pyrrha, and also the son of Minos and his heir as king of Crete. This second Deucalion had two sons: Idomeneus and Eurytion. We can consider two possible sources for the name, both of them based on *deuo*, 'to wet'. The first Deucalion we have mentioned made an ark which he entered with Pyrrha when Zeus said he would destroy mankind for the evil he had committed (shades of Noah here!). Deucalion and his wife duly floated on a flood for nine days and nights and came to rest on Mount Parnassus. The second Deucalion was the brother of Ariadne, who was the mother, by Dionysus, of various 'winy' children: Oenopion, Thoas, Staphylus, Phanus, Peparethus and Ceramus. So the 'wetting' can be sea or wine. *Pyrrha*, incidentally, means 'fiery red' (see the name) and is an adjective applied to wine in Greek – although this is unfortunately not the 'winy' Deucalion's wife.

Dexamenus was a king of Olenus who entertained Heracles. (Heracles somewhat abused his hospitality by raping Dexamenus' daughter Deïanira during his stay.) Dexamenus derives from *dexomai*, 'to entertain', 'receive hospitably'.

Dia was the daughter of Eioneus of Magnesia in Thessaly. She married Ixion, and bore him Pirithoüs. Her name appears to be a favourable one meaning 'godlike one' (*dia*). It was also a by-name of Zeus' wife Hera.

Diana, the Roman goddess equivalent to the Greek Artemis, has a name that very probably derives from Latin *deus*, 'god', as does the name of Zeus. Traditionally and popularly, she is not only the goddess of hunting but the goddess of the moon, for which, according to one mythologist, the old Latin name was Jana. Diana was invoked first as 'Deiva Jana' (the goddess Jana), which became 'Deivjana' and finally 'Diana'. Her name is thus related to that of

Janus. Be that as it may (and one suspects it may not), we must not overlook that behind these names, and even *deus* itself, lies the root *di-*, 'bright', so that the overall concept of bright = god = sky = day (Latin *dies*, which may also be behind her name) is a complex but powerful one in classical mythology.

Dictynna was an alternative name – a by-name – of Britomartis (whose name see). Somewhere behind the name may be a connection with *dictys*, 'net', since Britomartis was known as 'lady of the nets' and was the mistress of wild animals. But perhaps the more likely link is with Mount Dicte, in Crete, which is associated with her cult. The 'net' origin does, however, have a story to back it up. Minos fell in love with Britomartis and pursued her doggedly for nine months. When about to be overtaken by him, she jumped off a cliff into the sea, where she was saved in the nets of some fishermen.

Dictys was a fisherman who protected Perseus and Danaë from his brother Polydectes. As befits a fisherman, his name means 'net' (*dictys*). Compare **Dictynna**.

Dido was a famous queen of Carthage, the daughter of Mutto, king of Tyre in Phoenicia. She was the sister of Pygmalion and Anna, and of course she loved Aeneas (as music-lovers will know from Purcell's opera combining their two names). Most authorities agree that the name is a Phoenician one meaning 'brave', 'resolute', and that this epithet relates to her stabbing herself on her funeral pyre. Dido's other name was Elissa, which also appears to be Phoenician in origin (perhaps meaning 'wanderer').

Diocles was a king of Pherae who was instructed by Demeter in her worship and mysteries before she left Eleusis. His name appears to mean 'divine glory' or possibly 'glory of Zeus', from *dio-*, 'from the gods' or 'from Zeus' and *cleos*, 'fame', 'glory'. The name is suitable for a king who was also versed in religious matters.

Diomedes was the son of Tydeus and Deïpyle, and was a king of Argos. His name could mean 'divine ruler', from *dio-*, 'of the gods' and *medon*, 'ruler', or else perhaps 'divine cunning', with the second half of his name from *medos*, 'cunning'. Diomedes was also the original name of Jason (which see).

Dione was the name of an earth goddess who was a consort of Zeus, and also of the daughter of Atlas who married Tantalus.

115

The name is definitely 'divine' in some way, and may even be a feminine form of 'Zeus' (compare the genitive of Zeus, which is *Dios*). Thus, like Diana, the name is a complex of 'bright', 'sky', 'goddess' and 'Zeus'.

Dionysus has a difficult name to interpret. He was, of course, the Greek god of wine, corresponding to the Roman Bacchus. His parents are generally stated to be Zeus and Semele, and in view of his paternal origin his name of Dionysus has been deduced to derive from *Zeus* (genitive *Dios*) and the name of the city where he was brought up, *Nysa*. (According to some sources, too, his parents are said to have been Nisus and Thyme, with the former's name being incorporated into his own.) But this seems highly unlikely, and his name is almost certainly of Phrygian origin, as is that of his mother Semele. The Phrygian form of his name was Diounsis: the first part of this may possibly relate to *dio-*, 'of the gods', but the latter part is almost certainly not Nysa (as mentioned) but perhaps a word *nyso-* related to Greek *neos*, 'new', 'young' or *nyos*, 'daughter-in-law'. In other words we can perhaps suggest a meaning along the lines of 'divine son'. The name occurs more than once in the Linear B tablets of Knossos, so is at least certainly pre-Greek.

Dioscuri was the name, or perhaps rather the title, of the twins Castor and Pollux. It means 'the Zeus boys', from *Dios*, the genitive of Zeus, and *coros*, 'boy'. (More precisely, the name means 'the Zeus sons' since *coros*, when used with the genitive of proper names, means 'son' rather than just 'boy'.) It is interesting that for some reason the Romans did not translate the Greek word (*Dioscoroi*) into Latin. Not all versions of the stories about Castor and Pollux, however, give Zeus as the father of the twins. The constellation named Gemini (Latin *geminus*, 'twin') has immortalised the two brothers in the heavens.

Dirce was the wife of Lycus and the daughter of Helios. Her body was changed by Dionysus into a well on Mount Cithaeron. Her name seems to mean 'two' (*di-*) of something, though it is not clear what. Robert Graves suggests a possible derivation from *di-* and *creas*, 'flesh', in the sense 'cleft', this referring to some kind of erotic 'cleft' when she was in a Bacchic frenzy on Mount Cithaeron.

Dis (a name beloved of setters of cryptic crossword clues) was the god of the Underworld, the Roman equivalent of Pluto or Hades. All three names are really epithets, with *Dis* being a contracted

Dionysus at sea. Magnificent, bearded, the great god of wine lies in a sailing ship over which hang vines with huge grapes. Dolphins play round the ship.

form of *dives*, 'rich', itself a translation of Greek Pluto (*plouton*). It is just a coincidence that his name resembles the latter half of Hades. It is also a coincidence that the Roman name resembles the English word 'death', with which it is quite unconnected.

Dolon was the son of Eumedes, a Trojan herald. His name means 'craft', 'cunning', from *dolos*. Ironically, although sent out on a patrol by the Trojans (so that he could use his cunning), Dolon was himself captured by the Greeks and killed by Diomedes.

Dorippe was the wife of Anius and the mother of Andron, Elaïs, Oeno and Spermo (the 'winegrowers'). Her propitious name means 'gift horse' (or rather, 'gift mare' in her case), from *doron*, 'gift' and *hippos*, 'horse', 'mare'.

Doris was the goddess of the sea, the daughter of Oceanus and Tethys. She married her brother Nereus, by whom she had (traditionally) fifty daughters, the Nereids. Her name (especially in view of all those daughters) probably derives from *doron*, 'gift', meaning something like 'bountiful goddess'. It could, however, also mean 'Dorian girl', that is, a girl from the central Greek district of Doris. The modern girl's name Doris, popular from late Victorian times, was not directly inspired by the Greek goddess, although the meaning of the name is the same as hers.

Dorus was the son of Xuthus and Creüsa, the daughter of Erechtheus. His name means 'gift' (*doron*), and he gave his name to the district of Doris (see **Doris**) and to its inhabitants, the Dorians. It is intended as a 'good omen' name.

Dryads were tree nymphs, not so called by contrast to the 'wet' water nymphs or sea nymphs, but because the Greek for 'tree' is *drys*, a word that originally meant specifically 'oak tree'. (Linguistically, the Greek word is related to the English word 'tree'.)

Dryas was the father of Lycurgus. His name really means 'oak' (see **Dryads**), perhaps in reference to some ritual ceremony involving oak trees.

Dryope was a daughter of Dryops (or Eurytus). According to Ovid's *Metamorphoses* she once plucked the flowers of the lotus tree and was changed into this tree herself. Her name literally means 'woodpecker' (*dryops*), but perhaps we should break this word into

118

its component parts and interpret her name more suitably as 'tree face' or 'tree voice', from *drys*, 'tree' and *ops*, 'face', 'voice'.

Dryops was the son of Apollo or the river god Spercheius and Dia, the daughter of king Lycaon. He was the ancestor of the Dryopes, the people who lived in the valley of the Spercheius river and southward to Mount Parnassus. When he was a baby, Dryops was hidden in a hollow oak tree by his mother for fear of her father: hence his name, 'oak face', from *drys*, 'oak' and *ops*, 'face' (or of course 'oak voice' would be possible, and perhaps more apt for a baby in a tree).

Dymas was the name of at least two mythological persons: a Phrygian king who was the father of Hecabe and Asius, and the son of Aegimius, king of Doris. It is hard to find a satisfactory meaning for the name of these minor characters. Perhaps it is related to *dynamis*, 'powerful'.

Dysaules was the name assumed by Celeüs, exclaiming 'Mine is an unlucky house!' after the death of his sons Abas and Demophon. His name summarises his lament since it means 'of the unlucky house', from *dysaulos* (*dys-* is the same as 'un-', 'mis-', and *aule* is 'house', 'dwelling').

Dysponteus was one of the sons of Oenomaüs, together with his brothers Leucippus and Hippodamus and his sister Hippodamia. His name means 'rough sea', from the prefix *dys-*, 'un-', 'mis-' (it is actually the opposite of *eu-*, 'good', 'well') and *pontios*, 'of the sea'. We have no specific story linking him with the sea, rough or otherwise.

Echedemus is an alternative name for Academus (whom see). If we take this variant of the name it will mean 'he who knows the people', from *echo*, 'to know', 'to hold' and *demos*, 'the people', 'citizens'. This title would suit Academus as fittingly as any other.

Echemus was a son of Cepheus who became king of Tegea and married Timandra, the daughter of Tyndareus. He won the wrestling match at the Olympic games held by Heracles and later killed Heracles' son Hyllus in a duel. How much of this is reflected in his name is uncertain, especially if it derives from *echemythia*, 'silence'.

Echephron, with Promachus, was one of the two sons of Heracles

119

and Psophis. It is a fine propitious name, since it means 'possessing intelligence', from *echo*, 'to have' and *phronis*, 'wisdom'.

Echetus was a king of Epirus proverbial for his cruelty. His name does not reveal this, however, since it seems to mean 'possessor', from *echo*, 'to have', 'to know'. However, perhaps it implies 'possessing cruelty'. (*Echo* is a very versatile verb with several different meanings and shades of meanings.)

Echidna was a monster, the offspring of Chrysaor and Oceanus' daughter Callirrhoë. (Other accounts give her parents as Tartarus and Gaia, however, or Ceto and Phorcys.) She was part beautiful woman, part snake, and bore Chimaera, Hydra and Cerberus (a fearsome threesome!) to Typhon. She also bore the Sphinx by her brother Orthus. Her name simply means 'viper', 'adder' (*echidna*). By something of a semantic twist, the modern English word 'echidna' is used for the creature known as the spiny ant-eater, otherwise, as *Chambers' Twentieth Century Dictionary* describes it, 'a genus of Australian toothless, spiny, egg-laying, burrowing monotremes'. This sounds even more horrific than the original mythological monster.

Echion was the name of one of the Sown Men who married Agave and became the father of Pentheus. It was also the name of one of the Argonauts, a son of Hermes and Antianira. As with Echidna, the basic meaning is 'viper'. The direct link with the Sown Man is not clear here, but for the Argonaut the name may refer to the heraldic white ribbons on Hermes' staff which were later mistaken for snakes as he was the herald to Hades. However, the first Echion mentioned here was, like all the Sown Men, planted in the ground (as a dragon's tooth) by Cadmus, and Cadmus was eventually turned into a snake by Ares, so perhaps there is after all a sinuous link.

Echo was the nymph on Mount Helicon sentenced (forgive the word-play) by Hera to speak only when she was spoken to, and even then merely to repeat the final syllables uttered by another. She loved Narcissus, who spurned her – or according to another story was loved in vain by Pan. All in all, a frustrating life. Her name, of course, means what it says, although originally the Greek word (*echo*) meant 'sound', 'noise'. Let us perhaps compromise, and call her 'The Resounder'.

Eëtion was the father of Andromache. He and seven of his sons were killed by Achilles. His name seems to be based on *etes*, 'kinsman'. This may perhaps refer either to his sons or to the citizens of Cilicium whose king he was.

Egeria was a rather obscure Roman water nymph who was the 'patroness' of Diana's grove at Aricia. Her name means 'black poplar' (*aigeiros*), and doubtless these were the predominant trees in the grove. Persephone also had a grove of black poplars, trees associated with death. However, since she was a Roman goddess (or nymph) perhaps we should be looking for a Latin source for her name, and we could consider *egero*, 'to carry away' – perhaps as a kind of optimistic opposite of *infero*, 'to bring in' (suggesting something lower or inferior or even infernal).

Eidomene (or Idomene) was the wife of Amythaon and the mother of Bias and Melampus. Melampus was a famous seer, and thus Eidomene's name is appropriate for his mother, deriving from *eido*, 'to see', and *menos*, 'force', 'spirit', 'wish'.

Eidothea (or Idothea, or Ido) was the daughter of Proteus, the 'Old Man of the Sea'. Her name means 'divine form', from *eidos*, 'that which is seen', 'form' and *thea*, 'goddess'. This could mean either that she herself had a 'divine form', that is, a heavenly appearance, or that she saw things with the eyes of a goddess.

Eidyia (or Eidia, or Idyia) was an Oceanid, the wife of Aeëtes and the mother of Medea. Her name means 'the knowing one', from *eido*, 'to know', *eidyia*, 'knowing'. This is a very fitting name for the mother of cunning Medea (see her name).

Eileithyia (or Ilithyia) was the Greek goddess of childbirth whose Roman equivalent was Lucina (later Diana). As befits her speciality, her name means 'she who comes (to help)', from *elelytha*, 'she has come', since she came to the aid of women in labour. However, the 'light' meanings of her Roman names also suggests a possible derivation from *hele*, 'sunlight' and *thyo*, 'to move rapidly'. In the Knossos Linear B tablets her name appears as Eleuthia, which in turn suggests *eleutheria*, 'freedom', 'liberty'.

Eioneus was a king of Magnesia and the father of Dia who married Ixion. He may have been related to Ixion, and was indeed killed by him. His name seems to derive from *eon*, 'bank', with perhaps a reference to a river or its god – not that he was either.

121

Elaïs was one of the three daughters of Anius and Dorippe. Her name means 'olive oil', from *elaeon*, thus according with the names of her two sisters, Oeno and Spermo, which together promote the growth of oil, wine and grain.

Elatus was the name of several persons, including the son of Aries who was a king of Arcadia and married Laodice, a Centaur killed by Heracles, the father of Caenis, Ischys and Polyphemus (the Argonaut), a Trojan ally killed by Agamemnon, and one of Penelope's suitors. For all five the name Elatus seems to derive from *elater*, 'driver', that is, 'charioteer'. This could be suitable for almost all of them, although there is no record of a Centaur turning charioteer.

Electra was the name of three women: the daughter of Atlas and Pleïone, the daughter of Oceanus and Tethys, and (probably the best known) the daughter of Agamemnon and Clytemnestra who is the heroine of two well-known tragedies, respectively by Sophocles and Euripides. Her name conjures up 'electric', of course, but this is merely coincidental (although etymologically justified), since it really means 'amber' (*electron*) or, possibly, the word of which this is a derivative, 'the beaming sun' (*elector*). Exactly why this famous name should have the meaning it does is something of a mystery. We know that the Greeks valued amber highly, but the precise link with any of the Electras mentioned here is not clear. Perhaps the name is purely a 'bright and shining' propitious one. Stesichorus, a lyric poet of the fifth century BC, suggests – perhaps not all that seriously – another derivation. He takes the Doric form of Electra's name, Alectra, and makes it mean 'unmarried', from *a-*, 'not' and *lectra*, 'bed', that is, someone who is 'unbedded'. But he may have been echoing what another poet, Xanthus, had said two centuries earlier, when he pointed out that Agamemnon's daughter was originally called Laodice but had her name changed by the Argives as for a long time she was not married.

Electryon was a son of Perseus, whom he succeeded as king of Mycenae. His mother was Andromeda. Electryon married Anaxo, who bore him Alcmene (who became the mother of Heracles). Let us here stick simply to the 'beaming sun' that we proposed for Electra, and regard the name as just one of fair omen.

Elissa see **Dido**.

Elpenor was the youngest member of Odysseus' crew. He underwent a number of adventures (including falling from the roof of a house where he was sleeping off a hangover), but his name means simply, and rather charmingly, 'man's hope', from *elpis*, 'hope' and *aner*, 'man'.

Elymus was a friend of Acestes (otherwise Aegestes) who returned to Sicily with him after the Trojan War. His name seems to mean 'quiver' (*elymos*) which presumably is a propitious name for a warrior.

Empusa was a female monster, an 'amorous fiend' who assumed various shapes and like Lamia devoured her human lovers. Her name looks Greek enough, but is not so easy to explain. Perhaps it derives from *empoieo*, 'to put in', 'insert', with some sort of reference to her seductiveness or actual seduction.

Enalus was a young man who was rescued by a dolphin (like Arion) when he leaped overboard from a ship to join his love Phineïs. (She had been thrown into the sea to appease Amphitrite, and was herself also rescued by a dolphin – the mate of the one that rescued Enalus.) His name means 'one of the sea' – perhaps we should call him 'Young Man of the Sea' to counterbalance all those Old Men of the Sea – from *enalion*, 'of the sea' (*en*, 'in' and *hals*, 'sea').

Enarephorus was the son of Hippocoön and the nephew of Tyndareüs. He planned to abduct Helen when she was still a child, so the wary Tyndareüs entrusted her to Theseus to look after. In view of his failure as a cradle-snatcher, Enarephorus has a highly inappropriate name, since it means 'spoil winner', from *enara*, 'booty', 'spoil' and *phero*, 'to win'.

Enarete was the wife of Aeolus, to whom she bore six sons and six daughters (who to their parents' horror committed incest with one another). Perhaps Enarete's name is intended to offset all this wantonness, for it means 'virtuous' – literally 'in virtue', from *en*, 'in' and *arete*, 'virtue' (compare **Arete**).

Enceladus was a giant who fought against Athena (and lost when she flung the island of Sicily after him and crushed him as he fled). His name seems to suggest more noise than nous, for it basically means 'cheerer', 'urger on', from *enceleuo*, 'to cheer', 'urge on', 'shout huzzah'.

123

Endeïs was the wife of Aeacus and the mother of Peleus and Telamon. Her name would appear to derive from *endo*, 'to entangle', presumably meaning 'one who lives at cross purposes', or even 'enemy'. We do know that she hated her stepson Phocus (Aeacus' son by Psamathe) and that she and one of her sons killed him and hid the body.

Endymion was the son of Aëthlius, son of Zeus, and Calyce. He is usually described as a king of Elis. He was loved by the moon, Selene, and this is usually explained as the fact to which his name alludes, since it derives from *endyo*, 'to go in', 'enter' (the same verb as Latin *induco*), this referring to the moon's seduction of the king. It could also refer, of course, not to the moon but to the setting sun which 'enters' the sea, or else allude to the cave where Endymion met the moon. (In Hesiod's *Theogony* Night and Day live alternately in the same building, and some accounts tell of Endymion being a hunter who hunted at night and slept in a cave by day, so was thus always thought to be asleep.) So maybe it is the moon that 'enters' Endymion, or perhaps it is Endymion who finds himself 'entered', that is, encompassed or 'bathed' by his love the moon. The reference to sleep could be significant, too, since Selene put Endymion to sleep for ever so that he should not die (or according to another tale, Zeus gave him a wish and he chose to sleep for ever in a cave). It was this that some classical name-explainers had in mind when they derived his name from the Latin *somnum ei inductum*, 'the sleep put upon him'.

Enyo was the goddess of battle and the personification of war. She was also one of the Graiae. Her name seems to be a belligerent one meaning something like 'goader', 'inciter', from *nysso*, 'to prick', 'goad'. Enyo's Roman equivalent was Bellona (which name see).

Eos was the goddess of the dawn, and the daughter of Hyperion and Theia. She was the sister of Helios (the sun) and Selene (the moon). Her name is the Greek word (*eos*) which means either 'dawn' or 'east', although one theory suggests that her name could derive from *ao*, 'to blow', with reference to the cool morning breeze before sunrise. This is attractively poetic, but possibly smacks more of poetic licence than reality. In some stories Eos is also the name of one of the four horses that drew Helios in his chariot. Eos' Roman equivalent was Aurora.

Eosphorus was the god of the morning star and the star itself. He (or it) was the child of Eos by Astraeüs, the father of Ceÿx.

The name is readily translatable as 'dawn bringer', from *eos* (see Eos) and *phero*, 'to bring'. His Roman opposite number is Lucifer.

Epaphus was the son of Zeus and Io, and his name means 'touching', from *epaphao*, 'to touch', 'stroke', since Io became pregnant simply by a touch of the hand of Zeus. His name is actually a good example of 'wilful translation', since really he began life as the Egyptian bull-god Apis (with whom Herodotus equates him). To the name of Apis was added the prefix *pe-*, and this produced the 'Greek' word that translates as 'touches'.

Epeius was the son of Endymion who married Anaxirrhoë. There was also an Epeius who was the son of Panopeus and built the Trojan horse (with, of course, the help of Athena). The name means 'successor' (*epion*), and certainly Endymion's son won the race for the succession to the throne. The same word can also mean 'attacker', and this will do very well for the other Epeius.

Ephialtes was a giant who in the 'Gigantomachia' or battle between the giants and the gods was hit by arrows in each eye, from the bows of Apollo and Heracles. Most of the giants have sinister names, and this is no exception, since it means 'he who leaps on', from *epi*, 'on' and *iallo*, 'to put'. This seems to indicate a personified nightmare. There is, however, a later story that tells how he and his brother Otus ('pusher') piled up mountains, this being the 'putting on'. Of course, one who leaps on someone could perhaps be nothing more than some kind of personification of the wind.

Epicaste was the name Homer used for Jocasta (which see). It is not clear what it means: perhaps it comes from a word formed from *epi*, 'before' and *cazo* (in the form *cosmeo*), 'to adorn' (compare **Castor**). This could mean 'fore-adorned', with reference to her name being changed to Jocasta (the Greek form is *Iocaste*) when her fate changed. Robert Graves impressively suggests that the meaning could be 'upsetting over', with the name being a worn-down form of *epicatastrephomene*.

Epidaurus was the man who gave his name to the city so called on the east coast of Argolis. He was the son of Argus and Evadne (or else the son of Pelops or Apollo), and his name rather strangely seems to mean 'with shaggy hair', from *api*, 'over', 'with' and *daulos*, 'shaggy'. There is nothing in any story about him to justify this. Perhaps being hirsute (like Samson) could signify strength.

125

Epigoni was the title, rather than name, given to the sons of the Seven Against Thebes. Ten years after the original attack on Thebes by the Seven, their sons renewed the attack on the advice of the Delphic Oracle, mainly to avenge their fathers who had all been killed, except Adrastus. The names of the Epigoni were: Alcmaeon (their leader), Diomedes, Sthenelus, Euryalus, Promachus, Amphilocus and Aegialeus (son of Adrastus, who was the only one to perish as his father had been the only one to survive). The name means simply 'successors', more precisely 'those born after', from *epi*, 'after' and *gonos*, 'child', 'offspring'.

Epimedes was one of the Dactyls. His name boils down to meaning 'fool', from *epi*, 'after' and *medea*, 'plans', 'counsels', that is, one who makes plans too late. (Compare **Epimetheus**.) The Dactyls were a form of fingers, and in some western countries a nickname for the middle finger is the 'fool's finger'.

Epimetheus was the son of the Titan Iapetus who married Pandora. More relevantly as far as his name is concerned, he was the brother of Prometheus. His name thus means 'afterthought', from *epi*, 'after' and *medos*, 'plans', 'schemes', in other words he thought when it was too late, instead of planning in advance, as did his brother Prometheus (whom see). Epimetheus' big mistake was to marry Pandora; he did so in spite of the warning of his brother who saw the danger of accepting gifts from the gods.

Epistrophus, with Mynes, was the son of king Evenus. He was killed in a battle against Achilles (who was fighting the Trojans). *Epistrophe* means 'wheeling round', 'returning to the charge': no doubt this was Epistrophus' tactical error.

Epopeus was a king of Sicyon, of uncertain or disputed parentage. His wife was Antiope. His name means 'all-seer', from *epopao*, 'to look out', 'observe' (in turn from *epi*, 'over' and *ops*, 'eye'). This would seem to be a propitious name, suitable for one who is to be a king and oversee his people.

Erato was the Muse of lyric poetry or songs. Her name simply means 'lovely', 'passionate' (*eratos*).

Erebus was the son of Chaos and Nyx, and the father of Aether (the air), Hemera (the day) and Charon. He is almost more a place than a person, since his name means 'darkness', this being the region that was located above the even deeper Hades. The name is apparently related to the Gothic word *riqis*, 'darkness'.

Erechtheus was a king of Athens married to Praxithea. He is often confused with his grandfather Erichthonius, indeed, they may have been one and the same person. His parents were Pandion and Zeuxippe – or (according to Homer) he sprang straight from the soil without any human parents. He fought a war against the neighbouring people of Eleusis and was involved in a number of violent episodes, including the sacrifice of one of his daughters (Chthonia). His name may, of course, mean much the same as that of **Erichthonius** (which see), otherwise it could be a shortened form of Erechthochthonios, from *erechtho*, 'to shake' and *chthon*, 'earth', thus 'earth-shaker'.

Erginus was the son of Clymenus, king of the Minyans of Orchomenus in Boeotia. Another Erginus was one of the Argonauts, usually regarded as the son of Poseidon. The name may derive from *eirgo*, 'to confine', although in what sense is not clear. Perhaps it is a militant name for one who will capture prisoners.

Eriboea was the second wife of Alöeus. It was also another name for Periboea, the daughter of Alcathoüs. It seems to be a propitious name, meaning 'one who has much cattle', from *eri*, 'much' and *bous*, 'ox'. It could also derive from *eri*, 'much' and *bosco*, 'to feed', 'pasture', which is almost the same thing.

Erichthonius was both the name of an early king of Athens described as the son of Hephaestus and that of the son of Dardanus and Batia who married Astyoche and was the father of Tros. For the first Erichthonius there are several popular origins. One is to derive his name from *eris*, 'strife' and *chthon*, 'earth' with reference to the strife between his father Hephaestus and Athena: the story went that Hephaestus embraced Athena and made to possess her but she pushed him away and his semen fell on the earth. According to another version of this incident Hephaestus ejaculated against Athena's thigh when she pushed him away and in disgust she wiped off the semen with a piece of wool (*erion*), which she then threw to the ground (*chthon*). Another explanation of his name derives it from *eri*, 'very', 'much' and *chthon* 'earth' in the sense 'plentiful land', a suitable name for a king. But perhaps his name is really just an expanded form of **Erechtheus**. The two are sometimes confused. The second Erichthonius above was reputed to be

The birth of Erechtheus. Gaia, the Earth Goddess, hands Erechtheus to Athena in the presence of his father, Hephaestus.

very wealthy and to own three thousand mares: for him the 'plentiful land' definition seems best.

Erigone was the name of the daughter of Icarius and also the daughter of Aegisthus and Clytemnestra. The name could mean 'child of strife', from *eris*, 'strife' and *gonos*, 'child', 'offspring', or 'much offspring', from *eri-*, 'very', 'much' and the same *gonos*. For Icarius' daughter, at least, the first interpretation would be fitting since she hanged herself and prayed that all the daughter of Athens should do likewise. The second Erigone does not seem to merit either version, so we must perhaps settle for the propitious 'plentiful offspring' meaning for her. There is no record of this being fulfilled. But possibly another meaning altogether could be appropriate. One alternative is 'born in spring', from *ear*, 'spring' and *gonos*, 'child'. A spring child is clearly one born at a propitious and fruitful time.

Erinyes was the Greek name for the Furies, the female spirits of justice and vengeance. The derivation of the word is uncertain, although Hesiod claimed it meant 'the strong ones', presumably from the root *eri*, 'very', 'much'. Other conjectures have been *elinuo*, 'to rest', 'sleep' – hardly appropriate for angry beings seeking vengeance – and even the ingenious *en era naiein*, 'dwelling in the earth'. The Erinyes were said to have been born when the blood of the castrated Uranus fell on to Gaia, the earth.

Eriopis was probably the name of the daughter of Arsinoë or, according to some writers, of the daughter of Jason and Medea. If we take the *eri-* again as 'very', 'much', then we can try a meaning of either 'large-eyed' (from *ops*, 'eye') or 'very rich' (from *pion*, 'rich'). The former could suggest a gentle attractiveness, the latter be highly propitious.

Eripha was the name of a mare that belonged to Marmax, the first of the many suitors of Hippodamia (notice her 'mare' name, incidentally). Another mare who belonged to Marmax was Parthenia, and both poor horses were killed, together with their master, by Oenomaüs, who was systematically disposing of Hippodamia's suitors as he wanted her for himself. (Strangely, Oenomaüs was said to be fond of horses . . .) Eripha's name means 'kid', 'young goat' (*eriphos*), which seems somewhat out of place.

Eriphyle was the daughter of Talaüs and Lysimache. She was killed by her son, Alcmaeon, after she had been bribed by Polynices to send her husband Amphiaraüs to his death with the Seven Against Thebes. This was as a result of Eriphyle having become the arbiter between Amphiaraüs and her brother Adrastus. From this family dissension springs her name, meaning 'strife producer', from *eris*, 'strife' and *phyo*, 'to produce'. True, we could make her name mean 'many leaves' (*eri-*, 'many' and *phyllon*, 'leaf'), referring to some ritual or fertility rite, but this would be more speculative than suitable.

Eris was, as her name clearly indicates, the goddess of discord (*eris*). According to Hesiod she was the daughter of Nyx. She is famous for her part in the marriage of Peleus and Thetis: at the gathering she threw a golden apple inscribed 'for the fairest' among those present. Zeus suggested that the three goddesses who claimed the title, Hera, Athena and Aphrodite, should ask Paris to decide who was the rightful winner. Aphrodite was selected, and this was one of the main causes of the Trojan War. The apple was the proverbial 'apple of discord'. The Roman equivalent goddess was named, predictably, Discordia.

Eros was, of course, the god of love, corresponding to the Roman Amor or Cupid. Hesiod said he was born out of Chaos, together with Tartarus and Gaia. The Greek word *eros* specifies erotic (i.e. sexual) love.

Ersa was the daughter of Zeus and Selene (the moon). Her name means 'dew' (*erse*), which was believed to have been caused by the moon – compare the lines from *A Midsummer Night's Dream* where the Fairy sings: 'I do wander everywhere, Swifter than the moone's sphere; And I serve the fairy queen, To dew her orbs upon the Green', and where Oberon speaks of 'young Cupid's fiery shaft Quench'd in the chaste beams of the wat'ry moon'. Ersa's name was also doubtless metaphorical to denote a young and tender being, one born in the freshness of the morning.

Erymanthis, in the tale of Heracles' Fourth Labour, was the name of the mountain in Arcadia where the Erymanthian Boar lived. This mountain was said to have taken its name from a son of Apollo who had been blinded by Aphrodite because he had seen her bathing naked (compare the fate of Actaeon). The name seems to be based on *mantice*, 'divination' with the suffix *ery-* coming from *eryo*, 'to draw'. It thus means 'divining by lots', which is presumably intended as a powerful and propitious name.

130

Erysichthon was the name first of a son of Cecrops and Aglaurus and, second, of a son of Triopas, king of Dotion in Thessaly. This second Erysichthon dared to invade a grove of Demeter at Dotium, and began cutting down the sacred trees to provide timber for his new banqueting hall. Demeter punished him by making him perpetually hungry, so that he became a street-beggar, eating filth from the ground. The trouble here is that *eryo* means both 'to tear' and 'to guard', so his name can mean either 'earth tearer' (with the latter half of his name from *chthon*, 'earth') or 'earth guardian'. As a beggar he had to 'tear earth' in order to eat and survive, but we are not told how he guarded any land. Perhaps we can compromise and consider 'ploughman' (one who both 'tears' the earth and guards it). One theory suggests *erysibe*, 'mildew' as lying behind his name: mildew, after all, devours, and this represents Erysichthon's insatiable hunger.

Erythea was the name of one of the Hesperides (which see). Her name means 'red' (*erythros*), this obviously referring to the colour of the sun setting in the west.

Erytheïs was another of the Hesperides. Her name, too, means 'red'. See **Erythea**.

Eryx was a son of Aphrodite and Poseidon (or Butes), who became a king of part of north-west Sicily. His name seems to mean 'heather' (*ereice*) – compare the Latin botanical name for heather, *Erica*. Heather was a plant that had a special significance for the Greeks, perhaps because of some medical or magical association.

Eteocles is a name that one would expect to find belonging to a king, since it means 'true glory', from *eteos*, 'true', 'real' and *cleos*, 'glory'. And indeed we find that it was the name of a son of Andreus and Euippe who was an early king of Orchomenus in Boeotia, and of a more famous king of Thebes who was the son of Oedipus and Jocasta. The latter's brother was Polynices, and their names indicate clearly who was the 'good' brother and who was the 'bad' one. See **Polynices**.

Eteoclus has a name that means exactly the same as that of Eteocles, 'true glory'. He was one of the Seven Against Thebes.

Euanthes was the son of Dionysus and Ariadne. His name means 'blooming' or 'flowering', from *euanthes*, literally 'fine flower'. This

131

is a 'winy' name like those of his brothers: Oenopion, Thoas, Staphylas, Latronis and Tauropolus.

Eubuleus was the by-name, or rather the euphemistic title, of Hades – although sometimes he is said to be a brother of Triptolemus. The name means 'good counsel', 'prudence', from *euboulia* (*eu-*, 'good' and *boule*, 'counsel'). A name like this would be used not to anger the bearer of the real, fearsome name, in fact to avoid even mentioning his real name.

Euippe means 'good mare', referring not so much to the person so named (as a sort of 'fine filly') but as a propitious name for one who could possess several horses. One woman so called was the wife of king Pierus, who bore him nine daughters, the Pierides. Another was the daughter of Leucon who married Andreus, son of the river god Peneius.

Eumaeüs, in the *Odyssey*, was the name of Odysseus' swineherd who had been the swineherd of Odysseus' father Laërtes before him. His name is a good, honest one, meaning 'one who strives well', from *eu-*, 'good' and *maiomai*, 'to endeavour', 'strive'.

Eumelus was a king of Patrae in Archaea and the father of Antheas. He was also (as another Eumelus) the son of Admetus and Alcestis who became king of Pherae in Thessaly. The name is an agreeable one meaning 'sweet melody' or 'good tune', from *eu-*, 'good' and *melos*, 'song', 'melody'.

Eumenides was a euphemistic name used for the Erinyes (the Furies), whose real name was best avoided (compare **Eubuleus**). It apparently means 'well-minded', 'well-disposed', from *eu-*, 'good', 'well' and *menos*, 'spirit'. The name was first given to the avenging ladies by Orestes, the son of Agamemnon and Clytemnestra, and is familiar as the title of a play by Aeschylus.

Eumolpus was a son of Poseidon and Chione (or Dysaules and Baubo). It means 'sweetly singing', from *eu-*, 'good' and *molpe*, 'song', 'singing'. The name suggests some religious or mystical ceremony, and in fact Eumolpus was associated with the founding of the Eleusinian Mysteries. Lucian tells us that Eumolpus was a title adopted by the chief priest of the Eleusinian Mysteries when in office, since he was not supposed to use his own name at this time.

Euneo was a nymph who married Dymas, to whom she bore Hecabe. Her name is a favourable one, meaning 'good intelligence', from *eu-*, 'good' and *noos*, 'intelligence'.

Euneüs was the son of Jason and Hypsipyle, queen of Lemnos. His name seems to mean 'of the bed', from *eune*, 'bed'. Perhaps this is a favourable name for one born of a propitious marriage. (An echo of his name can be seen in the word 'eunuch', which means 'one who guards the bedchamber', from *eune* and *echo*, 'to protect'.)

Eunomus was the son of Architeles and the boy cup-bearer of Oeneus. He was accidentally killed, poor fellow, when Heracles boxed his ears. In spite of this, he obviously carried out his duties well, for his name means 'orderly', from *eunomes*, 'well-ordered'. Compare the fate of **Cyathus**.

Eupalamus must have been 'good with his hands', as they say – perhaps even an inventor. He was the son of Erechtheus and father of Daedalus (who was similarly gifted). His name derives from *eupalamos*, 'inventive', from *eu-*, 'good' and *palame*, 'palm of the hand', 'hand'.

Euphemus was the son of Poseidon and Europa (daughter of Tityus), who was also one of the Argonauts. His name must be the ultimate in propitious names, since it actually means 'of good omen', from *euphemos*, a word applied to people who used only words of good omen (or avoided words of bad omen).

Euphorbus was the son of Panthoüs, a Dardanian. His name is one more favourable one, meaning 'good pasture', from *euphorbia*, 'rich pasture' (with *phorbe* meaning 'pasture').

Euphrosyne was one of the Graces, and she has an appropriately agreeable name, meaning 'cheery' (*euphrosynes*).

Europa was the daughter of the Phoenician king Agenor and his wife Telephassa. Her main claim to fame, of course, is that she gave her name to Europe. So what does her name mean? A popular theory is that it means either 'broad-browed', from *eurys*, 'broad' and *ophrys*, 'brow', or 'broad face', from *eurys* and *ops*, 'face'. It could also mean 'she of the wide eyes', from *eurys* and *ops*, 'eye' or even, at a pinch, 'well watered' or 'fair-flowing', from *eu-*, 'good', 'well' and *rheo*, 'to flow'. Maybe the name of her mother (which means 'far-shining') is somehow significant. The actual name of the continent is generally held to mean 'west' (as opposed to Asia which is 'east'). The nineteenth-century French traveller and geographer Jean-Jacques Élisée Reclus wrote: 'Herodotus naively claims that not a single mortal has ever succeeded in discovering the true meaning of this word.' Europa is famous for her ride on the white bull (really Zeus) to Crete, where Zeus made love to her. She bore him three sons: Minos, Rhadamanthys and Sarpedon.

Eurotas was an early king of Laconia, and the father of Sparte. His purely propitious name means 'fair flowing', from *euroos* (*eu-*, 'well' and *rheo*, 'to flow'). This could suggest a rich and easy life or, more precisely, the gift of eloquence.

Eurus was the name of the east wind (more exactly, the southeast wind), who like the other winds was the son of Astraeüs and Eos. The obvious derivation is from *eos*, 'east' (see Eos), in spite of the name's resemblance to that of Europa, which (as the geographical name, at any rate) is thought to mean 'west'.

Euryale is one of the three Gorgons, and the mother of Orion by Poseidon. If we interpret her name as 'wide sea' (*eurys*, 'wide' and *hals*, 'sea'), this will accord well with the names of her son and husband.

Euryanassa was the daughter of the river Pactolus. Her name, as befits a riverine offspring, means 'wide-ruling queen', from *eurys*, 'wide' and *anassa*, 'queen'.

Eurybatus was the twin of Olus, with both brothers being the two Cercopes who harassed Heracles. His name means 'wide walker', from *eurys*, 'wide' and *baino*, 'to walk'. This is not so much a propitious name as a descriptive one, since he roamed abroad doing mischief. By a happy coincidence, the sense of 'wide' here is almost exactly that of the English word in the slang 'wide boy', where 'wide' (according to the *Concise Oxford Dictionary*) means 'skilled in sharp practice'. That was Eurybatus exactly.

Eurybia was the daughter of Pontus and Gaia. By the Titan Crius she was the mother of Astraeüs, Pallas and Perses. For one born of the sea and the land, her name is highly appropriate, since it means 'wide force', from *eurys*, 'wide' and *bia*, 'force', 'might'.

Euryclea was Odysseus' old nurse who recognised him on his eventual return from Troy. Her name means 'wide fame' (*eurys*, 'wide' and *cleos*, 'fame'), which is really more appropriate for her famous charge. But perhaps she was destined to bask in his glory.

Eurydamas was an Argonaut, the son of Ctimenus. His name would seem to be simply a favourable one, meaning 'wide tamer', from *eurys*, 'wide' and *damazo*, 'to tame'.

Eurydice was the name of more than one mythological female. First there was the famous Dryad who was loved by Orpheus (whose tale came to be told in several operas, plays and films), then there was Eurydice the mother of Danaë, thirdly there was the wife of Creon, and fourthly (and by no means last) there was Eurydice the daughter of Adrastus and wife of Ilus, king of Troy. The popular name means literally 'wide justice', from *eurys*, 'wide' and *dice*, 'right', 'justice', so thus loosely really means 'queen' or 'princess'. In this respect it is more of a 'title' name, like Creüsa.

Eurylochus was the leader of the 'recce party' that explored Circe's island when Odysseus and his crew landed there, and generally he was something of an aggressive character. Perhaps this is reflected in his name, which means 'wide ambush', from *eurys*, 'wide' and *lochos*, 'ambush' (compare the name of **Amphilochus**).

Eurymachus was the son of Polybus, a nobleman from Ithaca. He was the most favoured of the suitors of Penelope, Odysseus' wife, and was the second to be killed by Odysseus on his return. His name means 'wide fighter', from *eurys*, 'wide' (yet again) and *mache*, 'fight', 'battle'. His final battle with Odysseus is described in gory detail by Homer in the *Odyssey*.

Eurymedon was the giant who led his colossal colleagues in the 'Gigantomachia', the battle of the giants and the gods. His name appropriately means 'wide rule', from *eurys*, 'wide' and *medon*, 'rule' (as in Medusa, among other names).

Eurymedusa was the daughter of king Myrmidon who in spite of her name ('being of wide cunning') was seduced by Zeus disguised as an ant. Her name is a combination of *eurys*, 'wide' and **Medusa** (which see).

Eurynome was the name of two noted women: the daughter of Oceanus and Tethys who bore the Graces to Zeus, and the daughter of Nisus, king of Megara, who married Glaucus and bore Bellerophon to Poseidon. The name means either 'wide wandering' or 'wide rule', from *eurys*, 'wide' and *nomos*, 'district', 'range' or *nomao*, 'to direct', 'control'. Both senses are ones of good omen.

Euryphaëssa was a Titaness, the mother of Helios, Selene and Eos by Hyperion. Not surprisingly for one who bore such radiant offspring, her name means 'wide shining', from *eurys*, 'wide' and *phaeno*, 'to shine'. See also **Theia**.

Eurypylus was a name borne by several men, including a son of Poseidon who was a king in Libya, a son of Telephus who was a king of Pergamum, a former suitor of Helen from Thessaly, and another son of Poseidon who was another king (on the island of Cos). With such a wealth of lordly personages we must expect a rather grand meaning for the name, and it is in fact 'wide gates', from *eurys*, 'wide' and *pyle*, 'gate'. 'He of the wide gate' is obviously a suitable name for the king of a city.

Eurysaces was a son of Ajax and Tecmessa, and a king of Salamis. His warlike (or defensive) name means 'broad shield', from *eurys*, 'wide', 'broad' and *sacos*, 'shield'.

Eurysthenes was a son of Aristodemus, and a twin brother of Procles. His propitious name means 'wide strength', from *eurys*, 'wide' and *sthenos*, 'strength'. (Note the possibly even more propitious name of his father, which means 'best of people'.)

Eurystheus was a son of Sthenelus and Nicippe (or maybe Menippe), and he was the bitterest enemy of Heracles, who was enslaved to him while he carried out his Twelve Labours. A man to be reckoned with, therefore, as his name tells us, for it means 'widely powerful', for the same words as Eurysthenes. Note the echo of 'power' in his father's name.

Eurytion means 'widely honoured', from *eurys*, 'wide' and *tio*, 'to esteem', 'honour'. This is a suitable interpretation for the several people who bore the name, including a Centaur (who admittedly led a riot at the wedding of Pirithoüs and Hippodamia), a herdsman of the monster Geryon, and the son of Actor and Demonassa. If we are not too happy about the Centaur, then we can try another meaning for him, from *eu-*, 'good' and *rhytor*, 'drawer', meaning a good archer. However, even here it must be said that there was some doubt as to whether Centaurs actually used bows and arrows, although eastern artists represented them as archers.

Eurytus was a grandson of Apollo and the son of Melas. He became a king of Dechalia (possibly this was in Thessaly) and was himself the father of Iphitus. Eurytus was also the name of a giant who was struck down by Dionysus in the battle of the giants against the gods. It was, too, the name of one of the Moliones, a son of Actor and Molione. We can take our choice here, deriving the name from *eu-*, 'good' and *rheo*, 'to flow' (thus 'fair-flowing', like Eurotas), or from *eryo*, 'to keep guard', so 'holding fast', or even, like the Centaur Eurytion, from *eu-*, 'good' and *rhytor*, 'drawer', so 'good archer'. This last interpretation would certainly suit the grandson of Apollo, who himself was described by Aristophanes as *rhytor toxon*, 'drawer of bows', in his play *Thesmophoriazusae* (approximating to 'Women Celebrating the Festival of Demeter the Law-Giver').

Euterpe was the Muse of flute-playing, with her name meaning sweetly and simply 'delightful', from *eu-*, 'well' and *terpo*, 'to delight'.

Euthymus, in spite of cosmetic associations, has a name that means 'well-disposed', 'cheerful', from *eu-*, 'well' and *thymos*, 'soul', 'spirit'. He was the son of the god of the river Caecinus, and a famous boxer.

Evadne was the daughter of Poseidon and the nymph Pitane. Her name may be pre-Greek or it may be related to *euanthe* and so mean 'fair-flowering', from *eu-*, 'well' and *anthos*, 'flower'. It has a certain currency as a modern first name.

Evander was originally the name of Pan, meaning 'good man', from *eu-*, 'good' and *aner, andros*, 'man'. We can perhaps interpret the name more loosely to mean 'one who is good for men'.

Evenus was the son of Ares by Demonice, a mortal woman. He became the father of Marpessa. There was another Evenus who was the son of Selepus. He became king of Lyrnessus, near Troy. The name is fitting for a king or for one in authority since it means 'reining well' (no pun intended), from *eu-*, 'good' and *henia*, 'rein'.

Fates, otherwise Parcae, was the Roman title of the three female deities who supervised fate rather than determining it. Their names were Clotho, Lachesis and Atropos, and they were the daughters of Nyx. The Latin word *Fata* is a plural that is probably an adaptation of the singular word *fatum*, meaning 'that which is spoken'. In the course of time, however, the neuter plural noun *fata* became a feminine singular (not in classical Latin), and this is now seen in the Italian *fata* and French *fée*, 'fairy'. The Greeks called the Fates **Moirai** (which see).

Fauna was the wife or daughter (or even sister) of Faunus, which was the Roman name of Pan. She is often equated with Bona Dea. Her name, like that of Faunus, means 'she who favours' (*quae favet*). Her name and that of Flora are now traditionally combined ('fauna and flora') to denote the animal and plant life of a region.

Faunus, usually equated with the Greek Pan, was in Roman mythology the son of Picus and the grandson of Saturn. He is also associated or identified with Evander. His name is usually interpreted to mean 'he who favours' (*qui favet*). Linguistically, the names of Faunus and Pan seem to be related.

Faustulus was the name of the shepherd who found the babies Romulus and Remus in the she-wolf's lair. His name seems to be related to that of Faunus: if a god *favet* (favours), as Faunus did, he is *faustus* (lucky), as Faustulus was. Strictly speaking his name is thus a diminutive of *faustus*, meaning 'lucky little fellow'.

Flora was the Roman goddess of flowers (Latin *flos, floris*, 'flower'). She was the goddess who was responsible for the flowering of not just flowers but of all things, including plants and trees, and later, sex. See also **Fauna**.

Fortuna was a Roman goddess rather vaguely believed to bring her worshippers good luck, rather as a lucky mascot or Cornish pixy (or pisky) is believed to today. Her name may derive from *ferre*, 'to bring' or be a version of Vortumna, 'she who turns the year about' (from *verto* or *vorto*, 'I turn'). Her Greek equivalent was Tyche.

Furies (Latin *Furiae*) were the female spirits of justice and vengeance. They were said to have been born from the blood of Uranus that fell on Gaia when Cronos castrated him – or according to another version they were the offspring of Nyx. There are usually three of them: Alecto, Megaera and Tisiphone. They had the effect of sending their victims mad, hence their name, from *furor*, 'raving', 'madness'. Cicero and others identified them with a somewhat obscure Roman goddess called Furina or Furrina, who was believed to have had a grove on the banks of the river Tiber in Rome and to have been a kind of goddess of the spring. The Greek name for the Furies was **Erinyes**. See also **Eumenides**.

Gaia (or Ge) was the great primeval earth goddess, the first creature to be born from Chaos. The name is simply the Greek for 'earth', which usually appears in the form *ge* (as in 'geography') but also has the poetic form *gaia*, used for the name of the goddess, and occasionally *aia*. In Doric Greek, *ge* is sometimes *da*, but this does not seem to be the origin of the name Demeter (which see).

Galanthis (also Galanthias and Galen) was the slave girl of Alcmene. Her name means 'weasel' (*galen*) into which she was turned by Ilithyia when Galanthis tricked her into thinking that Heracles had been born (which Ilithyia had been trying to prevent).

Galatea was the daughter of Nereus and Doris, and as Handel's opera reminds us she was loved by Acis. Galatea lived in the sea off Sicily (where the Cyclops Polyphemus became infatuated by her), and doubtless a combination of this and the fact that she was beautiful is intimated in her name, which means 'milk white', from *gala, galactos,* 'milk'. (The Greek word gave the English 'galaxy', which in turn derived from the original Greek name for the Milky Way, *Cyclos galacticos,* literally 'milk circle'.)

Ganymede was the son either of Tros, the founder of Troy, or of Laomedon, the father of the Trojan king Priam. He was a beautiful boy, and according to Homer was abducted by the gods to live as a cup-bearer to Zeus. His name may well not have been Greek originally, but it must have suggested to a Greek ear *ganos*, 'beauty', 'delight' and *medos*. The latter word was used only in the plural (*medea*) as which it could mean either 'plans', 'cunning' or 'genitals' (in which sense it corresponded to Latin *virilia*). So his name means either 'delighting in cunning', or 'rejoicing in manhood' (i.e. in his own prospect of marriage), or even 'with delightful genitals'. (One hardly suspects that the gods abducted him for his cunning.) His name, in a rather perverse form, gave the Latin *Catamitus* which in turn produced the English 'catamite' as a word for what *Chambers Twentieth Century Dictionary* somewhat quaintly calls 'a boy kept for unnatural purposes'.

139

Gasterocheires was the collective name for the seven Cyclopes who built Argos and Tiryas. It derives from *gaster*, 'stomach' (as in 'gastric') and *cheir*, 'hand', presumably referring to their gonk-like appearance, so to speak 'bellies with hands'. They must not be confused with the Hecatoncheires, who were hundred-handed giants.

Geilissa was Orestes' old nurse. According to one story, she sent her own son to bed in the royal nursery so that he would be killed by Aegisthus instead of Orestes (who was then only ten years old). Her name means 'smiler', 'laugher' from *gelao*, 'to laugh'. This is an attractive name for an old nurse. In other accounts, she is named as Arsinoë or Laodamia.

Gelonus was one of three triplets (with Agathyrsus and Scythes), the sons of Heracles and Echidna. As with Geilissa, his name means 'laughing', from *gelao*, 'to laugh'. This is an agreeable name for the son of a disagreeable mother!

Gemini see **Dioscuri**.

Geryon (also Geryones or Geryoneus) was the son of Chrysaor and Callirrhoë, and he was a three-headed monster with rich flocks of cattle. Robert Graves suggests *geranos*, 'crane' as a possible origin of his name, but this has no relevance at all to the monster. Graves also proposes *tricephalon*, since Geryon was three-headed (*tri-* and *cephale*, 'head'), but this also seems too far removed from the name. Perhaps 'speaker', 'shouter', is more realistic, from *geryo*, 'to speak', 'utter', 'cry'. He would certainly have shouted at anyone trying to make off with his fine oxen, and fighting invariably involved war-cries.

Giants basically get their name from *ge*, 'earth', since they were the sons of Gaia. More directly, they were *gegenes*, 'earthlings', 'sons of the earth', and this word more closely approximates to English 'giant' and 'gigantic'. If Gaia was their mother, their 'father' was Uranus, since they sprang from the spot where the blood from Uranus' genitals, severed by Cronos, touched the ground. These were the giants 'proper' who fought in the 'Gigantomachia', the battle of the giants against the gods (in which they were all defeated or killed). More 'specialised' giants, also the offspring of Gaia, were the Titans and the Hecatoncheires. The names and numbers of those who fought the gods vary, but Apollodorus in his account of the battle includes: Alcyoneus, Porphyrion, Ephialtes, Eurytus, Clytius, Mimas, Enceladus, Pallas, Polybotes, Hippolytus, Gration, and Agrius and Thoas. (Another famous giant mentioned by Homer and Virgil is Titus.) The actual Greek word for 'giant' was *gigas*, plural *gigantes*. Attempts have been made to connect this with the root *gen-*, 'to be born', 'beget' (as in 'generate'), but this is apparently unrelated linguistically, say the experts. A pity, since the link between *ge* and *gigas* seems quite likely.

Glauce was another name (or perhaps the real name) of Creüsa, the daughter of king Creon of Corinth. It was also the name of the daughter of king Cychreus of Salamis, who was the first wife of Telamon. It appears to derive from *glaucos*, 'gleaming', 'bright' and thus be a kind of 'green light' name for a propitious future. (As a colour, *glaucos* did actually mean 'pale green'.) However, *glaucos* also means 'grey-eyed' and even sometimes 'blue-eyed', so perhaps Glauce was just that.

Glaucia was the daughter of the river Scamander (called Xanthus, 'yellow', by the gods) who conceived a child by Deïmachus but bore it after he had been killed in the Trojan War. She then fled to Heracles for refuge who entrusted her to Cleon, the father of Deïmachus. Meanwhile she had named her baby son Scamander (after her father), and he grew up to be a king of Boeotia and to name two streams in Boeotia respectively Scamander and Glaucia! Thus do names travel and propagate. Glaucia's name means 'grey-green' (*glaucos*), which cannot be anything other than the colour of the river. Scamander (father, grandson and stream) has a name that may well be interpreted in a 'rivery' way, too.

Glaucus is the name of several mythological characters, including the son of Anthedon and Alcyone (or Poseidon and Naïs), who was a sea god; the son of Sisyphus and Merope; a son of Minos; and a son of Hippolochus. For the first of these four, the name, meaning 'grey-green', is obviously suitable in view of his maritime nature. For the son of Sisyphus the name will also have connotations of the sea, since this Glaucus (in one story) leaped into the sea in grief for Melicertes (the son of Athamas). For the son of Minos, however, we must find a different explanation, since his chief claim to fame was that he chased a mouse, as a small child, and fell into a jar of honey and drowned in it. We cannot really see a 'grey-green sea' in this, so the best thing is to change the origin to *glaux*, *glaucos*, 'owl', for owls, after all, chase mice! In

141

general, however, Glaucus is a name that either denotes the sea or else has its primary sense of 'gleaming', 'bright' (as it did for Glauce) to indicate either a 'bright' future or the 'bright' eyes of a healthy and active person.

Glenus was the son of Heracles and Deïanira. His name means just 'wonder', from *glenos*, 'a thing to stare at' (from *glene*, 'eyeball'). Perhaps he was just that – a little wonder. (We are not told much about him.)

Gordius was the father of king Midas, and was the king of Gordium in Phrygia. He was the originator of the 'Gordian knot': he dedicated his chariot or ox-cart to Zeus with the yoke tied to the pole in a special knot; anyone who could find out how to untie the knot would rule all Asia. Alexander the Great (a historical character, of course) saw the knot at Gordium and simply solved the problem by cutting the knot with his sword. Unfortunately it is not quite so easy to solve the problem of Gordius' name. There are no Greek words starting *gord-* so we must consider some such derivation as *gryzo*, 'to grunt' (literally 'say "gry"'). Maybe Gordius grunted or muttered when he spoke?

Gorge was the daughter of Oeneus and Althaea, and she grew up to be the wife of Andraemon, king of Calydon. As with the Gorgons, her name means 'grim' (*gorgos*), which seems an unlikely name for an apparently blameless daughter and mother (of Thoas). But perhaps she was not so blameless after all, since some accounts say that she, not Periboea, was the mother of Tydeus and that she bore him to her own father, Oeneus, since Zeus had willed that Oeneus should fall in love with his own daughter.

Gorgons were the 'grim ones' (*gorgos*, 'grim', 'fierce'), three female creatures of frightening aspect. They were the daughters of Phorcys and Ceto, that is, the 'Old Man of the Sea' and his monstrous sister. Their names were Stheno, Euryale and (the most famous, and the only mortal) Medusa. The name has its origin where the very word *gorgos* does, and it seems that it may simply be meaningless – or rather, be intended to suggest something fearful. It is remarkable, in fact, that many English words starting 'gor-', 'gro-' or 'gr-' generally have unpleasant meanings. Among the best examples are 'gore', 'grime', 'grimace', 'grunt', 'groan', 'grief', 'grisly', 'grumble', 'grave', 'gorge', 'gross', 'gruesome', 'grovel', 'growl', 'gruelling', 'gruff', 'grumpy', and of course 'grim' itself! Even the Russian name of Ivan the Terrible (*Ivan Grozny*) has been

One of the Gorgons. Well may the name mean 'grim'! Note this Gorgon's hideous round face, serpentine hair, boar's tusks, fearful grin, snub nose, beard, lolling tongue, staring eyes and striding gait. No wonder that a glimpse of this could turn a man to stone. Perhaps this Gorgon is Euryale, 'wide-leaping'.

shown to be related to Greek *gorgos*. Of course, there are exceptions, but even 'gorgeous', it appears, has links – rather tortuously, via *gorgias*, an old French word for a kind of neck-scarf – with 'gorge', 'regurgitate' and other grim 'throaty' words.

Gorgophone was the name of the only daughter of Perseus and Andromeda. She became the wife of Perieres and, later, Oebalus. Her name literally means 'Gorgon-death', from *gorgos* and *phone*, 'murder', 'slaughter'. She did not kill any Gorgons, but of course her father did (Perseus slew Medusa), and her name is thus a commemorative one.

Graces (Latin *Gratiae*) were goddesses as pleasant as the Gorgons were unpleasant. They were usually said to have been the three daughters of Zeus and Euronyme, and their names, all with agreeable meanings (which see) were Aglaia (called Charis by Homer in the *Iliad*), Thalia and Euphrosyne. (Homer also introduced another Grace called Pasithea.) Their group name hardly needs interpreting: they were, after all, personifications of beauty and grace. The Greeks called them **Charites** (which see).

Graiae, however, were unpleasant, since they were the Gorgons' three weird sisters, also the daughters of Phorcys and Ceto. Their names were Enyo, Deino and Pemphredo (see the disagreeable meanings of these). If anything, they were even more sinister than the Gorgons since they were born *as old women*. Their name, thus, seems to be from the root of *grays*, 'old woman'. As Hesiod described it in his *Theogony*, 'They came into the world with white hair; that is why they are called Graiae by both gods and men.' (The English word 'grey' is not related to their name, even though the old women had grey hair.)

Gration was a giant who in the battle of the giants against the gods (the 'Gigantomachia') was shot by Artemis with her arrows. His name seems to mean 'scratcher', from *grapho*, 'to scratch' ('grave', in fact), although in what precise sense (with his hands?) is not clear.

Guneus was a king of Cyphus, near Dodona. He was the son of Ocytus and led twenty-two ships in the Trojan War. His name may refer to his kingly possessions, since it derives from *gounos*, 'fruitful land'.

Gyes was one of the Hecatoncheires, or 'Hundred-handed Giants', the offspring of Uranus and Gaia. Appropriately, his name derives from *gyion*, 'limb', so can be translated as something like 'many-limbed' or 'multi-membered'.

Gyges was a shepherd in the service of a remote king of Lydia, or possibly even the original ancestor of this particular royal family. His name means 'earth-born' (*gegenes*, compare **Giants**), which would be a suitable name for one who both worked on the land and was himself the progenitor of an important family or dynasty.

Hades was the infamous god of the dead, the ruler of the Underworld. In classical Greek, his name is always that of a person, never a place, although later, by extension, Hades came to be the name for the Underworld itself. (This happened through an elliptical use of the name in the genitive, meaning 'of Hades', with the missing but understood first word being 'house'.) The original form of the name was *Aïdes*, this meaning 'the unseen', from *a-*, 'not', and *eido*, 'to see' (this latter verb being ultimately connected with Latin *video*). This 'invisibility' was by implied contrast with the sun, Helios, who was clearly visible. In spite of this generally accepted derivation, however, there have been other suggestions regarding the origin of the name, one of them being a development from *aianes*, 'everlasting', 'wearisome', 'horrible'. This certainly conjures up an unpleasant endless torment in a version of Hell.

Haemon was the name of one or more of the sons of Creon of Thebes, and also of the son of Andraemon. The name seems to derive from *haema*, 'blood', and indeed the first Haemon came to a 'bloody' end when he was throttled by the Sphinx for being unable to answer her riddle. (For the man who finally outwitted her, see **Oedipus**.) But perhaps we must consider another origin as a possibility, this being *haimon*, 'skilful'. Such a generally commendatory name would be suitable for almost anyone.

Halia was a nymph who married Poseidon and bore him Rhode and six sons. When these wanton boys ravished their mother, Poseidon sank them underground, but Halia threw herself into the sea where she was deified as Leucothea. (This same story, incidentally, is also told about Ino.) So there are certainly enough maritime connections to justify her name, which means 'of the sea', from *hals*, *halos*, 'sea'. (The word is a base for several of the names that follow below.)

Haliartus was the brother of Coronus and the son of Thersander.

145

The story goes that he had been adopted by Athamas, son of Aeolus, when Athamas had been guided by the oracle to find food after a flock of sheep had all been devoured by wolves. Haliartus has a name that thus means 'bread of the sea', from *hals*, 'sea' and *artos*, 'bread', and so was a kind of 'manna in the wilderness' for Athamas.

Halirrhothius was a son of Poseidon and the nymph Euryte. He attempted to rape Alcippe, the daughter of Ares, but Ares killed him. (As a result of this, Ares was brought to trial by Poseidon on a hill at Athens that henceforth came to be called the Areopagus, or 'hill of Ares'.) As we know, Poseidon himself was not over-modest when it came to amatory advancement, and the name of Halirrhothius could be taken as referring to him in this regard, since it means 'roaring with waves', 'sea-beaten', from *halirrhothios* (*hals*, *halos*, 'sea' and *rhothos*, 'rushing noise as of waves', 'hoarse noise').

Halmus was a son of Sisyphus (with brothers Glaucus, Ornytion and Thersander). His name, too, appears to be connected with the sea, deriving from *halme*, 'sea' (more specifically, 'sea water that has dried', 'brine'). This would make him a seaman of some kind, or one who worked by the sea. Thomas Keightley suggests that the names of all four brothers may indicate the bustle of commerce since Sisyphus was a trader at Corinth.

Hamadryads were nymphs that some believed to be individual trees. As such, they died when their own tree did. This bonding is indicated in their name, which literally means 'together with a tree', from *hama*, 'together' and *drys*, 'tree'. See also **Dryads**.

Harmonia was the wife of Cadmus of Thebes. She was the daughter of either Ares and Aphrodite or Zeus and Electra (the daughter of Atlas). Her name is obvious, whether we interpret it as 'harmony', 'concord', 'union' or 'agreement'. It is, however, an unexpected name for one who was (in one account) the daughter of the god of war (Ares) and the goddess of love (Aphrodite). One would expect there to be anything *but* harmony here!

Harpalyce was the name of a daughter of Clymenus, king of Argos (who abducted her when she married Alastor), and of a daughter of Harpalycus, a Thracian king. The second Harpalyce clearly gets her name from her father. The first was involved in a violent situation – before she married Alastor, Harpalyce's father had incestuously raped her, and after he abducted her, she murdered the child she bore him – and this may explain her name which means 'ravening wolf', from *harpazo*, 'to ravish', 'abduct' and *lycos*, 'wolf'. (The name refers to her father's acts: compare Halirrhothius, whose name similarly relates to his father.)

Harpies were monstrous bird-like women. Traditionally, there were three or four of them and they were held responsible for anything that could not be found or had somehow disappeared. In Homer, they carried people off to their death, but later they mainly snatched away food. They seem originally to have been wind spirits. In any event, their name means 'snatchers', from *harpazo*, 'to carry off', 'snatch up' (compare **Harpalyce**). The English words 'rapt' and 'rapture' are related to the Greek word that gives their name.

Harpina (or Harpinna) was, according to some accounts, the mother of Oenomaüs, king of Pisa. The name was also that of a mare owned by Oenomaüs. It can mean either 'snatcher', from *harpazo* (see **Harpies**) or more likely 'falcon', from *harpe*. This would be a good descriptive name for a horse that was very swift (as the Harpies were). Admittedly, it is less fitting when applied to Oenomaüs' mother.

Hebe was the cup-bearer of the gods and the personification of youth, a kind of female equivalent of Ganymede. She was the daughter of Zeus and Hera and the sister of Ares, and there is evidence in a temple at Phlius (a town usually allied with Sparta) that she was locally actually called Ganymeda. Her name means simply 'youth', 'puberty', and the word *hebe* implied freshness, vigour, passion and the like – in fact, all the joys of youth. Her rather less exciting Roman equivalent was Juventas.

Hecabe has a name that to most people, almost entirely thanks to Shakespeare, is more familiar in its Roman form of Hecuba. She was the daughter of Dymas, king of the Phrygians, and became the wife of Priam, by whom she had nineteen children, including Paris, Hector and Cassandra. A lady of some consequence, therefore. Her name, however, is not so straightforward. Like that of Hecate (with whom she must not be confused), it may mean something on the lines of 'far off', from *hecas*, 'far'. This could mean she was 'distant' in some way – perhaps having an influence from a distance, or producing a distant effect. In one account she was stoned to death, and as she died turned into a bitch, later

One of the Harpies. This one flies off with a clutch of food that she has
snatched from the wretched, blind, half-starved Phineus (top left). She
is being vigorously pursued by Calaïs and Zetes, the winged twin sons
of Boreas. Calaïs' cap has fallen off in his haste and lies on the floor
(bottom left).

returning in this form to haunt the area where earlier her youngest son Polydorus had been murdered by the Thracian king Polymestor. This haunting could be regarded as a 'distant' influence.

Hecate was a Titaness and thus an earth goddess. She was associated by the Greeks with the moon, and her parents were Perseus or Zeus and Demeter. For a goddess associated with the moon (and later specifically with Artemis) her name can be more confidently interpreted as 'she who has power from afar'. This refers not only to the rays of the moon but to her special power as a giantess. The name was also one of the many by-names of Apollo (see Appendix III, page 323) and his sister Artemis. In this respect it is worth noting that the Greeks quite often formed names from the by-names of other gods (but only very rarely from the real names), and it might almost be that this particular by-name somehow became detached from Artemis and became a separate moon goddess. Robert Graves and others, however, derive her name not from *hecatos*, 'far' but from *hecaton*, 'hundred'. This could refer to a hundred of a number of significant things: victims on her altars, years during which unburied souls were detained, months of a king's reign, multiplicity of a harvest (a hundredfold), and the like. Either way, whether 'far-darting' or 'a hundredfold', she has a powerful and impressive name.

Hecatoncheires were the three hundred-armed giants Cottos, Gyes and Briareüs who were the offspring of Uranus and Gaia (who also bore the Cyclopes). Their name (from *hecaton*, 'hundred' and *cheir*, 'hand', 'arm') may be taken literally in view of their special status, or perhaps more metaphorically, for example because they acted a hundred more times more powerfully when they did anything than anyone else.

Hector was the great Trojan hero who was the son of Priam and Hecabe and the husband of Andromache. His name derives from *echo*, 'to hold fast', 'uphold', 'defend', since he was the Trojan war leader, the 'prop of Troy'. It is interesting that the name of his little son Astyanax has a similar meaning, reflecting his father's great powers of resistance. The English verb 'to hector' meaning to bully or bluster (or both) derives from his name, since this is how Hector was represented in medieval romances.

Hecuba see **Hecabe**.

Hegemone was one of the two original Charites, with Auxo. Auxo

149

Hector, the 'prop of Troy', with Priam. The old king of Troy, Hector's father, is urging him to attack the Greeks in the Trojan War.

represented the spring, and Hegemone autumn. Her name actually means 'leader', 'ruler', from *hegemon*, 'leader'.

Heleius (or Helius) was the son of Perseus and Andromeda. He plays only a small part in mythology, in spite of his famous parents, and his name means simply 'pity', 'mercy', 'compassion' (*heleos*).

Helen, best known as 'Helen of Troy', was the famous daughter of Zeus and Leda. She was the wife of Menelaüs, king of Sparta, and later of Paris, son of Priam. Her name in Greek is Helene, and most authorities derive it from *hele*, 'light', 'heat', although there are good grounds for regarding it as a non-Greek name, but as one associated with birds and trees in some way. In his *Aga-memnon*, Aeschylus ingeniously relates her name to *helenas*, 'ship-destroyer', since she 'took the ships' (*helein*, 'to take', *naus*, 'ship'). Her name may go back to Sanskrit *sarama*, 'born of the sky', fittingly enough for her, since she was the daughter of Zeus. What-ever the case, the modern girl's name Helen seems to owe its popularity not so much to her but to a more earthly Helen – St. Helena, the mother of the emperor Constantine. But inevitably some of the mythological Helen's charisma and beauty must rub off on modern Helens.

Helenus was the son of Priam and Hecabe, and the twin of Cassandra. He was a noted seer and warrior who figures in the *Iliad* of Homer. According to one account, he allowed the Greeks to capture him in the Trojan War because he was angry with the Trojans for giving Helen, whom he coveted for himself, to be married to Deïphobus. (But Deïphobus was killed before he could do so.) Perhaps we should translate his name as 'Helen man' in view of this.

Helicaon was the son of Antenor whose wife Laodice fell in love with Acamas. His name has no bearing on this, however, but is merely propitious, meaning 'burning sun', from *helios*, 'sun' and *caio*, 'to burn'.

Helice was the daughter of Selinus, king of Aegialus, and the wife of Ion. Her name appears to mean 'of the same age', *helix*, *helicos*, although we have no evidence that she was the same age as Ion, say, or anyone else. But perhaps she somehow linked up with Mount Helicon, either mythologically or linguistically.

Helios was the sun, of course, or rather its god. Originally he was

151

also known as Hyperion or Phoebus (which names see), but these became dissociated from him. His name means what he is, 'sun' (*helios*), in turn perhaps from *hele*, 'bright', 'hot' (see **Helen**). His Roman name is Sol, which is actually a variant of Helios since 'h' in Greek words often corresponds to 's' in their Latin counterparts (for example Greek *hepta*, 'seven' and Latin *septem*, Greek *hyle*, 'wood' and Latin *silva*).

Helle was the daughter of Athamas and Nephele. She was the girl who with her brother Phrixos fled on the golden ram from Athamas and her stepmother Ino, but fell off its back into the sea – which from then on was called the Hellespont ('sea of Helle'). Her name may well mean 'bright', from *hele*, 'bright', 'hot' (as with Helen). But *hellos* means 'young deer', 'fawn', and this could also be an apt name for her.

Hellen was the eldest son of Deucalion and his wife Pyrrha who gave his name to the Hellenes, otherwise the Greeks. As with Helen and Helle, his name may mean 'bright' and so be simply propitious.

Hemera was the daughter of Erebus and Nyx, that is, of Darkness and Night. Perhaps on the principle of 'two negatives make a positive' she therefore turns out to be Day, *hemera* (hence English 'ephemeral' for something that lasts only a day or a short time).

Hemithea was the daughter of Cycnus, king of Colonae, and a sister of Tenes. Her name, rather obviously, means 'half-divine', 'demi-goddess'.

Hephaestus was the Greek equivalent of Vulcan, the great smith and metal founder of the gods. He was the son of Hera – according to Hesiod, without a mate – and with Aphrodite as his wife became the father of Eros. As in so many cases, this is probably not a Greek name, although the root of his name certainly suggests 'to shine' (*phao*). Robert Graves thinks this, and proposes a derivation from a word *hemerophaestos*, 'he who shines by day', in other words – the sun! (For the first part of this word, see **Hemera**.) However, this may be over-ambitious, and we would do better to consider some sense of 'shining' or 'light' with the first two letters of his name unexplained. (Possibly they were simply added for euphony, which means his name is exactly the same as that of **Phaestus**, which see.) Hephaestus, like Vulcan, seems to have been some kind of volcanic god originally, so that the 'light' would have been a burning, fiery one.

Hera was the Greek equivalent of Juno. She was the wife of Zeus and also his elder sister, the daughter of Cronos and Rhea, and her divine status was that of 'Queen of Heaven'. As often, her name is no doubt pre-Greek, but traditionally there are two main contenders by way of an origin. The first is the meaning 'lady', with her name being a feminine form of *heros*, 'hero', 'warrior'. The second is a derivation from *aer*, 'air'. Both these, of course, are perfectly fitting for her. And if we consider her name jointly with that of Zeus we get a perfect combination for the two rulers of the heavens, with Zeus perhaps ruling the upper air (*aither*) and Hera the lower, denser air (*aer*) (see **Aërope**). Other proposed derivations have been *erao*, 'to love' (again, fitting for the goddess of marriage, as she was), and even *era*, 'earth' (the Latin *terra*), although this seems less justifiable. Perhaps the true meaning of her name is nearer 'protectress', since this seems to be the basic sense of the root of her name and that of 'hero', as Greek *heros* is linguistically related to Latin *servare*, 'to safeguard' (compare English 'servant'), with the original name being something like *Herwa*.

Heracles, of course, is the great Hercules, as the Romans called him, and here we have the most famous and popular of all Greek heroes. (With the Romans, he was more a god of physical strength, an image that he still popularly bears today, as a kind of classical Tarzan or 'Superman'.) His name has been the subject of much argument and speculation, with some sources saying flatly 'origin unknown' and others boldly asserting that it means 'Hera's glory'. This latter is indeed the widely held derivation, the interpretation being that he was 'one to whom Hera gave glory'. There is one serious drawback to this, however, as hardly any Greek god has a name that is compounded of that of another god or goddess. Since we are told in the tales about him (by Pindar and others) that his original name was Alcides, we may perhaps conclude that Alcides was his divine name and Heracles was his *human* name – in other words the 'glory of Hera' was the gift of a son to his parents. This is to suggest, in turn, that there may even have been a real man who became famous for his exploits, and that Heracles developed out of this folk hero. Even here, though, there are difficulties, since Hera actually persecuted Heracles and was in fact his lifelong enemy! As for his name Alcides, Pindar tells us that he was so named in commemoration of the name of his reputed

Heracles and Geryon. Heracles (below, in lion's skin) enacts his Tenth Labour. With his club he has already killed Orthus, the two-headed dog who guarded Geryon's cattle (above), as well as Orthus' master Eurytion (below, left). Note Geryon's three heads. Athena stands holding her *aegis* behind Heracles, aiding him.

father's father Alcaeüs, with Heracles' father being Zeus. As a name, too, Alcides echoes that of Heracles' mother, Alcmene, with its root *alce* meaning (most aptly for the great god) 'force', 'bodily strength'. (Compare other names starting *Alc-*.) Of course, there could well be a close link between the two names Alcides and Heracles, since the 'might' root (*alc-*) is present in both. In his chapter on Christian names in *Remains Concerning Britain*, William Camden interprets the 'might' somewhat differently, and his entry for 'Hercules' runs: 'Gr. Glory, or illumination of the air, as it pleaseth Macrobius [a fourth-century Latin grammarian], who affirmed it to be proper to the Sun, but hath been given to valiant men for their glory.' (Macrobius was here working on *aer*, as mentioned for Hera, and *cleos*, 'fame', 'glory': in other words, he was dividing the name not as Her/acles but as Hera/cles.) Before leaving the name, it seems worth pointing out that its meaning is almost certainly highly favourable, and that this is a characteristic of almost all names ending in *-cles*, even those of real people such as Sophocles (glory of wisdom) and Themistocles (glory of lawfulness). (Heracles' 'real' father, incidentally, was Amphitryon, the popular account of his birth stating that Alcmene had actually slept with Zeus when the latter was disguised as Amphitryon.) The Roman version of the name has a derivation that is exactly the same as those already considered for Heracles: he seems to have been one of the earliest gods to have been imported from Greece – in fact, he may even have been the first.

Hercules see **Heracles**.

Hermaphroditus has a name that perfectly reflects those of his parents, Hermes and Aphrodite. He was, furthermore, a hermaphrodite, that is, he combined the physical characteristics of both sexes. He was not originally so – he was born as a conventional baby boy – but became thus as a result of a total physical union (against his will, in fact) with the Naiad Salmacis when they embraced in a pool and their bodies joined together to form a single person (who had female breasts and proportions but male genitalia). Hermaphroditus had been a handsome young man, however, and his name can be interpreted less anatomically, to imply one who had inherited the best characteristics (and especially the beauty) of both his parents. Socio-historians like to see his name as symbolic of the transition in Greek society from matriarchy to patriarchy.

Hermes, the Roman Mercury, was the famed messenger of Zeus,

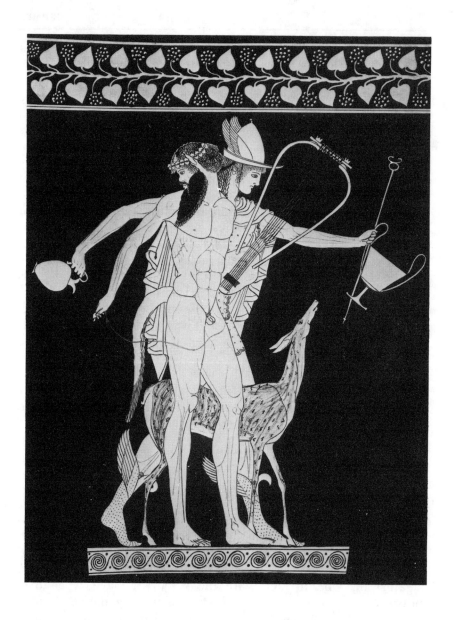

Hermes and Silenus. Hermes (otherwise Mercury) is shown in his traditional winged hat and shoes, holding his herald's staff with two snakes. In front of him is Silenus: note his snub nose and horse's tail and ears. Here, however, he is not pot-bellied and bald, as usually depicted, so this may be *a* Silenus rather than *the* Silenus.

the protector of travellers and bringer of luck. He was the son of Zeus and Atlas' daughter Maia, and he was the father of Pan. Maia was traditionally regarded as 'Mother of the Earth', so it is tempting to see Hermes' name as deriving from *era*, 'earth'. The widely held origin of his name, however, is not this but *herma*, 'rock', 'stone'. Hermes was (as a protector of travellers and a messenger) the god of roads, and at certain points on roads a stone heap would be placed to mark a holy spot (something on the lines of a Christian shrine such as the French *calvaire*). This stone heap conventionally became a pillar with the representation of a human bust (Hermes), and as well as being a religious or mystical symbol was also a phallic one. However, *herma* has the basic meaning 'prop', 'support', and the name can thus also be taken metaphorically. But, as so often, the name is very likely not of Greek origin at all.

Hermione was the daughter of Menelaüs and Helen. With Orestes as her husband she was also the mother of Tisamenus. Her name seems to be somehow connected with that of Hermes – perhaps not directly but in the sense that she was herself a kind of 'pillar girl' or 'supporting queen'. The modern girl's name Hermione derives not from her but from Shakespeare's Hermione, the queen in *The Winter's Tale*.

Hero, somewhat misleadingly, has a name that suggests 'hero', whereas it actually appears to relate to that of Hera, perhaps in the sense 'dedicated to Hera'. Hero was a priestess of Aphrodite whose name is traditionally linked with that of the man she loved, Leander.

Herse was the daughter of Cecrops and Aglaurus who bore Cephalus to Hermes (without being married to him). Her name is the standard word for 'dew' (*herse*), and this is simply an agreeable name, although perhaps also a propitious one if dew is regarded as heralding a fine day. (There may also be a suggestion of 'moon gift', since the moon was held to produce dew.) Compare the name of **Pandrosus**.

Hesione was a daughter of Laomedon, king of Troy, and thus a sister of Priam. She later became the slave of Telamon, to whom she bore Teucris. Her name is not easy to explain. Perhaps it relates to Asia, the daughter of Oceanus and Tethys, although it is hard to see how. On the other hand, she was chained to a rock

157

by the sea (a fate that happened to more than one hapless Greek damsel) and her name does contain a suspicion of *eion*, 'shore'.

Hespere has a name that clearly indicates her provenance, for she was one of the Hesperides (whose name see). *Hespera*, very suitably, means 'evening'. (The word is related to English 'vespers'.)

Hesperides was the collective name for the nymphs who were the daughters of Atlas and Pleïone (or Atlas and Hesperis, or even Erebus and Nyx), and who were the 'Daughters of the Evening' or 'Nymphs of the West'. They lived on an island in the west of the ocean and guarded the garden with golden apples that Gaia had given to Hera on her marriage to Zeus. They vary in number, depending on the source, but usually settle to four or seven. Originally, however, there were only three, who were Aegle, Erythea and Hespera. Later Hesperides were Arethusa, Hestia, Hesperusa and Hesperia. Of these, four names immediately and obviously relate to the collective name, which in turn simply comes from *hespera*, 'evening', 'west'. (There is even, etymologists tell us, a link between the Greek word – and the nymphs' name – and English 'west'.) The golden apples are significant in this, of course, since an apple, especially a ripe or ripening one, is the colour of the setting sun – red, yellow or gold. See also the names **Aegle**, **Erythea** and **Hestia**, which also relate to the sun and its colour.

Hesperus was the 'evening star' who was originally the son of Atlas. His Roman equivalent is Vesper (which is exactly the same name in Latin guise). Hesperus was carried away from his father's mountain by the wind and was turned into the evening star.

Hestia, apart from being one of the (later) Hesperides, is better known as the goddess of the hearth and home whom the Romans called Vesta. She was the eldest of the three daughters of Cronos and Rhea, and her name (etymologically and otherwise the same as Vesta) is simply the word for 'hearth of a house', *hestia*. The hearth was the main shrine of the house and the centre of Greek life, having much the same connotation that 'home' does in English, and thus being the focal point of a family house (as the English hearth and fire used to be before it was superseded by the quasi-Greek and Roman goddess Televisia). The actual Greek word *hestia* may be based on the *sta-* root that is present in many words denoting a fixed object: the Greek hearth was, after all, fixed as a *sta*tionary object in the centre of the room where the family gathered. Hestia's name, in meaning 'hearth', by implication suggests the low fire burning there, and this is the link with the Hesperides Hestia, whose name conjures up the red glow of the setting sun. The priestesses of Hestia were called the Vestal Virgins. For more about them, see **Vesta**.

Hicetaon was the son of Laomedon and Strymo (or Leucippe or Placia). He was thus the brother of Priam. He was also the father of Melanippus. As a Trojan elder he has a name that suggests his function, since it appears to derive from *hicetes* or *hictor*, 'suppliant'.

Hilaira (or Hiläeira) was the daughter of Leucippus. She was engaged to marry her uncle Lynceus but was abducted by Castor before she could marry him. Both she and her twin sister Phoebe (jointly known as the Leucippides) have 'shining' names that evoke the moon: *hilaros* (which was actually a by-name of the moon) means 'joyful', in turn linked to *hilaos*, 'gracious', 'cheerful' (and English 'hilarious').

Himerus was a rather vague god, sometimes said to be an attendant of Aphrodite, who was a personification of sexual desire. His name just means 'longing', 'desire' (*himeros*).

Hippalcimus (or Hippalmus) begins a run of 'horse' names, in his case 'horse strength', from *hippos*, 'horse' and *alce*, 'might', 'strength'. He was the son of Itonus and an (admittedly minor) Argonaut. His name is simply a propitious one.

Hippasus was the name of several characters, among them the son of Leucippe (note the resemblance between his name and hers), the son of Ceÿx, and the son of Admetus and Alcestis. The name just means 'horseman', *hippeus*, and is either descriptive or propitious (or both).

Hippe (sometimes appearing as Hippo) was the daughter of Chiron the Centaur. She had conceived a child, Melanippe, by Aeolus, and had been changed by the gods into a mare so that Chiron should not see her as a woman in childbirth. And 'mare' is exactly what her name means.

Hippocoön was a king of Sparta. He was the son of Oebalus and the Naiad Batia. His name, doubtless a desirable one, means 'horse stable' – literally 'horse house' from *hippos*, 'horse' and *oicos*, 'house'.

Hippodamia was a very popular propitious name borne by several ladies, among them the wife of Pirithoüs (a son of Zeus), and the daughter of Oenomaüs who became the wife of Pelops. It means 'horse tamer' from *hippos*, 'horse' and *damao*, 'to tame', and as a favourable name really means 'one who is high-born', 'one who owns many horses'. (Significantly, even today, in a different era and a different culture, the prestige of owning and riding a horse is still considerable, not least for a woman.) One should not overlook the 'taming' aspect of the name, either, which relates to the mastery of horses and chariots. (A goddess so named could give a person the power to tame horses.) There is a specific connection for Hippodamia the wife of Pelops, since she married her husband as the result of a 'rigged' chariot race which he won – and thus qualified to carry her off. Jane Harrison sees this story evolving from actual races which took place in the original Olympic games; in these, young men raced in chariots and girls (virgins) raced on foot.

Hippodamus was the son of Oenomaüs and Sterope. His name, like that of Hippodamia, means 'horse tamer', here in a propitious sense. Hippodamus' family had several 'horsy' connections: his brother was called Leucippus, his sister was Hippodamia, and his father was known to be fond of horses.

Hippolochus was a son of Bellerophon, and the father of Glaucus. His name on the face of it seems to mean 'horse ambush', from *hippos*, 'horse' and *lochos*, 'ambush'. This is not very satisfactory, however, and it would make more sense to take the other meaning of *lochos*, 'child birth'. He would then be 'one born from a mare'. There seems to be nothing 'mareish' about his mother, though, who is stated to be either Philinoë or Anticlea. Probably his name is simply one of good omen.

Hippolyta is best known as the queen of the Amazons, whose girdle Heracles had to fetch for his Ninth Labour (The Amazon's Girdle). Another Hippolyta was the daughter of Cretheus who became the wife of Acastus. The rather impressive name means 'horse releaser' or even 'one born of the stampeding horses', from *hippos*, 'horse' and *luo*, 'to release'. This name is just right for the Amazon queen. (See next entry for her son.)

Hippolytus was the famous son of Theseus and Hippolyta, queen of the Amazons (or of her sister Antiope), with whom Phaedra fell in love. Apart from the obvious connection with his mother's name,

Pelops abducts Hippodamia. According to one story, Hippodamia was already in love with Pelops when he abducted her, so here she gladly acts as 'horse tamer', as her name implies, while Pelops concentrates on the driving. Note his dark eyes and hair.

the meaning of the name ('horse releaser', as for his mother) is specific for Hippolytus: while riding along the seashore his chariot horses, frightened by a huge bull that reared up out of the sea, threw him out and dragged him to his death. Perhaps in view of this we should see his name as more 'loosed horse' than 'horse looser'. At the same time, even if he had not been killed in this way, Hippolytus would have been a fitting name for a charioteer, who 'releases horses'. Another character of the name was a giant, overcome in the battle of the gods against the giants by Hermes.

Hippomedon was one of the Seven Against Thebes. He was of doubtful parentage, but became the father of Polydorus. Like others of the name, he was a 'lord of horses', from *hippos*, 'horse' and *medon* (of which Medusa is the feminine), 'ruler'. The name is a favourable 'noble' one.

Hippomenes was the son of Megareus whose exploits seem to coincide with those of Melanion. He was also one of the suitors of Atalanta and won the race against her by decoying her (he rolled three apples that Aphrodite had thoughtfully given him off the course and Atalanta felt obliged to stop and pick them up). His propitious name means 'horse force', from *hippos*, 'horse' and *menos*, 'force', 'might'. Perhaps this favourable name helped him to win. (Of course, one can also read erotic overtones into the name.)

Hipponoüs was the original name of Bellerophon (whom see). It is a propitious name and means 'horse wisdom' (*hippos*, 'horse' and *noos* or *nous*, 'wisdom').

Hippothoë was the daughter of Mestor and Lysidice. She was abducted by Poseidon and bore him Taphius. Her name means 'active mare', from *hippos*, 'horse', 'mare' and *thoos*, 'quick', 'active'. This suggests (or promises) expertise in a number of directions.

Hippothoüs has a name that is the masculine counterpart of that of Hippothoë. He was the son of Poseidon and Alope. Apart from having a generally favourable connotation, the name is specifically relevant here since Hippothoüs as a child had been suckled by wild mares. Moreover, Poseidon was the patron of horses.

Hodites was one of the sons of Heracles and Deïaneira. His name means 'wayfarer', 'traveller' (*hodites*, from *hodos*, 'way', 'path'). We are told very little about him, but there is no reason why he should not have travelled a good deal – most Greeks did.

Hours (in Latin, *Horae*) were the daughters of Zeus and Themis representing either the three seasons, Spring, Autumn and Summer, or else the three ethical attributes of Law, Justice and Peace. Their name does not thus mean 'hours', or at any rate did not mean this as originally understood for the three. As seasons, the Hours were respectively named Thallo, Carpo and Auxo; as ethical names (in Hesiod) they were Eunomia, Dice and Irene (or Eirene). The origins of these six names are as follows: Thallo from *thallo*, 'to bloom', 'flourish'; Carpo from *carpos*, 'fruit'; Auxo from *auxe*, 'increase' (the summer is the season of fulfilment); Eunomia from *eu-*, 'good' and *nomos*, 'law', 'custom'; Dice from *dice*, 'right', 'order'; Irene from *eirene*, 'peace'. In his *Theogony*, Hesiod himself says the three 'watch over' (*oreuousi*) the works of mortal men – hence their name.

Hyacinthus was a beautiful boy loved by Thamyris (and then by Apollo). He was the son of Amyclas, king of Sparta, and Diomede. His name is almost certainly not Greek, as the *-inth* element testifies. However, his name is traditionally linked with the hyacinth, into which flower he turned, or rather his blood turned, when he was accidentally killed by a discus thrown by Apollo. The flower in the story is not our hyacinth but a type of iris. As with many plants, it was believed to have special properties, in this case its bulb was claimed to have the power of postponing a boy's puberty. This may have a bearing for Hyacinthus, whose puberty was 'postponed' indefinitely. The origin of the flower name itself, however, is still unknown. This is therefore one name that we shall have to leave, alas, without any proposed derivation as such. There is one nice little linguistic note that we can add, however, before altogether abandoning Hyacinthus: on the base of its petals the flower has marks that resemble the early Greek letters AI, and this is said to be either a cry of lamentation uttered by Apollo or else the first letters of the boy's name (in classical Greek it begins with the letter upsilon, γ).

Hyades was the collective name for the five (or seven) daughters of Oceanus and Tethys (or Atlas and Pleione) who were transformed into a cluster of stars (now several hundred stars in the constellation Taurus). There have been two main theories behind their name. The first derives it from *hyein*, 'to rain', since it was believed that when the constellation 'rose' simultaneously with the sun, rain and stormy weather would follow. The Romans, however, derived the name from *hys*, 'pig', and consequently translated it as Suculae (literally, 'piglets'). This unlikely interpretation sprang not merely from the resemblance of the word to the name but because the constellation was seen pictorially as a sow with her piglets. Pliny even combined both possibilities, saying that the rain presaged by the Hyades made the roads so muddy and miry that the stars seemed to delight in the dirt, like pigs! Another explanation says that the sisters wept copiously for their brother Hyas, who had been killed by a boar, and so were together known by his name. (In fact, as in many cases, his name was almost certainly invented to explain their name.) Yet another explanation rather ingeniously derives their name from its first letter, the Greek upsilon (see **Hyacinthus**), since the stars form a figure that resembles this letter.

Hydra was a monstrous water serpent with a hound's body, the offspring of two other monsters, Typhon and Echidna. It had anything from five to five hundred heads, and was killed by Heracles as his Second Labour (The Hydra of Lerna). Its name merely describes it, since *hydra* (from *hydor*, 'water') means 'water serpent'.

Hygea (or Hygiea) was a daughter of Asclepius and she is really an abstraction, having no mythology. As such she is the personification of health, the Greek for which is *hygieia*. Her name was also one of the by-names of Athena, as a result of the cures she brought about. Compare the name of her sister, **Panacea**.

Hylas was the son of Theodamas, king of the Dryopes, and the nymph Menodice. Heracles fought his father, abducted Hylas, and became his lover. His name derives, it seems, from *hyle*, 'wood', so that he is in some way connected with a wood (living in one or born in one, perhaps, although we are not given any specific connection). The poet Theocritus tells how Hylas had a festival annually at which his devotees would roam the mountains calling out his name. Perhaps this mourning or lamenting actually gave rise to his name, in other words it derives from the verb *hylao*, 'to howl' (which is related to the howling known attractively in English as 'ululation').

Hyllus was the son of Heracles and Deïanira who married Iole. A likely source for his name, but not a certain one, is *hyle*, 'wood', so perhaps we can think of him as 'woodsman' or 'forester'.

Hymen (or Hymenaeüs) was the god of marriage and its personification, described by a number of authors as a beautiful boy loved by Apollo (like Hyacinthus). His name seems to have evolved along the same lines as that of Bacchus, in other words it originated as a cry or shout. This shout, made at weddings, has been recorded as either *hymen o hymenaie* or *o hymen hymenaie*, a kind of meaningless refrain like 'hi-di-hi' or 'ee-I-ee-I-o' (to offer somewhat trivial equivalents). This was 'explained' as being an invocation to Hymen, the god of marriage. At the same time the word *hymen* existed as a separate word meaning, as it does in English, 'maidenhead', and it would seem reasonable to link this meaning with the wedding ceremony. Eric Partridge makes this connection and suggests that the wedding ceremony cry could thus represent the forthcoming loss of virginity. More generally, Hymen's name must be considered in connection with the verb 'to sing', *hymneo* (English 'hymn'), so that it actually means 'wedding song' while simultaneously *being* the song, or at any rate its refrain. The wedding song was in fact sung by the bride's attendants as they led her to the house of the bridegroom.

Hyperboreans were a mythical nation who lived far to the north (or possibly the east) of Greece. Traditionally, the name is interpreted as 'beyond the north wind' (*hyper*, 'over', 'beyond' and *Boreas*, the north wind – which see as a separate name). It could also, however, mean 'beyond the mountains' (*hyper* and *oros*, 'mountain') or even 'those who carry (goods) over' (*hyper* and *phoreo*, 'to carry'), in other words 'bearers', 'transporters'. The Hyperboreans tended to live in a rather splendid isolation, which added to their mystery: Apollo was said to spend the winter with them, and Perseus visited them when he was looking for the Gorgons. The idea of living *beyond* the north wind is rather a strange one, especially for the Greeks who associated the north wind with snow and cold. One would have expected them to locate this paradisian people in the warm south, and indeed Herodotus felt, logically, that if there were Hyperboreans, living beyond the north wind, there should also be Hypernotians, living beyond the south wind (*Notos*). But perhaps it was necessary to penetrate the icy north in order to emerge into a land where natural phenomena were of no consequence.

Hyperenor was one of the Sown Men of Thebes. His name means roughly 'Superman', from *hyper*, 'beyond' and *aner*, 'man'. This is obviously a nice straightforward propitious name.

Hyperion was a Titan, the son of Uranus and Gaia and the father of Helios (with whom he is often identified). His name means 'going over', 'one who walks on high', from *hyper*, 'over' and *ion*,

165

'going'. This is obviously a good name for a giant who 'walks tall', but the traditional association of the name is with the sun, which 'goes over'. (Homer actually calls the sun Hyperion in Book 19 of the *Iliad*.)

Hypermestra (or Hypermnestra) was the eldest of the fifty daughters of Danaüs, king of Argos, and the only one not to kill her bridegroom (Lynceus was the lucky man). Hypermestra was also the name of the daughter of Thestius who became the wife of Oïcles and the mother of Amphiaraüs. The name actually means 'superbride', implying an excess of wooing (or whatever else one wishes to call it), from *hyper*, 'over', 'above' and *mnesteira*, 'bride' (or *mnesteuo*, 'to woo', 'court'). This would seem to be an appropriate name, especially for the daughter of the prolific Danaüs.

Hypnos was the twin brother of Thanatos, and the personification of sleep, which is what his name means (*hypnos*, compare English 'hypnotic'). He was the son of Nyx, as one might expect. See also **Ker**.

Hypseus was the son of the river Peneius and the Naiad Creüsa. He became the father of Cyrene, Themisto and Astyagÿia, with his wife being Athamas, and he was also one of the kings of the Lapiths, in Thessaly. His name appears to be a complimentary one, meaning 'one on high', from *hypsos*, 'height' – which after all is suitable for a king.

Hypsipyle was a queen of Lemnos and the daughter of the king, Thoas. In spite of her various adventures (she saved her father when all the other men on the island were killed by the women, and later she was captured by pirates and sold to king Lycurgus) her name seems tu be simply a 'noble' one, meaning 'she of the high gate', from *hypsi*, 'high' and *pyle*, 'gate'. The reference is to the high gates of her city. (The name would also, in fact, be suitable for a queen of the Underworld.)

Hyrieus was the king and founder of Hyria, in Boeotia. In view of his unique method of fathering Orion (by urinating on a bull hide) it is tempting to derive his name from *hyo*, 'to wet', 'water', 'rain' (compare the **Hyades**), but this overlooks the 'r'. However, this letter may have appeared by association with the name of Orion (or with *ouron*, 'urine').

Iacchus was an obscure god sometimes called the son of Demeter

166

(or of Persephone) and often identified with Dionysus, although occasionally said to be his son. Dionysus' other name, of course, was Bacchus, and it is possible that Iacchus came to be identified with him because of a resemblance between the two names. Or again, as with Bacchus (and also Hymen) his name may have evolved from a ritual cry: he was always associated, as Dionysus was, with shouting and revelry. Furthermore, the verb 'to shout' is *iacho*, so he really seems to be a sort of personalised shout of joy ('Yahoo', so to speak).

Ialysa was one of the Danaïds, whose name seems to mean 'wailing woman', from *ialemos*, 'wail', 'lament', or rather *ialemizo*, 'to bewail', which gave *ialemistria*, 'wailing woman'. Her name is thus a 'worn-down' form, as are those of Cameira and Linda, also daughters of Danaë.

Iambe was a servant woman in the house of Celeus of Eleusis who consoled Demeter with her jokes. Her name seems to be closely linked to the iamb or iambus, the metrical foot in Greek verse that consisted of two syllables – a short one followed by a long one (as in the English word 'defeat'). Such verse was often jesting in nature, and it is not impossible that her name is the origin of the term for the foot. (According to some authorities, the Greek word for the foot, *iambos*, derives from *iapto*, 'to assail', 'shoot', that is, to lampoon.)

Iamus, the son of Apollo and Evadne, has his tale told by Pindar in his *Olympian Odes*. When a newborn baby, Iamus was fed by two snakes on the 'innocuous venom of bees' (*ios*, accusative *ion*, 'venom'), and at five days old he was found with his 'tender body bedewed with the yellow and red rays' of violets (*ion*, 'violet'), so his mother called him *Iamos*, 'violety'. A colourful origin, but it is disturbing that violets do not normally have 'yellow and red rays'. Perhaps Pindar had another flower in mind, such as the gillyflower.

Ianthe was the girl loved by Iphis (who was actually another girl disguised as a boy so that she could do this). Her name seems to mean 'violet flower', from *ion*, 'violet' and *anthos*, 'flower'. She was the daughter of Telestes of Crete, and her name would seem to be merely a 'pretty' one, with no special significance. (It resembles the name Iolanthe, familiar to lovers of Gilbert and Sullivan. This is not a name in Greek mythology, however. If it was, it too would mean 'violet', since it is really a form of Violetta via French Yolande.)

167

Iapetus was a Titan, so the son of Uranus and Gaia. He was the husband of Clymene, who bore to him the Titans Prometheus, Epimetheus, Atlas and Menoetius. His name apparently derives from *iapto*, 'to assail', 'strike' (see also **Iambe**), but whether it is of Greek origin or not, it is almost certainly related to the Biblical Japhet (one of the sons of Noah), whose own name is usually explained as meaning 'spacious' (or 'youthful' or 'beautiful'). It has on the other hand been pointed out that if his name is derived from *ipto*, 'to oppress', then it will have exactly the same meaning ('oppressed') as that of another Biblical character, Job. Perhaps he was intended to represent a man 'born to misery', or to symbolise mankind itself thus.

Iasion (or Iasius) was the son of Zeus (or Corythus) and Electra. He married Demeter and (possibly later) Cybele. His name seems to have something to do with dealing, since it resembles *iasis*, 'cure', 'remedy'. Such an interpretation, however, can only be a conjecture since we are not told much about him.

Iaso can be more positively connected with *iasis*, 'cure', since this daughter of Asclepius was a goddess of healing and health, like her sister Hygea.

Iasus, too, also appears to have been a healer (compare **Iaso**). He was king of Argos and the brother of Agenor and Pelasgus (or else a son of Argus). Another Iasus was a son of Lycurgus, who one story says was the father of Atalanta.

Icarius (not to be confused with Icarus) was the name of two mythological characters of note: the son of Oebalus and Batia (or Perieres and Gorgophone), and the father of Erigone. The first Icarius married Periboea who bore him two daughters, Penelope and Iphthime, as well as five sons. Although not the same person as Icarus, his name would seem to be of similar origin, and for the possibilities see the name of his better-known near namesake.

Icarus was the son of Daedalus who flew too near the sun so that his wax wings melted and he plunged into the sea, named the Icarian after him. In much that he did, Icarus was similar to his father, and for this reason it seems appropriate to suggest a derivation such as *eico*, 'to yield', 'obey', 'follow' for his name. The noun *eicon* (English 'icon'), 'figure', 'likeness', would also produce this sense.

Idaea was a daughter of Dardanus, king of Scythia. She married Phineus, and bore him Thynius and Mariandynus. Another Idaea was a nymph from Mount Ida who bore Teucer to Scamander. Doubtless her name reveals the meaning of Idaea – 'from Mount Ida'. (Although *ida* also meant 'wood', 'copse', and she might thus have been a wood nymph.)

Idas, with his inseparable brother Lynceus, was the son of Aphareus, king of Messenia, and Arene. His name suggests 'Ida', but we are not told of any connection with this famous mountain. He was an adventurous (and headstrong) person, however, so perhaps his name relates to *idea*, 'form', 'manner', 'fashion'. Or again, as with Idaea, possibly *ida*, 'wood', 'timber' may be more fitting. (One incident involving a tree was when Idas' lynx-eyed brother Lynceus spotted Castor hiding inside an oak; Idas promptly killed him. This was the culminating stage of Idas' long-running quarrel with the Dioscuri.) Idas married Marpessa, who bore him Cleopatra (who married Meleager).

Idmon was a son of Apollo and Cyrene who sailed with the Argonauts. He was a seer and predicted his own death on the journey. His name would therefore seem to derive from *eido*, 'to see', 'know', in a sense that Pierre Grimal translates as 'clairvoyant'.

Idomeneus, king of Crete, was the leader of the Cretan forces in the Trojan War. He was the son of Deucalion. Perhaps his name, like that of Idmon, derives from *idmon*, 'practised', 'skilled', 'knowledgeable'.

Iliona was the eldest daughter of Priam and Hecabe. She married Polymestor, king of Thrace. Priam was king of Troy, of course, and Iliona's name may therefore well mean 'lady of Ilium', since *Ilios* or *Ilion* was the alternative name for Troy (see **Ilus**).

Ilus was the son of Tros and Callirrhoë. He married Eurydice, the daughter of Adrastus, and she bore him Laomedon and Themiste. He founded the city of Troy (Greek *Ilios*, Latin *Ilium*) and in it, where the Palladium dropped (see **Pallas**), the famous temple for Athena. His name seems to derive from *ile*, 'troop', which seems appropriate.

Inachus was the god of the river Inachus and a king of Argos. He was the son of Oceanus and Tethys, and he married his half-sister

Melia, who bore him several children including Io. His name is difficult to interpret with any obvious relevance: *inodes* means 'sinewy', 'fibrous' (this could have an erotic connotation), while *einacis* means 'nine times' (with possibly some ritual allusion). His name may even somehow link up with that of his daughter Io.

Ino was the daughter of Cadmus and Harmonia who became the wife of Athanas. Her name is so short that we can only speculate on an origin: perhaps *is*, *inos*, 'sinew', 'force', with some erotic or orgiastic connotation in the root. We are certainly told that she and her sisters Agave and Autonoë were stricken with a Bacchic frenzy in which they tore to pieces Agave's son Pentheus who had been spying on them. After her death, however, Ino became known as Leucothea, and if this name (which see) relates to the white waves of the sea, then it is possible that Ino's original name was actually Ilo, and derives from *illo*, 'to roll'. But further suggestions will only be even more fanciful than this.

Io's main claim to fame is that she was turned into a white heifer by Hera or Zeus, and that when swimming through a section of the Adriatic Sea she gave her name to this as the Ionian Sea. (Later, still as a heifer and still swimming, she passed through the Bosporus, which as 'Oxford' – *bos*, 'ox' and *poros*, 'ford' – was also named after her.) She was originally the daughter of Inachus, first king of Argos, and Melia. Traditionally she is associated with the moon, which in a dialect of Argos was called Io, from *io*, *eimi*, 'to go'. Equally, she could have been regarded as the feminine equivalent of Ion, and thus as a forerunner of the Ionian race. Somehow the 'cow and moon' association seems the most attractive, since the inhabitants of Argos are said to have worshipped the moon as a cow, regarding the horned new moon as a source of water, and so of cattle food. There are those, even, who see the cow jumping over the moon in the 'Hey diddle diddle' nursery rhyme as symbolic of the changing seasons and the passing of the months. Iona and Peter Opie firmly discount such explanations in *The Oxford Dictionary of Nursery Rhymes*. (It is simply an agreeable coincidence that the female half of this husband-and-wife team has a name that itself may well link up with that of Io!)

Iobates was a king of Lycia whose daughter Stheneboea (or Antia) married Proëtus. If we pursue the 'moon' sense of *Io*, then we might have 'moon-goer' for his name, from *Io* and *baino*, 'to go'. This could be understood as 'he who travels with the moon', 'voyager'. However, most of the travelling in Iobates' experience was done not by himself but by Bellerophon, whom he persistently despatched in different directions in an attempt to get him killed (always unsuccessfully, since Bellerophon was aided each time by Pegasus).

Iolaüs was a son of Iphicles and Automedusa. He was also the nephew of Heracles and professionally was his charioteer. For his constant loyalty to Heracles and to the descendants of the hero we can perhaps see in his name a reference to the two meanings of *laos*, 'people', 'subjects' and 'of stone' (*laos* is a genitive of *laas*). He is thus a 'rock of the people'.

Iole was the daughter of Eurytus, king of Oechalia, who was won by Heracles as a prize (although she eventually married his son, Hyllus). All names starting Io- are difficult, and for Iole we can only suggest a 'moon' allusion (as for Io) with perhaps the latter half of her name being a shortening of *laos*, 'people' (which in its Ionic form was *leos*).

Ion was the son of Xuthus or Apollo by Creüsa. Popularly he has come to be regarded as the personification of the Ionians, hence his name. But Euripides in his play *Ion* makes Xuthus explain his name as deriving from *ion*, 'going', since he had been told by the oracle that the first man he met on leaving the temple, that is when 'going' from it, would be his son. Xuthus thus met Ion, assuming that he must be an illegitimate son (and that he would therefore have to break the news tactfully to Creüsa, who had never borne any children).

Iphianassa was the daughter of Proëtus and Stheneboea who was cured of her madness by Melampus. Another Iphianassa was the daughter of Agamemnon and Clytemnestra who is usually identified with Iphigenia (whom see). Either way, the name is a 'prestige' one, meaning 'mighty queen', from *iphi*, 'strongly', 'mightily' and *anassa*, 'queen'. See also **Iphinoë**.

Iphiboë, according to Apollodorus, was the mother of Augeas, king of Elis, by Helios. Her name means 'strength of oxen' (*iphi*, 'strongly' and *bous*, 'ox'). This could be simply a propitious name, but we are told that Augeas was indeed the possessor of a fine number of herds (which almost always produced female young).

Iphicles was the son of Amphitryon and Alcmene, and was said to be the twin brother of Heracles. Doubtless this prestigious family

171

connection is indicated in his name, which means 'famous might', from *iphios*, 'strong', 'mighty' and *cleo*, 'to be famous'. Like his brother, he was thus 'famous for his strength'.

Iphigenia was the eldest daughter of Agamemnon and Clytemnestra, and Homer generally refers to her as Iphianassa (which name see). Her name indicates her royal parentage, meaning 'of mighty birth', from *iphios*, 'strong', 'mighty' and *geno*, 'to bear'. Of course, the name could also indicate that she in turn would be the mother of mighty offspring, and in one story she is said to have married Achilles and borne him Pyrrhus. She also has an association with Artemis, who in one account carried her off to be her priestess at a temple where human sacrifices were performed. This suggests that Iphigenia may herself have originated as a by-name of Artemis, since it is certainly a highly suitable name for a great goddess.

Iphimedia was the daughter of Triops, and married his brother (i.e. her uncle) Alöeus. Later, however, she fell in love with Poseidon and bore him two giants, Otus and Ephialtes. In her association with Poseidon, she used to sit by the sea and wash its waters into her lap to achieve impregnation (Poseidon, of course, was the great god of the sea and waters). This, and the fact that she bore two giants, suggest an interpretation of her name as not so much 'strong ruler', from *iphi*, 'mightily' and *medeon*, 'ruler', which would be the traditional reading, as 'bearing mightily', from *iphi* and *medea*, 'genitals'. 'She who strengthens the genitals' is Robert Graves' rendering. Compare **Ganymede**.

Iphimedon could also have his name interpreted thus (as Iphimedia) but lacking further evidence it would be better to settle for a meaning that is simply propitious, 'mighty ruler'. He was the son of Eurystheus, and he and his brothers all have rather grand names, his brothers being Alexander, Eurybius, Mentor and Perimedes (see all these names, with Eurybius being the masculine form of Eurybia). In spite of their apparent power, the fine names did not save the five brothers from being killed in battle by the Athenians.

Iphinoë was the daughter of Proëtus and Stheneboea. Like her sister Iphianassa (whose name her own closely resembles) she was cured of her madness by Melampus. Her name means 'great mind', 'mighty intelligence', from *iphi*, 'mightily' and *noos*, 'mind'.

Iphis was the daughter of Ligdus, of Knossos in Crete, and Telethusa. She was brought up as a boy by her mother to deceive her father, who wanted a son. (This device was recommended by the goddess Isis.) When Iphis was thirteen Ligdus betrothed her, still in her male guise, to Ianthe, and the two fell in love. Telethusa attempted to postpone the wedding in view of the embarrassing situation, but eventually Isis once more came to the rescue and changed Iphis' sex into a boy so that all was well. None of this androgynous story seems to be reflected in the name of Iphis, which presumably simply means 'mighty', 'strong', from *iphios*. However, Ovid tells us (the story is, as might be expected, one of his *Metamorphoses*) that when Iphis changed sex 'her strength increased' and 'she showed more energy than a woman'. So her strength thus lay in her new-found manliness.

Iphitus was the name of several characters, including the son of Eurytus, the king of Phocis who entertained Jason, and a king of Elis. All three (and doubtless others) have a name that is a propitious one meaning 'mighty shield', from *iphios*, 'mighty' and *itys*, 'shield'.

Irene was one of the Hours and the goddess of peace. Her Roman equivalent was Pax. Irene's name is simply the word for peace, *eirene* (which spelling is also sometimes used for her name). The modern girl's name Irene was probably inspired by a more recent namesake, real or fictional, than the Greek goddess.

Iris has also found currency as a modern girl's name. Like Irene, she was also a goddess and was in effect (quite literally) a personified rainbow. As such she carried the messages of the gods to men across a multicoloured bridge on a kind of celestial shuttle service between sky and earth. She was the daughter of the Titan Thaumas and the Oceanid Electra. Her name actually means 'rainbow' (*iris*), and perhaps we should not overlook the significant name of her father (Thaumas means 'wonderful'). Twentieth-century Irises get their name not from the messenger of the gods but from the flower so called.

Irus was the name of two characters of note. One was the beggar in Odysseus' palace in Ithaca; the other was the son of Actor who became the father of the Argonauts Eurytion and Eurydamas. The name seems to be a masculine form of Iris, without any specific allusion to a rainbow or a messenger.

Isander was the son of Bellerophon and Philonoë. His name appears to derive from *isos*, 'equal' and *aner*, *andros*, 'man', probably in the desirable sense of being 'impartial', 'fair'.

Ischepolis was a son of Alcathoüs and Evaechme. His propitious name means 'strong city', from *ischys*, 'strength' and *polis*, 'city'. This nicely complements the name of his brother, Callipolis ('beautiful city'). The city would have been the one (Megara) of which their father was king.

Ischys was the son of Elatus. He loved Coronis at the time when she was pregnant with Asclepius by Apollo. His name means simply 'strength' (*ischys*). Robert Graves links the word with *ixos*, 'mistletoe', which plant was regarded as an all-healer. Asclepius, of course, was the god of healing.

Isis was one of the chief goddesses of Egypt whose cult spread to Greece, where Diodorus made her the daughter of Saturn and Rhea, while Herodotus identified her with Demeter. (Others again identified her with Io.) Plutarch says that she married her brother Osiris and that she reigned jointly with him in Egypt. Whoever she was as far as the Greeks were concerned, her name is obviously not Greek. It is in fact a version of an ancient Egyptian hieroglyph meaning 'throne'. As this was feminine, she symbolised the mother of the king since the throne 'created' the king. The modern name Isadora or Isidora is usually held to mean 'gift of Isis', with the latter half of the name being Greek *doron*, 'gift', 'present'. How the name was first popularised is not clear – probably through some literary character so called or as the feminine of a (real) man's name Isidorus, which was quite common in Greece. It is possible, however, that the first part of the name does not after all derive from Isis.

Ismene was the daughter of Oedipus and Jocasta, and the sister of Antigone. Thomas Keightley suggests that she may have been invented for sake of uniformity, in order to balance Antigone. There would then have been two brothers (Eteocles and Polynices) and two sisters. However that may be, we can contrive an origin for her to mean 'revealing strength', from *is*, 'strength', 'force' and *menyo*, 'to disclose', 'reveal'. Those of the 'ritual and historical' school, however, will probably derive the second half of the name from *mene*, 'moon'.

Itylus was the son of Zethus and Aedon who was killed by his mother by mistake (see **Aedon** for the story). Without stretching the credibility too far, we can make his name mean 'little nightingale'. We know that his mother's name means 'nightingale' and if we take his name as a diminutive of Itys (which see) it could refer to the song of a young nightingale and thus to the bird itself. Maybe little Itylus had a good singing voice. Whatever the case, it is significant that both Itylus and Itys suffered the same fate, for both boys were killed by their mothers. There seems little doubt that their names are linked in identity of fate, if not in actual meaning.

Itys was the son of Tereus and Procne. As mentioned (for Itylus) he was killed by his mother: not by accident, however, but deliberately, in order to deprive her husband of an heir (as revenge for his raping of her sister Philomela). Philomela was turned into either a swallow or a nightingale (depending which account one reads) as was Procne, and the song of the nightingale was represented by the Greeks as *ity, ity*. This lament was thus Procne (or Philomela) mourning the loss of Itys. His name, therefore, could mean something like 'song of the nightingale'. (There were two Greek words for the nightingale itself, both those of characters in mythology, *aedon* and *philomela*: see these as names.)

Ixion was a king of Thessaly, the son of Antion (perhaps) who married Dia, the daughter of Eioneus. We can interpret his name in a number of ways to suit different incidents in his life. He summoned Eioneus to come to him, saying that he would pay him a handsome sum for the hand of his daughter; instead, he treacherously murdered him. So perhaps his name comes from *hico*, 'to come' 'arrive', 'reach' (referring to the fate that came to Eioneus). Later, after attempting to seduce Hera, he was sentenced by Zeus (Hera's consort) to be tied to an endlessly revolving wheel. Here we have a possibility in *axon*, 'wheel' (relating to English 'axle'). Robert Graves, somewhat predictably, links his name with *ixos*, 'mistletoe' (see **Ischys**), saying that the name itself derives from *ischys*, 'strength' and *io*, 'moon' (see **Io**). Perhaps we can decide in favour of a compromise such as 'strong man', accepting that the base of his name is *is* or *ischys*, 'strength'.

Iynx was a nymph, the daughter of Pan and Echo (or Pertho). Her name is that of the bird into which she was turned by Hera for using magic to win the love of Zeus, either for herself or on behalf of Io. This bird was the wryneck, *iynx*, so named for its cry.

(The bird was believed to have the power to bring back lost lovers, among other things.)

Janus was the Roman god with two faces, the god of beginnings, doors, gates and passageways. Traditionally his name is derived from *ianua* (*janua*), 'door', 'entrance', or *ianus* (*janus*), 'doorway', 'covered passage'. Attempts have been made to link his name with that of Diana, but for various reasons this seems unlikely. First, although her name had the variant form Jana, the Roman name Dianus was relatively late, whereas it should be early if it is to link with her. Second, he is a native Roman god, whereas she was an imported goddess (from the Greek Artemis). Third, Diana seems to have no connection with doors or two faces. It could well be, however, that doors and gates came to be associated with Janus (rather than the other way round) because of the similarity between *ianua* and *ianus* and his name – which in this case will need another explanation. We do at least know that the month of January was dedicated to him, not because it was 'two-faced', looking back at the old year and forward at the new, but because it fell between winter and spring.

Jason (in its Greek form the name was Iason) was the popular hero of Thessaly, the elder son of Aeson (grandson of Aeolus) and either Polymede or Alcimede. He was reared by Chiron, who also named him, giving him a name that referred to the skill in medicine that he had taught him on Mount Pelion. His name thus means 'healer', from *iaomai*, Ionic *iesomai*, 'to heal' – although this attribute has come to be quite overshadowed by his great exploit to recover the Golden Fleece. But perhaps the 'healing' was more moral than physical. One point we must not overlook is that if Chiron named Jason when instructing him as a boy, he must have had an earlier name. He did, and this was Diomedes (which see, although the name is that of quite a different person). Curiously, Jason's name became very popular as a modern boy's name in the mid-twentieth century, although the inspiration for it is almost certainly not the hero of Thessaly but a modern folk hero such as a film or television actor so named, or even a cartoon character. Even so, the heroic image is still there.

Jocasta was the famous (or infamous) daughter of Menoeceus who first married Laius, king of Thebes, and then her son by him, Oedipus. Homer called her Epicaste (which name see). The Greek form of her name is Iocaste, and this is usually derived from *io*, 'moon' (see **Io**) and either *cazo*, 'to adorn' or *caio*, 'to blaze' (as perhaps in the name of Castor). This means that she was 'adorning moon' or 'shining moon'. But this seems too agreeable a name for her, unless it is intended propitiously. If we regard the initial 'io' as a cry of woe (*io* could be a cry of both joy and sorrow), then we can propose the more suitable 'woe-adorned' for her. After all, her troubles began when an oracle warned her first husband Laïus that any son she bore him would kill him. (This was how Oedipus got his swollen foot – see his name.) Then, after unknowingly marrying her son, Jocasta was so shocked that she took her own life (in Homer's account). Furthermore, at any rate according to Homer, her name was changed from Epicaste to Jocasta specifically to indicate a change in her fate.

Jove see **Jupiter**.

Juno was the Roman goddess of women and marriage, and the wife of Jupiter. Her name is of uncertain origin, but could well derive from the root of *juvenis*, 'young', in the sense of 'young bride'. On the other hand, her name may somehow link up with that of Jupiter, although one would expect a form Diuno or something like it, and there are no such names recorded. Somewhat curiously, the English adjective 'Junoesque', derived from her name, came to change its meaning in the latter half of the twentieth century from 'having stately bearing and regal beauty' to simply 'stout', 'well-built', especially in the phrase 'a Junoesque figure'.

Jupiter was the main Roman god, consistently identified with the sky. His Greek counterpart, of course, was Zeus, and the two names are actually the same in their linguistic origin, except that Jupiter has the word *pater*, 'father' (or a form of it) added. Jupiter is thus really '*Zeus pater*', or 'Father Sky'. The apparently unlikely identity of the names (one starting 'Ze-', the other 'Ju-') is acceptable when it is known that in Greek the genitive of Zeus was *Dios* (compare Latin *deus*, 'god'), and that the Ju- of Jupiter is related to the Sanskrit *dyaus* meaning 'sky', 'day', 'heaven'. (Sanskrit as a language has preserved some of the oldest forms of words that are today found in different Indo-European languages.) As for the form Jove, this too derives from a grammatical origin, since in Latin all cases of the nominative noun (name) *Jupiter* begin *Jov-* (for example, the genitive is *Jovis*). All three names so far mentioned (Jupiter, Zeus, Jove) are of course in turn related to that of Diana, which means that we have overall a prestigious and powerful blend of related names and words: Jupiter, Jove, Zeus and Diana all containing a root that means both 'sky', 'god', 'heaven' and 'day'. The original Greek name for the planet Jupiter was Phaëthon, 'shining' (see Introduction, p. 11, and also **Phaëthon**).

Juventas was the Roman goddess of youth, not so much of abstract youth or youthful beauty (as Hebe was) as more narrowly of the *juvenes*, the young men of military conscription age (17) including boys preparing for this, which they did at age fourteen on taking the *toga virilis*, the garment that proclaimed them to have reached 'manhood'. Latin *juvenis* (or *iuvenis*) simply means 'young' (compare English 'juvenile' and French *jeune*).

Ker is the sole representative of this letter of the alphabet that we shall have. (There is a spelling *Cer* but for some reason this is rarely used.) Ker was a female spirit of death resembling one of the Furies in her appearance and function. Hesiod says she is the daughter of Nyx without a male mate, and that her brothers were Moros ('Fate'), Hypnos ('Sleep') and Thanatos ('Death'). Generally, however, she is one of a group (Keres), as the Furies are. The name is usually derived from *ker*, 'destruction', 'doom', 'death', although it is more than likely that the word came from the name. It seems to be a rare coincidence that these spirits have a name that resembles that of the Valkyries, the Scandinavian goddesses who conducted the slain from the battlefield to Valhalla (their palace of bliss), all the more as they were similar in nature. But Valkyrie means 'chooser of the slain', from Old Norse *valr*, 'slain' (also the first element of Valhalla) and the root of *kjōsa*, 'to choose', and this Old Norse word can hardly be linked, at any rate meaningfully, with the Greek one.

Labdacus was the son of Polydorus (Cadmus' son) and Nycteïs. Robert Graves rather contrivedly offers *lampadon acos* as an origin for the name, this meaning 'help of torches' and referring to some torchlight procession heralding a symbolic ruler. Apollodorus, however, makes a rather neat suggestion: Labdacus, he says, starts with the Greek letter *lambda* (also called *labda*) (λ), and the name resembles the word for the letter; this letter follows the Greek letter *kappa* (K) in the alphabet, and *kappa* is the first letter of Cadmus' name! Alas, Labdacus' own son did not have a name that began with the next letter of the alphabet, *mu* (M) but was Laïus, the first husband of Jocasta and the father of Oedipus.

Lacedaemon was the son of Zeus and the mountain nymph Taÿgete. He married Sparte, and named his capital city of Sparta after her, himself being the mythical ancestor of the Lacedaemonians. His name strongly suggests 'lake demon', which although an English phrase derives from similar Greek words: *lacos* (or *laccos*), 'pond', 'lake' and *daimon*, 'god', 'demon'. This seems to point to some religious or magical ceremony, perhaps involving a sacrifice (to an underwater monster?).

Lachesis was one of the Fates, and her name literally means 'drawing of lots' (*lachesis*) from *lanchano*, 'to obtain by lot', 'draw lots'. She was thus the goddess who 'apportioned' a person's life, who laid down (or measured) what one's lot in life should be. Compare the names of the other Fates – **Clotho** and **Atropos**. Clotho, whose name suggests spinning, came to give the three a consecutive ordering of a person's destiny, with Clotho drawing the thread of life out, Lachesis measuring it, and Atropos cutting it off.

Lacinius was a robber who tried to steal Geryon's cattle (which in fact Heracles was trying to steal at the same time). His name could derive from *lacis*, 'tearing', 'rending', perhaps referring to his clothes (the word is related to *lacisma*, 'something torn', 'rags') or to his rough behaviour or violent nature.

Ladon was a hundred-headed serpent, the offspring of Typhon and Echidna. His main assignment was guarding the tree of golden apples that belonged to the Hesperides. His name can hardly derive from *ladanon*, 'ladanum' (a type of gum resin, not to be confused with laudanum, which is an invented word). Perhaps it is a worn-down form of some such name as Laodamon, meaning 'tamer of men'. Compare **Laodamas** and **Laodamia**.

Laelaps was an infallible dog that no beast could escape. It seems to have changed hands several times, originally (perhaps) being given by Zeus to Europa as a watchdog. To an English speaker the name may suggest 'lapdog' but this was certainly no pet Pom! Its name denotes its ferocious and speedy nature, since it means 'hurricane' or 'whirlwind', from *lailaps*, 'tempest', 'storm'. Perhaps Storm is actually the best English name for it.

Laërtes was the father of Odysseus, and himself was the son of Acrisius and Chalcomedusa (or Cephalus and Procris). His name apparently means 'people urger', from *laos*, 'people' and an old root *er-*, 'to urge on'. (His name appears in the Linear B tablets at Knossos as *Law-er-tas*.)

179

Laïus was the son of Labdacus. After an infatuation with the young boy Chrysippus, whom he kidnapped, he became the first husband of Jocasta, who bore him Oedipus. His name is so 'elemental' that a number of derivations can be proposed for him, all apt. Since the Thebans called him to the throne on the death of Zethus (who had usurped it), his name could be a shortened form of Laomedon and so be 'king of the people'. It could also be interpreted as 'unlucky', from *laios*, 'left', since his fate was to be killed by Oedipus, who was not aware that Laïus was his father. On similar sinister lines his name could be linked with that of Lethe, since Laïus was a kind of emblem of darkness. Or it could simply be a propitious name, from *leis*, 'herd of cattle', meaning 'one who is rich in cattle'.

Lamia was the daughter of Poseidon and Libya, but the name is best known for the bogeywoman (with the face and breasts of a woman and the body of a serpent) who had been deformed by Hera and in revenge lured strangers so that she could devour them. (Some mythologists equate both Lamias.) Her name is traditionally held to derive from *laimos*, 'throat', 'gullet', which would certainly be appropriate. However, there could also be a link with *lamyros*, 'voracious', 'gluttonous'. Perhaps the influence of both words is present in the name.

Lampetia has an obviously 'shining' name (from *lampo*, 'to shine'), and this is fitting for two of the best known: the daughter of Helios (the sun) who became the wife of Asclepius, and the daughter and chief herdswoman of Hyperion (which name see for its 'sun' link). Perhaps the latter half of the name is *etos*, 'year', so that she is the 'brightness of the year'.

Lampon was one of the four stallions (or mares) of king Diomedes, together with Podargus, Deinus and Xanthus. The name means 'bright', in reference to the horse's shining coat. Compare the name of **Podargus**, and see also the next entry.

Lampus was the son of Laomedon, and one of king Priam's brothers. Lampus was also an alternative name for Lampon (see previous entry). The name means 'bright', which for Laomedon's son was just a 'good omen' name.

Lamus was the son of Heracles and Omphale (and another Lamus was one of the many sons of Poseidon). Perhaps the name, like that of Lamia, means something like 'glutton', from *laimos*, 'throat'.

We are not given any information to support this, however, and we cannot assume that the name was originally Lampus.

Laocoön was the priest of Poseidon at Troy who was killed, together with his two young sons, by two huge sea-serpents who crushed all three in their coils. (The scene is portrayed in the famous Greek statue that stands in the Vatican Museum.) There was another Laocoön who was the son (or possibly the brother) of Oeneus, king of Calydon. The name, however, does not appear to relate to the serpentine fate, and it perhaps derives from *laos*, 'people' and some such word as *coinos*, 'common', meaning 'impartial to people', 'common to all the people'. If so, it is a generally commendatory name.

Laodamas was the son of Eteocles and a king of Thebes. As befits a king (at any rate, a classical Greek one), his name means 'people tamer', 'master of the folk', from *laos*, 'people', and *damao*, 'to tame', 'subdue'.

Laodamia was the name of two noted women: the daughter of Acastas and Astydamia who became the wife of Protesilaüs, king of Phylace, and the daughter of Bellerophon who became the mother of Sarpedon and who was slain by Artemis when she was still young. The name is a propitious one, meaning 'tamer of the people'. See **Laodamas**.

Laodice was the name of several women. Among them were the most beautiful daughter of Priam and Hecabe, the daughter of Agapenor, and the daughter of Agamemnon who later became Electra. Here is another stock propitious name on the lines of Creüsa, meaning 'justice of the people', from *laos*, 'people' and *dice*, 'justice'.

Laomedon was a king of Troy who was the son of Ilus (also king of Troy) and Eurydice. His name, appropriately enough, means 'ruler of the people', from *laos*, 'people' and *medon*, 'ruler'. If all names were as 'transparent' as this life would be not nearly so interesting!

Laonome has yet another 'people' name. She was the daughter of Guneus who according to some accounts married Alcaeüs and bore him Amphitryon and Anaxo. Her name means 'law of the people', from *laos*, 'people' and *nomos*, 'law'.

181

Laothoë was the mistress of Priam, king of Troy, and she was the mother of Lycaon. Her name seems to mean 'active among the people', from *laos*, 'people' and *thoos*, 'quick', 'active', although Robert Graves, without any explanation, derives it from *laas*, 'stone' and the same *thoos* to mean 'rushing stone'. It is hard to see the significance of this.

Lapiths were a Greek people who lived in the north of Thessaly. They traced their origin back to Ixion or (more obviously) to Lapithes, an obscure son of Apollo and Stilbe. They became famous through their battle with the Centaurs. They have been traditionally explained as 'pillagers', from *lapazo*, 'to plunder', 'carry off', but perhaps really they were 'stone-persuaders', from *laas*, 'stone' and *peitho*, 'to persuade', 'prevail', this being a poetic term for town builders.

Lara was a Roman nymph, the daughter of the river Tiber. She bore Mercury the Lares, the household gods of the Romans. Ovid seems to have invented her name to mean 'chatterer' (from Greek *laleo*, 'to chatter', 'babble') for the tale in his *Fasti* ('Calendar') in which she kept on blurting out all she knew about the amorous designs of Jupiter and so had her tongue cut out and was despatched by Mercury to the Underworld. The name does not seem to be connected with the city of Larisa (modern Larissa), in Thessaly, although oddly enough this could well be the origin of the modern girl's name Lara which acquired a certain vogue in English-speaking countries by way of the Russian name (and the popular 'Lara's Theme' in the film *Doctor Zhivago*). The modern name could also derive, again via Russian Larisa, of which it is a diminutive, from Greek *laris*, 'sea-gull'.

Lares were the Roman household gods: each Roman house had its *Lar* who was honoured together with the family's *Penates* (which see) and *Vesta*. These gods seem to have originated as the deified spirits of dead ancestors. Their name seems to be of Tuscan (or perhaps Sabine) origin, with possibly a meaning 'lord' (which English word, in spite of the resemblance, could not be related to them). Eric Partridge, however, relates the name to Latin *larva* or *larua*, 'ghost', 'mask', and thus to English 'larva', which resembles a mask.

Latinus was the son of Odysseus and Circe, or else of Heracles or Telemachus. He is said to have given his name to Latium, the homeland of Rome, although Latinus actually ruled, we are told, at Laurentum, which was refounded a short distance away as Lavinium, a name given in honour of Latinus' daughter Lavinia. More obviously, of course, the name relates to 'Latin', which properly was the name of the language spoken by the people (the *Latini*) who inhabited Latium. (Originally this was a small area in west Italy in which Rome lay.) It is possible that the name (and thus Latin and Latium) could be related to *latus*, 'broad', 'wide'.

Latona was a Titaness, the daughter of Coeüs and Phoebe. The name is the Roman equivalent of Greek **Leto** (which see).

Latromis was one of the sons of Dionysus and Ariadne. In view of the 'winy' interpretation that can be put on the names of all his brothers (Oenopion, Thoas, Staphylus, Euanthes, Tauropolus), we ought to look for one here. Perhaps it can be found in a blend of *latax*, 'drop of wine' and *rome*, 'strength'?

Laverna was the Roman goddess of thieves. Her name seems to derive from *lateo*, 'to lie hidden', 'lurk', with 't' an alternative for 'v'. (This happened quite frequently in equivalent Greek and Latin words, for example Greek *tillo* and Latin *vello*, 'to pull', 'pluck'; Greek *thelo* and Latin *volo*, 'to wish', 'want'; Greek *clitys* and Latin *clivus*, 'slope'. There are even similar doublets in English, as 'dale' and 'vale'.)

Lavinia was the daughter of Latinus and Amata (the second wife of Aeneas). Her name may have come from the town of Lavinium (see **Latinus**), although one late story says that she was the daughter of Anius, son of Apollo, and that she followed Aeneas east and died where *he* founded Lavinium. Furthermore, there is something of a pun here, since Latin *vinum* means 'wine' and Anius' name suggests the Greek for 'wine', *oeno*. (As added evidence, the collective name for Anius' daughters was the *Oenotrophoi*, 'wine-producers'!)

Leander was the young man who loved Hero, and loyally swam each night across the Hellespont to her, guided by the light of a lighthouse. (One night the light was out, and he perished in the stormy waves; Hero found his body on the beach the next morning, and in despair threw herself into the sea . . . .) His name, in spite of this sad fate, is a propitious one, meaning 'lion man', from *leon*, 'lion' and *aner*, *andros*, 'man'.

Leda was the daughter of Thestius, King of Aetolia, who became the wife of Tyndareüs, king of Sparta and the mother of the Dioscuri (Castor and Pollux) and Helen. She is usually associated with the fact that Zeus visited her disguised as a swan and coupled with her. Her name is said to mean 'lady', not from the English word but from a Lycian (i.e. Cretan) word, and to be related to Leto (or Latona). (Although Leto's name, which see, could mean 'darkness', in which case Leda's husband's name, Tyndareüs, could be complementary, since it means 'light'.)

Leiriope was a nymph, the mother of Narcissus. Her name seems to mean 'lily face', from *leirion*, 'lily' and *ops*, 'face', which is fitting when one considers the name of her son.

Lepreus was a son of Caucon and Astydamia. He founded the city of Lepreus, in Arcadia, which was said to be named from the leprosy that had attacked the first settlers. Lepreus, of course, was *the* first settler, which is why his own name means 'scabby', 'leprous', from *lepis*, 'scale', 'husk' (from *lepo*, 'to peel').

Lethe was the name of a river in the Underworld: the dead who went to Hades drank its waters and in doing so forgot their former lives. Thus the name, which Hesiod personified as the daughter of Eris, means 'forgetfulness', *lethe*. (Compare English 'lethal', and in fact 'latent' since *lethe* derives from a verb that means 'to lie hidden'.)

Leto was a Titaness, the daughter of Coeüs and Phoebe, and she bore Apollo and Artemis to Zeus. Her name may be a corruption of Lycian (that is, Cretan) *lada*, 'woman' (compare **Leda**). Some authorities, however, link her name with *lethe*, 'forgetfulness' (see **Lethe**) and also with *lateo*, 'to lie hidden' (see **Laverna**), thus interpreting her name as 'concealer' or even 'darkness' (see last sentence of entry **Leda**). This seems to be supported by the fact that one of her by-names is *Cyanopeplos*, 'dark-veiled'. Plato says her name comes *apo tes praotetos tes theon*, 'from the mildness of the goddess', apparently referring to some such root word as *lo*, 'I wish' or *leios*, 'soft', 'gentle'. But the real truth is that the name is almost certainly not Greek, and thus 'lady' is the best bet.

Leuca was a nymph whom Hades attempted to seduce. She was rescued (in the nick of time) by Persephone, who changed her into a white poplar. (Such metamorphoses were often extremely handy escape routes in tricky or dangerous situations.) It is perhaps not so surprising, therefore, to find that *leuce* means 'white poplar' (from *leucos*, 'white'). Compare the other 'white' names below.

Leucippe was the daughter of Minyas. In spite of her adventures and misadventures (her son Hippasus was torn to pieces and she was turned into a bat) her name has a propitious sense, 'white mare', from *leucos*, 'white' and *hippos*, 'horse', 'mare'. Compare the identical element in the name of her son.

Leucippus was the name of many mythological characters. Probably the two best known are the son of Perieres and Gorgophone who became joint king of Messenia with his brother Aphareus, and the son of Oenomaüs who dressed as a girl to win the friendship of Daphne (but who was exposed, in more senses than one, when her companions stripped him to make him swim with them). This is thus one of the several 'noble' propitious names, 'white horse' (see **Leucippe**), meaning someone who could have fine white horses for racing and the like. (Such names have their parallels several thousand miles away in the names of American (Red) Indian chiefs. There must have been more than one 'Big Chief White Horse'.)

Leucon was one of the four sons of Athamas and his third wife Themisto. The name means 'white' (*leucos*) and presumably is favourable in some way.

Leucos is best known for the fact that he seduced Medea, wife of king Idomeneus, during the latter's absence in the Trojan War, and then killed her. In view of this, he hardly lived up to his propitious name of 'white' (*leucos*).

Leucothea was a sea goddess, the daughter of Orchamos, into whom Ino was transformed (see **Ino**). Her name means either 'white goddess', an obviously propitious name, or 'runner on the white', from *leucos*, 'white' and *theo*, 'to run', in which case her name stands for the white waves of the sea (our 'white horses' – which the Greeks would have thought a highly favourable name!).

Liber was the ancient Roman god of fertility, often called Pater Liber ('Father Liber'). He was usually worshipped with Ceres and Libera (the latter being his wife), who are the Roman equivalents of Demeter and Persephone. He came to be identified with Dionysus (otherwise Bacchus), possibly because Iacchus, the companion of Persephone, was confused by the Greeks with Bacchus (see this name). His name seems not to derive from Latin *liber*, 'free', 'unrestricted', although there may be some sort of a link since one of Dionysus' by-names is *Lyaiüs*, 'deliverer', 'looser' (Greek *luo*, 'to loose', 'release'). Perhaps it relates more to *libo*, 'to give a taste of', 'make an offering or libation', in view of the fact that he was the god of fertility and that rain and dew help to make the land fertile. Reading his name this way, we can call him 'provider of moisture', even 'pourer'. His festival was called the Liberalia, and this became a favourite day for boys to don their *toga virilis* (their symbol of manhood) with an implicit pun on his name and Latin *liberi*, 'children'.

Libitina was a rather vague Roman goddess who was an equivalent to Venus. She presided over funerals and perhaps has a name related to *libero*, 'to set free' or (less likely) *libet*, 'it pleases', 'it is agreeable'.

Libya was the daughter of Epaphus and Memphis who gave her name to Libya. She bore the twins Belus and Agenor to Poseidon and seems to have a name that means something like 'rain', from *libas*, 'anything that drops or trickles', 'spring'. This could be a propitious name for a country or land where water was precious. The actual origin of the name of Libya is uncertain. The Greeks regarded it (or a region so called) as one of the three parts of the world, the other two being Europe and Asia.

Lichas was the herald of Heracles. When he brought a tunic dipped in poison to his master, Heracles flung him from a cliff into the sea (traditionally off north-west Euboea) and Lichas' body became the rock that still bears his name. The actual meaning of his name, or that of the Lichadian Islands, is not clear.

Licymnius was the son of Electryon, king of Argos, and his slave-girl Midea. He married Amphitryon's daughter Perimede, who bore him Oeonus, Argeius and Melas. His name suggests 'sweet singer' (*ligymnios*), from *ligys*, 'sweet' and *hymnos*, 'hymn', 'song'. We are not told anything to support this, however, although there could be a lost myth of some kind.

Linda was one of the three Danaïds (with Cameira and Ialysa) who named the three chief cities of Rhodes. In effect they are the three Fates with different names, Linda's being somehow related to *linon*, 'linen' – perhaps 'linen binder', from *linon* and *deo*, 'to bind'. Of the three Fates she would thus be closest to Lachesis, who 'paid out' the thread of a person's life. The modern name Linda is not from this minor Greek goddess but probably from an Old German word *lindi*, meaning 'serpent'. (The creature, unexpectedly, was a symbol of wisdom, as well as being slender and graceful.) However, there is a modern Spanish word *linda* meaning 'pretty', which is much more straightforward and obvious.

Linus was a musician, the son either of Apollo and Psamathe, or of Amphimarus and Urania. The popular derivation of the name is from *ailinos*, 'mournful dirge' (said to originate from *ai Linon*, 'alas for Linus' or *ai lanu*, 'alas for us'). But *linon* is 'linen' (see **Linda**) and there could well be a connection with linen or flax, especially since Psamathe's name means 'sand'. In fact Pliny says that Linus was the result of the flax plant being sown in sandy soil!

Lotus-eaters were the fabulous people who ate the lotus plant and as a result wanted to stay in 'Lotusland' for ever. Odysseus landed here and had to drag his men away by force. The difficulty is that no one really seems sure what the lotus in the classical stories actually was, even whether it was a herb, a root or a tree. Herodotus and Pliny thought it was some kind of fruit; Eustathius (a twelfth-century classical scholar) thought it was a herb, like the lily; Polybius (a Greek historian of about 200 BC) thought it was a tree with fruit like myrtle berries tasting like dates but 'of a far better smell'. Today many naturalists think it may have been the jujube-tree (*Zizyphus lotus*). The actual Greek word for the plant, however (*lotos*), is of obscure origin, but perhaps derives from a Hebrew word. The Greek name for the Lotus-eaters was *Lotophagoi*.

Luna was the Roman equivalent of Selene, that is, the goddess of the moon. Her name is simply the Latin for 'moon'.

Lupercus was the Roman Pan, a pastoral god who protected flocks (especially from wolves). Attempts have been made to derive his name from *lupos arcentes*, 'warding off wolves', which seems more contrived than appropriate. His name is directly linked with the festival called the Lupercalia, held annually in Rome on 15 February in honour of Pan. It took place near the cave of Lupercus, the Lupercal, believed by some writers to be the place where the she-wolf suckled Romulus and Remus. The exact connection between Lupercus and wolves and this festival (to say nothing of Pan and Romulus and Remus) is involved and uncertain.

187

Linus and Iphicles. Linus is teaching the 'strong' Iphicles how to play a 'mournful dirge' (*ailinos*) on the harp. The lettering above Iphicles is the name of the artist, and translates as 'Pistoxenus potter'.

Lycaon was the son of Pelasgus and Meliboea (or Cyllene). He became king of Arcadia and was the father of Callisto. For sacrificing a child on his altar to Zeus he was turned into a wolf (*lycos*). *Lycaiüs* is a by-name of Zeus, but is of uncertain precise meaning since it can be regarded as 'wolf-slaying' (from *lycos*), 'Lycian', i.e. relating to Lycia, a coastal district in south-west Asia Minor, or 'bright one' (from *lyce*, 'light'). This by-name could lie behind the name of Lycaon.

Lycomedes was a king of Scyros. Thetis brought her young son Achilles to him and asked him to bring him up as a girl in order to avoid the Trojan War. Lycomedes' name means 'wolf cunning', from *lycos*, 'wolf' and *medea*, 'cunning', 'craft'. This would seem to apply to the king himself rather than to Thetis' ruse; he would certainly have needed cunning to carry through the disguise.

Lyctaea was a daughter of Hyacinthus, and with her sisters (Antheïs, Aegleïs and Orthaea) was sacrificed by the Athenians in order to banish a spate of earthquakes. 'Wolf' (*lycos*) seems to be the root of the first half of her name; perhaps it is a corruption of 'Lycothea', 'wolf goddess', from *lycos* and *thea*.

Lycurgus was the name of several Greek persons, both mythological and real. Among the former were the son of a son of Dryas and a son of Aleüs. The name can be taken to mean either 'wolf work' or 'work of light', with the first half *lycos*, 'wolf' or *lyce*, 'light', and the second *ergon*, 'work'. Both these are complimentary and 'good omen' names.

Lycus means 'wolf' (*lycos*). It was the name of a king (more precisely a regent) of Thebes who was the son of Chthonius and the husband of Dirce, and of his son.

Lynceus was the name of a son of Aegyptus. When Danaüs' daughters killed all his brothers, his bride, Hypermestra, helped him to escape. He became king of Argos and was succeeded to the throne by his son Abas. Another Lynceus was the inseparable brother of Idas, the son of Aphareus and Arene. The name means 'lynx-like', and in particular 'lynx-eyed', from *lynx*, *lyncos*, 'lynx'. The second Lynceus was reputed to have vision so sharp that he could see what was hidden in the earth. In the case of the first Lynceus, the name is apparently a propitious one. We are not told that he escaped because of good sight or even foresight.

Lysianassa was the daughter of Epaphus. There was also another woman of the name who was the daughter of Polybus (and possibly the wife of Talaüs). The name means 'lady (or queen) who releases', from *luo*, 'to loose', 'release' and *anassa*, 'queen', 'lady'. This must be simply a favourable name, although Talaüs' wife 'released' (bore) a number of children (at least five).

Lysippe was the daughter of Proëtus and Stheneboea. She was cured of her madness by Melampus and married him, bearing him Abas, Mantius and Antiphater. Her name means 'horse releaser', which could be taken to be a 'powerful' name (for one who has power over horses), or else a 'chaotic' name (for one who loses control). If the latter, this could be a reference to Lysippe's madness. The two halves of her name are *luo*, 'to release' and *hippos*, 'horse', 'mare'.

Macar (or Macareus) was the son of Aeolus. He committed incest with his sister Canace and subsequently killed himself. Another Macar was one of Odysseus' seamen. The name, a more or less stock epithet for a god, means 'happy', 'blessed' (*macar*). In the case of Aeolus' son, the propitiousness of the name clearly proved quite ineffective! (In modern times, the same name, with the same meaning, became well known as that of Archbishop Makarios, the Cypriot head of state who died in 1977. This was of course his religious name, his real or lay name being Mikhail Khristodolou Mouskos.)

Macaria was the virgin daughter of Heracles and Deïanira who sacrificed herself to win a victory for Iolaüs and the children of Heracles (the Heraclids) in Attica. As for Macar, the name means 'blessed'.

Machaerus cut down Neoptolemus with his sacrificial knife for insulting Apollo at Delphi by burning down his temple. (In fact Orestes was planning to kill Neoptolemus but Apollo prevented him, foreseeing that he must die by the hand of someone else.) The name is a purely descriptive one, since it means 'butcher', *mageiros* (or else, also appropriately, 'large knife', 'sabre', *machaira*).

Machaon was the son of Asclepius by Epione, and a brother of Podalirius. He married Anticlea. We mentioned *machaira*, 'knife' for Machaerus, and this interpretation could also be valid for Machaon, since he was traditionally a surgeon while his brother Podalirius was a 'GP' (a 'practitioner'). The father of both brothers was of course a god of healing. But his name could also mean 'warrior' on the same basis, if we regard the *machaira* not as a surgeon's knife but as a weapon. And his name still works out as 'warrior' if we derive it from *mache*, 'battle', 'fight' (compare names ending in this word, such as Andromache). According to some accounts it was he who healed Philoctetes' wound (see **Phimachus** and also **Podalirius**).

Macris was a daughter of Aristaeüs. She nursed the baby Dionysus in Euboea, where she had taken him from Thebes or some place further away than this. Hera punished her by driving her from Euboea, and Macris took refuge on the island of Drepane, the home of the Phaeacians. The base of her name seems to be *macros*, meaning 'long' in space or time, so either 'tall' or 'far off'. The latter would make sense for travels and banishment.

Maeander was a river (now the Menderes) and its god who was the father of Samia (who married Ancaeüs). The name means 'seeking a man', from *mao*, 'to desire', 'seek after' and *aner, andros*, 'man'. Behind the name lies the following story: Maeander had made a vow that he would sacrifice the first person to congratulate him on his storming of the Phrygian city of Pessinus. This turned out to be his son Archelaüs ('ruler of the people'). Maeander, as he had vowed, killed him but then leapt into the river in remorse. The 'sought man' thus was his own son. A very similar story is told in the Bible, where in Judges 11 Jephthah 'vowed a vow' that he would give Jehovah his daughter as a burnt offering if he was successful in war. He was, and after a two-month period during which his daughter 'bewailed her virginity upon the mountains', he 'did with her according to his vow which he had vowed'. The river name, ancient and modern, gives the English word 'meander': the Maeander had a tortuous course.

Maenads were women who followed Dionysus in a state of ecstatic frenzy. Their name means 'madwomen', from *mainas*, 'mad', 'raving', 'frantic'. Compare the English word 'mania'.

Magnes gave his name to the people of Magnesia. He was a son of Zeus and Thyia (or else Aeolus and Enarete, or even Argus and Perimele), and was the father by a Naiad of Polydectes and Dictys. Most probably, his name actually evolved out of the name Magnesia, which was a place rich in minerals and also gave its name to 'the Magnesian stone', otherwise the 'magnet'.

Maia was prominent as two characters, one Greek, the other Roman. The Greek Maia was the eldest of the Pleiades (the daughters of Atlas and Pleïone) who was the mother of Hermes by Zeus. The Roman Maia was an obscure goddess who gave her name, it is generally believed, to the month of May. The Greek Maia's name has a meaning which ranges from 'mother' and 'dame' to 'nurse' and 'midwife'.

Manes were the Roman spirits of the Underworld, and thus of the dead. The name appears to be a euphemistic one, like that of the Erinyes (which see), since it derives from the old Latin word *manus*, 'good'. The spirits were sometimes called *Di Manes*, 'good gods'.

Mante (or Manto) was a prophetess, the daughter of Teiresias. She advised the women of Thebes to placate Leto and her children when Niobe mocked her for having only two children (Apollo and Artemis) when she herself had fourteen (seven sons and seven daughters). Mante's name indicates her role, since it means 'prophetess' (*mantis*, 'prophet').

Marathon was the son of Epopeus, king of Sicyon. He founded the town of Marathon to escape from his father's poor government. The town itself, famous for giving its name to the great race called the 'marathon' (the first such run being that of the messenger who ran 26 miles from Marathon to Athens to bring news of victory in 490 BC), is said to be so called since it was overgrown with fennel, *marathron*.

Marathus was the leader of the Arcadian contingent of the army of the Dioscuri (Castor and Pollux) against Athens. According to some accounts, it was he, not Marathon, who gave his name to the city so called. We must look to 'fennel', *marathron*, again for this name. Robert Graves points out that fennel stalks were used ritually for carrying the sacred fire from the central hearth to private hearths at the end of every year.

Marmax was the first of the many suitors of Hippodamia. He and his mares were killed by Oenomaüs. His name would appear to derive from *marmaros*, 'marble' and *anax*, 'king', in its full form *Marmaranax*, 'the marble king'. This was in fact the name of the white statue round which chariots were raced in the Hippodrome, so was almost a 'horse scarer', or at any rate 'one who rules the horses'. Compare the name **Hippodamia**. For Marmax such an interpretation can be regarded as propitious.

192

Maro or Maron was the son of Euanthes, and he was a priest of Apollo at Ismarus in Thrace. He gave Odysseus a large store of strong wine, which Odysseus later used to make Polyphemus drunk. According to Robert Graves, *maris* means a 'liquid measure of three pints', and this could therefore be the origin of the name.

Marpessa was a daughter of Evenus. She was wooed by Apollo but actually abducted by Idas. If we take *marpto*, 'to grasp', 'catch' as the basis of her name, then this could refer to either Apollo's unsuccessful attempt to carry her off or Idas' successful one!

Mars was the great Roman god of war, the father of Romulus. The well-known name, like a number of other well-known names, is still of uncertain meaning, although it is known that an earlier form of it had been *Mavors*, and in some dialects *Mamers*. Among attempts to interpret the name have been the following: from Greek *marnamai*, 'to fight', 'do battle', a suitably belligerent name; from Latin *mas*, 'virility', a literally masculine or male name; from an old Latin root *mar-*, 'to shine', appropriate for a sun god. Perhaps the name may ultimately link up with a Sanskrit word *mṛṇắti* meaning 'striker', 'crusher'. We can be certain, at least, that he gave his name to the month of March (Latin *Martius mensis*). The earlier Greek name of Mars the planet was *Pyroeis*, 'fiery' (compare **Pyrrha** and **Pyrrhus**), doubtless for its blood-red colour (see Introduction, page 11). This later became Ares, the name of his Greek counterpart, and finally Mars.

Marsyas was a satyr from Phrygia. He challenged Apollo to a flute-playing contest, using a double flute that Athena had discarded. Both players were doing equally well until Apollo defied him to play the instrument upside down. This could be done on the lyre, but not the flute, and Marsyas lost. Apollo thereupon flayed him alive and hung him from a pine tree (an unnecessarily grim fate, one would have thought, for merely failing to make music). In view of the contest, an appropriate name for Marsyas might therefore be 'battler', from *marnamai*, 'to fight'.

Matuta was the name of two Roman goddesses, one being the goddess of the dawn, and the equivalent of Eos, and the other being the counterpart of Ino, that is, Leucothea. *Manus* is the old Latin word for *bonus*, 'good' (see **Manes**), and is close in meaning to *clarus*, 'clear', 'bright', 'fair'. Matuta was also known as *Clara Dea*, 'the bright goddess', and this is certainly the meaning of the name Leucothea. But the exact root of Matuta's own name has not been precisely established. Possibilities are *manus*, 'good', *mater*, 'mother' (she was often called Mater Matuta), *maturus*, 'mature', 'seasonable', or (fittingly for the goddess of the dawn) *matutinus*, 'of the early morning'.

Mecisteus was a warrior from Argos, the son of Talaüs. Taking a little liberty, we can make his name simply the propitious *megistos*, 'the greatest'.

Meda was the wife of Idomeneus. While her husband was away fighting in the Trojan War, Meda had intercourse with an ambitious Cretan, Leucus. Then, before the return of Idomeneus (who was king of Crete), Leucus killed Meda and her daughters, usurped the throne, and drove out Idomeneus upon his eventual return. Probably behind all this scheming and cruelty there lay *medea*, 'cunning', although Meda was the subject of it, not the instigator.

Medea was the daughter of Aeëtes, king of Colchis, and Eidyia. She was the priestess of the Underworld goddess, Hecate, and had the power to work miracles for good or evil (like her aunt Circe). Her name undoubtedly means 'cunning' (*medea*), and this interpretation accords well with that for her mother (see **Eidyia**).

Medon was the name of several people, including the respective sons of Codrus, the last king of Athens, and of Oïleus, king of Locris. There was also a Medon who was a herald loyal to Odysseus. The name means simply 'ruler' (*medon*), a fitting name for an heir to a throne or generally as a name of good omen.

Medus was a son of Medea by either Aegeus or Jason. His name echoes that of his mother, and so means 'cunning' (*medea*).

Medusa was the famous Gorgon slain by Perseus. She was loved by Poseidon and was pregnant by him when Perseus killed her. Her name is the feminine of *medeon* or *medon*, so therefore means 'ruler', 'queen' (*medeousa*). This is a different kind of name to those of the other Gorgons (Euryale, 'wide sea' and Stheno, 'strength') since it denotes a direct 'human' status or position. For this reason, and to align it with the more allusive epithets of the other Gorgons, we could consider deriving Medusa's name from *medea*, 'cunning'. 'Ruler', however, is the popular explanation of her name.

Megaera was one of the Furies, and her name means simply 'grudger', from *megairo*, 'to grudge', 'refuse', 'deny'.

Megapenthes is a name that means 'great sorrow', from *megas*, 'great' and *penthos*, 'grief'. It was the name of, among others, the son of Proëtus and Stheneboea, and the bastard son of Menelaüs and his slavegirl Pieris (or Tereïs). For Proëtus' son the name could be taken as referring to the sorrow occasioned to their father by the madness of Megapenthes' sisters.

Megara (not to be confused with Megaera) was the daughter of king Creon of Thebes who married Heracles. Her name means 'temple', 'shrine', from *megaron* (literally 'large room', from *megas*, 'large'). We are not told with which particular shrine she may have been connected. She was not, however, the founder of the city of the same name. This was either Car, a son of king Phoroneus of Argos, or else possibly Megarus, a son of Zeus. Megara's name was, however, also spelt as Megera, and this could alter the interpretation of her name (see **Megera**).

Megareus, like Megara, has a name that means 'shrine'. He was a son of Poseidon by Oenope (or else of Onchestus, Aegeus, Hippomenes or even Apollo). He was king of Onchestus in Boeotia, and went to Megara (significantly) to aid Nisus in his war against Minos, king of Crete. His name could be taken to refer to one of the shrines at Megara, where perhaps he may have prayed for victory. (He was in fact killed in battle.)

Megera is another version of the name of Megara (which see). Instead of 'shrine', with this spelling we can suggest the very attractive meaning 'passing lovely', from *megeratos* (in turn from *megas*, 'great' and *eratos*, 'lovely'). This could well be a suitable name for a queen, as she was, as well as for the wife of Heracles.

Melampus starts a run of 'black' names. He was a seer, the son of Amythaon and Idomene, and his name means 'black foot', from *melas*, 'black' and *pous*, *podos*, 'foot'. We can interpret this in three different ways, literally, allusively, or historically. As a literal meaning, the name refers to an incident that occurred when he had just been born: Idomene put her baby in the shade but by mistake left his feet exposed to the sun, where they duly acquired an impressive tan. Allusively, he could have been a 'son of darkness', an 'obscure one', this being a reference to his powers of prophecy. Historically, the stories about Melampus could have originated in Egypt, where in fact *Melampodes* was a nickname for the Egyptians (who paddled in the black mud of the Nile when sowing their crops!). The choice can confidently be left to the reader, since each interpretation is as valid, or invalid, as the others.

Melaneus was a ruler in Messenia. He was said to be a son of Apollo because of his skill at archery. This does not quite explain his name, however, which simply means 'black one', 'murky one' (to be understood metaphorically rather than literally).

Melanion was a son of Amphidamas and became famous for his defeat of Atalanta in the race and for thus winning her as his bride. He may have been the father of Parthenopaeüs by her. His name seems to be 'black' in some way, but in what precise sense is not clear.

Melanippe was the daughter of Aeolus and Hippe, and of course her name links directly with that of her mother ('mare'). Melanippe's name means 'black mare', from *melas*, 'black' and *hippos*, 'horse', 'mare'. This must be a propitious name if it is not somehow connected, as any 'animal' name could be, with a religious or magical cult of some kind.

Melanippus is a 'noble' propitious name and a number of men were so called, including the lover of Comaetho, the son of Astacus and the son of Theseus and Perigune who was a famous runner. The name means 'black horse', or put another way 'he of the black steed', from *melas* and *hippos* (like Melanippe). Notice that Theseus' son was a runner, as is a horse (of any colour).

Melantheus (or Melanthius) was a goat-herd in the service of Odysseus at Ithaca. Disloyally, he sided with the suitors of Penelope against his master. His name, unexpectedly exotically, seems to mean 'black blossoms', from *melas*, 'black' and *anthos*, 'flower'. The Greek word *melanthos*, however, also meant 'black-coloured' generally, so perhaps for Melantheus it simply indicates 'swarthy man'. This could be appropriate for a goat-herd leading a largely outdoor life. See also **Melantho**.

Melantho was the sister of Melantheus, and a maidservant of Penelope. She was as disloyal as her brother, and she was also the mistress of Eurymachus, the most favoured of Penelope's suitors. Her name, too, can be taken to mean 'dark-skinned'.

Melas was a son of Portheus, king of Calydon, with another Melas being one of the four sons of Phrixus and Chalciope. (There were still others of the name.) The 'black' element is there (*melas*), but without further precise indication or interpretation it is impossible to say in what sense.

Meleager was a prince of Calydon, the son of Oeneus and Althaea (or Ares and Althaea). The popular (and obvious) interpretation of his name is 'guinea-fowl', from *meleagroi*, 'guinea-hens', into which birds his sisters were turned after mourning him at his funeral. (There seems little doubt that, as with so many names, this incident was invented to account for his name which resembled that of the bird.) However, it was Meleager who killed the famous Calydonian Boar, and his name can therefore also be understood as 'one who intends to hunt', from *mello*, 'to intend', 'design' and *agra*, 'catching', 'hunting'. There is even a third possibility for his name, with Meleager being a 'land-lover', from *melo*, 'to care for', 'tend' and *agros*, 'field', 'land'.

Melia was a daughter of Oceanus and Argia who married Inachus. She was an ash-nymph, as her name indicates (*melia*, 'ash-tree'). See **Meliae**.

Meliae were the nymphs of ash-trees (*melia*, 'ash-tree'), born from the drops of blood that fell when Cronos castrated his father Uranus. The ash-tree has long been regarded in many countries as a magic or mystic one, with one of the best known being Yggdrasil, the world tree of Scandinavian mythology that with its roots and branches binds together heaven, earth and hell.

Meliboea was a daughter of Niobe. Her name means 'sweet-voiced', 'honey-toned', from *meliboas* (*meli*, 'honey' and *boe*, 'cry'). Pausanias, however, says that Meliboea was also called Chloris because she turned 'pale' (*chloros*) when she was frightened! (The basic meaning of *chloros* is 'pale green', with the general sense of 'pale'. See also **Chloris**.)

Melicertes was the son of Athamas and Ino, and judging by his name seems to have been a bee-keeper since he is literally a 'honey-cutter', from *meli*, 'honey' and *ceiro*, 'to cut'. Alternatively, he could be a preparer of mead, if we take his name as meaning 'honey power', from *meli* and *cratos*, 'strength', 'might'. It has often been suggested, however, that his name is actually a Greek form of Melkarth or Melquart, the Canaanite equivalent of Heracles and the city god of Tyre (whose own name is said to mean 'lord of the city'). Like his mother, Melicertes became a sea deity, and as Ino was renamed Leucothea, so he became Palaemon (see this name).

Melissa was the daughter of Melissus, king of Crete, and the sister of Amalthea. She is said to have been the first person to find a way of collecting honey, so is named from the Greek for 'bee' and also 'honey' itself, *melissa*. We are told that she fed the infant Zeus with honey. Her name can be compared with that of Deborah, her Hebrew equivalent, since this also means 'bee'. Both names (especially the latter) have become fashionable as modern girls' names.

Melos has a name that (as *melon*) can mean both 'apple' and 'sheep'. These two meanings are woven into the story that is told about him. He was a young man of Delos who went to Cyprus. There he married Pelia, a relative of king Cinyras. From this marriage was born a son, also named Melos. When Adonis, the son of king Cinyras and a close friend of Melos, was killed by a boar, Melos (the father) hanged himself in grief from a tree, which thereupon took the name *melos* and became an apple-tree. Aphrodite, pitying him, turned Melos into an apple and Pelia into a dove. Meanwhile young Melos the son founded the town of Melos and became the first man to weave wool into clothes. He did this so expertly that sheep took a new name – *melon*.

Melpomene was the Muse of tragedy. Her name means simply 'songstress', from *melpomai*, 'to sing'.

Memnon was the son of Tithonus and Eos, and he became king of Ethiopia. His name means 'resolute', from *meno*, 'to stay', 'remain', which was a common name of kings. Compare the intensified form of it, **Agamemnon**.

Menelaüs was the younger son of Atreus, king of Mycenae, and Aërope, and, even more importantly, the husband of Helen (of Troy), with whom he is always associated in cult and literature. He was one of the leaders of the Trojan War, and his name is thus usually interpreted as 'withstanding men', from *meno*, 'to remain', 'stand' and *laos*, 'people'. Looked at rather differently, however, his name could derive from *menos*, 'force', 'strength' and *laos*, so that he is 'might of the people'. Yet again, another sense of *meno* is 'to await', 'expect', so that he could be 'he who awaits the people'. In this latter case, the 'wait' could refer to the famous 'long stay' of the army before Troy, and in this interpretation – as

Helen regained. Menelaüs (with shield) brings Helen home again after the Trojan War. Aphrodite helps Helen off with her cloak. Old Priam, king of Troy, sits on the right. By the handle of the vase (right) is the name of its potter, Hieron.

well as the others – his name suitably matches that of his elder brother Agamemnon (which see). Helen bore Menelaüs a daughter, Hermione.

Menestheus was the son of Peteüs and the great-grandson of Erechtheus. As with Menelaüs, we have the problem of deciding whether to interpret the first element of his name as *meno*, 'to stay', 'abide', 'await' or *menos*, 'strength', 'might'. If we take the latter half of his name as deriving from *theios*, 'divine', then it would seem to make better sense to say 'divine strength' than 'divine abider', especially as his 'strength' can be understood to mean the force of fifty ships that he led to Troy from Athens.

Menodice was the nymph who bore Hylas to Theodamas, king of the Dryopes. Here again we have the '*meno* versus *menos*' decision to make (see **Menestheus**), but perhaps *menos*, 'strength' is the one to choose, with *dice* meaning 'right'. Her name thus translates as 'right of might'.

Menoeceus was the name of two related men: the father of Creon and Jocasta, and this same man's grandson (i.e. the son of Creon and Eurydice). With such a family link, we must surely interpret the name as 'strength of the house', from *menos*, 'strength' and *oicos*, 'house'.

Menoetes was a herdsman who looked after the cattle of Hades. He actually dared to challenge Heracles to a wrestling match. He lost, however, when his ribs were broken, and he was saved only by the pleas of Persephone. The ill-fated match (or ill-matched fate) seems to be reflected in his name, if we interpret it as 'defying fate', from *meno*, 'to abide', 'stand by' and *oitos*, 'fate', 'doom'.

Menoetius may well have a name that means exactly the same as that of Menoetes ('defying fate'), but we have greater options here, if only because there were several of the same name. The two best known were the Titan who was the son of Iapetus and Clymene, and the Menoetius who was the father of Patroclus and himself the son of Actor and Aegina. The giant Menoetius was killed by a lightning strike from Zeus 'because of his savage insolence and overbearing boldness', as Hesiod tells us in his *Theogony*. Although 'defying fate' could be suitable here, perhaps 'doomed strength' might be more apt in view of the giant's sudden loss of power. This would give his name an origin in *menos*, 'strength' and *oitos*, 'doom'. Thomas Keightley also suggests a possible derivation from *menein ton oiton* for the 'defying fate' interpretation, these words literally meaning 'to await death' and referring to man's mortality.

Mentor was the old nobleman in Ithaca appointed by Odysseus to bring up his son Telemachus. Although the English sense of 'mentor' would be perfectly appropriate for one appointed to rear and educate another, the name appears to derive more directly from *meno* with its several meanings such as 'to stay', 'abide', 'await', 'expect'. Perhaps *menetos* (formed from this) is the origin, this word meaning 'patient', 'longsuffering'. On the other hand, perhaps the *men-* root found in such words as *mnemon*, 'mindful' and *mnaomae*, 'to remember' (and Latin *monitor*) might be the origin, so that Mentor's name means something like 'adviser'. And *menos*, 'spirit' should also be considered. The modern English sense of 'mentor' to mean 'experienced and trusted adviser' came not so much directly from the Ithacan nobleman's name as from the French, since in the romance *Télémaque* by the seventeenth-century writer Fénelon the part played by Mentor (as a counsellor) is much more prominent than in the original Greek classical stories. Compare **Mnemon**.

Mercury hardly needs an introduction as the famous Roman messenger of the gods and god of trade. His name derives from Latin *merx*, 'merchandise', with *merces* meaning 'reward', 'pay' (both words are related to English 'market'). The Romans needed a god for the success of their business transactions and therefore in about 495 BC 'imported' the Greek god Hermes, who of course was also the messenger of the gods. (Mercury did not, however, represent all the attributes of Hermes; for example he was not regarded as a god of fertility.) In his *Remains Concerning Britain*, William Camden, writing in the early seventeenth century, considers the Latin form of the name (Mercurius) and seems to derive it from a whole phrase: ' "Quasi medius currens inter Deos & homines," as the Grammarians Etymologize it, a mediate cursitor between Gods and men.' In spite of the slight similarity between the names of Hermes and Mercury (they have three letters in common) there seems to be no direct linguistic link, and Mercury's name is certainly nothing to do with the Greek boundary stone called *herma*. As for the planet Mercury, its early Greek name was *Stilbon*, 'shining', 'glittering', 'sparking', it being so called since it always accompanied the sun and thus resembled a 'spark' that had flown off from a larger fire. Moreover Mercury was also seen as the 'fastest' of the planets, and the Roman god was well known for his speed, which was indicated by his wide-brimmed winged hat and winged

Mercury the messenger. Compare this picture with the one of Hermes on p. 156. In addition to his winged shoes, Mercury here holds the short sword that he lent to Perseus.

sandals in pictorial depictions of him. Compare the former popular name 'quicksilver' for the metal mercury. The metal itself was named after the god.

Meriones was the son of king Idomeneus' brother Molus. He was famous as the next best archer after Teucer, and won the archery contest at Patrocles' funeral games. Perhaps his name refers to his skill as a bowman, and thus derives from *merizo*, 'to divide', either for his 'dividing' of the target or for winning a share of the total prize.

Mermerus, whether the son of Jason and Medea or their grandson, has a name that means 'care-laden' from *mermera*, 'care', 'trouble'. Perhaps one or both of them foresaw a tragedy or a defeat. Jason's son was murdered by his mother, according to Apollodorus (according to Pausanias he was killed by a lioness). Either way, his life was doomed to a fateful end.

Merope was a popular name, being that of: one of the Pleiades and the wife of Sisyphus; a daughter of Oenopion; the wife of Polybus and foster-mother of Oedipus; the daughter of Cypselus and wife of Cresphontes; the daughter of Pandareüs. The name literally means 'sharing the voice', from *meiromai*, 'to share', and *ops*, 'voice'. This usually meant 'endowed with speech' and therefore 'human', 'mortal' (as distinct from a god), although it could simply mean 'eloquent'. For the first Merope mentioned here, the name can be best seen as meaning 'human', since the lady in question married the mortal Sisyphus, and was indeed the only one of the Pleiades to have an affair with a mortal.

Merops has the standard word for his name (*merops*) that means either 'human' or 'eloquent' (see **Merope**). This could have been a propitious or simply descriptive name for those who bore it, such as the king of Egypt who married the nymph Clymene or the seer who was the father of Adrastus and Amphius.

Mestor was a son of Perseus and Andromeda, and the father of Hippothoë by Lysidice. His name means 'counsellor' (*mestor*) from *medomai*, 'to advise'.

Metanira was the wife of Celeüs, king of Eleusis in Attica. If we take the first element of her name *Meta-* to mean 'in the midst of' (*meta*) we then have the problem of 'in the midst of what' or 'in the midst of whom'. Robert Graves, without any supporting evi-

203

dence, interprets her name as 'she who lives among maidens', from *meta*, 'among', *a*-, 'not' and *aner*, 'man' (i.e. 'among those who are without a husband').

Metapontus was a king of Icaria and the husband of Theano. His name means 'across the sea', with *meta* here having the implication of 'change of place' (as it often did in compound words) and *pontos* meaning 'sea'. This is a suitable name for the king of an island that lies to the east of mainland Greece across the Aegean Sea.

Metion was the son of Erechtheus and Praxithea. The name may be simply a favourable one, since *metis*, from which it apparently derives, means 'counsel', 'wisdom'. Metion was thus (or could become) a 'wise man'.

Metis was the first consort of Zeus, herself the daughter of Oceanus and Tethys. She was renowned for her wisdom, and this is indicated in her name, since *metis* means 'thought', 'counsel'.

Metope was a river nymph, the daughter of the river Ladon. She married the river god Asopus, and bore him Thebe. Her name can be interpreted in different ways, but perhaps we can consider 'forehead' as a suitably propitious name for someone who is or should be 'ahead'. The source of the name would thus be *metopon*, 'forehead', 'front', literally 'space between the eyes' (*meta*, 'between' and *ops*, 'eye'). A variant of this could be *metopedon*, 'with the forehead foremost', 'fronting' and so 'headlong', a good epithet for a river.

Midas is popularly famous for his unique ability (not such a blessing as it first seemed) to turn to gold everything he touched – 'the Midas touch'. He was actually the son of Gordius and Cybele, and according to William Smith 'a wealthy but effeminate king of Phrygia'. His name seems to have been the title of a number of rulers of Phrygia, and it may possibly derive from *mita*, 'seed' or be identified with Mita, king of the Moschians. These were an ancient people inhabiting the western part of Thrace and famous for their riches.

Midea was a Phrygian slavegirl who became the mother of Licymnius by Electryon. Her name, presumably just a propitious one, may derive from *medea*, 'cunning'. Compare **Medea**.

Miletus was a son of Apollo by one of his mistresses (usually said

204

to be Acacallis), and the founder of the town that bears his name. His name is difficult, and Robert Graves tentatively suggests a meaning 'red earth' (*miltos*), referring to the fact that Cretans had a complexion that was redder than that of the Greeks!

Minerva was the Roman equivalent of Athena, the goddess of the household arts. She was possibly of Etruscan origin, and the most usual, if cautious, interpretation of her name is 'mindful' from the *men-* root that gave Greek *mnemon*, 'remembering', Latin *memini*, 'to remember', and ultimately English 'mind'. For her by-names (and those of Athena) see Appendix IV, page 327. Compare also **Mnemon**.

Minos was the possessor of the famous Minotaur, the 'Minos bull' that was the offspring of his wife Pasiphaë. He himself was the son of Zeus and Europa. His name is of uncertain meaning, but appears to be a 'title' name, perhaps in the sense 'king', on the same lines as Pharaoh or Caesar. If we can relate it to any Greek word at all, the most likely candidate would be *men*, 'month', this in turn relating to the twelve-monthly (or nine-yearly) despatch to him of seven boys and seven girls to be devoured in the labyrinth by the Minotaur.

Minotaur was the familiar half-bull, half-man who was the offspring of Pasiphaë and a bull and who was kept by king Minos in a labyrinth at Knossos. The name is really a title, meaning 'Minos' bull' (*Minos* and *tauros*, 'bull'). It sometimes comes as something of a surprise to learn that the Minotaur actually had a name – Asterius or Asterion (which see). The Minotaur was slain by Perseus, of course.

Minthe (or Menthe) was a Naiad, the mistress of Hades. Her name means 'mint' (*calaminthe*): she was trampled on by Persephone and turned into this plant. The more you trample on mint or crush it, the sweeter it smells.

Minyas gave his name to the Minyans, the legendary Greek people who originated in Thessaly. He was the son of Poseidon (or possibly Aeolus or Chryses) and the father of Alcithoë, Leucippe, Arsippe and Clymene. His name can be related to a number of possible origins: Robert Graves sees him as being a 'moon-man', with his name deriving from *mene*, 'moon'. This would be for some religious or magical cult of the moon.

Mnemon was a servant of Achillles and was his official 'remem-brancer' or 'reminder'. Achilles had been warned by Thetis that if he ever killed a son of Apollo, he in turn would be killed by Apollo. Mnemon's job was to remind Achilles of this – and of nothing else. But Achilles did kill a son of Apollo, Tenes, who was hurling rocks at the Greek ships. Realising too late what he had done, Achilles killed Mnemon because he had failed to remind him of Thetis' words. (There must be a moral in this story some-where.) Mnemon's name simply means 'remembering' (*mnemon*). Compare **Mentor**, **Minerva**, and the English word 'mnemonic'.

Mnemosyne was a Titaness, the mother by Zeus of the Muses. Her name is the actual word for 'memory', and she was so named, as Liddell and Scott nicely put it, 'because before the invention of writing, *memory* was the Poet's chief gift'. By a rather devious and suspect route she became identified with the Roman goddess of money, Moneta, who actually developed out of a by-name of Juno. Perhaps the Romans found Moneta (meaning 'mint') a rather ordinary name, so wanted to give it a more exotic meaning. The specific link between the names was made by the rather obscure third-century BC Roman poet and playwright (of Greek origin) Livius Andronicus, who translated and imitated Greek originals. In the beginning of his version of the *Odyssey* he explains that 'Moneta was the ancient Latin translation of Mnemosyne . . . *nam diva Monetas filia docuit*' ('for the divine daughter of Memory [Moneta] instructed'). Thus the 'divine daughter' of Uranus be-came the Roman mother of the Muses! Moneta's name has also been assigned a derivation from the Latin *moneo*, 'to remind', 'ad-vise', 'solemnly point out', and Cicero tells a far-fetched story about a voice in an earthquake at Juno's temple 'advising' that a pregnant sow should be sacrificed.

Mnesimache was the daughter of Dexamenus, king of Olenus, whom Heracles rescued from being raped by the Centaur Eurytion. Perhaps this experience gave rise to her name, which means 're-membering the battle', from *mnesis*, 'memory' and *mache*, 'battle'.

Moirai was the Greek collective name of the Fates (called also *Parcae* by the Romans). According to Hesiod, they were the daugh-ters of Zeus and Themis, and were named as Clotho, Lachesis and Atropos. Their name works out as 'allotters', from *meiromai*, 'to have a share', a fitting sense for the Fates who portioned out a person's life. Homer usually wrote of one single Moira, seeing her as a personification of fate. (In his *Iliad* she is shown as spinning out the thread of a man's life at his birth.) Her name is not, however, the origin of the modern girl's name Moira: this is a version of an Irish name that is the equivalent of Mary.

Molione was the wife of Actor (or of Poseidon) and the mother of Eurytus and Cteatus, known together as the Moliones. Her name has been variously derived from *molos*, 'battle', 'war', *molo*, 'to come', *myle* (Latin *mola*), 'mill', and the magic herb given by Hermes to Odysseus as an 'antidote' to the charms of Circe called *moly*. So she is a 'warrior', a 'comer', a 'mill-worker' (or 'crusher') or 'queen of the moly'. Very likely her name is not actually Greek in origin at all. But see, however, **Moliones**.

Moliones, as mentioned (for Molione), was the joint name of Eurytus and Cteatus, the twin sons of Actor (or Poseidon) and Molione. We can make them a plural form of all four meanings suggested for their mother's name. If, though, we settle on 'comer' for Molione, and bear in mind that Actor's name means 'bringer' (see his name), then the two brothers could be symbolic in some way of foreign trade. Such, at any rate, is the suggestion made by Thomas Keightley.

Molorchus was a poor man who offered hospitality to Heracles at Cleonae. The great man accepted, and used his humble cottage as a *pied à terre* when enacting his First Labour (The Nemean Lion). Molorchus' name probably relates to his occupation as a labourer, that of a tree-planter, from *orchos*, 'row of trees' (compare English 'orchard').

Momus was the son of Nyx and the personification of grumbling or blaming: he was a constant critic of the dispensations of the gods. His name actually means 'blame', 'censure' (*momos*).

Moneta see **Mnemosyne**.

Mopsus was the name of two seers: the first was the son of Ampyx by the nymph Chloris, and the soothsayer of the Argonauts, the second was the son of Apollo and Manto who with his half-brother Amphilocus founded Mallos in Cilicia (they eventually quarrelled and killed each other). Their name is not easy to interpret; perhaps it is a distortion of some such word as *mochthos*, 'toil', 'hardship' or *moschos*, 'calf' (relating to some sacrificial rite). There is no standard Greek word starting *mop-* or *mops-*. However, *moschos* could also mean 'young animal' in general, and even 'boy', so this seems the most promising candidate.

Moros has a name that is the masculine of Moira (see **Moirai**). He is the personification of fate and according to Hesiod is the brother of Ker, Hypnos and Thanatos (see **Ker**).

Morpheus was the son of Hypnos. He was a dream-god who caused human shapes to appear to dreamers. In spite of popular associations with sleep itself ('safe in the arms of Morpheus' and so on) his name actually means 'form' (*morphe*), the reference being to the 'forms' or shapes seen in dreams. In a sense, therefore, he is really a 'transformer'.

Mulciber is a euphemistic name (or by-name) of Vulcan, used in the hope that he will not savagely ravage by fire but gently aid and caress. The name probably derives from Latin *mulceo*, 'to touch lightly', 'caress', and is used extensively by Ovid.

Munippus was the baby son of Thyometes and Cilla, the sister of Priam. He and his mother were put to death after a pronouncement by the seer Aesacus that any royal Trojan woman bearing a child on that day must be killed together with her offspring. His name means 'lonely horse', from *monos*, 'alone' and *hippos*, 'horse'. This is probably not intended in a wistful sense, but more as a name of good fortune – 'lone stallion' perhaps is a better version of it.

Musaeus is a somewhat vague character, possibly a son (or a teacher) of Orpheus. If his name means anything at all, it must mean 'of the Muses'.

Muses were the daughters of Zeus and the Titaness Mnemosyne. They were the famed goddesses of the fine arts, music (the English word derives from their name), literature and, later, a whole range of intellectual pursuits. Traditionally there were nine Muses, Hesiod naming them as Calliope, Clio, Euterpe, Terpsichore, Erato, Melpomene, Thalia, Polymnia and Urania (see each of these individually). Their collective name is probably linked with the *men-* root that gives Greek *mnesis*, 'memory' and English 're-minder' and 'mind' (and of course 'memory' itself), the argument being that in early times poets had no books to read from so relied on their memories (compare **Mnemosyne**, and so also **Mentor**, **Minerva** and **Mnemon**). Other possible derivations have been offered, however, including an obsolete verb *mao*, 'to inquire', 'invent' and *manthano*, 'to learn', 'to understand'. The name gave English (and other languages) not only 'music' but also 'museum', the former word originally relating to all the arts (including painting and poetry) and the latter being an establishment that began as a 'seat of the Muses'.

Mygdon was a Phrygian king, the father of Coroebus. He fought with Otreus and Priam against the Amazons and is said to have given his name to the Mygdonians, a Phrygian race. We can only guess at the meaning of his name. It resembles both *amygdale*, 'almond' (the English word comes from the Greek) and *amygmos*, 'tearing', 'mangling', but failing further evidence it would be useless to suggest any special connotation for the name.

Myles was king of Laconia credited with having invented the mill. With no great surprise, therefore, we find that the word for 'mill' is *myle* or *mylon*.

Myrmex was a nymph who claimed that she had invented the plough when actually Athena had. As a punishment for such impertinence she was changed into an ant (*myrmex*).

Myrmidons are best known as the soldiers whom Peleus' son, Achilles, led to Troy (their story is told in the *Iliad*, in which account Achilles himself is their leader and king). Their name is popularly explained as meaning 'ant-men', from *myrmex*, 'ant'. This is what Aeacus is said to have called the people who originally inhabited Aegina, for their ant-like thrift, patience and tenacity. However, the name is also said to have derived from either Myrmidon, the son of Zeus and Eurymedusa, who was deceived by Zeus disguised as an ant, or Myrmex (see this name) – in other words, the Myrmidons had either Myrmidon or Myrmex as their ancestor. The best-known account concerning the origin of the Myrmidons is given by Ovid in Book 7 of his *Metamorphoses* where, in a dream described by Aeacus, ants turn into men. 'I called them Myrmidons', says Aeacus, 'giving them a name that did not conceal their origin.' The word came to be used as a derisory or semi-facetious term in English for policemen, so called 'myrmidons of the law' (with reference to the soldiers, although perhaps the expression has been influenced by other words such as 'minion' or even 'myriad').

Myrrha (or **Smyrna**) was a daughter of king Cinyras and Cenchreïs (or Metharme). When she grew up, Myrrha became

209

infatuated with her father, who had intercourse with her thinking she was a girl of Myrrha's age who had fallen in love with him. When he discovered his partner's true identity, he tried to kill her. Myrrha, however, fled and eventually was turned by the gods into a myrrh tree, as which she gave birth to Adonis. Robert Graves points out that myrrh is a well-known aphrodisiac.

Myrtilus was a son of Hermes. He was the charioteer of Oenomaüs, king of Elis, and after betraying his master was thrown into the sea by Pelops. His name obviously seems to mean 'myrtle' (*myrtos*), although he was not metamorphosed into one, for example. Perhaps his name is a blend of *myron*, 'oil' and *tylos*, 'lump', 'knob', this having some phallic reference.

Naiads were water nymphs, their name coming from *nao*, 'to flow'. Compare the **Nereids** and **Nereus**.

Narcissus was the son of the river Cephissus and the nymph Liriope, a beautiful boy who, having repulsed the love of many men and women, fell in love with his own reflection in a pool on Mount Helicon and gradually wasted away and died, whereupon the gods turned him into the flower that bears his name. There has been some dispute as to whether the flower took its name from him or the other way round. Pliny wrote that the name of the flower derived 'not from the boy in the myth' but from *narce*, 'stupor', as it had the power of 'burdening the head'. The numbing power that the plant was alleged to have can be seen reflected in the English 'narcotic'. So perhaps the best interpretation of the name is 'benumbed', alluding both to the plant and its power and to the 'benumbed' state of the boy as he pined away. The *-issus* ending of his name (also seen in that of his father), like the element *-nth-* (in Hyacinthus, for example, another good-looker), indicates that the name is probably not Greek at all.

Naucrate heads a short run of 'ship' names. Hers means 'ship power', from *naus*, 'ship' and *cratos*, 'strength', 'might'. There may be a historic reference here to the passing of sea power from Crete to Greece after the defeat of Minos in Sicily: Naucrate was one of Minos' slaves (and the mother of Icarus).

Nauplius was the name of two men who are sometimes confused. The first was the son of Poseidon (god of the sea) and Amymone, and a noted early navigator. The second was the son of Clytoneüs and a descendant of Nauplius No. 1. Either way, the name means 'navigator', 'seafarer', from *naus*, 'ship' and *pleo*, 'to sail'. Compare **Pleiades**.

Nausicaä was the young daughter of Alcinoüs whom Odysseus found playing ball with her maids when he was shipwrecked on an island on his way back to Ithaca. Her name seems to mean either 'burner of ships' or 'having ships that burn' (i.e. metaphorically, ships that are superior and conquer), from *naus*, 'ship' and *caio*, 'to burn', 'set on fire'. (Her name is also a reminder that English 'nausea' literally means 'boat' sickness.) Significantly, Nausicaä's brother Clytoneüs (who was also the father of Nauplius) has a name that could mean 'famous ship', from *clytos*, 'famous' and *naus*. Samuel Butler, the famous author of *Erewhon* and *The Way of All Flesh*, made a detailed study of the *Odyssey* and claimed that it had been written by Nausicaä! See also **Castor**, however.

Nausinoüs and Nausitheus were the twin sons of Odysseus and either Circe or Calypso. Nausinoüs' name fittingly means 'cunning sailor', from *nautes*, 'sailor' and *noos* or *nous*, 'mind'.

Nausitheus (see also **Nausinoüs**) was the helmsman of Theseus' ship when he set sail for Crete to kill the Minotaur. (Some accounts, however, say Phereclus was the helmsman.) His name literally means 'sailor god', from *nautes*, 'sailor' and *theus* (Doric form of *theos*), 'god'. Perhaps, since Theseus was the son of Poseidon, the sea god, we should interpret the name more precisely as 'sailor in the service of the sea god'.

Nausithoüs was a king of the Phaeacians and the son of Poseidon and Periboea. He became the father of Alcinoüs and Rhexenor, and was the grandfather of Nausicaä. His name means 'eager sailor', from *nautes*, 'sailor' and *thouros*, 'leaping', 'eager', 'impetuous'.

Neaera was a nymph, the consort of Helios. Another Neaera was the daughter of Pereus, who became the wife of Aleüs and mother of Auge and Cepheus. Her name seems to mean simply 'young', 'youthful', perhaps in the sense 'the younger', from *nearos*, 'young', 'recent'. There were others of the name, and they cannot all have been 'the younger' in a family. Perhaps the name is merely a complimentary one, almost an affectionate one, such as 'Young 'Un', 'Kid'.

211

Neïs was a daughter of Aedon and Zethus and (possibly) the wife of Endymion. Her name suggests that she was a water-nymph (from *nao*, 'to flow', see **Naiads**), although we are not told so directly in the stories about her.

Neleus was a son of Poseidon and Tyro. He was the twin brother of Pelias and he married Chloris, who bore him twelve sons and one daughter, Pero. Although his name suggests 'pitiless', from *neles* (meaning this), it is very tempting in view of all the 'watery' associations in the family to equate his name with that of Nereus and derive it from *nao*, 'to flow'. The head of the family tree is Aeolus, whose winds are needed for ships. Aeolus's son was Salmoneus, whose name could mean 'seaman' (see his name). Salmoneus' daughter was Tyro (maybe 'wearer away' like the sea) who became the wife of Poseidon, god of the sea. On the other hand modern evidence of his name in the Linear B tablets suggests that Neleus is a shortened form of Mycenaean *Nehe-lawos*, meaning 'saving the people'. There was apparently a real Neleus whose father Codrus was a king of Athens and saved the city from attack by the Dorians.

Nemesis was the goddess daughter of Nyx who was, and still popularly is, the personification of retribution for evil. Her name almost certainly comes from *nemo*, 'to distribute': originally Nemesis was a goddess who dealt or distributed appropriate gifts to her worshippers. Later she became more abstract and her 'distribution' was of anger at anything unjust. Today, in such phrases as 'overtaken by Nemesis', she appears less specifically as a dealer out of retribution, but more generally as some kind of fate or unpleasant consequence that will come upon one if a condition is not fulfilled or a deadline not met. Her Roman equivalent is Fortuna.

Neoptolemus was the son of Achilles by Deïdamia. His name means 'young warrior', from *neos*, 'young' and *ptolemos*, Epic Greek for *polemos*, 'war'. (The latter word is the origin both of the name of the Ptolemies, the Greek kings of Egypt, and of English 'polemic'.) This was the name given to him by Phoenix, son of Amyntor, either because of his youth or, more likely, because he joined the army late in the war against Troy, i.e. most of the soldiers were old stagers, while he was a new recruit. His name before this was **Pyrrhus** (which see).

Nephalion was one of the sons of Minos (with Eurymedon,

Chryses and Philolaüs). All four were killed by Heracles when they murdered two of his crew (on his visit to the Amazons, when he put in at the island of Paros). His name seems to mean 'sober', 'abstemious', from *nephalios*, 'drinking no wine'. *Nephalia meiligmata*, literally 'wineless propitiations', were offerings of water, milk and honey made to the Eumenides. (The second word in the phrase is related to *meli*, 'honey' and therefore to the name **Melissa**, which see.)

Nephele was the first wife of Athamas, and the mother of Phrixus and Helle. Her name means 'cloud' (*nephele*) and it was also borne by a number of other heroines. Clouds played a fairly important role in mythology. Aristophanes wrote a play called *Clouds* (in Greek *Nephelai*) ridiculing Socrates. In this he gave them their own genealogy: they are the daughters of Oceanus (like all water gods and goddesses) and live either on the peaks of Olympus, or in the Hesperides, or in the distant sources of the river Nile.

Neptune, to modern ears, is the best-known sea god, actually the Roman equivalent of Poseidon. Familiar though his name is, its origin is really very uncertain. One first seeks to link it somehow with water or the sea, and indeed attempts have been made to connect it with Greek *nao*, 'to flow' and *naio*, 'to dwell' (i.e. in the sea), and Latin *nato*, 'to swim' and *nauta* (earlier *navita*), 'sailor'. It may perhaps derive from some word such as Avestic (Zend) *napta*, 'damp' that links up with modern 'naphtha' (which is after all found in the sea). Leonard Ashley suggests a connection with *nephele*, 'cloud' (see **Nephele**). There have even been attempts to associate the name with 'potent' and 'despot', since Neptune was an 'earth-shaker'. The name of the planet Neptune, however, is as well-documented as that of the sea god is vague. The planet was discovered in 1846 as the result of mathematical calculations by the French astronomer Urbain-Jean-Joseph Le Verrier, and he himself proposed the name in a letter to the German astronomer Johann Galle suggesting he should search for the planet. (Galle observed it five days later.) The choice was a good one: the genealogical line Jupiter-Saturn-Uranus used for the previous three planets could not be continued since Uranus had no father. It was therefore logical to return to the brothers of Jupiter (Zeus). Thus the name of the god of the sea became that of the eighth planet of the Solar System. For consideration of the same name for the planet Uranus, see this name.

Nereids were sea nymphs, the fifty (*sic*) daughters of Nereus and his wife Doris. Among the better known were Thetis, whom both Zeus and Poseidon wanted to marry, Amphitrite, the wife of Poseidon, and Galatea. Their collective name of course derives from that of their father, so that we can similarly call them 'the wet ones'.

Nereus was a sea god older than Poseidon, and the son of Pontus and Gaia. His name almost certainly derives from *nao*, 'to flow', so that he is 'the wet one' or 'the watery one'.

Nessus was a Centaur who carried Deïanira across the river Euenos and who for his attempt to rape her on the way was shot by Heracles with a poisoned arrow. (This, much later, and via a tortuous route involving Nessus' blood being smeared on to Heracles' tunic, caused Heracles' own death.) Nessus' name could perhaps derive from *neossos*, 'young bird', 'young animal', although the exact relevance of this is hard to see. Perhaps in view of his riverside abode and the fact that he carried travellers over the river we should look for an origin *nao*, 'to flow'. (It may be no coincidence that the German for 'wet' is *nass*.)

Nestor was the only son of king Nereus to survive Heracles' attack on Pylos. Rather than *nao*, 'to flow' as the origin for the name it would be better to consider the old element *nes-*, 'to save', 'bring back safely', with the 'agent' ending *-tor* (as in Mentor, Castor and Hector). His name will then mean 'he who brings back safely'.

Nicippe was the wife of Sthenelus, the son of Perseus and Andromeda, and she was the daughter of Pelops. To Sthenelus she bore Eurystheus, Alcyone and Medusa (not, of course, the Gorgon so named). Her name, as many 'horse' names, is a propitious one, in her case meaning 'conquering mare', from *nice*, 'victory' and *hippos*, 'horse', 'mare'.

Nicostrate was an Arcadian nymph, a daughter of the river Ladon. She bore Evander to Hermes (although already married to Echenus) and went with Evander to Italy where he became a powerful king. She subsequently became Carmenta (whom see). Her name is a nice straightforward propitious one, 'victorious army', from *nice*, 'victory' and *stratos*, 'army'.

Nicostratus has a name that means precisely the same as that of Nicostrate. He was a son of Menelaüs and either Helen or a slavegirl.

214

Nike was the goddess of victory, which is exactly what her name means. The *nice* element that forms her whole name often occurs in other names, such as Eunice ('good victory'), Nicholas and Nicodemus (both 'victory of the people'), Berenice ('bringer of victory') and the like.

Niobe was the daughter of the Lydian king Tantalus and Dione, with another Niobe being the first woman – the daughter of Phoroneus (who was the first man). Her name can be derived either from *neos*, 'young', so that she is really 'Neobe', or from *nipha* (Latin *nivis*), 'snow'. In the latter case the 'b' of her name equals the 'v' in Latin *nivis* or the *ph* in Greek *nipha*. As 'snowy', her name is complimentary (like that of Snow White who was a beautiful maiden – compare **Chione**).

Nisus was a king of Nisa, a city that later became known as Megara. He was the son of Pandion, king of Athens, and the father of Scylla. His name may mean 'emigrant', from *nisomai*, 'to go away'.

Nomia was a nymph who made Daphnis promise to be faithful to her or else he would be blinded. Her rival, Chimaera, seduced Daphnis when he was drunk, so Nomia carried out her terrible threat. The point of the name seems to be not in this, however, but in the fact that Daphnis had many herds of cattle, for *nomos* means 'pasture'.

Norax was the son of Hermes and Erythea. He led a colony to Sardinia and there founded Nora, the island's oldest city. As it stands, his name has no obvious meaning at all. Robert Graves suggests it may be a miswriting of 'Norops', meaning 'sun face', literally 'flashing', this being some kind of complimentary or belligerent name ('face too bright to look at').

Notus was the god of the south wind (or more precisely the south-west), and was said to be the brother of Boreas (the north wind) and Zephyrus (the west wind). His name may perhaps derive from *nao*, 'to flow', so that he is the 'wet' wind. (Greek winds approximate to British ones in character.)

Nycteus was a king of Thebes and the eldest son of Chthonius. He married Polyxo who bore him Antiope and Callisto. His name appears to mean 'of the night', from *nyx, nyctos*, 'night'. There seems to have been nothing noticeably 'black' or evil about his life,

215

although Antiope fled from her father when she became pregnant by Zeus and either his anger or his grief at her departure could be regarded as 'black'. (According to one account, his grief was so great that he died of a broken heart.)

Nyctimene was the daughter of Epopeus, king of Lesbos, and when she was raped by her father took refuge in a forest, where Athena, pitying her, turned her into an owl. Her name thus means 'night strength', from *nyx*, *nyctos*, 'night' and *menos*, 'might', 'strength'. The owl is a bird whose strength is the night.

Nyctimus also has a 'night' name. He was the son of Lycaon, king of Arcadia, and in fact the only one of his sons to survive Zeus' thunderbolts. But perhaps the 'blackness' of his name indicates that he met his death in some other 'dark' way. He succeeded his father as king and it was in his reign that the notorious flood sent by Zeus occurred (in which Deucalion and Pyrrha were the only mortals to survive as they had built an ark).

Nymphs were female spirits of a divine or semi-divine origin. They were usually daughters of Zeus and were thought of as residing in particular 'natural' habitats such as rivers, mountains, trees and the ocean. Traditionally they were imagined as young and beautiful women, and were frequently associated with individual gods such as Pan, Hermes, Apollo, Dionysus and Artemis. They also accompanied Satyrs and the Sileni. (Later they became more 'folksy' and took on the general nature of rather 'twee' fairies.) According to where they lived, they were divided into 'orders' such as Dryads, Hamadryads, Meliae, Oreads, Naiads, Nereïds, Oceanids and the like (see these names). Their general name, which is related to English 'nubile' and 'nuptial', is simply the word (*nymphe*) for 'bride', 'young marriageable woman'. This may possibly have originated from a verb *nybo*, 'to cover', 'veil'. The diminutive word 'nymphet' is not of classical origin – it was devised as recently as 1955 by the author Vladimir Nabokov for his novel *Lolita* to apply to sexually attractive young girls who 'to certain bewitched travellers . . . reveal their true nature which is not human, but nymphic (that is, demoniac)'.

Nyx was the goddess of the night – and that is what her name means (compare **Nycteus**, **Nyctimene** and **Nyctimus** above). She was one of the very first created beings, and was the daughter of Chaos and sister of Erebus.

Oceanids were sea nymphs – the three thousand (!) daughters of Oceanus and Tethys, and sisters of the river gods. One famous one was Styx; another was Doris who married Nereus and bore the Nereïds.

Oceanus has a name that of course means whatever 'ocean' means. He was a Titan and a god of the river called Ocean, which Homer described as winding its way in a circle round the edge of the earth. His parents were Uranus and Gaia. The popular derivation of the name is from *ocys*, 'quick', 'swift' and *nao*, 'to flow', with a possible linguistic link-up with Latin *aqua* and Celtic *uisge*, both meaning 'water'. The actual origin of the word 'ocean' may lie in Sanskrit *asayanas*, 'lying over against'. It may be only a coincidence, however, that the names of the Aegean Sea and Ogygia (Calypso's island) also somewhat resemble the name.

Ocypete was a Harpy who with another, Aellopus, plagued Phineus. Both beasts were chased off by Calaïs and Zelus, sons of Boreas. Her name, fittingly, means 'swift wing', from *ocys*, 'fast', 'swift' and *pteron*, 'wing'.

Odysseus is one of the most famous names in Greek mythology – and of course also in Roman mythology as Ulysses. He was king of Ithaca and a son of Laërtes and Anticlea. The traditional story behind his name is told in Homer's *Odyssey* as follows: Euryclea, the baby's nurse, placed Laërtes' son in the lap of Autolycus (the child's grandfather) and suggested he should think of a name for the boy as no one else could. Autolycus suggested Odysseus (from *odyssomai*, 'to be angry') as he himself had collected many enemies in the course of his life – or alternatively, because he himself hated so many men. (In fact in the *Odyssey* Odysseus is not shown in such an 'angry' light as in other non-Greek tales.) Naturally, there have been other attempts to explain his name. Some have suggested the root of his name to be *hodos*, 'way', 'road', since he was a great traveller. One of the more fantastic explanations using this as a base is the story that Anticlea bore him on Mount Neriton one day when she had been caught in a rainstorm and was cut off by flood water. Zeus therefore had 'rained on the road' (in the original *cata ten hodon hysen ho Zeus*), and in this Greek phrase can be picked out the name of Odysseus! (Linguistically, it is actually unlikely that *hodos* would become *odos*.) His name has not yet been traced in the Linear B tablets at Knossos. Perhaps it would be best to settle for a meaning such as 'trouble-maker' – which is incidentally supported by the fact that Odysseus is traditionally described as having red hair!

Oeagrus was a Thracian king, possibly the father of Orpheus and Linus. We have little to go on here, since we are told little about him, but perhaps his name could mean 'lone hunter', from *oios*, 'alone' and *agreus*, 'hunter'.

Oeax was a son of Nauplius by Clymene (or Hesione, or Philyra). Nauplius was an Argonaut (and also a slave-trader), so it seems reasonable to interpret Oeax' name in a nautical way as 'rudder', 'helm' (*oiax*).

Oebalus was a king of Sparta who was the son of Cynortas or his son Perieres and who married Gorgophone. She (or maybe Batia) bore him Tyndareüs, Hippocoön and Icarius. It is difficult to suggest an obvious meaning for his name. Robert Graves, game as ever, offers (admittedly tentatively) *oebalia*, 'speckled sheepskin' (from *ois*, 'sheep' and *balios*, 'spotted') or *oecobalus*, 'threshold of the house' (from *oicos*, 'house' and *balos*, Doric Greek for *belos*, 'threshold'). The latter seems more generally acceptable.

Oedipus was the infamous king of Thebes who murdered his father, married his mother (both these unwittingly, it is true), and then 'when he saw what he had done' put out his own eyes and retired to Colonus near Athens led by his daughter Antigone. The meaning of his name, however, does not (apparently) lie in this fearful catalogue but in his babyhood. An oracle had warned Laïus, the child's father, that any son his wife Jocasta bore him would kill him. When therefore it was indeed a son that Jocasta bore, Laïus took the baby, pierced its feet with a spike, and abandoned ('exposed') it on Mount Cithaeron. As a name, thus, Oedipus means 'swollen foot', from *oideo*, 'to swell' and *pous*, 'foot'. How exactly Laïus came to decide on this grim expedient is not clear: possibly he thought it would hasten the child's death. Another explanation is that he thought it would prevent its ghost from walking (but how?). The story of course did not end there, since the shepherd who had been ordered to abandon the child actually gave it to another shepherd who took it to his king, Polybus. He, having no children of his own, adopted the child and named him Oedipus. There may be some erotic or phallic sense behind the name, so that Oedipus is perhaps the 'son of a swelling' (compare a similar sense for the Dactyls). It may be, too, that such a torturous start to the child's life was in some way symbolic

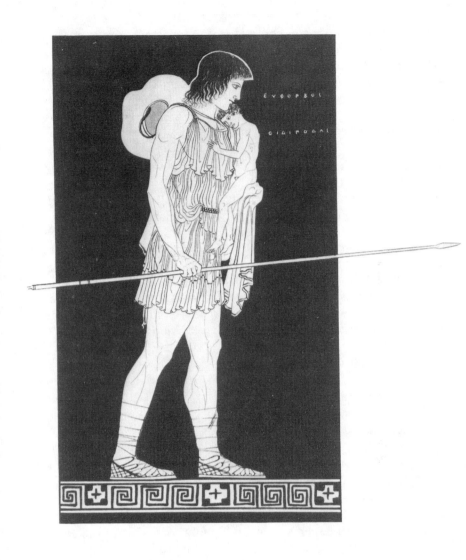

Baby Oedipus found by the shepherd. Oedipus does not appear to have a swollen foot as one might expect from his name. The shepherd is here aptly named Euphorbus, 'good pasture'.

of the terrible things to come. Oedipus became unjustly and unreasonably famous in the twentieth century for his association with the so-called 'Oedipus complex', whereby a boy child expresses a sexual desire for his mother (without being aware of it) and conversely a rejection of his father. (The opposite, a girl child's attraction for her father, is known as an Electra complex. Both terms were devised by Freud.)

Oeneus was a king of Calydon who was the son of Portheus and Euryte and the husband of Althaea. When Dionysus came to Calydon, Oeneus accommodatingly allowed him to sleep with Althaea, and the result of this union was Deïanira (who married Heracles). Dionysus repaid Oeneus his hospitality with the gift of viticulture, i.e. grape-growing, and according to some accounts even named wine (*oinos*) after him! Oeneus' name, therefore, cannot mean anything other than 'viny' (or 'winy'), and if we interpret his wife's name as 'full-flowing' (see **Eurytus**, the masculine form of it), we have a well-accorded couple. There is no doubt that the English word 'wine' is related to the Greek *oinos* (and Latin *vinum*), and 'oenophile' is a rather pretentious word for someone who is, or thinks he is, a connoisseur of wine.

Oeno was one of the three daughters of Anius by Dorippe. She promoted the growth of wine (*oinos*), just as her sisters Elaïs and Spermo promoted the growth of oil and grain (see their names).

Oenomaüs was the name of two noted characters. The first was a king of Pisa who killed all the suitors of his daughter, Hippodamia, until he was himself killed by Pelops. He was said to own an extensive fertile district of land where presumably there were vines, since his name seems to mean 'greedy with wine', from *oinos*, 'wine' and *margos*, 'raging mad', 'greedy', 'lustful'. The other character was a Trojan killed by Idomeneus. We have no evidence that he was 'lustful with wine' but that is what his name means.

Oenone was a nymph, the daughter of the river Cebren and the wife of Paris. Her name means 'wine lady', from *oinos*, and this can be taken to be a propitious name, indicating fullness, richness and gentleness, rather than drunkenness and wantonness.

Oenopion was a son of Dionysus and Ariadne. What other name could a son of Dionysus, the god of wine, have? It literally means 'wine face', from *oinos*, 'wine' and *ops*, 'face'. This can be taken as meaning 'liberal wine-drinker' or 'son of wine-man'. He winds up our short-list of 'winy' names.

Oeonus was a son of Licymnius, and a friend (and cousin) of Heracles. He was killed at Sparta by the sons of Hippocoön, and this may be reflected in his name which means 'omen', from *oiones*, 'solitary bird of prey' (from *oios*, 'alone'). The larger birds of prey, such as eagles and vultures, were observed for the omens they indicated. (They were thus distinguished from the 'ordinary' birds which were simply *ornithes*.)

Oïcles was an Arcadian seer and the father of Amphiaraüs. His powers of prophecy can be seen in his name, which means 'famous bird of omen', from *oiones* (see **Oeonus**) and *cleos*, 'fame'.

Oïleus was the son of Hodoedocus and Agrianome (a daughter of Poseidon) and a king of Locris. More importantly, perhaps, he was one of the Argonauts. His name seems to be a propitious one, and to derive from *ilaos* or *ileos*, 'gracious'.

Olus was the twin brother of Eurybatus, the two being the cheating, lying Cercopes who plagued Heracles (and constantly robbed him). The name may be a contraction of *olesypnos*, meaning 'sleep destroying' (from *ollymi*, 'to destroy' and *hypnos*, 'sleep'), on the lines of other 'destroying' words starting *oles-* such as *olesibolos*, 'earth-destroying' and *olesioicos*, 'house-destroying'.

Omphale was the daughter of Iardanus and the mother of Lamus. She was queen of Lydia, having married one of the country's early kings, Tmolus. When Heracles was sold into slavery she bought him and made him wear women's clothes. He carried out several valiant deeds for her, and she then married him. Her name means 'navel', *omphalos* (compare Latin *umbilicus* and English 'umbilical'). This may be a reference to a shrine that was somehow navel-shaped, or have the actual anatomical sense in view of the fact that for women, the navel was regarded as the seat of passion. Omphale thus had an 'umbilical' attachment to Heracles.

Oncus or Oncius was an Arcadian king and a son of Apollo. He is best known for his horse Arion, which he presented to Heracles. We are not told a great deal about him, and hardly enough to explain why his name seems to mean 'bend' or 'hook' (*oncos*). On the other hand, *oncos* could also mean 'bulk', 'weight', 'importance' (and conversely 'arrogance'), so perhaps he was either 'important' or 'conceited'.

Opheltes was a son of Lycurgus and Amphithea (or Eurydice). He was killed by a snake as a child and was posthumously renamed Archemoros (which name see for his story). We can consider two possible sources for his name. He was either 'helpful', from *ophello*, 'to help' or else he was 'crushed by a snake' (which we know he was), from *ophis*, 'snake' and *eilo*, 'to press tight', 'force together'. Either would suit him, the first possibly propitiously. (In fact 'helpful' is more an epithet than a real name, as indeed is his subsequent name, Archemoros.)

Ophion was a Titan and the husband of Eurynome. 'Snake' (*ophis*) seems to be the base of his name as well. Perhaps to make him sound more fearsome we could call him 'Serpent'. Eurynome was said to have had a shrine in Arcadia where she was depicted as a mermaid. This means that there was something of a scaly similarity between husband and wife.

Opis (or Upis) was a Hyperborean maiden who with Arge accompanied Leto, Apollo and Artemis to Delos. According to some accounts she was raped by Orion (who was then killed by Artemis for the affront). She may, however, have been a local goddess who came to be associated with Artemis, and this may account for her name meaning either 'reward' or 'punishment' (*opis*). Gods and goddesses reward or punish depending whether they are smiling or frowning on you.

Ops is the Roman equivalent to Rhea, so she is the goddess of plenty. Her name must be linked with *opes*, 'wealth', referring to the natural riches of the earth.

Orchamus was the father of Leucothea who 'ruled over Persia's cities', according to Ovid in his *Metamorphoses*. His name, thus, means 'ruler', from *orchamos*, 'first of a row', 'file-leader' (from *orchos*, 'row of trees').

Orchomenus was the name of two men who each gave his name to a Greek city. One was the son of Zeus and father of Minyas, whose city is in Boeotia; the other was the son of king Lycaon, with his city in Arcadia. (The latter Orchomenus was destroyed by Zeus in a flood.) His name literally means 'strength of the file', from *orchos*, 'line' (originally of trees), 'file' and *menos*, 'strength', 'might'. So we can interpret his name as 'strength of the battle-line'.

Orcus was a Roman name for Pluto or Hades. Marcus Verrius Flaccus, a first-century AD Roman scholar, maintained that Orcus' original name had been Uragus or even Urgus, and was thus derived from *urgeo*, 'to press', 'press forward', but this is hardly certain. Perhaps the name is somehow linked with 'ogre' (as Eric Partridge suggests in *Origins*) or the sea monster called an 'orc'.

Oreads were mountain nymphs. Their name simply derives from *oros*, 'mountain'.

Orestes was the son of Agamemnon and Clytemnestra who with his friend Pylades and the aid of Electra murdered his mother and her lover Aegisthus and thus avenged the murder of his father. His name appears to mean 'mountain dweller', from *oresteros*, 'mountainous' (from *oros*, 'mountain'). As a boy he grew up in Phocis which has high mountainous country around Delphi.

Orestheus was a king of Aetolia who was the son of Deucalion and an ancestor of Oeneus. Like Orestes, he is a 'mountain man' (from *oresteros*, 'mountainous'), not so much because he grew up on a mountain as for the fact that he was a hunter (and probably went coursing on the mountain with his bitch Sirius).

Orion was the great hunter. There are two main 'contenders' for his name and its origin. One is *ouros*, 'mountain' (the Ionic Greek form of *oros*), the other, bizarre though it may seem, is *ouron*, 'urine'. The 'mountain' origin could well be suitable for someone born in Boeotia, as Orion was – indeed it is a name that could apply to anyone from almost anywhere in Greece, which is a largely mountainous country. The 'urine' origin is, inevitably, much more specific. The story was that Hyrieus, a Boeotian king who had no children, was advised by Zeus that if he wished for a child he should urinate on a bullhide. He did so, and Hermes and Poseidon buried it. Nine months later, a boy was born from the hide. This was Orion. To support this account behind his name, Orion's name often featured in the form Urion. Yet a third explanation has been offered for the name, which derives it from *orino*, 'to be stirred', 'excite', with reference to his role as a hunter, or to the storms that he raised. The constellation of Orion was so named long ago, and certainly in Homer's time.

Orithyia or Oreithyia was an Attic princess, the daughter of
Erechtheus and Praxithea. She was abducted by Boreas (the north
wind) and carried to Thrace, where he forcibly married her. Her
name means 'mountain rusher', 'she who rages on the hills', from
oros, 'mountain' and *thyo*, 'to rush', 'storm', 'rage'. This suggests
that she was a priestess or at least a devotee of Bacchus, like her
aunts Procne and Philomela. It is also significant that the children
of Orithyia and Boreas had 'windy' (or 'rushing') names: Calaïs,
Chione and Zetes (see these names).

Orneus was the son of Erechtheus, king of Athens. His name
means 'bird', with *orneon* being the same as *ornis*. Precisely why,
we are not told. But see the name of his son, **Peteüs**.

Ornytion was the son of Sisyphus and father of Phocus. He was
perhaps not so much connected with birds (*ornis*, 'bird') as being
a 'rouser' or 'chaser', from *ornymi* or *ornyo*, 'to rouse', 'stir', 'cheer
on'. This could be a descriptive name or a wishful one.

Orpheus was the famous musician who was the son (or pupil) of
Apollo and the husband of Eurydice. Significantly, his mother was
Calliope, the Muse of epic poetry. There has been much discussion
regarding the origin of his name, often resulting in the verdict 'of
obscure origin'. The most common theory, however, is that his
name derives from *orphne*, 'darkness', 'night', since Orpheus was
connected with the darkness, both in his journey to the Underworld
and later when conducting his initiations by night. The English
word 'orphan' is related to Greek *orphne*, the common link being
the deprivation: darkness is deprived of light; an orphan is deprived
of his parents.

Orseïs was a nymph and the wife of Hellen, to whom she bore
Dorus, Aeolus and Xuthus. Her name appears to be based on
ornymi which has a wide range of meanings, from 'to rouse', 'stir'
to 'cause', 'excite', 'arise'. *Orso*, for example, means 'I will rouse'
(or any other of these meanings). It is difficult to be more precise
without some specific guideline.

Ortheia was one of the four daughters of Hyacinthus, all of whom
were sacrificed to Persephone. Her name is probably a commendatory one, meaning 'upright', 'straight', 'true' (*orthos*).

Orthus or Orthrus was a two-headed dog, the offspring of Typhon
and Echidna. It guarded Geryon's cattle and was killed by Hera-

cles. If we take the spelling *Orthus*, then we may have *orthos*, 'straight', 'true' as the meaning behind the name. If we prefer *Orthrus*, we may have *orthros*, 'dawn', 'early morning' as the root, with the general sense being 'early'. Both interpretations would suit a dog that looked after cattle, since it would have to be 'true' and work in the early morning. In his *Theogony*, Hesiod makes Orthus and Cerberus brothers.

Osiris was the husband of Isis, and the Egyptian god of the Underworld and the dead. In Greek mythology he was the son of Zeus and Niobe, and according to Plutarch he was murdered by his brother Typhon. The Greeks, too, linked him with Dionysus. His name appears to originate from the Egyptian city of Busiris that also gave the name of the king who in Greek mythology was regarded as the son of Poseidon and Lysianassa. Both Osiris and Busiris are names that have been popularly thought to mean, without much foundation, 'many-eyed'.

Otus and his twin Ephialtes were giants, the sons of Poseidon and Iphimedia (although actually called the Aloadae or 'sons of Alöeus' since he had been the husband of Iphimedia before she married Poseidon). Otus' name derives from *otheo*, 'to push', 'thrust', 'force back' (as in battle). This is a suitable name for a strong giant. (Ephialtes has a name with a similar meaning, which see.)

Oxylus was a son of Andraemon (or his son Haemon) and a king of Elis. His name may be a propitious one meaning 'sharp talker', from *oxys*, 'sharp', 'quick', and *laleo*, 'to talk'. (It could also, however, mean 'shrill talker' and even 'hasty talker'.)

Paeon (or Paean) was a physician of the gods, and subsequently one of the by-names of Apollo (see Appendix III, page 323). Homer mentions him as curing Hades when he was wounded by one of Heracles' arrows as he defended the entrance to the Underworld. His name has the same origin as that of Paeonius, that is, 'healer', from *paio*, 'to strike', 'drive away'. As a by-name of Apollo, Paeon (or Paean) was transferred to songs dedicated to him and to other gods, itself ultimately becoming the word for a battle, victory or festive song – a 'paean', in fact. The same name can also be seen in the peony (or paeony), a flower that used to be favourably regarded for its medicinal properties.

Paeonius was one of the Dactyls (together with Heracles,

225

Epimedes, Iasius and Acesidas). His name would appear to mean 'healer', from *paionios*, 'belonging to healing' (from *paio*, 'to strike'). If Dactyls are fingers, then this one has the healing touch.

Palaemon means 'wrestler', from *palaio*, 'to wrestle'. It was the name of several characters, including the son of Heracles and Autonoë (whose father certainly 'wrestled' with many a task), the son of Hephaestus (again for the exploits of his father), and (as a new name) Melicertes, son of Athamas and Ino, who aided sailors in distress. With regard to the first of these three, it should be remembered that Heracles was actually called Palaemon originally. As for Merlicertes, the new name was acquired at the same time as the conversion of his mother Ino to the sea-goddess Leucothea. It was given him by Sisyphus, who made the newly named Palaemon the protector god of the so-called Isthmic Games (those held on the isthmus of Corinth).

Palamedes was the son of Nauplius and Clymene. He was a gifted man, who was said to have invented draughts and dice games and even the letters of the Greek alphabet! Not surprisingly, his name reflects his cleverness, since it means 'ancient cunning', from *palai*, 'of old' and *medea*, 'cunning', 'skill'.

Palinurus was Aeneas' helmsman on his journey from Troy to Italy. His name seems to be a compound of *palin*, 'back', 'again' and *ouros*, 'fair wind', which is appropriate enough for one who has to steer a ship from A to B and back again.

Pallas is in fact two separate and distinguishable names. The first Pallas (genitive Pállantos) was a Titan, the son of Crius and Eurybia. The second Pallas (genitive Palládos) was the goddess Athena, for whom it was the best-known by-name (often used together with Athena, as Pallas Athena, but later used alone). The first Pallas (and various others of the name, including according to some accounts even the father of Athena) has a name that may mean simply 'young man' (*pallas*) or perhaps 'shaker', 'brandisher', from *pallo*, 'to wield', 'brandish'. Either meaning would be suitable for a giant. The second and more famous Pallas has a name that is variously explained. Some of the theories proposed are as follows. (1) That it was borrowed from the Titan Pallas as a 'powerful' name. (But, as mentioned, this is actually a different name.) (2) That it derives from the blow struck by Athena when she killed this Titan – or from some other blow (from *pallo*, 'to wield', 'brandish', 'leap', as for the Titan Pallas). (3) That it refers to the spear that she constantly flourished, and which she was brandishing even at the moment when she was 'born' by springing forth from the head of Zeus that Hephaestus had split open with an axe (*pallo* again). (4) That it refers to this actual blow by Hephaestus which enabled Athena to be born. (5) That it was taken in memory of a playmate of this name, a daughter of Triton, whom Athena accidentally killed as a girl. (6) That it simply means 'young maid' (*palla*), just as *pallas* can mean 'young man'. (Compare Latin *puella*, 'girl'.) Of all these possibilities, it is generally reckoned that the last explanation is the most likely. We also need to connect her name with the Palladium. This was a legendary statue of Pallas Athena, said to have been dropped down from heaven by Zeus to Dardanus, the founder of Troy, to ensure the city's protection. According to Virgil it was stolen by Diomedes and Odysseus, as a result of which the city was burned down. The London theatre called the Palladium seems to have been so named as the result of a misunderstanding: perhaps it was thought that the Palladium was not a statue but a type of theatre or circus like the Colosseum (which word may have confused the issue). The Colosseum, of course, was not even in Greece, but was the great amphitheatre at Rome, and far from mythological.

Pan was the god of pastures, famous for his pipes. He was the son of Hermes and Penelope (or Dryope), and his name has popularly long been regarded as meaning 'all' (*pan*). But all what, or all of what? Some writers have maintained that Penelope became the mother of Pan in the absence of Odysseus in the Trojan War, and that he was thus the offspring of *all* the suitors. Others say that he was so named since *all* the gods were pleased at his birth. Others again declare that he was a symbol of the universe, that is, of *all*. And a fourth group hold that his name embodies *all* sexual possibilities, since love conquered him and love conquers *all*, whoever they are. There is even a school that sees his anatomy as representing *all* aspects of nature, so that his horns are the sun and moon, for example, and his face the sky! But the truth is probably that in spite of the resemblance to the Greek for 'all' his name actually derives from the root *pa-* found in feeding and pasturing words such as Greek *pateomai*, 'to feed on', 'eat', Latin *pasco*, 'to feed', 'pasture', Latin *panis*, 'bread' and English 'pasture' itself (to which is even related 'feed'). He was thus 'Pan the Pasturer', 'Pan the Feeder'. Pan's name is also seen in the English 'panic': he may have been an apparently peaceful pastoral god but he had a nasty habit of suddenly startling unwary travellers, who therefore became panicky when they knew he was around.

227

Panacea was a daughter of Asclepius (as one might expect, with a name like that), her sisters being Iaso, Aegle and Hygea, among others. Her name means what English 'panacea' means, in other words 'all healer' (*pas*, neuter *pan*, 'all' and *acos*, 'cure', 'relief').

Pancratis was the daughter of Alöeus and Iphimedea. She and her mother were abducted by Thracian pirates to Naxos, where two of the pirate leaders killed each other in a duel over her. Her name means 'all strength', from *pas* (*pan*), 'all' and *cratos*, 'strength', 'might'. This was no doubt intended generally as a propitious name, but *she* was actually the winner of the trial of strength between the two men.

Pandareüs was a king of Miletus whose daughters (after his death) were carried off by the Harpies and turned over to the Furies. (One of the daughters was Aedon, who was changed into a nightingale.) Pandareüs' name appears to mean 'all-flayer', from *pas* (*pan*), 'all' and *dero*, 'to flay'. This is a 'strength-giving' name.

Pandarus (not to be confused with the above) was a son of king Lycaon of Zeleia in Lycia, and an ally of the Trojans. He disguised himself as Laodocus, a son of Antenor. Although not the same person as Pandareüs, his name has the same meaning – 'he who flays all'. He rather mysteriously features in later tales as the go-between acting on behalf of Troilus and Cressida, and became particularly prominent in this role in Shakespeare's *Troilus and Cressida*, where he says of the two lovers: 'If ever you prove false to one another, since I have taken such pains to bring you together, let all pitiful goers-between be called to the world's end after my name; call them all Pandars; let all constant men be Troiluses, all false women Cressids, and all brokers-between Pandars!' From this the word 'pander' (which should really be 'pand*a*r'), in the sense 'procurer', gained a firm place in the English language. (Its sense today has toned down considerably, so that as a verb it means little more than 'yield to', 'humour', as in 'pandering to the demands of a spoilt child'.)

Pandia was a daughter of Zeus and Selene. Her name, which reflects the attributes of her parents, means 'all-divine': *pan*, 'all', *dia*, 'godlike' (the feminine of *dios*, see **Pandion**).

Pandion was a son of Erichthonius and the Naiad Praxithea. He married his aunt Zeuxippe and she bore him Erechtheus and Butes as sons and Procne and Philomela as daughters. His name means 'all-divine', 'all-marvellous', from *pan*, 'all' and *dios*, 'godlike'. Thomas Keightley poetically suggests that this could be a reference to the sun in the spring when the swallow and nightingale (Procne and Philomela) appear. Another Pandion was the son of Cecrops and Metiadusa. He was the great-grandson of the first Pandion mentioned here.

Pandora was the first woman, made by Hephaestus and taken by Hermes to Epimetheus, who made the mistake of accepting her as his bride. Pandora brought with her a jar or casket (the famous 'Pandora's box') filled with all sorts of evils which she released, keeping only hope inside. Her name means thus 'all gifts' or 'all-giving', from *pan*, 'all' and *doron*, 'gift'. This can be interpreted in different ways: either she received a number of wicked traits from *all* the gods, or her 'box' contained not all evils but *all* good *gifts* for mankind (as some see it), or her casket contained *all* evils – although these are hardly gifts in the accepted sense. Of course, it could also be said that since she was the archetypal woman, and therefore endowed with perfect feminine attributes, the gods gave her *all gifts*, that is, good characteristics, not evil ones. Certainly Milton saw her name thus. In his *Paradise Lost* he compares Eve to her, saying she is

> More lovely than Pandora, whom the gods
> Endowed with all their gifts.

Allusively, too, her 'all-giving' could refer to the earth, from which she was made. There are in fact a number of parallels between Pandora and Eve (both, for a start, introduced evil into the world). There was also another Pandora. She was the daughter of Deucalion and the mother of Graecus by Zeus. Graecus was said to have been the ancestor of the Greeks. Pandora's name has found a small but steady demand as a rather chic modern girl's name.

Pandorus was the son of Erechtheus and Praxithea. His name, like Pandora's, means 'all-giving', in his case simply a propitious name.

Pandrosus was the daughter of Cecrops and Aglaurus. Her name means 'all-dewy' (*pan*, 'all' and *drosos*, 'dew'). Compare the name of her sister **Herse**.

Panopeus was the son of Phocus and the father of Aegle and Epeius. His name, presumably a 'powerful' one, means 'all-seeing', from *pan*, 'all' and *ops*, *opos*, 'eye'.

Panthoüs was the son of Othrys and father of Polydamas, Euphorbus and Hyperenor. He was also a priest of Apollo. His name means 'all-impetuous', from *pan*, 'all' and *thouros*, 'leaping', 'rushing', 'impetuous', 'eager'. This would be a favourable name rather than an unfavourable one.

Paris was a son of Priam, king of Troy, and Hecabe. His name is, of course, nothing to do with the French capital. It actually means 'wallet' (*pera*). As a baby, Paris had been abandoned or 'exposed' on Mount Ida. The shepherd Agelaüs, when checking to see if the child had died, found that it had been suckled by a she-bear. He therefore decided to take it to his farm, and he did so, carrying the baby there in a leather bag or wallet (in the original sense of the word). Homer called Paris **Alexander** (which name see).

Parnasus was the son of Poseidon who invented the art of augury. He is said to have given his name to Mount Parnassus (whose name is really probably pre-Greek). His name may perhaps mean 'scatterer' (of enemies), from *palyno*, 'to scatter'.

Parthenopaeüs was the son of Melanion and Atalanta (although his father could also have been Meleager, Ares or Talaüs). His name means 'virgin son', either for Atalanta's long-lasting virginity, or because she abandoned him on Mount Parthenium, or because she abandoned him to conceal the fact that she had lost her virginity. The elements of the name are *parthenon*, 'maid', 'virgin' and *pais*, 'child', 'son'.

Parthenope was the daughter of Stymphalus who bore a son, Everes, to Heracles. There was also a Siren of this name, which means, in a generally agreeable way, 'maiden face', from *parthenos*, 'maid', 'virgin' and *ops*, 'face'.

Pasiphaë married Minos and bore him many children. She succumbed, however, to her passion for a bull, and thanks to the ingenuity of Daedalus, who made her a hollow wooden cow, satisfied her desire and subsequently gave birth to the Minotaur. She herself was the daughter of Helios and Perse. Her name means 'all-shining', from *pas*, 'all' and *phaeno*, 'to shine'. 'She who shines for all' is a fine name, whether actually or propitiously, and it ties in well with the name of her father and her mother (perhaps) and her daughter Phaedra. See also **Phoenix**.

Passalus was one of the Cercopes (with his twin brother Acmon), both being the sons of Oceanus and Theia. His name clearly seems to mean 'peg' or else 'gag' (*passalos*). We know that Heracles tied both the dwarfish creatures to a pole and carried them off, head down, over his shoulder, and this could be the 'peg' reference, since *passalos* itself is based on the verb *pegnymi* meaning 'to fix in', 'to be fixed', 'to be impaled'. The 'gag' alternative seems harder to justify: Heracles certainly did not succeed in gagging the Cercopes, since even when suspended from his pole they made ribald jokes about his hairy posterior.

Patroclus was the son of Menoetius, king of the Locrians, and Sthenele, and a close friend of Achilles. His name means 'glory of the father', from *pater*, 'father' and *cleos*, 'fame', 'glory'. This is obviously a propitious name, although Robert Graves regards it as 'inappropriately patriarchal' and suggests that his actual name may have been Phoenix.

Pedasus was one of Achilles' horses (together with Balius and Xanthus). His name, a nice one for a horse, means 'bounder', from *pedao*, 'to spring', 'bound', 'leap'. He must not be confused with Pegasus.

Pedias was the wife of Cranaüs, the third mythological king of Athens. Her name means 'plain' (in the sense 'level tract of country'), and his means 'rocky' – a good basic blend for the royal couple.

Pegasus was the famous winged horse who sprang from the blood that flowed from Medusa's neck when Perseus killed her: Medusa was pregnant by Poseidon at the time, so Pegasus had Poseidon as its father. The popular origin of the name is *pege*, 'spring of water', and the origins of at least two springs in Greece were attributed to a stamp on the ground of the horse's hoof, the most famous being the Hippocrene or 'horse spring' (*hippos*, 'horse' and *crene*, 'well', 'spring') on Mount Helicon. Hesiod, in his *Theogony*, gives the other well-known 'spring' connection when he says that Pegasus was 'so named from the *pegai*, the springs of the Ocean' (i.e. Oceanus). On the other hand the horse's name may be derived in some sense from *pegnymi*, 'to make firm', 'fix', 'build', this possibly referring to the construction of a ship, in view of the name of his 'father'. Philologists point out, however, that the -*asos* ending of the name (*Pegasos*) shows that the real origin is pre-Greek.

Peirithoüs see **Pirithoüs**.

231

Pelagon was a king of Phocis who had rich herds of cows. One of these led Cadmus to the place where he was to found a city. This was Cadmeia, later to become Thebes in Boeotia (significantly 'Cowland', from *bous*, 'cow'). Pelagon's name immediately suggests 'sea' (*pelagos*), but it has also been understood as *pelogonos*, meaning 'born from clay' (*pelos*, 'clay', 'mud' and *gone*, 'offspring'). Both these are possibilities for one who lived in a 'sea' region (Phocis bordered the Gulf of Corinth to the west of Boeotia) and who was originally a 'bumpkin' herdsman, as Pelagon was before he became king.

Pelasgus gave his name to the Pelasgians, the aboriginal inhabitants of Greece. According to Aeschylus he was a king of Argos, possibly a son of Zeus and Niobe. His name is usually related to either *palaios*, 'ancient' or *pelagos*, 'sea'. Pelasgus would have been 'ancient' as the ancestor of the people who inhabited Greece before the Greeks; almost any Greek (or Pelasgian) could have regarded himself as someone whose life and destiny was never too far removed from the 'sea'.

Peleus was the son of Aeacus, king of Aegina, and Endeïs, and rather more importantly he was the father of Achilles. His name obviously suggests *pelos*, which means 'clay' (compare **Pelagon**). One story says that he had been covered in sepia-ink by Thetis, who had turned into a huge cuttle-fish when trying to escape his advances. In this state he would have been decidedly 'clayey' or 'muddy'. He was also the son of Endeïs, whose name (which see) could mean 'entangler', this being a synonym for a cuttle-fish. However, another explanation maintains that he was simply a 'man of Pelion', and it is true that his main adventures are centred round this mountain. Modern linguistic researches, on the other hand, suggest that his name may have originally been something like 'Teleus', and that thus he is 'from afar'. Compare **Telemachus**.

Pelias was the twin son, with Neleus, of Poseidon and Tyro. A story told by Apollodorus describes how as a baby he had been suckled by a horse that had trodden on his face and bruised it. This explains his name, from *pelios*, 'discoloured by a bruise', 'livid'. (Other accounts say a mare kicked him, but the result was the same.) For a name of similar origin, see **Pelops**.

Pelopia was a daughter of Thyestes and the mother by him of Aegisthus. Her name seems to mean 'dusky face', from *pelos*,

Peleus and Thetis. To win Thetis, Peleus had to capture her in a sea-cave and hold her or wrestle with her while she changed into different shapes and creatures. Here she has turned into a sea-serpent that grips Peleus by the leg.

'dark-coloured', 'dusky' and *ops*, 'face'. This could be descriptive rather than propitious. In any event it exactly echoes the name of her grandfather, Pelops.

Pelops was the son of the Lydian king Tantalus and Dione (or one of the Pleiades). The obvious interpretation of his name is the same as that of his grand-daughter (see **Pelopia**) – 'dark face'. Pelops is said to have emigrated from Lydia and to have given his name to the Peloponnese ('Pelops' Island'), the large southern peninsula (not actually an island) of Greece. Pelops had won a chariot race against Oenomaüs and as his prize was given Oenomaüs' daughter, Hippodamia, and this peninsula. There is no reason why Pelops, southerner or not, should not have been dark-faced, dark-eyed or dark-haired – or even all three.

Pelorus was one of the Sown Men of Thebes. His name (*peloros*) means 'monstrous', 'huge', 'giant', 'terrible'. This may be more a 'belligerent' name than a descriptive one.

Pemphredo was one of the Graiae. Her name means 'wasp' (*pemphredon*) which is a suitably unpleasant name for a spiteful and sinister old hag.

Penates were the Roman gods of the storeroom. In early Roman times the storeroom or pantry (*penus*) was at the centre of the house, and the Penates protected it. Their name thus comes from the word for 'pantry' which in turn is connected with the word for 'inside', *penes* (compare English 'penetrate').

Peneius was the god of the river Peneius in northern Thessaly, and the son of Oceanus and Tethys. The nymph Creüsa bore him Hypseus and three daughters: Cyrene, Daphne and Stilbe. His name comes from *pene*, 'thread', this referring to the windings or meanderings of the river.

Peneleüs was a Theban leader in the Trojan War. He was the son of Hipalcimus and Asterope, of whom nothing else is known. His name is difficult to interpret in terms of Greek words: the elements of his name appear to be *pene*, 'thread' (as for Peneius) and *leos*, 'people'. But it is not so easy to string these together and get a good sense. Perhaps the 'thread of people' were those on board the contingent of fifty ships that Peneleüs and Leïtus led to the Trojan War? Robert Graves sees the name as 'baneful lion' (*penthos*, 'sad' and *leon*, 'lion'), which sounds more like a cartoon character than a mythological hero.

Penelope, the famous and faithful wife of Odysseus, has a name that is still popular today. There are some agreeable stories to account for her name. One of the best known, and perhaps the most poignant, tells how Nauplius spread a false rumour that Odysseus had been killed in the Trojan War. Penelope, hearing this, tried to drown herself in the sea but was saved by some ducks. Her name therefore is a memorial to her rescuers, for *penelops* is a kind of duck. These birds sustained her and fed her – and she them. Another account derives her name from her weaving. For three years Penelope pretended to weave a shroud for her father-in-law, Laërtes, in order to keep her importunate suitors at bay. (She unravelled it at night, however, to spin out the work as long as possible. When the suitors discovered she was doing this, they forced her to finish it.) This explanation therefore sees her name as coming from *pene*, 'thread' (compare **Peneius**). Yet another origin has been offered in connection with her weaving, seeing her name as 'toiler', from *penomai*, 'to work', 'toil'. To what extent the duck and thread stories link up with totem birds and net clothes worn in orgies is not clear. Ducks were believed to have been regarded as protecting, kindly birds, and pictures of them have been found on old Greek vases, where they may represent benevolent goddesses. It may be no coincidence that in one story about Penelope she mated with Hermes and bore him Pan, whose name resembles her own. Perhaps her name was originally more like 'Panelopa', with altogether a different meaning? Another noteworthy fact is that although the modern Penelope (or Penny) owes her name to her, the Christian name itself was first used only in the sixteenth century. This may well have been due to William Camden's inclusion of it in his *Remains Concerning Britain*, published in its original form (in Latin, with the title *Britannia*) in 1586. Penelope acquired her name, he writes, 'for that she carefully loved and fed those birds with purpure necks, called Penelopes'.

Penthesilea was the legendary queen of the Amazons killed by Achilles, who did not triumph, however, but grieved over her. She was the daughter of Ares and the Amazon queen Otrere. The latter element of her name is not certain, but the first indeed suggests *penthos*, 'grief', 'sorrow'. Compare **Pentheus**.

Pentheus was the second (or possibly third) king of Thebes. He was the son of Echion and Cadmus' daughter, Agave. He came to

Penelope and Telemachus. Mother and son are waiting for the return of Odysseus. Telemachus seems at least eighteen years old, so they will not have long to wait. Note Penelope's weaving, as her name implies.

a fearful end. He was spotted hiding in a tree by Agave and her sisters, where he was trying to spy on the women in their bacchic (or dionysiac) revels. In their madness, the women assumed he was a wild beast, so pulled him down and tore him to pieces. This was the revenge of Dionysus on Pentheus, who had refused to honour Dionysus and had attempted to ban such revels. Since he was doomed to this fate at the hands of Dionysus, Pentheus can thus be regarded as a 'man of woe' and his name interpreted as 'grief' (*penthos*).

Penthilus was the illegitimate son of Orestes and Erigone, and he was the father of Echelas and Damasias. His name seems to mean 'assuager of grief', from *penthos*, 'grief' and *leios*, 'smooth', 'gentle'. It is not clear if this interpretation has a specific reference.

Perdix was a nephew of Daedalus, and like his uncle, a gifted man. He invented the saw, the chisel and the compasses. The story goes that Daedalus became jealous of his skills, so threw him down from the temple of Athena on the Acropolis at Athens. As he fell he was changed by Athena into a partridge, *perdix*. Robert Graves points out that this bird was a symbol of mating (from the dance of the cock before the hen) and that it was sacred to Aphrodite.

Pereus was a brother of Aleüs, who married his (Pereus') daughter, Neaera. He is best known for his attempt to get rid of his niece Auge, after she had been seduced by Heracles. But his name probably does not relate to her, even though it seems to mean 'slave dealer', from *perao*, 'to sell slaves'.

Pergamus was the youngest son of Neoptolemus and Andromache, and the founder of Pergamum. As a city founder, it is appropriate that his name should derive from *pergama*, 'citadel'. *Pergamos* was the specific name of the citadel of Troy.

Periboea is a 'rich' propitious name. It was that of the wife of Polybus (also called Merope), who was the foster mother of Oedipus, and also that of the daughter of Hipponoüs, who married Oeneus. It means 'surrounded by cattle', from *peri*, 'around' and *boes*, 'cattle'.

Periclymenus is a propitious name if ever there was one. It means 'very famous', 'heard of all round', from *peri*, 'round' and *clytos*, 'famous'. The name was that of a son of Poseidon who was a Theban champion in the war of the Seven Against Thebes, and also that of one of the twelve sons of Neleus, an Argonaut who had the power of changing his shape and who fought against Heracles. With regard to Poseidon's son, it is worth noting that one of the by-names of Poseidon himself was Clytos.

Perieres was a son of Aeolus and Enarete. He married Gorgophone and she bore him Aphareus and Leucippus. Another Perieres was the charioteer of Menoeceus. The first element of the name seems to mean 'round' (*peri*), but the question is 'round what?' or 'surrounded by what?'. Perhaps the second half of the name derives from *ercos*, 'entrenchment', 'bulwark'. 'Surrounded by bulwarks' is certainly a good 'protective' name.

Perigune, the daughter of Sinis and Sylea, was the mistress of Theseus, to whom she bore Melanippus. Her name, which is composed of the elements *peri*, 'round' and *gounos*, 'fruitful land', can be interpreted in two ways. Either it is a purely propitious name, bringing wealth and fruitfulness, or it refers to the episode where Perigune fled from Theseus, hid in the vegetable garden, and begged the plants there to rescue her. So either 'fruitful land all round' or 'round the vegetable garden'.

Perimede means 'very cunning', 'cunning all round', from *peri*, 'round' and *medea*, 'cunning', 'craft'. This propitious name was that of at least four mythological women, including the three respective daughters of Aeolus, Oeneus and Eurystheus, and the sister of Amphitryon.

Perimedes was a son of Eurystheus, and his name means exactly the same as that of his sister just mentioned (see last entry).

Periopis was a daughter of Pheres, king of Pherae. According to one account she was the mother of Patroclus by Menoetius. Her name means 'very rich', from *peri*, 'around' and *pion*, 'rich', 'wealthy'. This may have been a descriptive name or a 'wish fulfilment' one.

Periphetes was the son of Hephaestus (or Poseidon) and Anticlea. He had the habit of belabouring any travellers he met with an iron club, which distinctive feature earned him the nickname Corynetes ('club-wielder'). Eventually Theseus slew him and appropriated his club for his own use. Periphetes was also the name of other, fairly minor, characters, and it means 'notorious', from *peri*, 'around' and *phatis*, 'fame', 'report'.

Pero was the pretty daughter of Neleus, king of Pylus, and Chloris. She was much sought after by the young men of Messene, but the lucky man to win her was Bias, together with the aid of his brother Melampus. (Maybe Bias' name helped, too.) Her name appears to derive from either *pera*, 'wallet', 'bag' or *peros*, 'maimed', 'deficient'. There is no obvious connection between Pero and a wallet, at least not one that has come down to us. (Compare **Paris**, where there was a specific link with this word.) Nor is there a direct association between Pero and any kind of deficiency: in fact, just the reverse, since she attracted suitors in plenty and as a mother produced several children. There is an oblique reference that might be made here, however. This is that Iphicles had become impotent through being frightened as a child and he was later cured by Melampus – who was a rival for Pero in marriage! But perhaps such a tenuous connection is best disregarded and another source should be sought. This might be from *pero* or *peiro*, 'to penetrate', which in Pero's case, as mentioned, could well have a sexual significance.

Perse or Perseïs was the daughter of Oceanus and Tethys, and the mother of Perses by Helios. To judge by the next three names, including the famous Persephone and Perseus, Perse's name ought to mean 'destruction', from *pertho*, 'to destroy'. But we are given no reason for preferring this meaning, and perhaps it is best to say that she simply acquired the name from her son. The only other thing we can do is to link her name somehow with *phero*, 'to bear', 'bring', 'produce', 'gain'.

Persephone was the famous daughter of Zeus and Demeter who was carried off by Hades (alias Pluto) to live with him in the Underworld for a third of the year every year, returning to earth for the remaining eight months. She was the symbol of the rebirth of the crops in spring after their 'death' in the winter, and as such she featured centrally in many sacred rituals. During these she was not referred to by her name but was spoken of simply as Core ('maiden'). If we translate her name in Greek terms we get 'bringer of death', from *phero*, 'to bring' (see **Perse**) and *phone*, 'murder', 'slaughter', this referring to her attributes as queen of the dead in the Underworld. She is a contradictory character, however, bringing death in the winter and life in the spring, and for this reason her name has also been interpreted as deriving from *phero*, 'to bear' (i.e. bear fruit) and *phao* or *phaino*, 'to shine', 'show', so that she is a 'fruit-shower'. There have also been attempts to link the first part of her name with *pyr*, 'fire', as well as *phao*, 'to shine', as already mentioned. In this case, retaining the sense of *phone*, 'murder', she would be a 'light-destroyer', admittedly an apt name for the queen of the dark, dead Underworld, but a highly unlikely one in origin. Her name also existed in the forms Persephassa and Persephatta, the latter variant being derived by some from *pertho*, 'to destroy' and *ephapto*, 'to fix', so that she is a 'destruction-fixer'. Other spellings of her name included Pherephassa, Pherephatta and Phersephonia, for all of which similar etymologies have been proposed. The Romans knew her as Proserpine, which was probably simply a distorted pronunciation of one of the Greek forms of her name. Inevitably, they tried to read some meaning into the name, and popularly derived it from Latin *proserpo*, 'to creep forth' (with the latter part of this word related to 'serpents' which creep). This, they said, referred to a goddess who made the plants 'creep forth' in spring! The many forms of her name, together with the pre-Greek -*ss*- in some of them, suggest that she is a very old goddess and that she could even be a blend of more than one goddess. This would explain her ambivalent nature. Somewhat similar problems of interpretation arise over the name of **Perseus**, which see.

Perses was the name of several characters, among them the son of Helios by Perse (significantly), the eldest son of Perseus (again significantly) and Andromeda, who was said to have been the ancestor of the Persian kings and a son of the Titan Crius and Eurybia. The name is usually associated, either generally or specifically, with *pertho*, 'to destroy'.

Perseus was the famed and powerful son of Zeus and Danaë. He rescued Andromeda (who was chained naked to a rock) and married her, as well as enacting a number of other impressive feats, usually involving the slaying of an evil or important character, such as the Gorgon Medusa or the sea-monster that would have devoured the captive Andromeda. He also killed his grandfather Acrisius and his (Acrisius') twin brother Proëtus. His name is almost always regarded as deriving from *pertho*, 'to destroy' (the 's' is seen in the future of this verb: *perso*, 'I will destroy'). And undoubtedly, as mentioned, he certainly was a destroyer. However, as with Persephone, there is also scope for a 'light' or 'fruitful' interpretation (see her name for the roots), since there were times when Perseus was constructive rather than destructive. Nor should we overlook that Andromeda bore him a son Perses, among others. One association that never seems to be mentioned is that when

Perseus cut off Medusa's head he put it, and kept it, in a wallet, *pera* (see **Paris** and **Pero**).

Peteüs was the son of Orneus and the father of Menestheus. Bearing in mind the ornithological name of his father (which see) we may perhaps suggest an origin for him in *peteenos*, 'able to fly', 'winged'. Of young birds this meant 'fledged', which is even more appropriate for the son of Orneus. But there seems to be no other justification than this family connection for interpreting the two names in this birdlike way.

Phaea was the name of the so-called Crommyonian Sow, the offspring of Typhon and Echidna. It ravaged the town of Crommyon, on the isthmus of Corinth, until Theseus killed it. *Phaios* means 'grey', 'dusky', which could refer to its colour. On the other hand, Apollodorus tells us that the animal was actually owned by an old woman named Phaea. She in turn may have been so called since she was grey-haired. Either way, 'grey' suggests ghosts and the dead. It does not seem likely, as Robert Graves reads the name, that the origin is in *phaos*, 'light'.

Phaedra was the daughter of Minos and Pasiphaë and she became the wife of Theseus. Her propitious name means ·'bright', from *phaeno*, 'to shine'. Compare the name of her mother (and even *her* mother).

Phaënon was a beautiful boy created by Prometheus. When Prometheus had moulded a man out of clay, he usually presented him to Zeus for the great god's approval. Since Phaënon was outstandingly good-looking, however, he neglected to send Phaënon for the usual check (perhaps because he knew of the god's fondness for beautiful boys). Eros 'ratted' on this oversight, however, and Zeus promptly sent Hermes to fetch Phaënon. In the event Hermes managed to persuade Zeus that Phaënon would be better off as an 'immortal' and so carried him off to heaven where he became the planet Jupiter. Some say, however, that Jupiter was called Phaëthon, and that Phaënon became the planet Saturn (see the names of both these planets). At all events, as befits handsome boy and glowing planet, his name means 'shining', from *phaeno*, 'to shine'. The story is told by Hyginus in his *Poetica Astronomica*.

Phaestus was a Cretan, the son of the bronze man Talos. His name seems to mean 'made to shine', from *phaeno*, 'to shine' and *istemi*, 'to set', 'place'. This must be simply a wishful name.

Phaëthon or Phaëton was the name of several characters, including the sons of Helios and Eos (the latter Phaëthon was abducted as a boy by Aphrodite) and, rather unexpectedly, the leader of the herd of twelve bulls that belonged to Augeas (whose stables Heracles cleaned out for his Fifth Labour). For all these, and appropriately indeed for Helios' son, the name means 'shining', from *phaetho*, 'to shine'. Eos, as goddess of the dawn, was also, of course, the daughter of Helios, so in these relationships 'their shining names are told' quite clearly. Phaëthon was also a byname of the wretched Apsyrtus, who was so called since he 'outshone' all the other Colchian youths. Phaëthon the son of Helios came to grief while driving his father's chariot, and this incident produced the word ('phaeton') used in English for a type of open four-wheeled carriage.

Phaëthusa was the daughter of Helios who with her sister Lampetia guarded her father's cattle in Sicily. The name was also that of the daughter of Danaüs, who became the mother of Myrtilus by Hermes. The meaning of the name is 'bright being', from *phaetho*, 'to shine' and *ousia*, 'being'. For Helios' daughter this is clearly an appropriate name.

Phalerus was one of the Argonauts, the Athenian son of Alcon. The origin of his name appears to be *phalaros*, 'having a patch of white', 'white crested', the Ionic form of which was *phaleros*. This in turn derives from *phalos*, which was the word for a part of the helmet as worn by Homeric heroes – perhaps the metal ridge on the crown in which a plume was fixed. This could therefore allusively or propitiously be a 'power' name. The city and port of Phaerum was said to have been named after him.

Phanus was also an Argonaut. With his brothers Staphylus and Oenopion he was the son of Dionysus and Ariadne. His name appears to mean 'torch' (*phanos*), which does not accord with the 'winy' names of his brothers and his father. Perhaps it makes more sense to base the name less narrowly and to look for its origin in *phaino*, 'to show', 'display', 'be clear', 'shine forth'. This could relate to the colour or 'glow' of grapes or wine. It could also, of course, be merely a favourable name.

Phegeus was a king of Psophis in Arcadia, and the father of

Temenus, Axion and Arsinoë. The only Greek word closely resembling his name is *phegos*, 'esculent oak', i.e. one whose fruit could be eaten (compare **Aesculapius**). We do not have a specific reference to such a tree or fruit in the stories about him, but doubtless there could be a connection with some ritual or religious ceremony, perhaps on the lines of those associated in other western mythologies with the mistletoe (which also grows on oak trees).

Phemius was a minstrel in the household of Odysseus. His name is really just an ordinary 'good-omen' one, meaning 'famous', from *phemis*, 'speech', 'reputation'. Of course, he was certainly in famous company.

Pheres was a name borne by a number of characters, including the son of Cretheus, king of Iolcus, and Tyro, and the son of Jason and Medea. It must derive from the verb *phero* which has a number of meanings, the most general being 'to bear', 'carry'. Almost all senses of the verb are favourable, however, and have to do with producing and being generally progressive.

Philammon, because of its *phil-* element, can only have a favourable sense, as will those names below also starting thus. The element means 'to love' (*phileo*), and in the case of Philammon means 'lover of the race-track', with the second element being *ammos*, 'race-track'. (The better-known word for this course was *hippodromos*.) Philammon was a famous minstrel, the son of Apollo and Chione (and so the half-brother of Autolycus). The name simply implies that he enjoyed either watching horse races or participating in them. There are many twentieth-century Philammons who share his pleasure.

Philemon was the elderly husband of Baucis, the pair being a symbol of married bliss, a classical Darby and Joan. The affectionate base of the name is *philema*, 'kiss' (in turn from *phileo*, 'to love').

Philoctetes was the son of Poeas, king of the Malians, and Demonassa. He was a 'lover', too, and he greatly treasured a bow presented to him by Heracles. He was thus a 'possession-lover', from *phileo*, 'to love' and *ctetos*, 'something that can be gained', 'held as property', 'possessed'. There is a Philoctetes in almost all of us.

Philoetius was the faithful cowherd of Odysseus in Ithaca. His name means 'friendly fate', from *philia*, 'love', 'friendship' and *oitos*, 'fate'. Philoetius was constantly loyal to his master and joined Eumaeüs, the swineherd, in support of Odysseus' battle with the suitors on his return from Troy.

Philolaüs was one of the sons of Minos. He and his brothers were killed by Heracles when they murdered two members of his crew during their journey to the Amazons. His propitious name means 'loved by the people', from *phileo*, 'to love' and *laos*, 'people'.

Philomela was the daughter of Pandion, king of Athens. She is famous as the sister of Procne (whose name see). Her melodious name means 'sweet song', from *philos*, 'dear', 'loving', 'pleasing' and *melos*, 'song'. This is more than just a pleasantly propitious name, however. The basic story behind her is this: Pandion, at war over a border dispute with Labdacus, called Tereus to his aid. With his help, he won the war and gave his daughter Procne to Tereus as a bride. Procne in due course bore a son to Tereus, and this was Itys. After a while Procne wanted to see her sister again, and at her request Tereus went to Athens and persuaded Pandion to let him escort Philomela back to Procne, in Thrace. On the way, however, he raped her, and then cut out her tongue to prevent her telling anyone what had happened. She managed to communicate with Procne, however, and after further misadventures the two sisters fled together from an angry Tereus. As he was on the point of catching up with them, they prayed to the gods to change them into birds: Procne was changed into a nightingale and Philomela into a swallow. This latter bird was the appropriate one for Philomela, the gods decided, since she had lost her tongue and so could not speak or sing but merely chatter, like a swallow. And yet her name means 'sweet song'! This is because the story was told and repeated in several variations, until Roman authors, who probably preferred the sound of her name to that of Procne, told it the other way round: Procne was now the swallow and Philomela the nightingale, which of course sings sweetly. (The name can also be translated as 'song lover', which is also appropriate.) In the midst of all these metamorphoses another explanation for Philomela's name has been made. This is that it derives not from *melos*, 'song' but *mela*, 'flocks of sheep' (from *melon*, 'sheep'). Such a name, it is pointed out, is suitable for a swallow since it nests in byres and farm buildings. Whichever bird we prefer (and does it really matter in the end?), *philomela* was the standard Greek word for 'nightingale' together with *aedon* (see **Aedon**). In view of the popularity of the name in classical times, as well as its general attractiveness, it is a little surprising that it has never really caught on as a modern first name, even in Victorian times. Perhaps it needed a flesh-and-blood saint or martyr Philomela to give the name a boost.

Philonoë was the wife of Bellerophon, to whom she bore Isander, Hippolochus and Laodamia. She herself was the daughter of Iobates. Her name means 'loving thought', 'kindly mind', from *phileo*, 'to love' and *noos*, 'mind', 'thought'. This is a general but agreeable name.

Philyra is not, as might be thought, a 'loving' name, since it means 'lime-tree' (*philyra*). This daughter of Oceanus and Tethys was discovered on an island in the Black Sea one day by Cronos, and he coupled with her in the form of a stallion, so as to deceive his wife Rhea. Philyra later bore the offspring of this union and was horrified to see it was a monster with the body of a horse from the waist down. Deeply ashamed, she asked Zeus to change her into a lime or linden tree, and thus obtained her name.

Phimachus was a shepherd in the service of king Actor. He sheltered Philoctetes on the island of Lemnos and for ten years dressed his wound that he had received as the result of being bitten by a snake. Phimachus thus has a name that means 'pain muzzler', from *phimos*, 'muzzle' (as for a dog), 'nose-bag' (for a horse) and *achos*, 'pain', 'ache'. No doubt it was necessary to 'muzzle' the wound since the bite had festered and so gave off an unpleasant stench. (It was as a result of this that Agamemnon had ordered Philoctetes to be 'isolated' on Lemnos.) Philoctetes' wound was finally cured by either Machaon or Podalirius.

Phineïs was the girl who loved Enalus. She was thrown into the sea to appease Amphitrite, but was rescued by a dolphin, as Enalus was. Her name seems to be that of a kind of sea-bird, perhaps a type of vulture, the Greek for which is *phene*. Perhaps in the original story Enalus had been rescued by a dolphin and Phineïs by a sea-eagle or other big bird.

Phineus was the name of a brother of Cepheus, the uncle of Andromeda, and of the blind soothsayer of uncertain parentage who became the king of Salmydessus, in Thrace. Although the name is quite well known, and occurs both in the Bible and in literature, as well as being a historical name and a rarish modern first name, its origin is unclear. There are no words starting *phin-*

245

in Greek, so all we can do is to consider the same sea-bird as for Phineïs (which see) or some such origin as *phthino*, 'to decline', 'waste away'. But there is no evidence that either of the two characters mentioned here did that. Other derivations for the name in general that have been proposed are an Egyptian word meaning 'dark-complexioned' and a Hebrew word meaning 'mouth of brass' or 'oracle'. Harry Long derives the name from Hebrew *pi*, 'mouth' and *nahash*, 'hisser', so that Phineus is a 'snake-mouth' or tempter.

Phlegyas was the son of Ares who gave his name to the Phlegyans of Boeotia. He was the father of Ixion and Coronis. His name means 'fiery', from *phlego*, 'to burn', 'blaze up' and this is suitable for the son of the god of war!

Phlogius was also 'fiery', and we know that he aided Heracles in his battle with the Amazons. He was the brother of Autolycus (not the thief but the son of Deïmachus). The change of vowel in his name does not affect the meaning, since *phlox*, genitive *phlogos* means 'flame', 'blaze'. The flower phlox is so called for its 'flaming' colour – its name is an ancient one and can be traced back to Pliny (although this would not have been the flower as we know it today but some other plant).

Phobos was the son of Ares and Aphrodite and the brother of Deimos ('Fear'). His name means 'panic' and is the personification of the emotion felt in war. (Deimos as a name means more 'terror'; Phobos' name indicates rather the outward show of fear.) The two small satellites of the planet Mars (i.e. Ares) are named Deimos and Phobos. In mythology, the brothers were constant 'satellites' of their father and often drove the chariot into battle. (The planetary brothers were discovered and named as recently as 1877 by the American astronomer Asaph Hall. The choice of names could hardly be better.)

Phocus was the bastard son of Aeacus, king of Aegina, and the Nereïd Psamathe, who had turned into a seal (*phoce*). There were others of the name, including a son of Poseidon or Ornytion, both of whom, of course, had close links with the sea.

Phoebe was a popular name, being that of a Titaness, the daughter of Uranus and Gaia, of a daughter of Leucippus, and of a daughter of Tyndareüs and Leda, among others. It means 'bright', 'pure', 'radiant' (*phoibos*), which is obviously a good name to have. Note that the Titaness married her brother Coeüs, whose name could be interpreted as 'lucid' (see his name). Phoebe was also a by-name of Artemis in her capacity as goddess of the moon. In this respect see the name of Leucippus' other daughter, Hilaira.

Phoebus was one of the best-known by-names of Apollo. Like Phoebe (which see) it means 'bright', and it was often preferred to Apollo's 'standard' name. Apollo was not originally identified with the sun, although this name promoted his association with it. Some classical writers maintained that he came to be so called since his grandmother was named Phoebe (this is the Titaness Phoebe mentioned in the previous entry). In more recent times Phoebus has come to be simply a poetic name for the sun, without any hint of the name belonging to Apollo. No doubt Shakespeare started the trend, with his 'Hark! hark! the lark at heaven's gate sings, And Phoebus 'gins arise' (probably the best-known quotation from one of his least-known plays, *Cymbeline*). For more by-names of Apollo, see Appendix III, page 323.

Phoenix was the son of Agenor and Telephassa. He was also the brother of Cadmus, the father (some say) of Europa, and gave his name to the Phoenicians. Another Phoenix was the son of Amyntor, king of Ormenium, and Cleobule. The name means 'blood-red' (*phoinos*), and doubtless referred to the moon. Many of the names of the family of Minos relate to the moon or other heavenly bodies, or could be interpreted this way. Europa, for example, is 'broad face' and the daughter of Phoenix and Telephassa ('far-shining') as well as being the mother of Minos. Moreover she married Asterion ('starry'). Meanwhile the wife of Minos is Pasiphaë ('all-shining'), who herself is the daughter of Helios (the sun). In turn, Pasiphaë's daughter is Phaedra ('bright'). Neither Phoenix considered here is anything to do with *the* Phoenix, the fabulous bird of Arabian (or Egyptian) mythology that was said to set fire to itself and rise from the ashes every five hundred years. Tales of this bird were introduced to the Greeks by Herodotus. Its name also means 'blood-red', 'purple', either with reference to the colour of its plumage (or part of its plumage) or to the flames of the fire on which it perished. The tales and origins of the Phoenix are so complex that they deserve a book of their own.

Phoenodamas has a name that literally means 'blood-red tamer' from *phoinos* (as for Phoenix) and *damao*, 'to tame'. This means he was a 'subduer of slaughter'. His story involves Hesione. Poseidon had sent a sea monster to punish Laomedon, Hesione's father, for failing to pay his fees when the walls of Troy were built and when

Poseidon and Apollo tended his flocks. To appease the two gods, and as advised by an oracle, Laomedon tied Hesione to a rock as a sacrifice. However, he did not do so readily, and at first tried to force Phoenodamas to sacrifice one of *his* daughters, who had been kept safely at home. Phoenodamas made a careful speech saying that Laomedon was the one to blame. To decide the matter, they cast lots – and Laomedon lost. (Hesione was tied to the rock but was rescued by Heracles.) Later, Laomedon killed Phoenodamas and sold his three daughters to Sicilian merchants. Aphrodite, however, rescued them from this fate. The moral of this rather lengthy story about a minor character is that Phoenodamas chose to talk rather than to commit himself to a murderous act – in other words he was the 'dove' to Laomedon's 'hawk'. And although he lost his own life, neither Hesione nor his own daughters were sacrificed, as they might otherwise have been.

Pholus was a Centaur who lived on Mount Pholoë. He was accidentally killed by Heracles after an argument over the wine that he had provided for his eminent guest. His name perhaps derives from his home, *pholeos*, 'den', 'lair', or from such a place that he frequented or visited. Robert Graves thinks his name was originally 'Phobus' and that it therefore means 'fear' (like **Phobos**).

Phorbas was a Lapith, the son of Lapithes or his son Triopas. He is confused (or identified) with another Phorbas who was the father of Actor. A third Phorbas was a man from Panopeus in Boeotia who used to terrorise travellers by challenging them to box with him and then killing them. The name may derive from either *phorbas*, 'feeding', 'giving food' or (more suitably for the third one mentioned) *phobos*, 'fear'.

Phorcys was an ancient sea god, one of the original 'Old Men of the Sea'. He was the son of Pontus (or Nereus) and Gaia, and the father of a number of monsters by Ceto, including the Graiae, the Gorgons, Echidna, and so on. His name may well link up with the sea monster called an 'orc' (see **Orcus**) or else be a 'brutish' name related to Latin *porcus*, 'pig'. On the other hand his name could be associated with *phero*, 'to bear', 'carry', this being a reference to the motion or current of the sea. But this hardly seems unpleasant enough for one who fathered such a horrific clutch of monsters. (Among his other offspring, according to some writers, was Scylla.)

Phoroneus was the son of Inachus, the river god, and Melia (or else Argia). He was the founder of Argos, which he called Phoronea. According to Apollodorus he was the first man, while Pausanias describes him as building an elemental society and providing its members with fire, the products of the earth, and social institutions. With this background, we can propose a derivation for him from *phero*, 'to feed', with perhaps the latter half of his name being based on *onesis*, 'profit'.

Phosphorus was the personification of the morning star. He was the son of Astraeüs (or Cephalus) and Eos, and his name can be interpreted either as 'light bringer' (*phos*, 'light' and *phero*, 'to bring') or 'dawn-bringer' (*eos*, 'dawn', as for Eos, and *phero*). His Roman equivalent, whose name means exactly the same as the first of these, is Lucifer. The chemical substance took its name not from him but independently from the Greek adjective *phosphoros*, 'light-bearing'.

Phrasius was a seer of Cyprus who advised Busiris to sacrifice strangers so as to relieve a drought. His name means 'speaker', from *phrazo*, 'to tell', 'declare' (which word is related to English 'phrase'). This is of course a name that one would expect a great soothsayer to have.

Phrixus and Helle were the children of Athamas and Nephele. Phrixus travelled with Helle on a miraculous ram to Colchis, and although Helle fell off (into what became the Hellespont), he stayed on. When he reached his destination the ram asked him to sacrifice it. Phrixus did so and hung its golden fleece on an oak in the grove sacred to Ares. This was *the* Golden Fleece that became the object of the voyage of the Argonauts. Phrixus has a name that derives from *phrix*, 'bristling', in turn from *phrisso*, 'to bristle' (of hair or a mane). This could mean 'bristling with horror' but it seems much more logical to apply it to the Golden Fleece and see it as a 'ruffling' of the rich coat of the ram.

Phylacus was king of Phylace in Thessaly and a son of Deïon and Diomede. His wife was Clymene, who bore him Iphiclus and Alcimede, the mother of Jason. Phylacus was famous for his fine herds that Melampus tried to steal. It can therefore be appreciated that for him his name, meaning 'guardian', 'watcher' (*phylax*), was specially significant.

Phylas was the name of more than one character, including a king of the Thesprotians who seduced Pylas' daughter Astyoche (or

249

Astydamia), a king of the Dryopes of Mount Parnassus, and the father of Polymele (who may be the same as one or other of the first two here). Whoever he was, Phylas has a name that means 'guardian', as for Phylacus. This could be merely a generally descriptive name for a king or a desirable name for anyone.

Phyleus was the son of Augeas. He married Timandra, the daughter of Tyndareüs, who bore him Meges. His name means 'army leader', from *phyle*, 'division in the army', 'number'. He himself was a king, as his father was.

Phyllis was the daughter of Sithon or of Lycurgus, king of Thrace. According to whichever story one reads, she married either Acamas or Demophon. Whoever it was, when her husband sailed away and did not return to her by the time he had promised, she hanged herself in despair and was changed into an almond tree. This tree, says the Demophon version (as told by Apollodorus), had no leaves. When Phyllis had changed into the tree, Demophon returned to Thrace and hugged it, whereupon it sprouted leaves. From this incident, we are told, the Greek word for 'leaves', formerly *petala* (the plural of *petalon*, which is probably related to 'petal'), became *phyllas*. Hence her name. It was this Phyllis, via English Renaissance and later poets, that gave her name to modern Phyllises (who are less common now than they were fifty years ago).

Physcoa came from Elis, and she was the mother of Narcaeüs by Dionysus. Her decidedly unpropitious name appears to derive from *physce*, which means 'large intestine', 'black pudding', 'sausage', in other words the embodiment of an ancient Greek haggis. Still, her paunchy state could perhaps be blamed on the bibulous father of her child, whose own name (Narcaeüs) seems to come from *narce*, 'stiffness', 'numbness'. This again is hardly an agreeable name.

Phytalus was an Athenian who welcomed Demeter to his house and was given a fig tree by her. This gift lies behind his name, it seems, for *phyton* means 'plant', and thus Phytalus was a 'planter'. No doubt in time he had a whole orchard of fig trees.

Phytius was the son of Orestheus and according to one genealogy the father of Oeneus (whose father is more usually given as Portheus). As with Phytalus, his name means 'planter', from *phyton*, 'plant'. The story goes that Orestheus had a bitch Sirius (mentioned earlier in his entry, which see) who gave birth to a piece of wood. Orestheus buried it, and from it in due course there grew a fine vine. Because of this miracle, Orestheus named his son Phytius.

Picus was a son of Saturn and the father of Faunus. The sorceress Circe fell in love with him but he did not respond to her approaches. As a result she lured him to a forest and turned him into a woodpecker, Latin *picus*. In some stories he appears as a soothsayer who made use of a woodpecker in his predictions. The bird was in fact regarded as having powers of prophecy, no doubt for its ability to 'tap out' the future. It may be no coincidence that Circe's name means 'hawk'.

Pielus appears to have a purely descriptive name. It seems to mean 'plump' (*pion*, feminine *pieira*), although this could of course be seen as a 'good omen' name in the sense 'fat', 'rich', 'prosperous'. He was the son of Neoptolemus and Andromache, so was high-born enough to justify such a name anyway.

Pieris was a slave-girl from Aetolia, who though not married to Menelaüs bore him the twins Nicostratus and Megapenthes. As for Pielus, her name means 'rich', 'fat' (*pieira*), in a literal or metaphorical sense. This same word also meant 'juicy', which although strictly speaking applied to pine-wood could also, one would think, be used of a person.

Pimplea was a nymph loved by Daphnis. She was abducted by pirates and taken as a slavegirl to Phrygia, where Daphnis found her. Here, with the help of Heracles, Daphnis won a contest against the king, Lityerses, and as a result the king was killed and Daphnis took his place with Pimplea as his queen. (Some accounts tell the same story with the nymph's name being Thalia.) Pimplea to English ears sounds a mean name, but it is actually the opposite since it derives from *pimplemi*, 'to fill up', so that she is the 'filler-up', the 'satisfier'.

Pirithoüs (or Peirithoüs) was a king of the Lapiths and a close friend of Theseus. He was a son of Zeus by Ixion's wife Dia. The story went that when Zeus was attempting to rape Dia, he ran round her in the guise of a horse. His offspring was thus named for this incident, from *peritheio*, 'to run round' (*peri*, 'round' and *theo* or *theio*, 'to run'), as if his name was really 'Peritheüs'.

Pittheus was a son of Pelops and Hippodamia who founded a city

251

that he named for his brother, Troezen. He is said to have taught the art of oratory, and even to have written a book on it. This prompts one to derive his name from *peitho*, 'to persuade'. Supporters of the ritualist school, however, prefer the origin 'pine god', from *pitys*, 'pine' and *theos*, 'god'.

Pitys was a chaste nymph chased by Pan. She escaped, as many Greek maidens did such a fate, by changing into a pine tree (*pitys*). A nice touch to the story says that Pan took a branch of this tree and wore it as a necklace. (Two thousand years later he would have kept a lock of her hair in a locket.) For a similar story, in which Pan also gave chase, see **Syrinx**.

Pleiades means 'daughters of Pleïone', and was the collective name for the seven sisters born to Atlas and this daughter of Oceanus. The seven daughters were: Maia (mother of Hermes by Zeus), Electra (mother of Dardanus and Iasion by Zeus), Taÿgete (mother of Lacedaemon by Zeus), Celaeno (mother of Lycus by Poseidon), Alcyone (mother of Hyrieus, Hyperenor and Aethusa by Poseidon), Sterope (mother of Oenomaüs by Ares) and Merope (who bore Glaucus to Sisyphus, the only mortal husband of the seven). These seven names are today the names of the seven stars visible to the naked eye in the star cluster called the Pleiades. (Many people can make out only six stars of the seven, and extra keen sight is needed to be able to spot the seventh, Sterope. See her name in this respect.) There are two rival derivations for the name. The first takes it from *peleia*, 'pigeon', 'dove', so that the seven are a flock of pigeons. Zeus, it seems, set the seven sisters in the sky as seven pigeons to save them from the lust of Orion. (This story overlooks the fact that Orion went too, and today the constellation that bears his name can still be seen 'chasing' the Pleiades across the sky!) A variant of this, with no reference to pigeons, is that the sisters were so distressed at the death of the Hyades, who according to one story were also the daughters of Atlas and Pleïone, that they killed themselves. Zeus therefore transformed them into stars. The second theory derives their name from *pleo*, 'to sail'. This is because the seven stars 'rise' in the spring which marked the start of the sailing season for the ancient Greeks. Other explanations for the name say that it comes from the phrase *to pleion*, and so means 'the full ones', since the stars are visible at a time when the earth is 'full' of crops, or that the origin is in *to polein*, 'the turners' (*poleo*, 'to go about' or *pelo*, 'to be in motion', as English 'pole'), since they 'turn' in the sky or in time. There is also the completely unimaginative explanation, of course, that the seven get their name from their mother! As an astronomical name, Sterope is today known in the form Asterope for the faintest star in the cluster.

Pleïone was the daughter of Oceanus and Tethys, and the mother of the seven daughters known as the Pleiades (see entry above). Her name can mean any of the root words proposed for the Pleiades, so that she can be a 'sailor', a 'dove', a 'full one' or a 'turner'. All of these are suitable in their way. From the astronomical point of view it is worth pointing out that when the telescope had been invented, and the Pleiades were found to number far more than seven, the names of Pleïone and her husband Atlas were assigned to two more stars in the cluster. This was thanks to the observations made in the seventeenth century by the Italian astronomer Giovanni Riccioli, and he it was who added the names of mother and father to those of their offspring.

Pleisthenes was either the son of Pelops or the son of Pelops' son Atreus, and he was the husband of either Aërope or Cleolla. His name is a propitious one, meaning either 'greater strength' or 'sailing strength', from *plein*, 'more' or 'sailing' and *sthenos*, 'strength'.

Plexippus was the son of Thestius, with another of the name being the son of Phineus, king of Salmydessus. The name suggests a richly caparisoned or decorated horse, from *pleco*, 'to plait', 'weave' (as in English 'complex' and 'duplicate') and *hippos*, 'horse'. This suggests a 'power' name or a royal one.

Pluto was the notorious god of the Underworld. His name derives from *ploutos*, 'wealth', with Liddell and Scott explaining, 'because corn, the wealth of early times, was sent from beneath the earth as his gift'. However, there are other 'gifts' to be found below the ground apart from corn, and Pluto's wealth must surely have also included the precious metals that even in classical times were mined from below the earth. A more modern school of mythologists suggests that the god's name, like that of the Eumenides, was a euphemistic one for Hades, and that it was borrowed from Plutus (whom see). The planet Pluto was discovered and named quite recently. The American astronomer Percival Lowell, who died in 1916, deduced that it must exist, and it was actually first discovered by another American astronomer, Clyde Tombaugh, in 1930. Several names were suggested for the newly found planet, with Pluto finally chosen by 11-year-old Venetia Burney of Oxford, England.

It is a most suitable name, since Pluto was the brother of Poseidon (Neptune) and Zeus (Jupiter), and these two planets were already present in the line of planets that now numbered nine. Furthermore, Pluto is a fitting name for the planet that is the farthest from the sun and so in an 'eternal night' like that of the Underworld. Finally, there is a nice tribute in the name to the astronomer who calculated its existence, since the first two letters of Pluto are also the initials of Percival Lowell! One wonders if the little girl who proposed the name was aware of all these happy parallels and coincidences. The Romans borrowed the name from the Greeks both in its untranslated form and also as Dives ('riches') which was contracted to Dis (see this name). (There was also in fact a Titaness named Pluto who became the mother of Tantalus. Her name has the propitious 'riches' sense as well.)

Plutus was the son of Demeter and Iasion. Demeter, of course, was the corn goddess, and Plutus therefore has a name (*ploutos*, 'riches') that symbolises the wealth of the harvest. Many mythologists maintain that Pluto derived his name from Plutus.

Podalirius was the son of Asclepius and Epione, and a brother of Machaon. Like his father, he had medical skills, and according to some accounts it was he, not Machaon, who finally healed Philoctetes' wound (see **Phimachus** for details of this). His name is rather difficult. It seems to be composed of *pous, podos*, 'foot' and *leirion*, 'lily', which makes him something like 'lily-footed'. Perhaps this refers to the healing properties of the plant, so that Podalirius took his medical skills with him as he walked, or used medicines or drugs derived from the lily in his work.

Podarces was the younger son of Iphiclus, and it was also the original name of Priam, the youngest son of Laomedon. Hesiod tells us that Iphiclus' son could run so quickly over cornfields that he did not even bend a stalk and that the boy was so named by his father for his fleetness of foot (*podoces*, 'swift-footed'). However, this ignores the 'r' in the name, which gives it an apparent meaning of 'bear-foot', from *pos, podos* and *arctos*, 'bear'. This could be a 'power' name for one who will crush his enemies under foot. We are told in the *Iliad* that Podarces, the son of Iphiclus, took command of a fleet of forty ships in the Trojan War. Priam's original name could have had either of these senses.

Podarge was a Harpy who was raped by Zephyrus (the west wind). The result of this union were the two horses, Balius and

Xanthus, who were Poseidon's wedding gift to Peleus and Thetis. Podarge's name means either 'bright foot' or 'swift foot', from *pous, podos*, 'foot' and *argos*, 'bright', 'swift' (see **Argus** for the connection between these two senses). This is of course a suitable name for a fast-moving creature, even though she moved by her wings, not her feet, but perhaps the 'swiftness' refers to the snatching carried out by means of her talons.

Podargus was one of the four savage horses of Diomedes that had to be captured by Heracles in his Eighth Labour (The Mares of Diomedes). The horse's name means 'bright foot' or 'swift foot', like that of the Harpy Podarge. Indeed, the name may have been borrowed from her. The other three horses in this team were Lampon, Xanthus and Deinus. By what cannot be a mere coincidence, the horse named Xanthus that Poseidon gave to Peleus was the offspring of Podarge, together with its twin Balius.

Poeas was the son of Thaumacus who married Demonassa. She bore him Philoctetes. We know that Poeas was a king and that he had fine herds of sheep, and this doubtless explains his name as something like 'owner of pastures', from *poia* or *poa*, 'grass'.

Poene was a Harpy sent by Apollo to the city of Argos as a punishment for a double murder – of Linus, the baby son of Apollo and Psamathe, and then of Psamathe herself. Her name expresses her fate, since *poine* means 'ransom', 'vengeance' and so 'punishment'.

Poliporthis was the young son of Odysseus and Penelope. He was born while Odysseus was away, so his father saw him for the first time only on his return. What Odysseus had been engaged in, of course, was the war against the Trojans, and this had involved the sacking of a number of cities. Poliporthis, thus, has a name that commemorates this, since it means 'sacker of cities', from *polis*, 'city' and *porthesis*, 'sacking' (from *portheo*, 'to destroy', 'ravage').

Polites is one of the more ordinary names in classical mythology, since it simply means 'citizen' (*polites*, compare English 'politics'). So named were the son of Priam and Hecabe, and a comrade of Odysseus.

Pollux is the Latin version of the Greek name, **Polydeuces** (which see), of the twin brother of Castor, both of them the brothers of

255

Helen and Clytemnestra. Jointly the twins were known to both the Greeks and the Romans as the **Dioscuri** (which name also see).

Polybus begins a longish run of 'Poly' names, in which this first element means 'many' (*polys*). There were two kings of note named Polybus. One was the king of Corinth who was married to Merope and who adopted Oedipus. The other reigned over Sicyon and was a son of Hermes and Chthonophyle. The name is a 'power' or royal one, meaning 'many oxen', the second element being *bous*, 'ox'.

Polycaon was the first king of Messenia who married Messene. His name means either 'killer of many' or 'much burning', from *polys*, 'many', 'much' and either *caino*, 'to kill' or *caio*, 'to burn'. Both are 'power' names, fitting for a king.

Polycaste was the daughter of Nestor and Anaxibia who married Telemachus. The second element of her name is not immediately translatable – 'many of what?' or 'much what?'. Perhaps we can consider, as for Castor and Epicaste, the origin *cosmeo*, 'to adorn'. She will then be 'much adorned'. This seems a reasonable name for a princess, since she was the daughter of a king, after all.

Polydectes was a king of Seriphos, the son of Magnes and a Naiad. He it was who sent Perseus to fetch Medusa's head. He seems to have been a hospitable man, at any rate in some accounts, since his name means 'receiving many', from *polys*, 'many' and *dectes*, 'receiver'. The second element of his name may be related to that of his brother, Dictys, especially since the latter's name means 'netter', i.e. a kind of 'receiver'.

Polydeuces, better known to many by his Roman name of Pollux, was the twin brother of Castor. His name appears to mean 'much sweetness', from *polys*, 'much' and *deucos*, 'sweet'. The latter word was a variant of *gleucos*, which meant 'sweet new wine' (what the Romans called *mustum*, in English, 'must'). The concept as a whole could relate to some religious or other festival when much new wine was drunk. However, in considering the name of Castor we mentioned an interpretation 'light' for him. If we then see him as representing the day in some way, it seems logical that Polydeuces, his twin, could symbolise the night. To get such a sense, we can derive the latter half of Polydeuces' name not from *deucos* but from *deuo*, 'to wet', 'soak', this referring to the dew of the night. (This is perhaps not to go quite so far as the nineteenth-century German philologist Friedrich Welcker, who made Castor the same as 'Aster', 'star', and Polydeuces the same as 'Polyleuces', 'much light', in other words Castor was the sun and Polydeuces the moon!)

Polydora has a nice straightforward propitious name, meaning 'many gifts' or 'much-gifted', from *polys*, 'many' and *dorea*, 'gift'. She was the daughter of Peleus and Antigone who first bore Menestheus to the river Spercheius, then married Borus.

Polydorus means exactly the same as Polydora (above). There were two notable characters so called. One was a king of Thebes who was said to be the only son of Cadmus and Harmonia. The other was the youngest son of king Priam. (His mother, according to the *Iliad*, was Laothoë, the daughter of king Altes.) This is an obvious and actual royal name. The 'many gifts' of the Theban king seem to have been literary, since he was the son of Cadmus who had introduced the letters of the Greek alphabet from Phoenicia. Moreover he was nicknamed Pinacus, meaning 'writing-tablet man' (*pinax*, *pinacos*, 'notice board' and its diminutive *pinacion*, 'writing tablet'). His son was Labdacus, whose name see for more on the letters of the alphabet.

Polygonus, with Telegonus, was a son of Proteus. The pair rashly challenged Heracles to a wrestling match in which they were killed. Polygonus' name means 'having many children', from *polys*, 'many' and *gonos*, 'child' (as for Antigone). This must have been a propitious name, since we are not told of Polygonus having any children (or even of his marrying), and Proteus was not known to have been a prolific father.

Polyidus (or Polyeidus) was an Argive seer whose advice helped Bellerophon to tame Pegasus. He also foresaw the death of Minos' son Glaucus who was drowned in a jar of honey (see **Glaucus**). His name means 'many shapes', from *polys*, 'many' and *eidos*, 'something seen', 'form', 'shape'. This is an appropriate name for a seer.

Polymede was the daughter of Autolycus and the mother of Jason. Her name means 'much cunning', from *polys*, 'many' and *medea*, 'schemes', 'cunning'. No doubt she inherited her wiles from her father. Some tales equate her deeds with those of Alcimede.

Polymele was the mistress of Hermes, to whom she bore Eudorus. Her mellifluous name means 'many songs', from *polys*, 'many' and *melos*, 'song'. She must have been a happy soul. She was married to Echecles ('fame possessor', from *echo*, 'to have', 'possess' and *cleos*, 'fame').

Polymnestor (or Polymestor) was king of the Bistones (a Thracian people). He murdered Polydorus, Priam's son, to whose eldest sister, Ilione, he was married. His name could mean 'many suitors' or 'mindful of many things', from *polys*, 'many' and *mnester*, 'suitor' or 'mindful'. 'Many suitors' hardly seems appropriate, so 'mindful of many things' is the better sense for him. No doubt one of the things of which he was all too mindful was that he could win a vast sum of money and the hand of Agamemnon's daughter Electra if he murdered Polydorus . . .

Polynices (or Polyneices) was the elder son of Oedipus and Jocasta, and so the brother of Eteocles. According to Aeschylus, in his drama *Seven Against Thebes*, Polynices was quarrelsome from birth, the very opposite of the 'nice' Eteocles. In view of this, and Polynices' belligerence, it is not surprising to find that his name means 'much strife', from *polys*, 'much' and *neicos*, 'quarrel', 'strife'. He married Argia, who bore him Thersander.

Polypemon see **Procrustes**.

Polypheides was a seer, the son of Mantius, also a seer (*mantis* means 'prophet') and grandson of the greatest seer of all, Melampus. His name means 'much thrift' from *polys*, 'much' and *pheido*, 'thrift'. Polypheides' son Theoclymenus was also a seer.

Polyphemus was famous as the Cyclops who was made drunk, and then blinded, by Odysseus (who had disguised himself as a stranger called Nobody). He was a son of Poseidon by the sea-nymph Thoösa, and he lived with other Cyclopes on the island of Sicily. He must have made quite a name for himself there, for Polyphemus means 'many tales' (i.e. notorious) or else 'many loud cries' (i.e. brash and boastful), from *polys*, 'many' and *pheme*, 'words', 'rumour', 'reputation'. This was perhaps a propitious name for the Argonaut Polyphemus who was the son of Eilatus and Hippea.

Polyphontes was a descendant of Heracles who usurped the throne of Messenia, killed the two elder brothers of Aepytus, the former king, and also his father, Cresphontes, and forced Aepytus' mother Merope to marry him. All this violence can be seen in his name, which means 'murderer of many', from *polys*, 'many' and *phone*, 'murder'. Later, it should be added, Aepytus returned with supporting forces to Messenia and in turn killed Polyphontes and recovered the throne. Another Polyphontes who features in the *Iliad* was a Theban warrior who was the son of Autophonus. The 'murder' element (*phone*) is also present here in the names of **Cresphontes** (which see) and Autophonus (literally 'self-killer', meaning not 'suicide' but 'killing one's own family').

Polypoetes was the eldest son of Pirithoüs and Hippodamia, and the name was also that of a king of Thesprotia who was a son of Odysseus and Callidice. It is a favourable name, meaning 'maker of many things', from *polys*, 'many' and *poietes*, 'maker' (from *poieo*, 'to make'). This latter word gives English 'poet', who was originally a 'maker'.

Polyxena was a daughter of king Priam and Hecabe. Her name means 'very hospitable', literally 'many guests', from *polys*, 'many' and *xenos*, 'guest', 'stranger'. Sadly for such an agreeable sounding person, she was put to death by Neoptolemus as the result of a request by Achilles' ghost after the fall of Troy that she should be sacrificed on his grave.

Polyxenus has a name that means precisely the same as that of Polyxena (above). He was a son of Agasthenes, king of Elis, and led some of the Elean forces in the Trojan War.

Polyxo was the name of at least three women. One was a prophetess who was an old nurse of queen Hypsipyle, another was the widow of Heracles' son Tlepolemus, and a third was the mother of Antiope by Nycteus. The name seems to be a contraction of 'Polylyxo' and thus means 'much light', from *polys*, 'much' and *lyce*, 'light'. Robert Graves, however, derives it from *polys* and *xyo*, 'to scrape', so that it means 'much itching'. But in what precise sense – there's the rub.

Pomona was the Roman goddess of fruit and its cultivation, with her name deriving from Latin *pomum*, 'fruit', 'apple' (compare French *pomme*). The story of how she spurned the love of Vertumnus is told by Ovid in his *Metamorphoses*.

Porphyrion was a giant who fought Hera and Heracles. When he tried to rape Hera, he was killed by Zeus. His name appears to be a threatening one, from *porphyreos*, 'purple', 'dark' (originally of the sea), although Pindar called him king of the giants and the 'purple' could indicate royal power.

Portheus (or Porthaon) was a king of Calydon, the son of Agenor and Epicaste. By Euryte he was the father of Oeneus, among others. His name is a 'powerful' one, meaning 'destroyer', 'sacker', from *portheo*, 'to destroy' (related to *pertho*, 'to sack', 'destroy'). Compare the names of **Perseus** and **Poliporthis**.

Poseidon was the chief Greek god of the seas and waters, the equivalent of Neptune. He was the son of Cronos and Rhea, and a brother of Zeus. The Doric form of his name was Poteidan, and this is usually understood as meaning 'husband of Da', Da being, perhaps, an old pre-Greek name of the earth goddess who later became Demeter. He is thus, as god of the sea, complementary in his powers and attributes to the goddess of the land, and one of his best-known by-names, Gaieochos, supports this, since it means 'earth-holding', from *gaia*, 'earth' and *ochos*, 'that which holds'. The sea therefore 'holds' the earth. Those who feel that such an association with 'earth' can be ambiguous, prefer to derive his name from an exclusively 'watery' source, such as *pontos*, 'the open sea', *potos*, 'drinking' or *potamos*, 'river', all linked to the root *po-* which relates to drinking and water (as in English 'potion').

Praxithea (otherwise Prasithea or Pasithea) was the wife of Erechtheus, king of Athens. Lycurgus writes that she favoured sacrificing one of her daughters to gain a victory against Eumolpus, as Erechtheus had been advised to do by the Delphic oracle. In the light of this, her name can be interpreted as 'exacting a sacrifice', from *praxis*, 'doing', 'business', 'exacting' and *thyo*, 'to sacrifice'. Robert Graves sees the name as meaning 'active goddess' from *prasso*, 'to pass through', 'practise', 'be active' and *thea*, 'goddess'.

Priam (or Priamus) was a king of Troy. He was the son of Laomedon of Troy and Strymo (or Placia, or Leucippe), and by his first wife Arisbe and various successive wives and mistresses had anything up to fifty children. His name was originally Podarces, a standard propitious name meaning 'swift foot' or 'light foot', from *pos*, *podos*, 'foot', and *argos*, 'bright', 'swift' (see **Podarge**). The story went that as a child he had been ransomed from Heracles by his sister Hesione, and so was named Priam from the word *priamai*, 'I buy'. Others saw his name meaning something like 'chief', 'leader' and deriving from *peri* (Latin *prae*), or *prin* (Latin

Gaia, Poseidon and Polybotes. The giant Polybotes ('many oxen') was killed by Poseidon (otherwise Neptune) as he was walking across the Aegean. Note Poseidon's trident. The artists' names are below: 'Erginos potter, Aristophanes painter'.

prius), both meaning 'before' (the former in place, the latter in time). In fact his name is almost certainly not Greek at all.

Priapus was a Phrygian god of fertility, and was associated with gardens, vineyards and agriculture generally. He was borne by Aphrodite to Dionysus or Hermes, and was represented as an ugly scarecrow-type man with huge genitals. The origin of his name is obscure. Attempts have been made to link it with *prio*, 'to saw', this being a reference to his gardening activities as a pruner of trees, and Robert Graves sees him specifically as a 'pear-tree pruner', from *prio* and *apios*, 'pear-tree', this being a tree sacred to Hera. One theory refers to the by-name Briepyos used of Ares by Homer in the *Iliad*, this meaning 'shouting loudly' (from *bri-*, an intensive prefix, and *epyo*, 'to shout'), and maintains that Priapus' name was originally something like 'Briapus' with this same sense. All the evidence points to his name being at any rate erotic or phallic in some way, resembling the senses of the names of other phallic deities such as Orthanes ('erect'), Conisalus ('dust whirler') and Tychon ('he who hits his mark'). If Hermes was his father, then here is another phallic link. Maybe after all Priapus originated as an orgiastic by-name, whatever its meaning, of Dionysus. Understandably, the name has not passed on to any heavenly body, nor has it become a personal forename. Its only use is as a medical term, 'priapism', to refer to a persistent erection of the penis. This word derives from the Greek verb *priapizo*, 'to be lewd', 'to be like Priapus', which itself came from his name.

Proclea was the wife of Cycnus and the mother of Tenes. Her name means 'challenger', from *procaleo*, 'to call forth', 'defy', 'provoke'. This is presumably a good 'positive' name.

Procles was a Spartan king, the son of Aristodemus and the twin brother of Eurysthenes. His name, like that of Proclea (which see), means 'challenger'.

Procne was the famous sister of Philomela and mother of Itys by Tereus, both girls being the daughters of Pandion, king of Athens. She was turned into a swallow (for the story of this, see **Philomela**), so the first part of her name may be *pro*, 'before', 'beforehand' or *proi* 'early', 'early in the day' to refer to a swallow who announces the spring or the dawn. The trouble is, of course, that the nightingale also announces the spring! And what does the second half of her name mean? It may perhaps be simply a random ending, although the *-cne* could be linked with *cineo*, 'to move', 'arouse' or even Latin *cano*, 'I sing'. This whole theory is propounded by Thomas Keightley. Robert Graves, seeking a simpler derivation, prefers *progone*, 'the elder' (*pro*, 'before' and *gonos*, 'child').

Procoptas see **Procrustes**.

Procris was the daughter of Erechtheus and the niece of Procne and Philomela. She married Cephalus, and on marrying both she and he took a vow of everlasting faithfulness. This vow may be expressed in her name, which derives from *procrino*, 'to choose before others', 'prefer' (*pro*, 'before' and *crino*, 'to choose'). Or of course the name could apply to her, meaning 'she who is chosen above others'. The resemblance between her name and that of Procne is curious, and may be significant.

Procrustes, the infamous scoundrel, was said to be a son of Poseidon. He was notorious for his habit of lying in wait for strangers who passed by his house on the road from Eleusis to Athens, inviting them in, and then fastening them to a bed (a long one for short people and a short one for tall) and stretching them or 'lopping' them to fit it accordingly. His name was actually a nickname, 'stretcher out', from *procrouo*, 'to hammer out', with his real name being either Polypemon ('much suffering', from *polys*, 'much' and *pema*, 'suffering'), Procoptas ('cutter away', 'lopper', from *pro*, 'away' and *copto* 'to cut') or Damastes ('subduer', 'tamer', from *damazo*, 'to tame'). It is possible, however, that one or more of these were also nicknames, since they are obviously descriptive. On a kind of 'eye for an eye' basis, Theseus treated Procrustes as he had treated others, and killed him by fastening him to a short bed and lopping off his head. His name survives today in the term 'Procrustean', to mean 'seeking to enforce uniformity by violent methods'.

Proëtus was a king of Tiryns and a son of Abas, the king of Argos, and Aglaia. His twin brother was Acrisius. He married Stheneboea (called Antia by Homer), who bore him three daughters, Lysippe, Iphinoë and Iphianassa, and one son, Megapenthes. His name seems to mean 'first', from *protos*, 'first' or *proteion*, 'first place', this being both a 'powerful' name and a suitable one for a king.

Promachus was the son of Parthenopaeüs, with another of the name being the son of Aeson by Alcimede (or Polymede), and so

263

the younger brother of Jason. The former Promachus was one of
the Sown Men, and was probably killed at Thebes. The name for
both men is a belligerent one, meaning 'champion', literally 'fighting in front', from *pro*, 'before' and *mache*, 'battle', 'fight'. For the
younger brother of Jason this had to remain a propitious name,
since he was killed by Pelias while still a boy.

Prometheus was the famous Titan who was the son of Iapetus
and Themis (or Clymene, or Asia). He is best known for being the
champion of men against the gods, and according to Hesiod was
a master-craftsman at creating men from clay. He used to submit
his models to Zeus for his inspection and approval (but omitted to
do so in the case of Phaënon, whose name see). To help the men
he had created, who were still poorly off, he also undertook the
risky mission of stealing fire for them so that they could cook their
food and keep warm. (Until that time fire had been reserved for
the gods alone.) From his fire-stealing, attempts have long been
made to link his name with the Sanskrit *pramantha*, 'fire stick', but
this seems an unlikely origin for such a patently Greek name.
Prometheus, in fact, has a name that is the ordinary word, *pro-
metheia*, for 'forethought', from *pro*, 'before' and *metis*, 'counsel',
'wisdom'. This simply summed up his character – he had knowledge of what was to come. According to Aeschylus he was viewed,
too, as bestowing the gift of knowledge on mankind. Compare the
opposite meaning of the name of his brother, **Epimetheus**.

Proserpine (or Proserpina) see **Persephone**.

Protesilaüs was king of Phylace, in Thessaly, and a son of Iphiclus. He was the first one to leap ashore in the Greek expedition
to Troy, in spite of the fact that the oracle had said that the first
Greek to tread Trojan soil would also be the first to die. His name
thus comes from *protos*, 'first' and *laos*, 'army', or perhaps *protos*,
'first' and *luo*, 'to loose'. This could, of course, be regarded as
merely a propitious or belligerent name, not a rash one.

Proteus (not to be confused with Proëtus) was an ancient sea-
god, a so-called Old Man of the Sea (*halios geron*), who was
occasionally described as a son of Poseidon or Nereus (the latter
according to Euripides). His name would appear to mean simply
'first' (*protos*) in any appropriate sense, such as 'first to rule',
'first-born', 'first in time' and the like. Thomas Keightley suggests
that the name should really be 'Ploteus' and so mean 'floater',
'swimmer', from *plotos*, 'sailing', 'floating', 'swimming'.

Psamathe was a Nereid (i.e. a daughter of Nereus) who bore Phocus to Aeacus and later, having married Proteus, bore him Theoclymenus and Eido. Her name means 'sand' (*psamathos*) – in modern terms we can call her Sandy Shore – for her associations with the beach and the sea. She had turned herself into a seal while trying to escape from the embraces of Aeacus. Significantly, the name of her son by him was Phocus ('seal')!

Psyche was the beautiful daughter of some king who has not been identified. The somewhat fairy-like or folk-storyish tale about her love for Cupid (otherwise Eros or Amor) was told by Apuleius in *The Golden Ass*. Her name means 'soul' (*psyche*), and in his tale Apuleius hints at an allegory of the soul seen in pursuit of divine love.

Psylla was a mare obtained by Oenomaüs from Ares (together with its companion, Harpinna). Its name means 'flea' (*psylla*), presumably for its agility and high leaps!

Pterelas was the name under which Procris disguised herself (as a handsome boy) for fear that Pasiphaë might bewitch her for having given Minos a drugged draught to prevent him from impregnating her with reptiles and insects when he was on the point of seducing her. She was the wife of Cephalus, of course, but Artemis made her think that Cephalus was visiting his former love, Eos, when he crept out one night to hunt. She went after him – and he, with his dog Laelaps and his magic dart (both dog and dart being presents from Minos to Procris), killed her. Haunted by her ghost he plunged into the sea calling on her name of Pterelas, as whom he had loved her most, not realising that all along she had been his wife. In view of all these rather bizarre incidents (retold in condensed form here), what does the name mean? It appears to relate to the culminating point of the account, where Cephalus dives into the sea, and so to derive from *pteron*, 'feather', 'wing' and either *elasis*, 'riding', 'driving' or *las*, 'stone'. Cephalus was thus either a 'wing-rider' or a 'feather that fell like a stone'. Yet really, of course, we would expect the name to apply in some way to Procris rather than her husband, particularly as she chose it specially for her disguise.

Pterelaüs has a name very similar to the one above. He was king of the Taphians, and a son of Taphius as well as a grandson of Poseidon. His distinctive feature was a single gold hair which, so long as he bore it, would ensure that he could not die; as soon as it was pulled out, he would die or a city would be captured. If we regard this hair as a 'feather' (*pteron*), then we can perhaps see the name as meaning 'feather release', from *pteron* and *luo*, 'to release', 'loosen'. Admittedly, this is not too convincing, but any other interpretation is difficult.

Pygmalion was a king of Cyprus who (according to Ovid) carved a statue of his ideal wife and fell in love with it. In answer to his prayer, Aphrodite brought the statue to life and Pygmalion married her. The name, however, hardly seems to relate to this romantic tale, at any rate if it derives from *pygme*, 'fist' or *pygon*, 'elbow'. The only possible suggestion one can make is that Pygmalion made a scale model of his ideal woman, since both *pygme* and *pygon* were measures of length, the former being the distance from elbow to knuckles (i.e. just over one foot) and the latter being from the elbow to the first joint of the fingers (i.e. about 15 inches). The word *pygme* gave the name of the pygmies, the dwarf peoples of Equatorial Africa. Robert Graves' solution to the name is 'shaggy fist', from *pygme* and *malion*, 'hair'. But no shaggy fist comes into the stories about Pygmalion.

Pylades was the son of Strophius and Anaxibia, Agamemnon's sister. He was brought up with his cousin and close companion, Orestes, and assisted him in most of his adventures and doings, including his murder of Neoptolemus. The first part of his name seems to mean 'gate' (*pyle*). Could this be the 'gate of Hades'?

Pylas (or Pylos, or Pylon) was first king of Megara, then king of Pylus (which took its name from him). His name just means 'gate', the important entrance to the town that he as king protected. His daughter was Pylia (see next entry).

Pylia was the daughter of Pylas (above) and the wife of Pandion. Her name naturally reflects that of her father the king, as well as standing for her own allegiance to 'the gate', *pyle*.

Pyramus was the well-known lover of Thisbe. Their story was retold by Shakespeare ('the most lamentable comedy, and most cruel death of Pyramus and Thisbe') in *A Midsummer Night's Dream*. Since the story originated in ancient Babylon – as Ovid admits, when he tells it in his *Metamorphoses* – the name of Pyramus may well not be Greek. It may somehow be connected with 'pyramid', an Egyptian word, or with *pyramous*, a Greek word for a kind of cake given as a prize to a person who kept awake the longest in a night watch. (This up to a point ties in with the long night whisperings through a chink in the wall that Pyramus and Thisbe had to resort to since their families would not allow them to marry.)

Pyrrha was a daughter of Epimetheus and Pandora who married her cousin Deucalion. Her name seems to be a descriptive one, probably referring to the colour of her hair, so that she was a 'redhead', from *pyrrhos*, 'flame-coloured', 'red', 'tawny'. The same name was given to Achilles for his red hair by the daughters of Lycomedes when he was brought up as a girl in Lycomedes' house.

Pyrrhus was the original name of Neoptolemus (whom see). He was so named either (simply) because he was red-haired (see **Pyrrha**), or because he was the son of Achilles and his father had been called Pyrrha as a boy (again see), or simply because he blushed easily!

Python was a monstrous serpent in Delphi. It gave the place its first name, Pytho, allegedly because either its body, or the body of Delphyne (which see), had rotted there beside the sacred spring after it was killed by Apollo. Its name, together with the ancient name of Delphi and the word 'python', thus derives from *pytho*, 'to rot', 'decay'.

Quirinus was the name under which Romulus was worshipped after he became a god, or else that of an early Roman war god resembling Mars. He may have originated as a Sabine god from the town of Cures, and get his name from there, and some authorities say that the Latin word *Quiris*, which came to mean 'citizen', also came from this town. After the union of the Sabines and the Romans, the latter called themselves (as civilians) *Quirites*. On specially solemn occasions they were called *Populus Romanus Quirites*, 'the Roman people, citizens'. William Smith reminds us that it was a reproach for soldiers to be called *Quirites* instead of *milites*. Other sources maintain that the name of Quirinus is connected with *quiris* or *curis*, 'spear', which was originally a Sabine word. Quirinus was certainly often represented with a spear. A third theory is that his name was originally something like *covirium*, 'assembly of men'.

Remus was the son of Mars and Rhea Silvia, and the famous twin brother of Romulus. The *Oxford Classical Dictionary* suggests that the name may derive from some local place-name, such as *Remona*, or even *Roma*, 'Rome'.

Rhadamanthys (or Rhadamanthus) was a judge of the dead, and a son of Zeus and Europa, or a brother of Minos and Sarpedon, or even a son of Phaestus. His name looks Greek and meaningful enough, but it is not straightforward. If we bear in mind that he was a judge, then the second half of his name may relate to *mantis*, 'soothsayer', 'seer'. If this is so, the first half of his name can perhaps be derived from *rhabdos*, 'rod', 'wand', so that he is a 'rod diviner', that is, he divines by means of a rod or wand. But would a judge actually divine? Again, as the name of a member of the family of Minos, one would expect a 'shining' name (see **Pasiphaë**), but Rhadamanthys does not seem to relate to the moon or the sea, for example. It has been pointed out that Hesychius uses a verb *rhadameo*, 'to make grow', and if this combined with *anthos*, 'flower', we can get a sense something like 'flower-grower', in other words a sort of masculine Flora. But the truth of the matter is that the name is almost certainly pre-Greek.

Rhea was a Titaness, the daughter of Uranus and Gaia and the consort of Cronos, her brother, to whom she bore Hestia, Demeter, Hera, Hades, Poseidon and Zeus. It is a pity that for such an important character we have such an uncertain name. Attempts have been made to associate it with that of Hera, by means of a kind of transposition, as well as to derive it from *rheo*, 'to flow', this latter interpretation being made by the third century BC Greek philosopher Chrysippus ('Golden Horse'!) 'because rivers flow from the earth'. Leonard Ashley sees the name, however, as meaning 'thingness', which is about as basic – or as vague – as one can get. She does really seem to have been an earth goddess, however, as the name of her Roman equivalent Ops suggests (see this name), so perhaps it is best to return to Hera and decide in favour of one of the origins we considered for her name – that of *era*, 'earth'.

Rhea Silvia was the mother of Romulus and Remus, and so not a Greek goddess at all. Indeed, her name often appeared as *Rea Silvia*, and it is possible that the spelling *Rhea* was introduced by writers or editors who were thinking of the Greek Rhea in the entry above. If she is Rea Silvia, then the first part of her name may be nothing more than *rea*, 'one accused', 'one condemned', perhaps referring to the 'guilt' of her giving birth to Romulus and Remus. (One account tells how her uncle Amulius 'exposed' the twin brothers after Rhea had given birth to them, and then imprisoned her; she was released many years later by her sons.) Silvia suggests 'of the forest' (latin *silva*). In an early version of her story, in which Rhea is said to be the daughter of Aeneas, she is called Ilia, after his homeland of Ilium (i.e. Troy).

Rhesus was a Thracian king and an ally of king Priam of Troy. He was a son of Eioneus or the river-god Strymon and one of the Muses. His name seems to be a 'belligerent' one, from *rhexis*, 'breaking', so that he is a 'breaker'. The king's name came to be applied, apparently with no logical connection at all, to the so-called rhesus monkey. This monkey was widely used in medical experiments, and so passed its name in turn to such expressions as the 'rhesus factor' of blood.

Rhexenor was the eldest son of Nausithoüs, king of the Phaeacians. He was the father of Arete, who married his brother Alcinoüs. His name is a warlike one, *rhexenor*, 'breaking through ranks of warriors', from *rhexis*, 'breaking' (see **Rhesus**) and *aner*, 'man'.

Rhode (or Rhodos) was a nymph, the daughter of Poseidon and Amphitrite (or Aphrodite), who is said to have given her name to the island of Rhodes. Her name may be linked, prettily enough, with *rhodea*, 'rosy', and *rhodon*, 'rose' has also been suggested as the origin of the name of the island. In fact both its name, and hers, are probably pre-Greek or even pre-Indo-European.

Romulus, the twin brother of Remus, was the mythical founder of Rome in 753 BC. As possibly for Remus' name, Romulus is a name that almost certainly derives from that of Rome itself, so that it simply means 'Roman'. The actual name of Rome is disputed: it may derive from an early name of the river Tiber that flows through it, this being *Ruma* or *Rumon*, or something similar, and itself perhaps related to Greek *rheo*, 'to flow'. The important thing here is that Romulus did not found Rome, Rome 'founded' him!

Sabazius was a Thracian or Phrygian god who came to be identified with Dionysus. His name is rather more straightforward to interpret than that of Dionysus – if, as seems likely, it comes from *sabazo*, 'to shatter', 'destroy'. Sabazius would thus be a 'destroyer' with a powerful, belligerent name.

Salmoneus was a son of Aeolus and Enarete and a brother of Sisyphus. His first wife was Alcidice, who bore him Tyro, and later he married Sidero. He was a king of Salmonia, in Elis, and there

269

is a good case for regarding his name as 'Halmoneus' and so making him a 'seaman', from *halme*, 'salt water', especially as Elis was a coastal district on the Ionian Sea. The 'good case' here is that 's' often took the place of 'h' in Greek, especially in the Aeolian dialect, and a similar interchange took place between Greek and Latin words, such as Greek *hys* and Latin *sus*, 'pig', Greek *hals* and Latin *sal*, 'salt', Greek *hex* and Latin *sex*, 'six', Greek *hepta* and Latin *septem*, 'seven', Greek *herpo* and Latin *serpo*, 'to crawl', and so on.

Sarpedon was a son of Zeus and Europa, and he was a brother of Minos and Rhadamanthys, with whom he was reared by the childless king Asterius (who had married Europa). On the basis that 'h' could often replace 's' in Greek (see **Salmoneus**) we have good grounds for reading his name as 'Harpedon' and so for regarding his name, perhaps, as deriving from *harpage*, 'seizure', 'rape', this referring to his abduction of Europa. Compare the name of the **Harpies**.

Saturn was the Roman god of agriculture, the husband of Rhea and the father of Jupiter. His name is usually derived from the root *sat-* that means 'sowing' (seen in the verb *sero*, 'to sow' itself, where *satus* means 'sown'), but there is also a possibility that the name connects with *saturo*, 'to fill', 'satiate' and that the original form of the name was something like 'Saturinus', meaning 'satisfier'. On the other hand the Romans identified Saturn with Cronos who is certainly an early god, and the name Saturn itself may thus derive also from an ancient Etruscan or even oriental god. As a planet, Saturn was originally called *Phainon*, 'shining', by the Greeks (compare **Phaënon**), and subsequently, when names of gods were given to planets, Cronos (see Introduction, page 11). Saturn, of course, is the planet next to Jupiter, so it is perfectly logical that father should be placed next to son!

Satyrs were woodland creatures in the form of men with some animal features. They were usually young and vigorous (today they would be called randy) and traditionally accompanied the Maenads in the revels of Dionysus. Hesiod says that they were descended from the five daughters of one Hecaterus, who had married an Argive princess, the daughter of king Phoroneus. The Romans identified them with their own woodland spirits, the fauns, and it was thus the Romans who gave them the familiar goats' legs and horns with which they are depicted in post-Renaissance paintings. Popularly they were thought of (the image still lives) as

270

perpetually pursuing maidens through the woods. Their name has been associated with *ther*, 'wild animal' (Euripides certainly referred to them as *theres*) but it may actually be derived from some ancient Peloponnesian dialect word meaning 'the full ones', this referring to their 'abundant' or sexually excited condition. Eric Partridge suggests that possibly the 'sowing' root of *sat-* (see **Saturn**) may lie behind the name.

Scamander (or Scamandrus) was a Trojan river and its god, this river being the Maeander (today the Menderes) whose god Maeander we have already considered (see this name). Scamander was the son of Oceanus and Tethys, and the father of Teucer by the nymph Idaea, as well as of Callirrhoë and Strymo. The name seems to derive from *scazo*, 'to limp' or perhaps *scaios*, 'left', 'awkward' and *aner*, *andros*, 'man', thus being a 'limping man' or a 'clumsy man'. This would refer to the many bends and winds ('meanders') of the river, which does not run straight and true but 'limps' its way along. Scamander was also known as **Xanthus** (which see).

Schoeneus was a king of Orchomenus, in Boeotia, the son of Athamas and Themisto. He is chiefly known for being the father of Atalanta, an honour that many writers ascribe instead to Iasus. The base of the name appears to be *schoinos*, 'rush'. This could make Schoeneus a 'man of the rushes', so named for the swamps that were the haunts of Atalanta, as well as the mountains. On the other hand the suggestion has been made that the word refers to the measured race that Atalanta ran: in ancient Greece the *schoinos* was a land measure equal to 60 *stadia*, that is, approximately seven miles. There was another Schoeneus who was the son of Autonoös and Hippodamia. For the 'rushes' in his name, see **Acanthis**.

Sciron was a famous robber, a son of Poseidon or Pelops. He had developed the idiosyncratic practice of forcing passing travellers to wash his feet as he stood on a cliff-top by the sea on the border between Attica and Megaris on the isthmus of Corinth. As they did so, he gave them a hefty kick and sent them into the sea, where a giant turtle devoured their bodies. (Theseus eventually put an end to this by paying him back in his own coin – he booted *him* off the cliff into the sea.) We have a choice here: *sciron* means 'parasol', *sciros* means 'gypsum'. The former may refer to a type of sacrifice in which a victim was pushed from a cliff-top into the sea carrying a token parachute; the latter could mean 'limestone' and refer to the rock of the cliff. Parasols were by no means unfamiliar objects

271

to the Greeks: at an annual women's festival in Athens, priestesses processed carrying parasols. (This ceremony was called the *Scirophoria*, 'parasol-bearing', and gave its name to one of the Greek months, Scirophorion, which corresponded to the latter half of June and the first half of July.)

Scylla was the infamous sea monster who devoured sailors as they passed through the Strait of Messina. She had earlier been a beautiful nymph of variously recorded parentage, but Circe (out of envy of all the suitors she attracted) turned her into a monster with a woman's head and six dogs for legs – or something on similar lines, depending which account one reads or prefers. She lay low on a promontory opposite a whirlpool called Charybdis (which see) – hence the phrase 'between Scylla and Charybdis' to refer to an unpleasant dilemma. She was said to bark like a dog or whine like a puppy, and thus her name may mean 'whelp', 'puppy' (*scymnos*). However, she also used to tear her prey to pieces, and this suggests an origin in *scyllo*, 'to flay', 'rend'. Another Scylla was the daughter of Nisus, king of Megara, who has sometimes been confused with the monster. Yet she did some 'rending' too, for she is said to have torn her father's body to pieces after she had caused his death by cutting off the golden hair on his head that ensured he would live. (In his *Art of Love*, Ovid positively identifies the monster with this second Scylla.)

Scythes was the mythical ancestor of the Scythians. He was the son of Heracles and a 'woman with a snake's tail' who is usually identified as Echidna. His name, and that of the Scythians, has been linked with *scythros*, 'angry', 'sullen', 'gloomy', but the word is probably not Greek at all.

Selemnus was a handsome youth who loved the sea-nymph Argyra. She tired of him, and when he died of heartbreak, Aphrodite changed him into the river Selemnus. If his name derives from *selas*, 'bright' (as for Selene), then it closely approximates the origin of Argyra's own name (which see). The story seems to have originated from a spring called Argyra that was located near the river Selemnus in Achaea.

Selene was the goddess of the moon (not the only one, of course). She was the daughter of Hyperion and Theia (or of Pallas or Helios and Euryphaëssa). Her name undoubtedly comes from *selas*, 'bright light', 'brightness', to which word are also related *hele*, 'light of the sun' (compare **Helios**) and German *hell*, 'bright'.

Selene, Moon Goddess. The pair of winged horses draw Selene's moon chariot. The moon itself rises above her head like a halo.

(For alternation between 'h' and 's' see **Salmoneus**.) The Roman equivalent goddess was Luna, whose name means 'moon' just as *selene* means 'moon' in Greek.

Semele was a daughter of Cadmus and Harmonia, and the mother of Dionysus. There are two rival origins for her name. One is as a corruption of Selene or 'Seleme', so meaning 'bright'. The other is as a non-Greek word meaning 'earth'. The 'bright' derivation makes sense if we consider Selene's name (or even that of Selemnus), and if we regard her name as similar to the 'bright' names of water-nymphs such as Electra, Galatea, Glauce and Ianthe (to say nothing of her sister Ino, who became Leucothea and a goddess of the sea). The 'earth' sense could derive from a Thracian word *zemelo*, 'earth' (compare modern Russian *zemlya*, with identical meaning), so that she was an earth goddess with a name something like 'Zemelo'. She was also known as Thyone (which see). The latter does seem to be a Greek name.

Sibylla was a prophetess (the original sibyl) who lived at Marpessus near Troy and was devoted to serving Apollo, who inspired her to make her predictions. She gave her name to all the prophetesses called sibyls, so that the meaning of her name will be the meaning of this word. Unfortunately, the derivation is not easy. Plutarch proposed an origin in *Dios*, 'of Zeus' and *boule*, 'counsel', so that the name means 'counsel of Zeus'. Saint Jerome saw the name as originating in *theou boule*, 'divine counsel', with this being an Attic Greek expression for which the Doric would have been *Siobolla*. Eric Partridge favours a link with Latin *sibilus*, so that her name may mean 'the hisser' (presumably mouthing predictions). In any event, her name first appears in the writings of Heraclitus, the Greek philosopher who lived in the sixth and fifth centuries BC. The name was steadily popular until quite recently (often with the spelling Sybil) as a Christian name. Its 'boost' in the nineteenth century may have owed something to Disraeli's novel *Sybil* published in 1845.

Sicyon was the son or grandson of Erechtheus. He married Zeuxippe, who bore him Chthonophyle – who in turn bore Polybus to Hermes. He is said to have given his name to the city of Sicyon on the Gulf of Corinth. If his name derives from *sicyos*, 'cucumber', then this may be either a 'fertility' name (even a phallic one) or else refer to some incident that has not come down to us.

Side was the first wife of Orion. When married to him, she offended

Hera and was sent down to the Underworld. Her name means 'pomegranate' (*side*), a fruit that has links with the Underworld, since it was the food that Persephone had thoughtlessly eaten there when she should have eaten nothing (for Demeter to be able to win her back from Hades, who had carried her off there). See **Ascalaphus** for this.

Sidero was the second wife of Salmoneus and the step-mother of Tyro. She was hard-hearted towards her step-daughter, and that is why her name derives from *sideros*, 'iron'.

Sileni were the sons of Silenus and a number of nymphs. They resembled the satyrs, except that on the whole they were older, wiser and drunker – a distinction both formidable and exciting. For the origin of their name, see **Silenus**.

Silenus was an elderly companion of the Maenads in the revels of Dionysus, a cross between a dirty old man and a chronic alcoholic – yet also wise and possessing powers of prophecy. He is usually regarded as being a son of Pan or Hermes and a nymph. He may originally have been a river god, in which case his name can perhaps be derived from *eilo* or *illo*, 'to roll'. In this respect it may be no coincidence that Latin *silanus* means 'fountain', 'jet of water'. Some writers, too, say that Silenus was the son of Gaia, which further suggests a fountain or stream that springs from the earth. Whether this 'moisture' connection can be extended to the wine that he drank and that Dionysus symbolised is another matter.

Sillus, with Triballus, was one of the twin brothers Cercopes who plagued Heracles (their names were also recorded as Passalus and Acmon, or Olus and Eurybatus). His name means 'mocker', from *sillaino*, 'to insult', 'mock', 'jeer', and this is exactly what he was.

Silvanus was a Roman woodland god who was frequently identified with Pan. With the growth of his cult, he was 'promoted' and became more a god of agriculture than one simply of forests. His name means 'of the forest', however (Latin *silva*). In view of the adjectival form of his name, perhaps the noun *Faunus* should be supplied.

Simöeis was a son of Oceanus and Tethys, and the father of Astyoche and Hieromneme. He was a god of the river Simöeis which flowed from Mount Ida (and is today called the Dombrek). His name, disconcertingly, means either 'flat', or 'steep', or 'hollow', 'concave' (*simos*). In view of the location of the river, and its source on Mount Ida, the last sense seems the most appropriate, referring to the channel worn by the river in the mountain-side.

Sinis was a notorious brigand, the son of Polypemon and Sylea. He was nicknamed Pityocamptes ('pine-bender') for his habit of tying his victims' limbs to pine trees that he had bent low, and then releasing the trees. This either catapulted the victims to their deaths or rent them asunder – a hideous quartering without a previous hanging or drawing. Theseus killed him, as he often did, by applying the dastard's own devices to himself. Sinis' name means 'destroyer', 'ravager', 'robber' (*sinis*).

Sinon was a young Greek spy related to Odysseus. He allowed himself to be captured by the Trojans so that he could tell them a false story about the Wooden Horse, and thus persuade them to allow it inside their walls. His names means 'hurt', 'harm', 'damage' (*sinon*), which was certainly his objective.

Sinope was the daughter of Asopus, and according to some accounts was carried off by Zeus to the city of this name on the Black Sea (today in Turkey). Others say that it was Apollo who abducted her, and that she bore him Syrus, the ancestor of the Syrians. Her name appears to contain the element that means 'face' (*ops*), but the first half of her name is difficult to interpret with any certainty. It can hardly be from *sinos*, 'harm', 'mischief' (see **Sinon**). Robert Graves makes the name mean 'moon-face', with the *sin-* element presumably deriving from *selene*, 'moon'.

Sirens were bird-like women, not unlike Harpies, who lured sailors with their songs. They had various names and their numbers also varied, as did their parents. Traditionally, they lived on the island of Anthemoëssa ('flowery') near the straits where Scylla and Charybdis lurked. They are first mentioned in the *Odyssey*, where Odysseus is told, 'your next encounter will be with the Sirens, who bewitch everybody that approaches them'. Their name is of uncertain origin, but is popularly derived from *seira*, 'chain', for their 'binding' power. (In Greek the name is spelt *Seirenes*, singular *Seiren*.) There is a theory, however, that traces their name back to *seirios*, 'hot', 'scorching', which was a word used of heavenly bodies causing heat (compare **Sirius**). This might mean that the Sirens had some sort of power to dry up pastures in the hot summer months. Plato divided the Sirens into three categories and assigned them as being under the rule of Jupiter, Neptune and Pluto res-

Sirens try to lure Odysseus with their songs. Odysseus has had himself bound to the mast to prevent him from responding to their lure. The crew's ears have been plugged with wax to prevent them hearing the bewitching singing.

pectively. The modern ship's or factory siren is named after them, and the word was specially chosen for the first siren, invented by the Frenchman Cagniard de la Tour in 1819 ('The Syren, a new Acoustical Instrument . . . In consequence of this property of being sonorous in the water this instrument has been called the Syren'). The word was in general use in English before this, however, to mean 'dangerously seductive woman'. The mythological Sirens have often been popularly confused with mermaids, which of course they are not: Sirens were half-woman, half-bird; mermaids were half-woman, half-fish.

Sirius was the favourite dog of Orion, the hunter (and also, apparently, of Orestheus). He was placed in the heavens as Canis Major, the Dog Star, where he was the brightest star in the sky. His name is said to derive from *seirios*, 'hot', 'scorching', since he appeared in the night sky at the time of greatest heat, July and August, and it was thought that this heat came from Sirius, not the sun. The Romans called him *Canicula*, 'little dog', in an affectionate manner, but they also noticed that he appeared at the hottest time of the year, and this gave the English expression 'dog days' (Latin *dies caniculares*).

Sisyphus was the son of Aeolus and Enarete. He founded Corinth, at first called by him Ephyra, and he was 'the most crafty of men', as Homer called him. His name is usually thought to be a reduplication of *sophos*, 'wise' (perhaps in the form 'Se-sophos' or 'Si-sophos'), this having the effect of intensifying the sense, so that he is 'very wise', even 'too wise'. Significantly, his father Aeolus was also crafty and cunning (see this name). In the Trojan War, Odysseus was given the nickname Sisyphides for his devious schemes, especially the brilliant one that resulted in the Wooden Horse. Sisyphus has given his name to the term 'Sisyphean' to denote an everlastingly laborious undertaking: he was condemned in the Underworld to roll a heavy stone up a hill and start all over again when it rolled down from the top.

Smicrus was a lost child descended from Apollo who was taken as a servant into the household of a rich man named Patron, whose daughter he eventually married. His name means 'small' (*smicros*, Ionic Greek and old Attic for *micros*).

Smyrna see **Myrrha**.

Soloön was one of three brothers (the others were Euneüs and

278

Thoas). He was a companion of Theseus when he visited the Amazons. Having fallen in love with Antiope, but not daring to approach her personally, he drowned himself in the river Thermodon out of unrequited love. His name seems to be a blend of *solos* and *oon*, 'egg'. The *solos* was a mass of iron used as a weight for throwing in games, like a discus but spherical. So he was, or he represented, an 'egg-weight'! This presumably refers to some sporting contest rather than being a personal Humpty Dumpty-style epithet.

Somnus was the Roman god of sleep, identified with the Greek Hypnos. Like him he is little more than an abstraction. His name actually means 'sleep' just as that of Hypnos does.

Sosipolis was a divine child brought by an unknown woman to Olympia and offered by her as a future champion to the Eleans. When the Eleans faced the Arcadians in combat, they placed the naked child at the head of their army. Upon the attack of the Arcadians the child changed into a serpent, at which the Arcadians fled in terror. The child then vanished. The Eleans dedicated a temple to the child and named it 'saviour of the state', from *sozo*, 'to save', 'preserve' and *polis*, 'city', 'state'.

Spermo was one of the three daughters of Anius and Dorippe, together with her sisters Elaïs and Oeno. She promoted the growth of grain, so her name means 'of the seed', from *sperma*, 'anything sown', 'seed'. Compare the names of her sisters.

Sphaerus was the charioteer of Pelops, and in this position it is obviously appropriate for him to have a name that derives from *sphaira*, 'ball', 'sphere', referring to the wheels of his chariot. (He could, however, have been a sportsman, even a boxer, from *sphairomacheo*, 'to box', literally 'glove-fight'.)

Sphinx was a female monster, the daughter of Typhon and Echidna. Her name means 'throttler', from *sphingo*, 'to throttle': she asked a riddle of young Theban men who passed by the walls of the citadel where she was advantageously perched; if they could not answer it (and they usually could not), she strangled them. Oedipus, however, found out the answer to her riddle and answered it correctly, whereupon the mortified Sphinx threw herself from the citadel and perished. (She had wings, but on this occasion was presumably too shocked to use them.) In art the Sphinx is represented as having a woman's bust on the body of a lioness.

279

This Greek Sphinx is quite distinct from the Egyptian sphinxes, which are the huge rock carvings in the desert (notably the one at Giza) of a lion with a Pharoah's head. These sphinxes pre-date the Greek one by several centuries.

Staphylus was the name of two characters of note. The first was the son of Dionysus and Ariadne, who went with the Argonauts. The second was a goatherd in the service of Oeneus who was alleged to have discovered the grape. For both men there are obvious 'winy' associations, so it is hardly surprising to find that the name means 'bunch of grapes' (*staphyle*). The brother of the first Staphylus mentioned here was Oenopion (which see for yet another vinous name).

Stentor was a proverbial herald of the Greeks at Troy, whose voice was said to be equal to that of fifty men. The modern English word 'stentorian', meaning 'extra loud' (of a voice), comes from his name, which in turn derives from some Indo-European root such as *ston-* or *sten-* denoting a loud voice (compare Greek *steno*, 'to groan', Latin *tonare*, 'to thunder', Russian *ston*, 'groan', etc.). There may also be an influence of Greek *tonos*, 'stretching', 'straining of the voice', which word is reflected in English 'tone'.

Sterope was one of the seven Pleiades, and the mother of Oenomaüs by Ares. Her name could, perhaps, mean 'stubborn face', from *stereos*, 'stiff', 'stubborn' and *ops*, 'face', but in view of her celestial role it would make better sense to derive it from *sterope*, 'lightning', 'glare'. In astronomy her name is used in the form Asterope to apply to the faintest of the seven stars in the Pleiades that are visible to the naked eye. (Some ancient stories say that Merope was the name given to the faintest of the seven, since of the seven sisters she was the only one to marry a mortal – Sisyphus. The fact remains that Sterope today is the faintest.) Sterope was also the name of the daughter of Cepheus and Neaera, and the daughter of Acastus and Astydamia (or Hippolyta), together with Laodamia and Sthenele. It was also the name (usually in the form Asterope) of one of the four horses that drew the chariot of Helios.

Steropes was a Cyclops, the offspring, with Argos and Brontes, of Uranus and Gaia. His name means 'lightning', or 'stubborn face', or even 'cruel eye' (which might be more fitting), from either *sterope* (see **Sterope**) or *stereos*, 'stiff', 'stubborn', 'cruel' and *ops*, 'eye', 'face'.

Stheneboea was the wife of Proëtus who failed to seduce Bellerophon and so tried to bring about his death. When she failed she
committed suicide (although according to Euripides, Bellerophon
killed her). Homer calls her Antia. Her name is a propitious one,
meaning 'strength of cattle', from *sthenos*, 'strength', 'might' and
bous, 'ox'.

Sthenelus is a propitious name meaning 'strong one', 'forcer',
from *sthenos*, 'strength', 'might', 'force'. There are at least half a
dozen characters with the name, including the son of Perseus and
Andromeda who married Pelops' daughter Amphibia (or Nicippe),
a companion of Heracles when he fought the Amazons, and the
son of Capaneus and Evadne.

Stheno also means 'force', 'strength' (see **Sthenelus**) and this was
the name of one of the three Gorgons, the others being Euryale
and Medusa.

Strophius was a king of Phocis and a son of Crisius. According to
some accounts he was the husband of Agamemnon's sister Anaxibia (or Astyoche). His name literally means 'turning', 'twist'
(*strophe*), but perhaps we should take this in a metaphorical sense
and call him a 'twister' or 'slippery' customer. To be fair, however,
the stories we have about him do not indicate any marked shiftiness
or deviousness in his doings.

Strymo was the daughter of the river Scamander and the wife of
Laomedon. Her name may derive from *stryphnos* and mean 'harsh',
'austere'.

Strymon, like Strymo, has a name that could mean 'harsh', or
'austere'. He was a river god, and the father of Rhesus by either
Calliope or Euterpe.

Stymphalus was the son of Elatus and a king of Arcadia. According to Robert Graves, the name 'suggests erotic practices', and
could derive from *styma*, Aeolian Greek for *stoma*, 'mouth' and
phallos, 'phallus'. The name is also seen in the Stymphalian Birds
who were the objective of Heracles' Sixth Labour. These birds
were pests who infested the woods around Lake Stymphalus, in
turn named for the city founded in north Arcadia by Stymphalus.
They were voracious creatures and even attacked (and ate) men,
and they were armed with brazen wings from which they shot at
people with steel-tipped feathers. (Heracles scared them off with

bronze castanets or a rattle and killed a number as they flew off.) Stymphalus was the father of Parthenope (an innocent name in the midst of all this evil and eroticism) – and she bore Heracles a son, Everes.

Styx was the main river of Hades, and its goddess. Like most river deities, she was a child of Oceanus and Tethys, and she married Pallas, the Titan, to whom she bore Zelus, Nike, Cratos and Bia. The waters of the Styx were fatal to life, so that 'crossing the Styx' meant death and was to be feared and abhorred. Her name, thus, means, 'hated', 'abhorrent' (*styx*, *stygos*). (The word is not actually related to English 'stigma', as stated by some sources.)

Syleus was an outlaw in Lydia who forced passers-by to till his vineyard. Heracles killed the rascal with his own hoe. His name means 'robber', from *sylao*, 'to strip', 'plunder'. Oddly enough, his brother Dicaeus has a name that means 'just', 'fair', and his daughter's name was Xenodice, 'fair to strangers' – which he himself certainly was not.

Syrinx was an Arcadian nymph who hunted with Artemis. Pan (characteristically) pursued her, whereupon she turned into a bed of reeds. From these, Pan made his famous 'Pan pipes', which he named after his fleeting love. The Greek for 'pipe' is *syrinx*.

Talaüs was a king of Argos and the father of Adrastus and Eriphyle by his wife Lysimache. He himself was the son of Bias and Pero. His name is a propitious one and means either 'endurer', from *tlao*, 'to endure', or possibly 'flourishing', from *thallo*, 'to bloom', 'flourish'. The latter interpretation links up with the name of his son, since Adrastus may mean 'fruitful', and even his horse Arion, whose name could mean 'flowing'.

Talos was a bronze giant who guarded Crete. He had a single vein in his body which ran from his head to his ankles and contained so-called *ichor*, the blood of the gods. He was killed by Medea, who pulled out the nail in his foot that sealed the bottom of the vein, whereupon he bled to death. In reference to this, or to combats undertaken in his lifetime (he had the task of repelling invaders), his name is said to mean 'sufferer', from *talas*, 'enduring', 'patient', 'wretched'.

Talthybius was the chief herald of the Greeks in the Trojan War. It seems reasonable to look for a 'belligerent' origin here, and perhaps it lies in *talas*, 'enduring' (as for Talos) and *bios*, 'life', or else *thyella*, 'storm' (from *thyo*, 'to rush', 'storm') and *bios*, so that his name expresses an 'enduring life' or a 'stormy life'. The first element in the name, if it derives from *talas*, can mean not just 'enduring' but also 'suffering', 'wretched' and even 'headstrong'. All these are suitable for a man who was forever carrying out disagreeable duties, such as taking Cassandra into slavery and snatching the child Astyanax from his mother Andromache so that he could be murdered.

Tantalus was the son of Zeus and the Titaness Pluto. His grotesque fate of having to stand up to his chin in water with fruit overhead that receded whenever he tried to reach it has given us the word 'tantalise'. There seems little doubt that his name is based on the *talas* or 'suffering' root that we considered for both Talos and Talthybius and saw in the names of Atlas and Telamon. Plutarch derived it from the superlative of *talas* – *talantatos*, 'most wretched'. But *talanton* means 'balance', 'pair of scales', and this may refer to his riches for which he was famous, so that he is a kind of personified greed: having much, he ever wishes for more. There was even a Greek saying about the 'talents of Tantalus' (*Tantalou talanta*) which came to mean more or less the same as the 'riches of Croesus'. (In this respect, his mother's 'rich' name is significant.) A somewhat more complex theory, although on the same lines, sees his name as meaning 'flourishing', and as being a reduplication (as for Sisyphus) of *thallo*, 'to flourish'. This again refers to his wealth and his insatiable desire for more. The reduplication would have caused an original name such as 'Thalthalos' to become Tantalus, with 'th' alternating with 't', and 'l' with 'n', as they sometimes did (for example, Ionic *aythis*, 'again', 'back' for *aytis*, and Attic *litron* for Doric *nitron*, 'soda').

Taphius was the king of the Taphian islands near the mouth of the Gulf of Corinth, with his son Pterelaüs succeeding him to the throne here. He was the son of Poseidon and Hippothoë, and his name seems to mean 'tomb', from *taphos*, 'burial', 'tomb', an element seen in the English word 'cenotaph' (which literally means 'empty tomb'). It is not clear to which burial or tomb the name refers, if a specific reference was intended. However, there may be a prophetic reference to Pterelaüs, who was sent to his 'tomb' or death when Comaetho pulled out the single golden hair that kept him alive.

Tartarus was originally a place, situated as far below Hades as

283

heaven was above the earth, to which rebellious Titans were sent. Later it became synonymous with Hades, and later still it was personified by Hesiod in his *Theogony* as the offspring of Chaos, together with Gaia (earth) and Eros (love). The name looks easy, but is actually difficult to interpret. It may be a Cretan word, and somehow linked to one of the place-names containing *tar-* that lie to the west of Greece, for example Tartessus, an ancient kingdom and sea port near the mouth of the river Guadalquivir in south-west Spain (modern Andalusia). The name also had its influence on the spelling 'Tartar' (with an 'r') for a member of the race whose name is more correctly spelt Tatars (itself of Persian origin). (The other 'tartar' meaning 'wine sediment' seems to be related to neither Tartarus nor the Ta(r)tars, but apparently derives from a medieval Greek word *tartaron* of uncertain origin.)

Tauropolus, after Tantalus and Tartarus, is a relatively straightforward name to explain. It is a 'fighting' name, i.e. propitiously belligerent, meaning 'bull slayer', from *tauros*, 'bull' and *apollymi*, 'to slay' (see **Apollo**). Tauropolus was one of the 'winy' sons of Dionysus and Ariadne.

Taÿgete was one of the Pleiades, so was a daughter of Atlas and Pleïone. After Zeus had seduced her (an attempt by Artemis to turn her into a doe having failed), she bore Lacedaemon. Her name has no obvious Greek derivation, and although 'properly' it should be spelt Taügete, the first half of the name does not appear to be derived from *tauros*, 'bull'. Robert Graves inventively boils it down from a word *tanygenuetos*, 'long-cheeked', from *tanyo*, 'to stretch' and *geneus*, 'both jaws', 'cheek'. This presumably could be a complimentary epithet, as 'cow-eyed' was. (There were similar words for physical characteristics, such as *tanyetheiros*, 'long-haired' and *tanypous*, 'long-legged'.)

Tecmessa was the daughter of the Phrygian king Teleutas. She became the mistress of Ajax and bore him Eurysaces. Her name seems to come from *tecmairomai*, 'to judge', 'decree', so that she is an 'ordainer' or even a priestess or goddess.

Tectamus was a king of Crete and a son of Dorus. He married a daughter of Cretheus and sailed for Crete with an army of Aeolians and Pelasgians. He seems to have been a resourceful and practical man, since his name indicates 'craftsman', from *tectainomai*, 'to build', 'plan', in turn from *tecton*, 'carpenter', 'builder'. This could have a metaphorical sense, however, and mean more 'planner', 'plotter'.

Tegyrius was the Thracian king who gave shelter to Eumolpus and his son Ismarus when they were exiled from Ethiopia. His name could well mean 'bee-keeper', from *tegos*, 'roof', 'covering' and *hyron*, 'beehive' (compare **Hyrieus**). Bee-keeping and honey-production were an important industry in ancient Greece.

Teiresias was a blind seer (however contradictory that may seem) of Thebes, the son of Everes and the nymph Chariclo. When Zeus and Hera were disputing whether man or woman derives the greater pleasure from the sex act, Teiresias was called in as an impartial arbiter, since as a result of striking a pair of coupling snakes he had earlier been transformed for seven years into a woman. His verdict was that women experienced a satisfaction nine or ten times greater. This reply angered Hera, who blinded Teiresias, but at the same time gave him the gift of prophecy. His name is thus based on *teirea*, 'heavenly bodies', 'signs', the Epic Greek plural of *teras*, 'sign', 'wonder', 'portent', and we can call him 'interpreter of portents', 'sign-reader'.

Telamon was the son of Aeacus, king of Aegina, and Endeïs. He was the brother of Peleus and he married Hesione. His name can be interpreted in two ways: either as 'bearer', 'endurer', from *talas*, 'enduring' or *tlao*, 'to bear' (compare **Talos** and **Talthybius**) or, more readily, 'supporting strap', from *telamon*. Before marrying Hesione (who bore him Teucer), Telamon had married Periboea, daughter of Alcathoüs, and she had borne him Ajax. Ajax was famous for the great shield that he carried, and this could be the reference to the 'carrying strap'. Thomas Keightley, however, who likes lining up family names on a common theme, sees a possibility for an origin in *helos*, 'marsh', so that Telamon, his brother Peleus, his wife Hesione, and his father Aeacus, all have 'watery' names.

Telchines were magicians who lived at Ialysus, on the island of Rhodes. According to Diodorus they were children of Thalassa ('sea'). Greek grammarians derived their names from *thelgo*, 'to charm', but there is a chance that the name actually relates to the Tyrrhenians or Tyrsenians, the people who were later known as the Etruscans.

Teledamus begins a short run of 'far' names, with the element *tele*, 'far' (as in many modern scientific words such as telephone

Telamon, Heracles and the Amazons. In the battle, Telamon ('the endurer') has struck down one Amazon (left) while Heracles, in his lion's skin, brandishes his club to challenge others.

and television). With Pelops, Teledamus was the twin son of Agamemnon and Cassandra. His name is a propitious one, meaning 'far tamer' from *tele* and *damazo*, 'to tame'.

Telegonus was the son of Odysseus and Circe, and was born to his parents during the year that Odysseus spent on Circe's island of Aeaea. According to Apollodorus, Telegonus killed his aged father in error and then married Penelope, Odysseus' former faithful wife. His name means 'far born', 'born far off', from *tele*, 'far' and *gonos*, 'child', 'offspring'. This is because he was born far from Odysseus' native land of Ithaca. Another Telegonus was a king of Egypt, whom Io married. He, too, could have been 'far born'.

Telemachus was a son of Odysseus and Penelope. He was only a baby when his father went off to the Trojan War, and as he grew up, his mother was besieged by suitors who were convinced that Odysseus would never return to Ithaca. Telemachus was too young and weak to counter the suitors, so Athena instilled manly power into the growing boy. His name means 'far fighter', from *tele*, 'far' and *mache*, 'fight', 'battle'. This could refer to his father, who was a 'far fighter' in the Trojan War, or to his own special strength, given by Athena, to fight from afar for his father on behalf of his mother. There have been attempts to make his name mean 'final battle', from *teleo*, 'to complete', 'fulfil', 'finish', but although this seems appropriate, Telemachus' name is spelt in Greek with the letter eta (η), not the letter epsilon (ε), so that the 'far' sense is the better one.

Telephassa was the wife of the Phoenician king Agenor, to whom she bore five sons (including Cadmus and Phoenix) and one daughter, Europa. Her name is an agreeable one for a queen, meaning 'far shiner', from *tele*, 'far' and *phao*, 'to shine', 'beam'.

Telephus was the son of Heracles and Auge. His name immediately suggests 'far shiner', as if contracted from 'Telephanes' (compare **Telephassa**, above), but it is traditionally derived from a blend of *thele*, 'teat' and *elaphos*, 'doe'. This refers to the account which tells how some shepherds discovered him as an abandoned baby being suckled by a doe.

Tellus was the Roman earth goddess, the equivalent of the Greek goddess Gaia (or Ge). Her name is simply Latin *tellus*, 'earth' (used more of the planet than to mean 'land'). This Latin word does not seem to be related to the better-known *terra*, 'land', yet the Roman goddess was also known as Terra.

Temenus was a son of Aristomachus and a descendant of Heracles. After the conquest of the Pelopennesus he was allocated Argos as the result of a drawing of lots, and became its king. His name means 'portion of land' (*temenos*), from *temno*, 'to cut', 'draw a line', and this could be an indication of the land that he won. Another Temenus was a son of Pelasgus who is said to have reared Hera in the Arcadian city of Stymphalus (see **Stymphalus**). There he built three shrines to celebrate three different aspects of the goddess (as Maiden, as Bride, and as Widow), and for him *temenos* is also appropriate since apart from meaning 'portion of land' it also meant 'piece of land sacred to a god', 'precinct'.

Tenes was a son of Cycnus and Proclea (although some accounts say his father was Apollo). Falsely accused by his father of rape, Tenes was locked in a chest and flung into the sea (for some reason, with his sister Hemithea). The chest floated ashore on an island, brother and sister escaped, and Tenes named the island Tenedos for himself. His name may be based on *tenon*, 'sinew', 'tendon', from *teino*, 'to stretch', perhaps referring to the 'tension', physical and metaphorical, that existed in his relationship with his father (and which continued even when he had settled on the island).

Tereus was a son of Ares and a king of the Thracians. He it was who raped Philomela and then cut out her tongue to prevent her revealing what he had done (see her name in connection with this). Perhaps with reference to this incident, or to his nature in general, his name can be derived from *teros*, 'guard', 'watch'. Thomas Keightley prefers an origin in *thereutes*, 'hunter', from *thereuo*, 'to hunt', 'run down'. (But could this be a reference to his chase after Philomela and Procne, and their consequent metamorphosis into a nightingale and a swallow? See the sisters' names for more about this.)

Termerus was a man who killed travellers by challenging them to a butting match, which he always won. However, he met his match in Heracles, who out-butted him and killed him. His name may have a symbolic or prophetic sense if it derives from *terma*, 'end', 'finishing point'! Compare **Terminus**.

Terminus was the Roman god of boundaries and frontiers, these being specifically sacred boundaries of landed property marked by stones and consecrated by Jupiter. On such boundaries sacrifices were offered annually to Jupiter at the festival called the Terminalia. His name is direct Latin for 'boundary line', with the word related to Greek *terma* (see **Termerus**).

Terpsichore was the Muse of lyric poetry or dance, with her name attractively (and even musically) meaning 'delighting in the dance', from *terpo*, 'to delight' and *choros*, 'dance' (the latter word giving English 'chorus').

Terra see **Tellus**.

Tethys was the daughter of Uranus and Gaia and the wife of Oceanus, to whom she bore a vast number of offspring, including most of the river-gods and their three thousand (!) sisters, the Oceanids. Her name is popularly derived from *tethe*, 'grandmother' (perhaps more 'grand mother'), a word apparently related to *tittho*, 'nurse', 'teat', or *tithene*, 'nurse'. On the other hand her name could also be linked with *tithemi*, 'to place', 'put', 'order' (compare **Themis** and **Thetis**), so that she is a 'determiner' or 'disposer'.

Teucer was the first mythical king of Troy, the son of the river god Scamander and the nymph Idaea. Another Teucer was the son of Telamon by Hesione. We can look for a sense 'craftsman' in the name, from *teucho*, 'to make', 'construct', or else propose a 'watery' name to match derivations suggested for Hesione ('shore') and Telamon ('marsh'). Such an origin might be in *deuso*, 'I will wet', 'I will soak', from *deuo*, 'to wet', 'soak'. Compare **Deucalion**.

Teuthras was a king of Teuthrania (to which he gave his name), in Mysia. He bought Auge as a slavegirl and either adopted her or married her, making Telephus, her son by Heracles, his heir. His name seems to derive from *teuthris*, 'cuttle-fish', but in what precise sense is not clear.

Thalia was the Muse of comedy, with her name meaning 'festive', 'cheerful', as one might expect, from *thallo*, 'to flourish'.

Thamyris was a Thracian bard or minstrel, the son of Philammon and the nymph Argiope (and allegedly the first man to love a boy – Hyacinthus). He even dared to challenge the Muses to a 'music and poetry' contest. Predictably, they won, and exercising their right to deprive the loser of the contest of anything they wished, took away his sight as well as his poetic gift. The root of his name appears to be *thama*, 'together in crowds', 'close', 'thick'. This is difficult to apply to one person, so perhaps it is better to consider the other sense of the word, which is 'often', 'frequent'. This could refer to his frequent singing and lyre-playing: perhaps indeed his name is a contraction of something like 'Thamalyris', so that it contains not just the *thama* element but also *lyra*, 'lyre'.

Thanatos was the son of Nyx (night) and the brother of Hypnos (sleep). He was the personification of death (*thanatos*). The first part of his name is seen in the modern word 'euthanasia' ('easy death').

Thasus gave his name to Thasus, the large island in the north Aegean Sea. He was the son of Agenor, or Cilix or Poseidon. Perhaps his name is based on *thasso*, 'to sit', 'sit idle', though we have no evidence that he was unusually dilatory or indolent.

Thaumas was an ancient sea-god or Titan (we cannot be quite sure what his functions were), the son of Pontus and Gaia. He married Electra, who bore him Iris and the Harpies. *Thauma* means 'wonder', 'marvel' so no doubt he was a 'sea wonder'. He rather sketchily features in Hesiod's *Theogony*.

Thea has a divine name – literally, since *thea* means 'goddess'. She was the daughter of Chiron the Centaur and was a noted prophetess. She was raped by Aeolus and for a while after this was disguised by Poseidon as a mare named Euippe, as whom she bore the foal Melanippe (these names meaning respectively 'fine mare' and 'black mare').

Theano was the wife of Metapontus, king of Icaria, with another Theano being the wife of Antenor. Her name, like that of Thea, means 'goddess', with the base word *thea*.

Thebe was the Boeotian nymph who gave her name to Thebes, which before this had been called Cadmia, after Cadmus. Her name could be based on *thauma*, 'wonder', so that she is 'admirable'.

Theia (not to be confused with Thea) was a Titaness, the daughter of Uranus and Gaia. She is said to have borne Helios, Eos and Selene to Hyperion, and to have been the mother of the Cercopes by Oceanus. Her name most obviously means 'goddess' (*thea*, see

Thea), but it could also mean 'swift', from *theo*, 'to fly', 'run'. Both interpretations would be suitable for her. She features in some stories as **Euryphaëssa** (which name see).

Theias was one of the possible fathers to whom Myrrha (Smyrna) bore Adonis. His name appears to mean 'diviner', from *theiazo*, 'to practise divinations'.

Theiodamas (or Theodamas) was a king of the Dryopes and the father of Hylas. When he refused to give one of the bulls with which he was ploughing to Heracles, the latter killed him and carried off his handsome son Hylas to be his escort. His name means 'divine tamer', from *theos*, 'god' and *damazo*, 'to tame'. This would have been a propitious name.

Themis was a Titaness, the daughter of Uranus and Gaia and the second consort of Zeus (after Metis). She was originally, like her mother, an earth goddess, but later became more and more special-ised until she became a goddess of order, being particularly as-sociated with assemblies. The Greek word *themis* means 'law', 'right', but both it and her own name may derive from a root *the-* meaning 'put', 'make fast', as in *tithemi*, 'to set', 'settle', 'de-termine'. Her name is certainly related to English 'theme' and 'thesis', and possibly also to 'doom': as Jane Harrison points out, Doomsday is Judgment Day.

Themiste was the daughter of Ilus, king of Troy, and she was the mother of Anchises by Capys. Her name has the same basis as that of Themis, and may be specifically linked to *themisteuo*, 'to give laws', 'give oracles', 'govern'. This is an appropriately 'comman-ding' name for a princess.

Themisto was the daughter of Hypseus, king of the Lapiths. She married Athamas, king of Orchomenus, and bore him a number of sons, including Erythrius and Schoeneus. As with Themiste, her name is an 'authoritarian' and powerful one, from *themis*, *themistos*, 'law', 'right', 'sanctions'.

Theoclymenus was an Argive seer or prophet descended from Melampus (whose name see). Another of the name was a king of Egypt, the son of Proteus. For both, the name is a propitious one, meaning 'famous as a god', from *theos*, 'god' and *cleos*, 'fame' (or *cleinos*, 'famous').

291

Theogone was the wife of Ares and mother of Tmolus. Her name means 'divinely born', 'child of the gods', from *theos*, 'god' and *gonos*, 'child', 'offspring'. This is a somewhat high-powered propitious name for a relatively minor character. However, she *did* marry Ares.

Theonoë was the later name of Eido or Eidothea, the daughter of Proteus, king of Egypt and Psamathe. Her name means 'divine mind', from *theos*, 'god' and *noos*, 'mind', 'purpose'. For her original name, see **Eidothea**.

Theophane was the daughter of king Bisaltes, who reigned in Thrace. She was known for her beauty and had many suitors, but Poseidon carried her off to the island of Crumissa (or Crinissa) where he metamorphosed her into a ewe and coupled with her himself as a ram. (This was a ruse to foil the suitors who had tracked her down on the island.) Her name means 'divine showing', from *theos*, 'god' and *phaino*, 'to show'. This could mean either 'she who appears as a goddess' or 'she who makes a god appear'. The former would refer to her beauty; the latter to Poseidon.

Theras was the son of king Autesion of Thebes. He led parties of Spartans and Minyans to the island of Calliste ('beautiful'), which thereupon became known as Thera. His name means 'hunter', 'chaser', 'seeker', from *thera*, 'hunting', 'pursuit', 'chase'. This could denote his 'pursuit' for a territory of his own, since although Theras ruled Sparta, he did so on behalf of his nephews Procles and Eurysthenes. When these twins came of age and were able to rule Sparta jointly, Theras sought his own kingdom, and found it on Calliste.

Theronice, with Therophone, was the twin daughter of Dexamenus, king of Olenus. She married Cteatus, one of the Moliones. Her name seems to mean 'wild beast tamer', from *ther*, 'animal' and *nice*, 'victory'. This would be intended metaphorically as a propitious or 'power' name rather than a literal one. The name of her sister has a similar sense, meaning 'animal slayer', from *ther*, 'animal' and *phone*, 'slaughter'.

Thersander was a son of Polynices and Argia, and a king of Thebes. Another Thersander was a son of Sisyphus. The name means 'encourager of men', from *tharsyno*, 'to encourage' and *aner*, *andros*, 'man'. An alternative interpretation might be 'warm men', from *thermos*, 'warm', 'hot', 'rash', 'hasty' and *aner*, *andros*. This could be purely descriptive in an allusive sense, referring to busy activity such as commerce, or else to rashness of action. Either of these two shades of meaning could refer specifically to the son of Sisyphus, since Sisyphus himself was noted for his activity and enterprise, as well as his cunning.

Thersites was a Greek soldier in the Trojan War who was given to mocking the Greek leaders, especially Achilles and Odysseus, to make his audience laugh. In spite of this characteristic, which eventually cost him his life (Achilles killed him for his ridicule), his name means simply 'courageous', from *tharsos*, 'courage', 'boldness'. This must have been a propitious name that never quite worked out.

Theseus, king of Athens, was the great Attic hero who was the opposite number of Heracles, the Dorian hero. He was the son of either Aegeus or Poseidon and Pittheus' daughter Aethra. His name can be interpreted on a general level as 'orderer', 'regulator', on a more specific basis as 'settler', 'civiliser', or with a purely local and incidental reference, as 'putter', 'depositor'. All of these senses derive from *tithemi*, 'to put', 'place', 'set', 'determine', 'deposit' and the like – the verb has at least ten basic meanings. The first two of these interpretations, the general and the specific, are self-explanatory, especially in view of the hero's method of dealing with evil or unscrupulous persons (he was a great slayer of villains, among them Sinis, Procrustes and, most famous of all, the Minotaur). The third interpretation, the incidental one, refers to the sword and sandals of Aegeus that were 'deposited' or simply 'put' for him under a boulder as tokens. True, in this case it was Aegeus who was the putter or depositor, but it could be argued that he was doing so symbolically and prophetically, since the sword would be used by Theseus for civilising and settling, and the sandals for travelling and adventuring in order to bring order and stability. For Theseus all is theme and thesis, putting and settling, and of all mythological characters his name is unique in exploiting to the full the many meanings of a single highly significant verb. (Among other characters whose names also derive from *tithemi* see **Themis** and **Thetis**.)

Thespius was the king and namer of Thespiae, a city west of Thebes. His name is based on *thespis*, 'inspired', 'prophetic', 'divine' (from *theos*, 'god' and *epos*, 'word', 'prophecy'), and indicates an actual or desirable oracular or prophetic gift. The word 'Thespian', often used facetiously to mean 'actor' or 'actress', de-

Theseus, the 'orderer'. Here he 'orders' or puts paid to four evil characters (from top left): Cercyon, the Minotaur, Sciron and Procrustes. Note that Theseus dispenses with dress and weapons to enact his feats: the axe he holds is for paying Procrustes in his own coin, by 'lopping' him as he had 'lopped' others.

rives not from him but from a real person, Thespis, the sixth-century BC actor who was called the Father of Greek Tragedy.

Thesprotus, whose name passed to Thesprotia, a region in southern Epirus, gave shelter to Pelopia, the daughter of Thyestes. We are told little about him, but perhaps we may risk interpreting his name as 'first law', from *thesmos*, 'rule', 'law' and *protos*, 'first'. Admittedly, it is hard to see what precisely this 'first law' was or could be.

Thessalus was the son of Jason and Medea who gave his name to Thessaly. All one can suggest here is an origin somehow in *thessasthai*, 'to pray for'. This could, of course, be a name of good omen and of optimism.

Thestius (not to be confused with Thespius) was a king of Pleuron in Aetolia, and the son of Ares and Demonice (or of Agenor and Epicaste, in which case Demonice was his sister). By Eurythemis, Leucippe or some other woman he was the father of a number of children, including two sons Toxeus and Plexippus and daughters Althaea, Hypermnestra and Leda. His name may be a kind of masculine equivalent of Hestia (whom see), so that he is a domestic or 'hearth' god.

Thestor was perhaps the father of Calchas, and he came from either Megara or Mycenae. We have very little to help us here, so all we can do is propose some meaning such as 'diviner', from *theiazo*, 'to practise divinations'.

Thetis, though only a minor sea-goddess (a Nereid), played an important part in many stories. She was brought up by Hera, and was the daughter of Nereus and Doris and, more importantly, the mother of Achilles by Peleus. Her name seems to have the *the-* root seen also in Theseus and Themis (and also Tethys), so that she could be another 'disposer'.

Thisbe was loved by Pyramus, as both Ovid and Shakespeare tell and retell. The names of both lovers may well be of Asiatic origin, with an assimilation to Greek. Perhaps Thisbe's name approximates to that of Thespis, so that she is 'divine' or 'prophetic'. (Oddly enough, there was a town Thisbe in Boeotia, not too far from Thespia, both places being at the foot of Mount Helicon.) It sounds the sort of classical and romantic name that ought to have become a vogue modern first name, but somehow it has never caught on.

295

Thoas, meaning 'quick-moving', 'nimble', was the name of a number of characters including the son of Dionysus and Ariadne and his grandson (the son of Jason and Hypsipyle), the son of Andraemon and Gorge, and a giant who was the brother of Agrius. Its origin is in *thoazo*, 'to move quickly', 'hurry along'.

Thoösa was a sea-nymph, the mother of Polyphemus the Cyclops by Poseidon. She herself was the mother of Phorcys. Her name means 'quick', 'nimble' (*thoos*), which must be a good name for a sea-nymph or indeed any kind of nymph.

Thyestes was a son of Pelops and Hippodamia. By him (and so incestuously) his daughter Pelopia bore Aegisthus (who killed Agamemnon). His name suggests anger, from *thyo*, 'to rage', 'storm', and we know that with his brother Atreus he killed their half-brother Chrysippus. An identical verb *thyo*, however, means 'to sacrifice', and this may refer to the many flocks and herds he was said to possess.

Thymbraeüs was the twin brother of Antiphas, both children being the sons of Laocoön. They and their father were crushed to death by sea-serpents. His name may be derived from *thymbra*, 'savory', a fragrant but bitter-tasting herb. One can only guess at the implied significance of this (the crushing of a young life seen as both fragrant and bitter). Thymbraeüs was also one of the by-names of Apollo (see Appendix III, page 323), but this derives from the town of Thymbre, not from Thymbraeüs.

Thymoëtes was one of the elders of Troy and, according to Virgil's *Aeneid*, the first to suggest that the Wooden Horse should be moved inside the walls of Troy. His name could derive from *thymoeides*, 'high-spirited', 'courageous' (from *thymos*, 'soul', 'courage' and *eidos*, 'form', 'shape', 'figure'). This could be both a suitably 'belligerent' name for a warrior and also a descriptive one for this particular man.

Thyone was the new 'heavenly' name of Semele when she was taken up to heaven by Dionysus, her son. The name is based on *thyo*, 'to rush', 'rage', so means 'raging', 'storming', suggesting a powerful ecstasy.

Thyreus was one of the four sons of Oeneus and Althea. His name, like that of Tydeus and Thyone, is based on *thyo*, 'to storm', 'rage', although in his case not so much ecstatically as impetuously.

Timandra was the daughter of Tyndareüs. She married Echemus but left him for Phyleus. Her name reads rather ironically in view of this, since it means 'honoured by man', from *timao*, 'to honour' and *aner*, *andros*, 'man'. It is hardly any better if interpreted as 'honouring man'!

Tiphys was a helmsman of the *Argo*, the son of Hagnias or Phorbas and possibly Hyrmina. He was in charge of the launching of the *Argo* and steered it safely through many dangers. Appropriately, his name means 'pool' (*tiphos*).

Tisamenus was a king of Sparta and Argos, and a son of Orestes by Hermione. He was overthrown by the Heraclids (the descendants of Heracles) when they invaded the Peloponnese, and led a band of followers to the north where, however, he was killed fighting the Heraclids or in some other battle. Another Tisamenus was a king of Thebes, the son of Thersander and Demonassa. His reign was markedly uneventful, and he was succeeded by his son Autesion. The name of both kings is inappropriate for their actual lives and reigns, since it means 'strength of revenge', 'retribution', from *tisis*, 'penalty', 'punishment', 'reward' and *menos*, 'strength', 'spirit'. Of course, in the case of Orestes' son the name could more broadly indicate the continuing feud between the house of Thyestes and that of his brother Atreus.

Tisiphone was one of the Furies, with her decidedly 'furious' name meaning 'avenging murder' or 'vengeful destruction'. The two elements in the name are *tisis*, 'penalty', 'punishment', 'retaliation' and *phone*, 'murder', 'slaughter'. Avenging the murder of members of a family was precisely the role played by the Furies or Erinyes, a notable example being the revenge they wrought on Orestes and Alcmeon. The Furies drove these young men insane for having murdered their mothers.

Titans were the giant gods who were the offspring of Uranus and Gaia. Hesiod lists twelve of them in his *Theogony*, namely Oceanus, Coeüs, Crius, Hyperion, Iapetus, Theia, Rhea, Themis, Mnemosyne, Phoebe, Tethys and Cronos. These names are a mixed bunch of Greek and non-Greek origins, some expressing abstract concepts (such as Themis and Mnemosyne), others being more specific and 'concrete'. The collective name Titans was said by Hesiod to derive from *titaino*, 'to stretch', 'strain' with a blend of *tisis*, 'vengeance' (see **Tisiphone**), this referring either to their procreative efforts or being an allusion to their relations with their

297

father (Cronos overthrew Uranus for his high-handed behaviour). Needless to say, there have been many attempts since Hesiod to explain the name, ranging from Jane Harrison's *titanos*, 'white earth', 'chalk' (so that they were originally men who painted themselves white to perform initiation rites) to Thomas Keightley's reduplicated *taia*, itself an alleged variant of *aia* or *gaia*, 'earth' (so that they were 'earth men'). Current thinking proposes, albeit tentatively, that the name may derive from *tio*, 'to esteem', 'honour', 'respect', so that they are 'the honoured ones'. Their name lives on in the English 'titanic' to mean 'gigantic', 'colossal'.

Tithonus, a handsome youth, was snatched from the palace of his father, king Laomedon, by Eros, goddess of the dawn. His mother was either Strymo, Placia or Leucippe. Some writers say Eros turned him into a cricket, and that his name comes from the Greek word for this insect, *tettix*. Again, Zeus made Tithonus immortal (but not ageless) so that this extension of his life may be reflected in his name if it contains the element *teino*, 'to stretch'. A more likely source would be *tithemi*, 'to put', 'set', 'order' (as for Themis, Thetis and Theseus), referring to one who was 'ordered' by the goddess of the dawn, who reigns daily in a preordained manner. One of the more obscure explanations is offered by the *Classical Manual*, where the name is 'said by some to be derived from two words implying "the mount of the sun" . . . Tithonus being nothing more than a tower, sacred to the sun'. Compare this same tome's explanation for **Triton**.

Tityus was a giant, said to be the son of Zeus and either Gaia or Elare (the daughter of Orchomenus). He is chiefly known for his attempt to rape Leto. For this offence he was taken to Hades and stretched helpless on the ground while two vultures ate his liver, which grew again with each new cycle of the moon. The liver was the supposed seat of lust, and if Tityus is regarded as a kind of personification of lust, his name can be seen as a reduplication of *thyo*, 'to rush on', 'rage', such a reduplication resembling those considered for Sisyphus and Tantalus. There certainly seems to be something phallic or erotic in his name even if one derives it instead from *titycomai*, 'to prepare', 'aim at'.

Tlepolemus was the son of Heracles and Astyoche, and he was a king of Ephyra in Thesprotia. His name is simply a propitious belligerent one, meaning 'enduring in battle', from *tlao*, 'to endure', 'hold out' and *polemos*, 'war'.

Tmolus was a god or a king associated with Mount Tmolus who decided the musical contest between Apollo and Pan. According to some accounts he was the husband of Pluto (the daughter of Cronos) and the father of Tantalus. His name is almost certainly not Greek in origin, and the only Greek word remotely resembling his name is *tmego*, 'to cut', 'be divided'. This is so general that it could apply in a number of ways according to whim: for example the musical contest could be said to be 'cut' or 'divided' by Tmolus.

Toxeus was the name of one or two characters. If two, they were the son of Thestius and brother of Althaea, and his nephew who was the son of Oeneus and Althaea. For one or the other (or both) the name is simply descriptive, and means 'archer', from *toxon*, 'bow'.

Triballus was the twin brother of Sillus, and one of the two Cercopes who made Heracles' life such a misery. (For their other names, see **Sillus**.) His name seems to derive from *tribo*, 'to rub', 'wear out', 'waste time', 'oppress', in other words he was a 'harasser' or 'time-waster'.

Triops (or Triopas) was the name of several characters, including a number of kings of Argos, Thessaly and Rhodes. One Triops was a son of Phorbas, another was the son of Poseidon and Canace, a third was the son of Helios and Rhode. For these and many more the name means either 'three-eyed' or 'three-faced', from *tri-*, 'three' and *ops*, 'face', 'eye'. The 'three-eyed' reading makes sense for the son of Phorbas, who was engaged by Temenus as a guide when conquering the Peloponnese. For the others the reference may be a generally divine or magical one, alluding to an ancient sky-god, perhaps. One of the by-names of Zeus was Trioculus, and of Apollo was Triopius (see their respective Appendices V and III, pages 330 and 323). See also Zeus' by-name Infernalis, page 333.

Triptolemus was a young Attic man chosen by Demeter to be the medium through which her gift of the plough and agriculture (which he is said to have invented) could be passed to men. The easiest way to interpret his name is to make him a 'triple warrior', from *tri-*, and *ptolemos*, the Epic form of *polemus*, 'war' (compare the name of Neoptolemus, who was a 'young warrior'). This would suggest he was originally some kind of war god on the lines of Ares. Or perhaps he was a 'threefold ploughman', from *tri-* and *poleuo*, 'to plough'. This accords well with his agricultural speciality and his association with Demeter.

Triptolemus and Demeter. Triptolemus (note his 'three-fold' ear of grain) sits in Demeter's magic chariot. Behind him stands Persephone.

Triton was a minor sea god, a merman, in effect, who was the son of Poseidon and Amphitrite. By muddled association with Neptune (his father), who is usually depicted holding a trident, his name also suggests 'trident'. But Triton, in fact, is usually depicted holding a large shell or conch, and he is not associated with a trident at all, either pictorially or linguistically. There may, however, be a link between his name and that of his mother, Amphitrite. In considering her name (see her entry) we mentioned both *tritos*, 'third' and *tryo*, 'to wear out' as possible sources. These can equally well apply to Triton with the same application, i.e., the sea as the third element and as a corrosive force. The 'sea' link certainly seems the most promising, and is supported by words in some languages that actually mean 'sea', such as Old Irish *triath*, genitive *trethan*. The *Classical Manual* proposes an etymology similar to the one it offers for Tithonus: 'some say a corruption of *Tirit-On*, and to have meant "tower of the sun"'.

Troezen was a son of Pelops and Hippodamia. It is also the name of a city in south-east Argolis, which Pittheus, his brother, is said to have named in his honour, combining the two former towns of Hypereia and Antheia ('Upper Town' and 'Flower Town'). Robert Graves says the name is apparently a worn-down form of *trion hezomenon*, '(city) of the three sitters', from *tri-*, 'three' and *hezomai*, 'to sit'. This, he says, refers to the three thrones that served 'Pittheus and two others' as seats of justice.

Troilus was the son of Priam (or Apollo) and Hecabe. His name can be read as either 'Trojan' or 'descendant of Tros'. The latter, of course, gave his name to Troy (see his name). Troilus' name is more familiar from Shakespeare's play *Troilus and Cressida* than it is from the brief references to him by classical writers such as Homer and Virgil. In his play, Shakespeare seems to enjoy the name:

Cressida. And is it true I must go from Troy?
Troilus. A hateful truth.
Cressida. What, and from Troilus too?
Troilus. From Troy and Troilus.

Trophonius was a son of Erginus, king of Orchomenus, and he was renowned for being a fine architect and builder. His brother was Agamedes (see his name for an object lesson in crime not paying). Trophonius' name apparently means 'feeder' (*trophos*), whereas one might expect it to allude somehow to his architectural

301

achievements. Perhaps originally he was a kind of 'nourishing' or earth god. The English word 'trophy' is not related to his name, but comes from Greek *tropos*, 'turning'. (Turn an enemy and you get victory; get a victory and you get a trophy.)

Tros, predictably, was a king of Troy, and his name is inextricably linked with the name of the city. He married the river-nymph Callirrhoë, and she bore him Ganymede. At its basest level, we can only interpret his name as 'Trojan'. The actual origin of the city name is still unresolved. All we do know is that so called 'troy' weight derives not from the Greek city but from the French town of Troyes. This is rather disappointing. The French are luckier: their word *truie*, 'sow' derives from the Greek city via Latin *porcus troianus*, 'Trojan pig'. It seems that in the twelfth century, a type of game stuffing was so called in humorous allusion to the Wooden Horse, which was 'stuffed' with Greek soldiers to capture Troy.

Tyche was the goddess of fortune, answering to the Roman Fortuna. She was the daughter of Oceanus (or Zeus) and Tethys. The name comes from the verb *tynchano*, 'to hit', and reflects its various shades of meaning, such as 'to hit on by chance', 'obtain', 'gain one's end', 'happen to be', 'befall', 'chance to be' and the like. In other words the 'hit' or fortune could be good or bad. Tyche played an important role in situations where chance really mattered, as in athletics, drawing lots, love, seafaring, and so on. In all these, as in life itself, a good 'hit' can result in supreme success and happiness, while a bad 'hit' can end in disaster. Tyche also had an important influence on whole cities, as well as on individuals.

Tydeus was a son of Oeneus, king of Calydon, by his second wife Periboea or his daughter (sic) Gorge. He was a warrior with the Seven Against Thebes, and his belligerence may be indicated in his name if we derive it from *thyo*, 'to rush along', 'dart along' (compare **Thyreus**). But if we are looking for an 'incident' name, we may be able to find it in *tymma*, 'thump', 'blow', for Tydeus killed his brother Melanippus when out hunting, although he maintained that this was accidental. Compare **Tyndareüs**, below.

Tyndareüs was a king of Sparta, the son of Batia or Gorgophone. He married Leda. His name may be related to the family of words connected with *daio*, 'to burn', 'blaze' and Latin *taeda*, 'torch' that are to do with light and heat. One of these (say, *taeda*) would then have an inserted 'n' as (perhaps) Lynceus has, from *lyce*. This could be a propitious name for a king, who metaphorically radiates light and warmth to his people. But this theory is suspect – in spite of English 'tinder', that seems to support it. Perhaps it would be better to settle for a belligerent name, and we would have this, as for Tydeus, in *tymma*, 'thump', 'blow'. As a Spartan hero and the father of Castor and Pollux, Helen (of Troy) and Clytemnestra, Tyndareus must have been involved in a good deal of 'thumping' and must have been responsible for many 'blows'. Indeed, he was indirectly responsible for the Trojan War, since he made Helen's suitors take an oath that they would support the chosen bridegroom, whoever he was to be, and protect his marriage rights. It was this oath that led the Greeks, some years later, to go to Troy to win back Helen from Paris who held her there, having won her as his wife as a result of a gift from Aphrodite.

Typhon was a monster, the offspring of Tartarus and Gaia. It was said to have had a hundred burning snake heads ('those of a dreaded dragon') and to speak with both men's and animals' voices. It was eventually overcome by Zeus, who after a few ineffectual lightning-strikes managed to crush it with a mountain. The creature seems to have had its origin in the god that personified either a volcano or a fierce wind, such as the sirocco. Moreover, and not merely from the similarity of the names, it was sometimes confused with the Python. It seems to be oriental in origin (which is why its name relates to 'typhoon'), although Greek *typho*, 'to smoke', 'smoulder' seems relevant.

Tyro was the daughter of Salmoneus and his first wife Alcidice. Her name may be linked to that of Tyrrhenus (which see) and so to *tyrsis*, 'tower', with reference to her father's kingship of Elis. (This word does not, *pace* Robert Graves, seem to be related to 'tyrant', which is strictly speaking the Doric equivalent, *tyrannos*, of *coiranos*, which in turn comes from *cyros* or *cyrios* and means 'lord'.) It seems less likely that Tyro's name comes from the *tryo* element meaning 'to wear out' that we considered for Triton and Amphitrite. The English word 'tyro', incidentally, meaning 'beginner' or 'novice', seems to have no relation at all to her name. It apparently derives from Latin *tiro*, 'military recruit'.

Tyrrhenus was a son of the Lydian king Atys. He gave his name to the Tyrrheniåns (the people known later as Etruscans) and to the Tyrrhenian Sea. His name is also spelt Tyrsenus, which suggests that it may derive from *tyrsis*, 'tower' (compare **Tyro**). This would be a fitting name for a prince, whose family lived in a walled city.

303

Udaeüs was one of the Sown Men. Appropriately, his name means 'of the earth', from *oudas*, 'ground'.

Ulysses (or Ulixes) was of course the Roman name of the great Odysseus, king of Ithaca. The names are sufficiently different for us to look for a separate origin for Ulysses. Robert Graves suggests one in Greek *oulos*, 'wound' and *ischea*, 'thigh', referring to the boar-tusk wound in his thigh that Odysseus received when he went out hunting on Mount Parnassus as a boy with the sons of Autolycus. This wound stayed with him all his life, and it was because of it that Euryclea, his old nurse, recognised him when he eventually returned to Ithaca from Troy. On the other hand, if the Latin form of the name did gradually evolve from the Greek, it must have been through an Attic variant such as 'Olysseus'.

Urania was the Muse of astronomy, her name simply meaning 'heavenly' from *ouranos*, 'heaven'. See **Uranus**.

Uranus was the son of Gaia, without a mate. Having borne him, she then mated with him and produced the Titans. Uranus is the god of the sky, of course, and the popular origin of his name is *ouranos*, 'heaven', 'sky'. This seems so obvious that no doubt many writers have felt there should be a more complex derivation for the name. Eric Partridge, for example, suggests an association with *ouron*, 'urine', with the sense-link being the rain that falls from the sky. Robert Graves proposes 'king of the mountains', this being a masculine form of *Ur-ana*, 'queen of the mountains'. (Presumably the *Ur-* here is the first element in the name of the Ural Mountains.) Yet another theory offers the Sanskrit root *var-*, 'to veil', 'cover', since Uranus was a personification of the heavens that cover the earth. The planet Uranus was discovered by the English astronomer Sir William Herschel in 1781. Herschel was not much of a professional namer, however, and he proposed calling the planet *Georgium Sidus*, 'George's Planet', in honour of King George III. The name 'Georgian' actually lived a hesitant life for about fifty years on and off, while in France the name 'Herschel' was used for the newly discovered planet. Meanwhile some astronomers were not too happy about Herschel's name. In 1783 the Swedish-born Russian astronomer A.I. Lexell presented a report about Uranus to the St Petersburg Academy of Sciences, in which he stated that Herschel's name was 'not fully appropriate' and that it would be more fitting 'to name this body "Neptune of George III" or "Neptune of Great Britain" in memory of the great feats undertaken by the English fleets over the past two years'.

Uranus, thus, was nearly called Neptune! But already two years before, in the year of discovery, the German astronomer Johann Elert Bode had suggested Uranus as an appropriate name, since this god was, after all, the father of Saturn, who in turn was the father of Jupiter. Jupiter and Saturn were the two planets already in existence, of course, next to Uranus, and this latter name was therefore the one to be accepted. It was notable for being the first Greek planet name, since there is no Roman equivalent name for Uranus.

Urion see **Orion**.

Venus was the Roman goddess of fertility and gardens, the equivalent of Aphrodite. Her name is traditionally derived from Latin *venus*, *veneris*, 'desire', 'grace', 'charm', 'sexual love', a word which is related to English 'venerate' and even 'winsome'. It also seems to link up with *venia*, 'grace or favour of the gods', and *venenum*, 'magic drug', 'charm' (English 'venom'). As is to be expected, there have been a number of other attempts to explain the name, including *vanus*, 'empty' and *venio*, 'to come'. This latter interpretation was the one favoured by William Camden in his *Remains Concerning Britain*, although in citing it, he disapprovingly mentioned yet another etymology that had obviously been current: 'Coming to all, as Cicero derived it, à veniendo, a fit name for a good wench. But for shame it is turned of some to Venice.' However, the name is actually almost certainly pre-Roman, as pointed out by Varro, the Roman scholar born in 116 BC, who wrote, *cuius nomen ego antiquis litteris . . . nusquam inveni*, 'whose name I nowhere found in previous writings'. The original Greek name of the planet Venus was either *Hesperos* ('evening', see **Hesperides**), *Phosphoros* ('light-bearing', see **Phosphoros**) or *Eosphoros* ('bearing the dawn', see **Eos** and **Phosphoros**). More than one name was used of the planet since Venus can be observed in both the evening and the morning, and the Greeks thought that they were seeing two separate 'stars'. (It was Pythagoras, incidentally, who first suggested that it was actually a single heavenly body.) Of these three names, *Hesperos*, of course, was the planet's evening one, while *Phosphoros* and *Eosphoros* were alternative morning names. Later, when the Greeks were eventually convinced that Venus was only a single planet, her name of Aphrodite appeared, this being recorded by Aristotle and his teacher Plato in the third century BC. Finally the Roman name came, although not before the Romans in turn had abandoned their own 'morning' and 'evening' names for the planet of Lucifer ('light-bringer') and Vesper ('evening', as English 'ves-

305

pers'). (It was much later than this that Lucifer came to be a nickname of the Devil in Christian mythology.) For some of the many by-names of Venus, see Appendix II, page 319.

Vertumnus (or Vortumnus) was a Roman god of fertility, especially as evidenced in the changing seasons. According to Ovid, he won the love of the fruit goddess Pomona. His name derives from *verto*, 'to turn', referring to the seasons, but this in turn is probably a translation of a Tuscan name.

Vesta was the Roman goddess of the hearth, the equivalent of the Greek Hestia. The names are linguistically related, and for the basic origins see **Hestia**. In a Roman household, much as in a Greek one, her shrine was the hearth, actual or symbolic, and Romans offered prayers to her before the main meal. The attractively alliterative Vestal Virgins were Roman priestesses whose duty it was to attend the sacred hearth-fires. Traditionally there were six of them, serving in the temple of Vesta at Rome. They were elected by lot from a short list of twenty girls and officiated for at least thirty years: ten of learning and initiation, ten of actual ministration, and ten in turn teaching the initiates. They really were virgins, and if they lost their virginity during their term of office the penalty was death by being buried alive. There seems to have been another Vesta of some kind, perhaps a kind of earth goddess, who was said to have been the wife of Coelus and even the mother of Saturn. Her name, according to some, was nothing to do with Hestia's, but was from the earth being clothed (*vestita*) with plants, or else from the stability of the earth, so that *sua vi stat*, 'it stands by its strength'!

Victoria was the Roman opposite number of Nike, so was (obviously) the goddess of victory. Her cult associated her with Jupiter (one of whose by-names was Victor), and even more often, with Mars. She was most fervently favoured, understandably enough, by soldiers in the army.

Virbius was a Roman god associated with the worship of Diana. When Diana was identified with Artemis, Virbius was identified with Hippolytus, and it was explained that he had been raised from the dead by Asclepius and brought to Rome by Artemis. In view of this 'rebirth', many writers have not been able to resist the temptation to derive his name from *vir bis*, 'a man for a second time'! Almost as unlikely is a link that has been proposed with *verbena*, in spite of the religious associations of this herb. More likely is a derivation from something like *hiros*, 'holy' and *bios*, 'life', with the 'h' becoming 'b' as in the Hestia and Vesta doublet.

Voluptas hardly needs any explanation. She was the daughter of Cupid and Psyche, and the personification of pleasure, *voluptas*.

Vulcan was the Roman god of fire, the equivalent of Hephaestus. He gave his name to the volcano, which epitomises the kind of natural, uncontrolled fire that he personified. (He was not associated, for example, with fires that were deliberately lit or kept burning for a special purpose, such as a sacred fire.) His name (in Latin Vulcanus) may derive from a Cretan god of fire called something like Welkhanos, this actually meaning 'god of fire'. It has been suggested that this name in turn may be related to Latin *ignis*, 'fire', especially as there was an Asian fire god Agni. (The latter, unlike Vulcan, was a god of the sacred fire, and worship was offered at his altar.)

Xanthus was the immortal horse of Achilles, just as Balius was. He was the son of Zephyrus (the west wind) and the Harpy Podarge. As a colour, *xanthus* basically means 'yellow', but for a horse's coat, as here, it can also mean 'bay', 'chestnut' or 'golden'. Perhaps, though, the colour refers more specifically to the horse's mane, in which case he could even be a 'palomino'.

Xuthus was a son of Hellen and the nymph Orseïs, or else of Aeolus and Enarete. He was a king of Athens and married Creüsa, the daughter of Erechtheus. Robert Graves derives his name from *strouthos*, 'sparrow', which stretches the credulity for both word and sense. More likely, the name is a variant of Xanthus, so that the king was 'yellow-haired'. However, there is another colour *xouthos*, described by Liddell and Scott as 'between *xanthos* and *pyrros*', i.e. between yellow and red, so meaning 'tawny', 'dusky'. This seems the best reading of his name, and refers either to his skin, his complexion, his hair – or all three.

Zagreus is a somewhat obscure Cretan god identified with Dionysus. Although his name is almost certainly not Greek, it has been approximated to *zao*, 'to live' and has been interpreted as 'mighty hunter', from *za-*, an intensive like *ari-* (see **Ariadne** and **Arion**), and *agreo*, 'to hunt'.

Zelus was a constant companion of Zeus, together with his brothers Bia and Cratos and his sister Nike. His fidelity is expressed in his name, which means 'emulation', 'zeal' (*zelos*).

Zephyrus was the god of the west wind, the only son of Astraeüs and Eos. According to some stories, he caused the death of Hyacinthus through jealousy of the beautiful boy's love for Apollo. His name may relate to *zophos*, 'darkness', 'west' (darkness comes from the west when the sun sets), just as Eurus (which see) means 'morning', 'east'.

Zethus was the twin brother of Amphion, both being the sons of Zeus and Antiope and joint rulers of Thebes. As for Zetus, Euripides connected the name with *zeteo*, 'to seek', 'search out', although if we interpret Amphion's name as 'he who goes round', from *amphi*, 'round' (see names starting with this), and regard him as representing the sun, then Zethus could have a name originating in *zeo*, 'to boil', 'heat', and share his twin's representation. The idea is fanciful, of course, yet the brothers' mother was Antiope, whose 'face opposite' name could allude to the moon – and the twins *were* the sons of the great sky-god Zeus!

Zetus (or Zetes) with Calaïs, was one of the twin sons of Boreas and Orithyia. His name is best derived from *zao*, 'to blow', especially in view of his parents' 'windy' names (see them) and his own function, with Calaïs, as a winged chaser of the Harpies when these monsters were plaguing their brother-in-law, king Phineus. Even an origin based on *zeleo*, 'to search out', would also be fitting. According to an ancient theory, Calaïs' name meant 'he who blows gently', while Zetus' meant 'he who blows hard'.

Zeus was the supreme ruler of the Greek gods, the Roman Jupiter or Jove, and his name is one of the few major Greek god-names that we can definitely say is Indo-European. It contains the root for 'sky' or 'day' in a number of languages, for example the actual word for 'day' in Latin (*dies*), French (*jour*), German (*Tag*), Russian (*den*) and English 'day' itself. The name is reflected in those of other similar 'sky' gods, too, such as the Scandinavian Tiw or Tiu, whose name comes in our 'Tuesday'. More importantly, his name is 'god' itself, as in Latin *deus*, Greek *theos* and French *dieu*. In fact, we get the same powerful amalgam that can be found in the name of Diana (which see). In addition, there have been attempts to associate his name with *zao*, 'to live'. Aeschylus was a supporter of this origin. In short, for this greatest of gods, the sky's the limit when it comes to basic interlinguistic associations.

Zeuxippe was a Naiad. She married her nephew Pandion, king of Athens, and bore him twin sons, Erechtheus and Butes, and twin daughters, Procne and Philomela. Her name may be simply propitious, since it means 'she who yokes horses', from *zeugos*, 'yoke of beasts', 'pair of horses' and *hippos*, 'horse'. (Greek *zeugos* and English 'yoke' are related words.) But could not this 'pair of horses' actually refer to her two sets of twins?

APPENDICES

The seven Appendices that follow are designed both to supplement and complement the main text of the Dictionary, and they can thus be regarded as suitable for reference, for interest, or simply for browsing.

Appendix I lists some of the most common elements that can combine to form classical Greek names, with both the actual elements and the names themselves taken from the Dictionary. (The names are purely by way of example, and not all the names in the Dictionary containing the particular element are given.) The overwhelmingly 'propitious' nature of the elements, as shown by their basic English senses, is immediately apparent. Here are 'king', 'bright', 'self', 'beautiful', 'good', 'horse', 'gold', 'abiding', 'loving', 'fame', 'strength', and many more. With twentieth-century reservations over the more obviously belligerent epithets, almost all the senses are ones that appeal to man today, more than two thousand years since the age when they expressed the Greek ideal. Who does not wish for fame, power, health, wealth and beauty, even if for another? The lists, in an admittedly selective way, serve as a mirror to man's agelong aspirations, and epitomise the values that he holds most dearly and the goals that he aims to attain.

At a more practical level, the elements here listed can enable the reader to 'crack' a number of Greek names fairly readily. This holds good for both mythological names and 'real' ones, which otherwise do not figure in the book, of course. It is thus possible to deduce that Demosthenes, the great Athenian orator and statesman, has a name that means 'power of the people', and that the equally well-known statesman Pericles, who lived a good century before him, has 'fame all round'. (The names of other great Greeks can be similarly translated with the help of the main entries in the Dictionary, so that a combination of Archippe and Diomedes will reveal that Archimedes was potentially an 'excellent ruler', and a blend of Hippolytus and Naucrate or Pancratis will show the famous physician Hippocrates to be 'superior in horse'.)

Appendix II is a select but fairly comprehensive list of the by-names of Aphrodite (otherwise Venus). As explained in the Introduction (page 12), a 'by-name', as here understood, is a specific name for a god or goddess, often used together with his or her main name. It usually either describes a desired or desirable attribute, or derives from a particular place sacred to the deity, or applies in a particular way to an event in the deity's life or to a characteristic feature. Thus a desired or desirable attribute of Aphrodite is Charidotes, 'giver of joy' (which her worshippers desired her to be or which she desirably was anyway). She was specially worshipped in Cyprus (her 'birthplace'), so was called Cypria, and she was both 'born from the sea' (as Aligena) and 'bright-haired' (as Comaetho). All four types

313

of name occur in a number of varieties to give us a good, all-round picture of the nature of the goddess and of her special characteristics and associations – mainly, as to be expected, love and beauty.

Appendix III, on similar lines to those of Appendix II, gives a reasonable selection of the by-names of Apollo. Here, too, we can obtain a fullish picture of the god: what his worshippers wanted him to be or what he was already believed to be (as Exacesterius), where he was worshipped (as Delius), what happened during his life (as Pyctes), and what physical or special characteristics he had (as Euchaites). The overall image he presents is mainly of one of power, handsomeness and belligerence.

Appendix IV offers some of the by-names of Athena (Minerva). Her general picture is one of an almost Amazonian blend of belligerence and beauty, which one must own is rather alluring.

Appendix V is predictably the longest list of by-names – those of Zeus or Jupiter. He, after all, was the god of gods, the embodiment of all that man would be, yet could never be. His special association is the storm, hence the several names relating to thunder and lightning. He can come to aid both to drive away troublesome flies (Myiodes) and to win booty in battle (Praedator); he brings health (Salutaris) and wealth (Plusius); he presides over banquets (Epipinates), marriages (Gamelius), houses (Herceus) and laws (Nomius); he is both saviour (Soter) and preserver of life (Zenogonos). In short he is perfect (Teleius).

Appendix VI is the most down to earth (in more senses than one) of the lists. Here are the names – not by-names but actual individual names – of forty of the hounds of Actaeon. Apart from the few famous horses in mythology, notably Pegasus, Heracles' horse Arion, Achilles' horses Balius and Xanthus, and the Mares of Diomedes (Deinus, Lampon, Podargus and Xanthus), they are the most extensive animal names we have in Greek mythology. Most of the dogs' names are mentioned by Ovid in his *Metamorphoses*, in the story about Actaeon. This hapless hero was changed ('metamorphosed') into a stag by Diana (or Artemis), whom he had accidentally seen bathing naked, and so attacked and killed by his own formerly faithful hounds. Traditionally there were fifty hounds (what modern huntsmen would call 'twenty-five couple') but the names of all fifty have not been reliably recorded. Forty names, however, enable us to see how the Greeks named their hunting dogs, and the list reveals that dog names (Barker, Spot, Shaggy) have hardly changed over the ages. These were 'working' dogs, of course, not pets, so it is to be expected that many of the names will refer to their business-like potential as trackers, runners and killers, hence such names as Ichnobates, Dromas and Nebrophonos. Even so, names for the dogs' physical characteristics, such as the colour of their coat or their strength, are also popular.

Appendix VII, placed last in order for ease of reference as a kind of 'index', is a list of the parallel Greek and Roman names of mythological characters who came to be identified as one and the same – or as sharing common attributes or characteristics. As mentioned in the Dictionary in many of the respective entries, the Roman doubles who evolved out of the Greek originals frequently acquired a specialised or even changed persona. This does not invalidate the fact that the two names have come to be generally identified as referring to one and the same character. Some Roman names are patently latinised adaptations of the Greek name (as Heracles and Hercules). Most of the names are quite dissimilar, how-ever, and these are the ones for which a check-list such as this will probably be most useful. (The English form of the Roman name is given if this is the traditional one. This applies for Saturn, Cupid, Vulcan, Mercury, Proserpine and Neptune, whose Latin forms are properly Saturnus, Cupidus, Vulcanus, Mercurius, Pro-serpina and Neptunus.)

In Appendices II to VI cross-references are given, wherever it is felt to be helpful or interesting, to names either in other Appendices or in the main body of the Dictionary. In Appendices II to V, (G) indicates a Greek name and (L) a Latin one.

APPENDIX I

Common Elements in Greek Mythological Names

(A) *To begin name*

A-	'not'	Acamas, Acastus, Achilles, Adrastea, Alecto, Amazons
Aege-	'goat'	Aegaeon, Aegeus, Aegimius, Aegina, Aegisthus
Aga-	'very'	Agamedes, Agamemnon, Agapenor, Agathyrsus
Alc(i)-	'might'	Alcestis, Alcidice, Alcimedes, Alcinoüs, Alcippe, Alcmaeon
Alex(i)-	'averting'	Alexander, Alexiares, Alexirrhoë
Amphi-	'around'	Amphidamas, Amphilocus, Amphinomus, Amphitrite, Amphitryon
Anax-	'king', 'queen'	Anaxagoras, Anaxarete, Anaxibia, Anaxo
Andro-	'man'	Androclea, Androgeüs, Andromache, Andromeda
Anti-	'against'	Anticlea, Antigone, Antilochus, Antinoüs, Antiope
Arg-	'bright'	Argia, Argiope, Argo, Argus
Aster-	'star'	Asterius, Asterodea, Asterope
Asty-	'city'	Astyanax, Astydamia, Astyoche, Astypalea
Auto-	'self'	Autolycus, Automedon, Automedusa, Autonoë
Calli-	'beautiful'	Callidice, Calliope, Callipolis, Callirrhoë
Chrys-	'gold'	Chrysaor, Chryseïs, Chrysippus, Chrysothemis
Cleo-	'fame'	Cleobis, Cleobule, Cleodice, Cleopatra, Cleothera
Cly(t)-	'fame'	Clymene, Clytemnestra, Clytius
Deï-	'spoil'	Deïanira, Deïdamia, Deïleon, Deïmachus, Deïpyle
Demo-	'people'	Demonassa, Demonice, Demophon
Dio-	'divine'	Diocles, Diomedes, Dionysus(?)
Epi-	'after'	Epigoni, Epimedes, Epistrophus
Eri-	'very'	Eriboea, Erigone, Eriopis
Eu-	'good'	Euanthes, Euippe, Eumenides, Euphemus, Euphorbus, Euthymus
Eur(y)-	'wide'	Europa, Euryale, Eurydamas, Eurydice, Eurysthenes

Hippo-	'horse'	Hippocoön, Hippodamia, Hippolytus, Hippomedon, Hippothoë
Hyper-	'over'	Hyperboreans, Hyperenor, Hyperm(n)estra
Iphi-	'strong'	Iphianassa, Iphiboë, Iphicles, Iphigenia, Iphimedon
Lao-	'people'	Laodamia, Laodice, Laomedon, Laothoë
Leuc-	'white'	Leucippe, Leucothea, Leucus
Lyc-	'wolf'	Lycaon, Lycomedes, Lycurgus
Mel-	'black'	Melampus, Melanippe, Melantheus, Melantho
Meli-	'honey'	Meliboea, Melicertes, Melissa
Men(o)-	'abiding'	Menelaüs, Menodice, Menoetes
Nau(s)-	'ship'	Naucrate, Nauplius, Nausicaä, Nausithoüs
Nyct-	'night'	Nycteus, Nyctimene, Nyctimus
Oeno-	'wine'	Oeneus, Oenomaüs, Oenone, Oenopion
Pan-	'all'	Pancratis, Pandarus, Pandora, Pandrosus, Panthoüs
Peri-	'around'	Periboea, Periclymenus, Perieres, Perigune, Perimedes
Phae-	'shining'	Phaedra, Phaënon, Phaëthusa, Phaëton
Phil(o)-	'loving'	Philammon, Philoctetes, Philolaüs, Philomela
Pod-	'foot'	Podalirius, Podarces, Podarge
Poly-	'many'	Polybus, Polycaste, Polydora, Polygonus, Polyphemus
Pro-	'before'	Proclea, Procne, Procris, Prometheus
Sthen-	'strength'	Stheneboea, Sthenelus, Stheno
Tele-	'far'	Teledamus, Telegonus, Telemachus, Telephassa
Theo-	'god'	Theoclymenus, Theogone, Theophane
Tri-	'three'	Triops, Triptolemus, Triton

(B) *To end name*

-agoras	'market'	Aechmagoras, Anaxagoras
-(a)nassa	'queen'	Demonassa, Euryanassa, Iphianassa, Lysianassa
-ander -andra -anira	'man'	Alexander, Cassandra, Deïanira, Leander, Timandra
-anthe -anthe(u)s -anthis	'flower'	Acalanthis, Euanthes, Galanthis, Ianthe, Melantheus
-boe(a)	'cattle'	Alphesiboea, Meliboea, Stheneboea
-casta -caste	'adorned'	Epicaste, Jocasta, Polycaste
-clea -cles	'fame'	Androclea, Anticlea, Euryclea, Heracles
-damia -damas -damus	'tamer'	Amphidamas, Astydamia, Eurydamas, Laodamia, Teledamus
-dice	'justice'	Alcidice, Callidice, Eurydice, Laodice

317

-dora -dorus }	'gift'	Pandora, Polydora, Polydorus
-enor	'man'	Antenor, Elpenor, Hyperenor, Rhexenor
-gone -gonus }	'offspring'	Antigone, Erigone, Polygonus, Telegonus
-ippe -ippus }	'horse'	Aganippe, Anippe, Chrysippus, Melanippe, Plexippus, Zeuxippe
-loc(h)us	'ambush'	Amphilocus, Antilochus, Eurylochus, Hippolochus
-mache -machus }	'battle'	Andromache, Deïmachus, Eurymachus, Mnesimache, Telemachus
-meda -medon }	'ruler'	Andromeda, Automedon, Eurymedon, Iphimedon
-mede(s)	'craft'	Agamedes, Alcimede, Diomedes, Ganymede
-mena -mene(s) -men(e)us }	'might'	Alcmene, Aristomenes, Clymene, Hippomenes, Orchomenus
-m(n)estra	'bride'	Clytemnestra, Hyperm(n)estra
-noë -noüs }	'mind'	Alcinoüs, Antinoüs, Arsinoë, Hipponoüs
-one	'queen'	Chione, Hermione, Hesione, Oenone
-ope -ops }	'face', 'eye'	Aërope, Aethiops, Asterope, Cecrops, Sterope
-pha(ë)ssa -pha(n)e }	'shining'	Euryphaëssa, Pasiphaë, Telephassa, Theophane
-phon(e) -phontes }	'killer'	Bellerophon, Cresphontes, Gorgophone, Persephone*
-phor(us)	'bearing'	Enarephorus, Eosphorus, Phosphorus
-polis	'city'	Callipolis, Ischepolis, Sosipolis
-p(t)olemus	'war'	Neoptolemus, Tlepolemus, Triptolemus
-pus	'foot'	Aellopus, Melampus, Oedipus
-pyle -pylus }	'gate'	Deïpyle, Eurypylus, Hypsipyle
-rrhoë	'flowing'	Alexirrhoë, Callirrhoë
-sthenes -sth(e)us }	'strength'	Aegisthus, Eurysthenes, Eurystheus, Menestheus
-thea -theus }	'god'	Eidothea, Erythea, Nausitheus, Praxithea
-thoë -thoüs }	'quick'	Alcathoüs, Hippothoüs, Laothoë, Peirithoüs
-usa	'being'	Acidusa, Medusa, Phaëthusa

* For Demophon the -phon will mean 'killer' with an omicron (o), 'voice' with an omega (ω).

APPENDIX II

By-Names of Aphrodite/Venus

Acidalia	fountain of Orchomenus in Boeotia
Acraea	worshipped at Acra, Cyprus
Aligena	'sea-born' (G)
Amathontia ⎱	
Amathusa ⎰	worshipped at Amathus, Cyprus (now Limassol)
Amathusia	
Ambologera	'postponer of old age' (G)
Amica	'friend' (L)
Anadyomene	'emerging from the sea' (G), in allusion to birth
Androphonos	'man killer' (G), for affliction of Thessalians with plague
Anosia	'impious', 'cruel', 'unholy' (G) (compare Androphonos)
Antheia	'flowery' (G)
Apaturia	'skilled in deception' (G) (compare same name for Athena)
Aphacite	temple and oracle at Aphaca, Phoenicia
Apostrophia	'turner away', 'preserver' (G) so named by Cadmus for 'preserving' lovers by turning away from them
Appias	temple to her, and four other gods, near Appian Way, Rome
Area	'like Ares' (G), represented armed like him, especially in Sparta
Armata	'armed' (L) (see Area)
Aurea	'golden' (L), for her beauty (also a by-name of Fortuna)
Baiotis	'little ears' (G), regarded as a beautiful feature
Barbata	'bearded', 'hairy' (L), restored to Roman women hair they had lost as result of epidemic
Basilea (Basilis)	'queen' (G), i.e. of love
Byblia	worshipped at Byblia, Syria
Calligloutos ⎱	'beautiful backside' (G) (as statue in Museo
Callipygos ⎰	Nazionale, Naples)
Calva	'bald' (L) 'a name under which she was worshipped at Rome in consequence of the women having cut off their hair to make bowstrings for their husbands' (*Classical Manual*), or 'prayed to by women to prevent their hair falling off' (Ashley), or 'because she was represented bald' (Lemprière) (but compare Euplocamos!)
Candarena	worshipped at Candara, Paphlagonia
Charidotes	'giver of joy' (G)
Chryseë	'golden' (G) (see Aurea)
Chrysenios	'golden bridled' (G)

319

Cloacina	'purifier' (L) or temple near Cloaca Maxima ('biggest sewer'), Rome (confused with next)
Cluacina	'hearing (petitions)' (G), 'the name under which a statue was raised to her in the spot where peace was concluded between the Romans and the Sabines' (*Classical Manual*) (confused with foregoing)
Cnidia	statue by Praxiteles at Cnidus, Caria
Colaena	temple at Colaen, near Sardis
Comaetho	'bright-haired' (G) (compare same name in Dictionary)
Cypria	worshipped in Cyprus
Cytherea	long worshipped in island of Cythera, Ionian Islands
Despoina	'lady', 'mistress' (G) (compare same name in Dictionary)
Dionea	mother of Dione
Dolometes	'propitiated by gifts' (G)
Elephantine	worshipped at island of Elephantis, Nile River, Upper Egypt
Elicopis	'black-eyed', 'with beautiful eyes' (G)
Enoplios	'bearing weapons' (G) (compare Area, Armata)
Epipontia	'on the sea' (G), i.e. goddess of it
Epistrophia	'turning inwards' (G), i.e. as patroness of sex, even incest (but compare Apostrophia!)
Epitragia	'turned into a goat', 'sitting on a goat' (G), goats were sacrificed to her
Epitymbia	'on the graves', 'on the tombs' (G) (compare Androphonos)
Erycina	temple on Mount Eryx, Sicily, or 'of the heather' (G) (Graves)
Etaira	'mistress' (G)
Euplea	'good sailing' (G)
Euplocamos	'well tressed' (G) (but compare Calva!)
Eustephanos	'well garlanded' (G)
Exopolis	'outside the city' (G), statue was outside city walls at Athens
Frugia Fruta Frutis	'honest', 'frugal' (L) (although 'Frutis' said to be corruption of 'Aphrodite')
Genetrix	'mother' (L), Caesar built temple to her under this name at Rome
Golgia	worshipped at Golgos, Cyprus
Harma	'joins' (G), hence Harmonia, her extension (see her in Dictionary)
Helicoblepharos	'quick-glancing', 'quick-winking' (G) (compare Elicopis, Paracyptousa)
Hetaira	'whore' (G), i.e. patroness of them
Hippolyteia	temple so named consecrated to her by Phaedra, when in love with Hippolytus (see these two names in Dictionary)
Hortensis	'(worshipped) in gardens' (L)
Idalia	worshipped in Idalium, Cyprus
Junonia	statue in Laconia, linking her with Juno (see her in Dictionary)

Libertina }	'freedwoman' (L), either for dedication to her of toys by
Libitina }	girls who had grown out of them, or 'gratifying libertines', or 'connected with the dead', from *libertinarius*, 'undertaker'
Limnesia	'of the sea' (G) (*limne*, 'lake', used by Homer for 'sea')
Lysemelas	'care-loosing' (G)
Marina	'of the sea' (L)
Mascula	'bold', 'masculine' (L) (also a by-name of Fortuna)
Mechanites	'contriver', 'machinator' (G), allusion either to 'love will find a way' or many artifices practised in love
Melaenia	'black' (G), according to Pausanias, since most love-making takes place at night (compare Scotia)
Melissa	'bee', 'priestess' (G)
Morpho	'shapely' (G), represented thus at Sparta, veiled and with chains on her feet
Myrtea	'myrtle' (G), which was sacred to her
Nicophore	'victory-bringing' (G) (compare Area, Armata, Victrix)
Nympha	'bridal' (G)
Obsequens	'compliant' (L), i.e. she would grant requests
Pandemia	'all people' (G) over whom she had power, or as opposed to 'heavenly' Aphrodite, or for 'common' pleasures
Paphia	worshipped at Paphos, Cyprus (said to be named for Paphus, son of Pygmalion)
Paracyptousa	'side-glancer' (G), i.e. looking askance at us
Paregoros	'giver of comfort', 'soother' (G) (compare English 'paregoric')
Pasiphaëssa	'far-shining' (G), like moon goddess (see Pasiphaë in Dictionary)
Peitho	'persuasion' (G), so called on Lesbos
Pelagia	'sea-born' (G)
Peribasia	'walking about' (G)
Persephaëssa	as queen of Underworld (see Persephone in Dictionary)
Phallommeda	'phallus-attracted', 'lover of genitals' (G), from foamy birth
Phila	'amiable' (G)
Pithyionice	'bringing victory in the Pythian games' (G)
Pontia }	'sea-born' (G)
Pontogenia }	
Porne }	'whore' (G) (see Hetaira, and compare English 'pornography')
Praxis	'business, doing' (G), i.e. success, love
Psithyros	'whisperer' (G) (also a by-name of Cupid)
Saligenia	'sea-born' (G) (*salos*, 'the open sea')
Schoenis	'of the rush basket' (G) (see Schoeneus in Dictionary)
Scotia	'darkness' (G) (compare Melaenia)
Speculatrix	'spectatress' (L), at temple built by Phaedra (see Hippolyteia) she 'saw' Hippolytis
Symmachia	'alliance', 'auxiliary' (G), in military sense
Telessigama	'presiding over marriages' (G) (*telos*, 'fulfilment', *gamos*, 'marriage')
Thalamon	'inner room', 'bedroom', 'bridal chamber' (G)

Thalassia	'of the sea' (G)
Tritonia	Libyan lake Tritonis, where Athena was said to have been born
Tymborychos	'gravedigger', 'grave robber' (G), as if she had power to bring dead back to life
Urania	'celestial', 'heavenly' (G), as goddess of sacred or pure love
Verticordia	'turning hearts' (L), i.e. (of women) to cultivate chastity
Victrix	'victorious' (L), i.e. in love or war (compare Nicophore, Symmachia)
Zephyria	worshipped on Zephyrum, promontory on Cyprus
Zerynthia	worshipped in Zerynthus, Samothrace

APPENDIX III

By-Names of Apollo

Abaeus	temple and oracle at Aba (Abae), Phocis
Acersecomes	'with unshorn hair' (G), hence by extension 'ever-young', since Greek boys wore their hair long till they reached manhood
Acesius	'healing' (G), as god of medicine
Acraephnius	worshipped at Acraephnia, Boeotia
Acritas	'height' (G), for temple on a hill at Sparta
Actius	worshipped at Actium
Aegletes	'lightning' (G), for averting dangers that threatened Argonauts when they ran into a storm
Aegyptius	as son of Osiris and Isis
Agreus	'hunter' (G)
Agyieus ⎫ Agyleus ⎭	'street' (G), for sacrifices offered to him on public streets, of which he was guardian
Alexicacus	'keeping off evil' (G), for delivering Athenians from plague during Peloponnesian War (between Athens and Sparta, 431–404 BC)
Amphryssius	river Amphrysus, Thessaly, near which fed flocks of Admetus
Amyclaeus	worshipped at Amyclae, Laconia
Anaphaeus	worshipped on island of Anaphe, Cretan Sea
Aphetor	'one who gives oracles' or 'one who shoots arrows' (G)
Apotropaeus	'one who averts evil' (G)
Arcitenens	'bearing the bow' (L), for killing Python by arrows
Argurotoxus	'having a silver bow' (G)
Asterusius	worshipped on Mount Asterusius, Crete
Averruncus	'one who averts evils' (L)
Basses	worshipped in Bassae, Arcadia
Boedromius	'running to aid' (G) or being worshipped in month Boedromion (latter half September–first half October)
Branchides	for Branchidae, priests at Didyme, near Miletus, who were so named from temple of Apollo's son Branchus (see him in Dictionary)
Cataonius	worshipped at Cataonia, Cappadocia
Cerdoüs	'gainful' (G), from profit gained from his predictions
Chrysaorus	'having a golden sword' (G)
Chrysochaites	'golden-haired' (G)
Chrysotoxus	'having a golden bow' (G)
Cillaeus	worshipped at Cilla, Aeolia
Cirrhaeus	worshipped at Cirrha, Phocis

Citharodos	'singer to the lyre' (G)
Clarius	worshipped at Claros, Ionia
Coelispex	'heavenly watcher' (L), so called among astrologers
Comaeus	'flowing hair' (G)
Corypaeus	worshipped at Corypae, Thessaly
Culicarius	'driving away midges' (L) (*culex, culicis,* 'gnat', 'midge')
Curotrophus	'protecting young people' (G)
Cynthius	worshipped on Mount Cynthus, Delos
Daphnaeus	worshipped at Daphne, beauty spot near Antioch
Decatephore	'bearing ten' (G), for statue at Megara, made from tenth part of enemy spoils
Delius	worshipped on island of Delos, where traditionally born
Delphicus	worshipped at Delphi
Delphinius	'dolphin' (G), as which accompanied colonising ship to Crete
Didymaeus	'double' (G), for double light: from himself and from moon
Dionysiodotes	'gift of Dionysus' (G)
Diriadiotes	worshipped at Diras, region belonging to Argos
Dromaeus	'runner' (G), so worshipped in Crete (compare Boedromius)
Eleleus	'giving a war cry', 'ululating' (G)
Epibaterius	'mounting up' (G), for escape rendered from tempest
Epicurus	'helper' (G)
Epidelius	'for Delos' (G) (compare Delius)
Euchaites	'well-haired' (G)
Eupharetres	'having a beautiful quiver' (G)
Exacesterius	'one who averts evils' (G)
Gryneus	worshipped at Gryneum, Asia Minor
Hebdomagenes	'born on the seventh day' (G), all seventh days were sacred to him
Hecatebeletes	'far-shooting' (G)
Hecatombaeus	'one to whom hecatombs are offered' (G) (see same by-name of Zeus p. 332, for meaning of 'hecatomb')
Helius	'sun' (G)
Hermapollo	for statue combining Apollo and Hermes
Horion	'boundary' (G), 'Pausanias supposed it was . . . assigned to him upon some happy termination of a dispute respecting the division of land' (*Classical Manual*)
Horus (Orus)	as son of Osiris and Isis
Hyperboraeus	worshipped in Hyperborean region (see Hyperboreans in Dictionary)
Hyperion	'one who goes over' (G) (see this name in Dictionary)
Hysius	worshipped at Hysia, Boeotia
Ichnaeus	worshipped at Ichnaea, Macedonia
Ilios	for cry '*e, e*' ('what ho!') (G), to call attention to something
Ismenius	temple on borders of river and mountain Ismenus, Boeotia
Laossoös	'people-rouser' (G)
Larissaeus	worshipped at Larissa, Ephesus

Latoüs	for mother Latona
Leschenorus	'converser', 'debater' (G), so worshipped by philosophical students
Leucadius	worshipped on promontory Leucaste, island of Leucadia (now Santa Maura), Ionian Sea
Loimius	'pestilence' (G), so worshipped as god of medicine, Lindus, Rhodes
Loxias	'oblique' (G), for obliqueness of course or of 'crookedness' of oracles; may refer to stance of archer when shooting
Lycaeus	'wolf' (G), for delivering either Argive territory or flocks of Admetus from wolves (compare Lycoctonos)
Lycegenes	'born in Lycia' (G), in fact widely worshipped there (compare Lycius)
Lycius	'of Lycia' (G) where had famous oracle
Lycoctonos	'wolf-slayer' (G) (compare Lycaeus)
Marmarinus	worshipped at Marmarion, Euboea
Metageitnius	'between neighbours' (G), from month Metageitnion (latter half August–first half September) when traditionally people moved to a new neighbourhood; temple so named near Athens, allegedly for removal of inhabitants of Melite suburb to that of Diomea
Milesius	worshipped at Miletium, Crete
Musagetes	'leader of the Muses' (G)
Myricaeus	'tamarisk' (G), for branch of this as his emblem of divination
Napaeus	'groves', 'glens' (G) where worshipped
Neomenius	'new moon', 'new month' (G) when specially invoked
Nomius	'belonging to shepherds' (G) for tending of cattle of Admetus (compare same name for Zeus)
Orchestes	'dancer' (G)
Ortygia	worshipped on Ortygia, ancient name of Delos (compare Delius)
Paean	'hymn' (G) especially one sung after he had slain Python
Palatinus	temple to him on Palatine Hill (Mons Palatinus), Rome
Parnopius	'locust', 'grasshopper' (G), for delivering Athens from swarm of them
Patareus	worshipped at Patara, Lycia, where had temple and oracle
Patrius	'father-like' (G); to all Athenians he was a paternal figure
Phanaeus	'appearing' (G), from promontory Phanaeum, Chios, from where Latona first saw Delos
Philalexandrus	'friend of Alexander' (G), for freeing of his statue from its gold chains, before Alexander the Great sacked Tyre (332 BC)
Philesius } Philius }	'friendly', 'affectionate' (G)
Phoebus	'bright', 'splendid' (G) (see this name in Dictionary)
Phylleus	worshipped at Phyllos, Arcadia
Phyxius	'fugitive' (G), for his protection of them
Platanistius	'plane-tree' (G), for temple at Elis, Peloponnese, surrounded by them
Poliris	'grey-haired' (G), so depicted at Thebes

325

Proöpsius	'foreseeing' (G)
Prostaterius	'standing before', 'guarding' (G), i.e. of houses
Ptous	worshipped at Ptous, mountain in Boeotia
Pyctes	'boxer' (G), for victory over robber Phorbas (see him in Dictionary)
Pythius	for any of: (1) slaying Python, (2) slaying some man Pythius, (3) *pytho*, 'to putrefy', referring to body of Python (see Dictionary), (4) *pynthanomai*, 'to ask', 'enquire', for oracular power, (5) *Pytho*, oldest name of Delphi
Salganeus	worshipped at Salganae, Boeotia
Saligena	'born from the sea' (G) (*salos*, 'the open sea'), for birth on floating island Delos
Smintheus	either worshipped at Sminthia, district of Troy, or for destroying rats (Phrygian *sminthai*) in Phrygia
Soractis	worshipped on Mount Soracte, near Rome
Sosianus	'healing the mad' (G) (*sos*, 'healthy', *anous*, 'foolish')
Spelaites	'cave', 'grotto' (G) where worshipped
Spodius	'ashes' (G), perhaps for altar over ashes of sacrifices to him
Tegyraeus	worshipped at Tegyra, Boeotia
Telchinius	association with Telchines (see in Dictionary)
Temenites	worshipped at Temenos, Syracuse
Theoxenius	for Theoxenis, festival held in honour of all the gods at which Apollo was allegedly host to the other gods (G) (*theos*, 'god', *xenos*, 'host')
Thermius	'warm' (G) as the sun (compare Helius)
Thorates	'engendering' (G) (*thoros*, 'semen')
Thurius	worshipped at Thurium, Boeotia
Thymbraeüs	temple on plain of Thymbra, district of Troy (see Thymbraeüs in Dictionary)
Thyraeus	'door', 'entrance' (G) (Greek *thyra*, German *Tür*, English 'door'), where his altars were often placed
Toxophorus	'bearer of the bow' (G)
Triopius	worshipped at Triopium, Caria
Ulius	'healthy' (G) (*oulos*, 'whole', 'perfect')
Vulturius	for delivering shepherd from underground cave by means of vultures; shepherd built temple to him on Mount Lissus, Ionia
Zerynthius	worshipped at Zerynthus, Samothracia
Zosterius	'belt' (G) (*zoster*, 'belt', 'girdle'), as if engirdling the world, or as if girt for battle (compare Athena's by-name Zosteria)

APPENDIX IV

By-Names of Athena/Minerva

Aedon	'nightingale' (G) (see also this name in Dictionary)
Aetherea	'sky' (G), for the Palladium, which fell from heaven (or the skies)
Ageleia	'she who carried off the plunder' (G) (*ago*, 'to drive', *leia*, 'plunder') for her help in gaining booty (e.g. cattle) in a victory
Aglaurus	for the wife or daughter of Cecrops, who nominated her as goddess over his kingdom (see Aglaurus in Dictionary)
Agorea	'market' (G) over which she presided
Agrotera	worshipped at Agrae, Attica, or 'huntress' (G)
Aithyia	'seagull', 'shearwater' (or some sea bird) (G), as which she carried Cecrops to Megara
Alalcomenes	'guardian', 'parrier', literally 'strong defender' (G) (*alalcein*, 'to defend', *menos*, 'strength'), either as general or specific protectress (e.g. of buildings), or for Alalcomenae, Boeotia, where allegedly born, or for supposed sculptor of statue of her, Alalcomene
Alcideme	'strength of the people' (G)
Alcides	'strength' (G), as whom worshipped in Macedonia
Alea	for temple allegedly built by Aleus, son of Aphidas, king of Arcadia
Amphira	according to Greek poet and grammarian Lycophron (283–246 BC), who so named her, 'divine influence' (G)
Anemotis	'wind influencer' (G)
Apaturia	from Apaturia, annual festival at Athens when Athenians had mature sons enrolled as citizens (maybe from *pater*, 'father' or *phaetria*, 'clan', properly 'brotherhood', with initial *a-* for euphony)
Area	'like Ares' (G) (compare same name for Aphrodite)
Armifera (Dea)	'(goddess) bearing arms' (L) (compare Area)
Armipotens	'powerful in arms' (L)
Astyra	worshipped at Astyra, Phoenicia
Atrytone	'unwearied', 'invincible' (G)
Aulis (Aulon)	'flute' (G) which some say she invented
Axiopaenas	'worth vengeance' (G) (*axios*, 'worth as much as', *poene*, 'price paid')
Bellipotens	'powerful in war' (L)
Bulaea	'counsel' (G) (*boule*)
Caesia	'grey-eyed' (L), this said to denote ferocity or belligerence
Carya	worshipped at Carya, Arcadia

Catuliana	for Catulus, Roman admiral (consul in 242 BC), who dedicated standard to her (this man not to be confused with better known Catullus, poet)
Cecropia	for Cecropia, original name of Athens
Celeuthea	'road', 'street' (G) (*celeuthos*), Odysseus said to have dedicated statue to her under this name in celebration of his victory over suitors of Penelope, Athena having promised him such a victory in a particular street
Chalcioeus	for temple at Chalcis, Euboea
Chalinistes	'bridler' (G), for having bridled Pegasus for Bellerophon
Chrysolonchos	'bearing a golden lance' (G) (*chrysos*, 'gold', *lonche*, 'spear', 'lance')
Coresia (Coria)	for birth from head of Zeus (see Coryphagenes), or *core*, 'maiden' (compare Parthenos)
Coryphagenes	'head-born' (G) (*coryphe*, 'head', *genea*, 'birth'), for birth from head of Zeus
Coryphasia	worshipped on promontory of Coryphasium, Peloponnese
Cratia	worshipped at Cratia, Bithynia
Cyparissia	worshipped at Cyparissia, Peloponnese
Cyrestes	'authority' (G) (*cyros*)
Eirenophore	'bearer of peace' (G)
Ergane	as goddess of handicrafts, from *ergon*, 'work' (G)
Erysiptolis	'protecting the city' (G) (compare Poliuchos)
Frenales	'bridler' (L) (*freno*, 'to bridle') (compare Chalinistes)
Gigantophontis	'giant-killer' (G), for her assisting Zeus against giants
Glaucopis	'grey-eyed' (G) (see Caesia)
Gorgonia	for Perseus being armed with her shield when he conquered the Gorgon
Gorgophora	'Gorgon-bearer' (G), from her aegis, on which was head of Medusa
Gorgopis	'Gorgon-faced' (G) (see Gorgophora)
Hephaistion	for association with Hephaestus (whom see in Dictionary)
Hippia	'horse' (G), for skill in horsemanship
Hippoletis	worshipped at Hippola, Laconia
Hoplosmia	'fully armed' (G) (*hoplon*, 'arms', 'armour')
Hospita	'hostess' (L)
Hygieia	'health' (G) of which goddess
Ismenia	worshipped by river Ismenus, Boeotia
Laossoös	'people-rouser' (G)
Larissea	worshipped by river Larissus, Peloponnese
Lindia	worshipped at Lindus, Rhodes
Luscinia	'nightingale' (L), for inventing the flute (see Aulis)
Machinatrix	'contriver', 'inventress' (L) (compare Mechanica)
Mechanica	'skilful', 'inventive' (G), invoked as such for building of towns
Medica	'medicine' (L), as goddess of which invoked at Rome
Metis	'counsel' (G) (compare Bulaea)
Montana	'mountain' (L), as such worshipped on mountain in Phrygia
Musica	'music' (G), for invention of flute (see Aulis)
Narcea	for Narcaeus, son of Dionysus and Physcoa, said to have built temple to her in Elis

Nike	'victory' (G), as whom had temple in Athens, built to commemorate victory of Theseus over Minotaur
Ophthalmitis	'eye-preserving' (G)
Organa	'working', 'fashioning' (G)
Oxyderce	'sharp-sighted', 'quick-sighted' (G) (compare Perspicax)
Pacifera	'bearer of peace' (L), found so named on medal of Marcus Aurelius
Pallas	(see this name in Dictionary)
Pallenis	worshipped at Pallene, Attica
Panacheis	'all Achaians' (G), i.e. protectress of all Greeks (see Achaeus in Dictionary)
Pandrosia	for Pandrosus (whom see in Dictionary), or 'all dewy' (G)
Parthenos	'virgin' (G), for her perpetual maidenhood
Perspicax	'sharp-sighted', 'perspicacious' (L) (compare Oxyderce)
Polias	'city (protectress)' (G), i.e. Athens
Poliporthos	'town destroyer', 'city sacker' (G), as war goddess (compare Poliporthis in Dictionary)
Poli(o)uchos	'city protectress' (G) (*polis*, 'city', *echo*, 'to hold', 'protect')
Praestes	'presiding', 'protecting' (L) (compare same name for Zeus)
Promachorma	'hastening to battle' (G)
Pronaia	'before the temple' (G) (*pro*, 'before', *naos*, 'temple'), for her statue at Delphi in front of temple of Apollo
Pronoia	'providence' (G)
Pylotis	'of the gate' (G) (*pylos*, 'gate'), i.e. as protectress of cities (with her image over main city gate)
Salpinx	'war trumpet' (G) (see Salpiga), for her temple at Corinth allegedly built by Hegeleus, son of Tyrrhenus, the latter being the inventor of the trumpet (according to Hyginus' *Fabulae*)
Salpiga	'war trumpet' (G) (*salpinx*), for inventing the flute (compare Audon, but also compare Salpinx)
Soteira	'preserver', 'saviour' (G)
Sthenias	'strong' (G)
Stratea	'warfare' (G) (compare Area)
Telchinia	for the Telchines, who were descended from her and Apollo (see their name in Dictionary and compare Apollo's by-name Telchinius)
Tithronia	worshipped at Tithronium, Phocia
Tritogenia } Tritonia }	either as born near a river Triton or Tritonis (of uncertain location), or for some association with Triton (whom see in Dictionary) or water
Unigena	'single birth' (L), as daughter of Zeus alone without a mate
Virago	'manly maiden' (L) (compare English 'virago')
Zosteria	'belted' (G), i.e. girt for battle (compare Apollo's by-name Zosterius)

APPENDIX V

By-Names of Zeus/Jupiter

Adultus	for being invoked by adults on marriage
Aegiochus	'aegis-holding' (G) (see *aegis* in Technical Terms, page 13)
Aegyptius	worshipped by Egyptians
Aether	'air' (G), a poetical name
Aethiops	as worshipped in Ethiopa
Aetneus	for association with Mount Etna, volcano in Sicily
Agetor	'leader', 'guide' (G) (*ageter*, Doric for *hegeter*), as whom invoked at start of military campaign or battle
Agoreus	'market' (G) over which presided
Alastor	'avenger', literally 'not forgetting' (G) (*a-*, 'not', *lanthanomai*, 'to forget')
Almus Alumnus	'feeder', 'nourisher' (L) (*alo*, 'to feed', 'nourish')
Altius	worshipped in sacred grove Altis, round his temple at Olympia
Ambulius	'walker' (L), allegedly from statue in portico at Sparta, where people walked (but strange to have Latin name in Sparta!)
Ammon	either 'sand' (G) (*ammos*), for supporting Dionysus with water when he was travelling through African desert, or for Egyptian god Ammon (Amun), identified by Greeks with Zeus and Romans with Jupiter
Apatenor Apaturius	'deceiver', 'tricker' (G) (*apatao*, 'to cheat', 'trick')
Apemius	'propitious', literally 'doing no harm' (G) (*a-*, 'no', *pema*, 'misery')
Aphesius	'releaser' (G); story was that in a drought Aeacus (whom see in Dictionary), having sacrificed victim to Zeus in Aegina, brought part of body to cliff-top here and threw ('released') it into sea to propitiate Zeus
Apobaterius	'disembarker' (G) (*apobaino*, 'to step off'), so invoked by sailors leaving ships to conquer a land
Apomyius	'driver-off of flies' (G) (*apo*, 'away', *myia*, 'fly'), for dispelling flies that plagued Heracles during a sacrifice (compare Apollo's by-name Culicarius)
Arbitrator	'judge, 'arbitrator', so invoked at Rome
Asterius	for king of Crete so named (whom see in Dictionary), with whom associated or confused
Asteropetes	'lightener' (G)
Astrapaeus	'of lightning' (G) (*astrape*, 'flash of lightning')
Athous	worshipped on Mount Athos

Basileus	'king' (G), i.e. of sky (compare Aphrodite's by-name Basilea)
Brontaeus	'thunderer' (G) (*bronte*, 'thunder')
Buleus	'counsellor' (G), i.e. would advise all who asked him (compare Athena's by-name, Bulaea)
Capitolinus	for temple on Capitoline Hill (Mons Capitolinus), which was named for temple, Rome
Cappautas	'subsider' (G) (*cappeson*, Epic for *catapipto*, literally 'to fall down'), for stone on which Orestes was sitting when his madness left him (but this name confused with next)
Cappotas	'down-pourer' (G) (*cata-*, 'down', and *po-* root meaning 'water'), i.e. causing heavy rain (but this name confused with foregoing)
Catachthonius	'subterranean' (G) (*cata-*, 'down', *chthon*, 'earth'), by contrast with bright sky and peak of Olympus
Cataebates	'coming down' (G), i.e. descending to earth in thunder and lightning
Catharsius	'purifier' (G) (compare English 'cathartic')
Celainephes	'black-clouding' (G) (*celainos*, 'dark', 'gloomy', *nephos*, 'cloud')
Celestinus	'heavenly', 'celestial' (L)
Centipeda	'hundred-footed' (L) for stability
Ceraunius	'thunderbolt' (G), i.e thunder and lightning ('thunder' alone is *bronte*, see Brontaeus; 'lightning' alone is *asterope* or *sterope*, see Astrapaeus, and compare Asterope and Sterope in Dictionary)
Charisius	'favouring', 'giving grace' (G), i.e. as god who enables men to find favour with one another
Chthonius	'earthly' (G) (compare Catachthonius)
Clerius	'by lot' (G) (*cleros*, 'lot'), so worshipped at Tegaea, Arcadia, as sons of Arcas (see him in Dictionary) settled their inheritances by drawing lots here
Conius	'dusty' (G) (*conis*, 'dust'), for dust inside his temple at Megara, Achaia, which had no roof
Conservator	'preserver', 'conserver' (L)
Cosmetes	'orderer', 'arranger' (G) (*cosmeo*, 'to order', 'arrange')
Crescens	'growing' (L), so known in representations of him as child on goat
Ctesius	'property protector' (G) (*ctesis*, 'possession')
Custos	'guardian', 'custodian' (L)
Damascenes	worshipped at Damascus
Dapalis	'presider over religious feast' (L) (*daps, dapis*, 'religious feast', 'sacrificial feast')
Depulsor	'thruster-aside', 'repeller' (L), i.e. in battle
Descensor	'descender' (L) (compare Cataebates)
Dictaeus	worshipped on Mount Dicte, Crete
Diespiter	'father of day' (L) (more an alternative name than a by-name)
Dodonaeus	for his famous oracle at Dodona, Epirus
Eleus	worshipped at Elis
Eleutherius	'liberator' (G) (*eleutheros*, 'free'), a name said to have been given him after defeat of Persians at Plataea (479 BC)

Elicius	'drawn out', 'elicited' (L), i.e. by prayer or incantation
Endendros	'in the trees' (G) (*en*, 'in', *dendron*, 'tree'), probably for location of his temples in groves
Epidotes	'generous' (G) (*epidosis*, 'giving over and above')
Epiphanes	'appearing' (G) (*epiphanes*, 'coming to light'), presumably for his ready response to prayer
Epipinates	'presiding over banquets' (G) (*epi*, 'by', 'over', *pino*, 'to drink' or *pinax*, 'board', 'plate', 'dish')
Epistius	'presiding over harbours' (G) (*epistion*, 'dock')
Erceus	see Herceus
Erigdupus	'thundering' (G) (literally 'loud-sounding')
Euanemus	'fair wind' (G) (*eu*-, 'good', *anemos*, 'wind'), i.e. either calming stormy winds or bringing favourable ones
Europaeus	for his flight with Europa (see her in Dictionary)
Euryopa	'wide-seeing' (G) (compare Europaeus and Europa)
Exacesterius	'thoroughly curing' (G) (*exacesis*, 'complete cure')
Expiator	'atoner', 'expiator' (L), i.e. of mankind
Fagutalis	'among the beech trees' (L) (*fagus*, 'beech-tree'), as which worshipped on Aventine Hill (Mons Aventinus), Rome, at temple surrounded by beech grove
Feretrius	one or more of: (1) 'striker' (L) (*ferio*, 'to strike'), (2) 'bearer' (L) (*fero*, 'to carry'), (3) 'bier', 'carrying frame' (L) (*feretrum*); if latter, maybe reference to booty of king Acron, slain by Romulus, that was carried triumphantly into Rome
Fluvialis	'presiding over rivers' (L) (*fluvius*, 'river')
Forensis	'market' (l) (*forensis*, 'of the market', from *forum*, 'market-place) over which presided (compare Agoraeus)
Fulgens Fulgur Fulgurator	'lightning', 'splendour', 'effulgence' (L) (*fulgare*, 'to flash')
Fulminans Fulminator	'thunderbolt' (L) (*fulmen*)
Gamelius	'presiding over marriages' (G) (*gamos*, 'wedding', 'marriage') (compare Adultus)
Genethlius	'presiding over births' (G) (*genethle*, 'birth')
Genitor	'father', 'creator' (L)
Hecatombaeus	'one to whom hecatombs are offered' (G) (a hecatomb was properly a sacrifice of a hundred oxen, from *hecaton*, 'hundred' and *bous*, 'ox', although it could be any large number)
Heliconius	worshipped on Mount Helicon
Heraius	'of Hera' (G), i.e. as her brother and husband
Herceus	'protector of houses' (G) (*herceios*, 'belonging to the *hercos* or courtyard'), i.e. 'household' god, with his statue standing in the courtyard in front of a house
Hicesius	'of suppliants' (G) (*hicetes*, 'suppliant'), for response to those who ask his help
Homagyrius	'presiding over public assemblies' (G) (*homos*, 'common', *agyris*, Aeolian form of *agora*, 'assembly', 'gathering')
Horcius	'guardian of oaths' (G) (*horcos*, 'oath')
Hospes Hospitalis	'hospitable', 'favourable to hosts and guests' (L)

Hyetius	'rain-bringer' (G) (*hyetos*, 'rain')
Hypatus	'highest', 'supreme' (G) (*hypatos*)
Hypsizygos	'high-enthroned', 'sitting up high' (G) (*hypsi*, 'high', *zygon*, 'cross-bench' (in a ship), literally 'yoke')
Icesius	see Hicesius
Icmaeus	'showery', 'moistener' (G) (*icmas*, 'moisture')
Idaeus	worshipped on Mount Ida
Ileus	'propitious' (G) (*ilaos*, Attic *ileos*)
Imperator	'ruler', 'commander' (L)
Infans	'child' (L), so worshipped at Aegium on isthmus of Corinth (compare Crescens)
Infernalis	'infernal', 'of the Underworld' (L), so worshipped in a temple at Argos, where his statue had three eyes as symbolic of his triple power (over earth, sea and sky)
Inventor	'discoverer', 'inventor' (L)
Invictus	'invincible' (L)
Laoetas	'of the people', 'plebeian' (G) (*laos*, 'people')
Lapideus	'stone' (L) (*lapis*, *lapidis*), for the stone swallowed by Cronos in place of Zeus (when he swallowed his children one by one as they were born to Rhea)
Larissaeus	for temple at Larissa, Asia Minor
Latialis ⎫ Latiaris ⎬ Latius ⎭	worshipped in Latium (see Latinus in Dictionary)
Leuceus	'shining', 'clear', 'white' (G) (*leucos*)
Liberator	'deliverer', 'liberator' (L) (compare Eleutherius)
Locheates	'of child-birth' (G), for birth of Athena, or as god of births (compare Genethlius)
Lucerius ⎫ Lucetius ⎬	'of light' (L) (*luceo*, 'to be light', 'shine', compare Leuceus)
Lycaius	'wolf' (G) (*lycos*), as said to have changed Lycaon into a wolf (see this name in Dictionary)
Maimactes	'boisterous', 'stormy' (G) (*maimasso*, 'to burst forth'), as god of storms
Maius	'greater' (L), i.e. than other gods
Marinus ⎫ Maritimus ⎬	'of the sea', 'maritime' (L), as presiding over the sea
Martius	'war-like', 'martial' (L)
Maximus	'greatest' (L), i.e. of the gods
Mechaneus	'contriver', 'instrumental' (G) (*mechane*, 'machine'), as god of all undertakings and enterprises
Meilichius	'mild, 'gracious' (G) (*meilichios*)
Melissaeus	for Melissa, sister of Amalthea, one of his nurses (see her in Dictionary)
Metietes	'counsellor' (G) (*metis*, 'counsel') (compare Bulaeus)
Minianus	'vermilion', 'red oxide of lead' (L) (*minium*), allegedly for painting of his statues on festival days with vermilion
Moiragetes	'ruler of the Fates' (G) (see Moirai in Dictionary)
Morius	'mulberry-tree' (G) (*moron*, 'mulberry'), as protector of this tree which was sacred to Athena
Muscarius	'driver-off of flies' (L) (*muscarium*, 'fly-flap', from *musca*, 'fly' (compare Apomyius and Myiodes)

Myiodes	'driver-off of flies' (G) (*myia*, 'fly')
Nemetor	'judge' (G) (*nemetor*) (compare Nemesis in Dictionary)
Nephelegeretes	'cloud-collector' (G) (*nephele*, 'cloud', *ageiro*, 'to collect')
Nicaeus	'victorious' (G)
Nicephorus	'bringing victory' (G) (compare Aphrodite's by-name, Nicephore)
Nomius	'presiding over laws' (G) (*nomos*, 'law')
Olympius	worshipped at Olympia
Opiter	
Opitulator	'helper' (L) (*opitulor*, 'to bring aid')
Opitulus	
Optimus Maximus	'best and greatest' (L)
Palaestes	'wrestler' (G) (*palaistes*), for having wrestled with Heracles
Panarius	'supplier of bread' (L) (*panarium*, 'bread-basket', from *panis*, 'bread'); story was that when Romans were besieged in Capitol by Gauls, they inspiredly threw down loaves so that the enemy would think they were well stocked with provisions (compare Pistor)
Pancrates	'ruler over all', 'omnipotent' (G)
Panhellenius	'protector of all Greece' (G)
Panomphaeus	'all-oracular' (G) (*pan*, 'all', *omphe*, 'divine voice', 'oracle'), as source or inspirer of all oracles
Panoptes	'all-seeing' (G)
Pater	'father' (G, L)
Pelorius	for a man named Pelorus (not the Sown Man in the Dictionary) 'who during the celebration of a Thessalian festival . . . communicated the intelligence that the mountains of Tempe had been separated by an earthquake, and that the waters of the lake . . . had found a passage into the Alpheus, and left behind a beautiful and extensive plain' (*Classical Manual*)
Pentapylon	'five gates' (G), for a temple at Rome (as Jupiter Arbitrator)
Phegoneus	'beech-tree' (G) (*phegos*, 'oak' or 'beech'), for presiding over groves at Dodona (see Dodonaeus)
Philius	'friend' (G), for protection of friends
Phratrius	'of a kindred race' (G), as protector of related families in Athens
Physicus	'presiding over nature' (G)
Phytalmius	'nourishing' (G), as god of nature (compare Physicus)
Phyxius	'fugitive' (G) (*phyxis*, 'flight'), as protector of fugitives
Pistius	'faithful' (G) (*pistis*, 'faith'), rewarded those who were faithful to him, or himself was always faithful
Pistor	'baker' (L) (for story see Panarius)
Plusius	'bestower of riches' (G) (*plousios*, 'rich', 'wealthy'; compare Pluto in Dictionary)
Pluvius	'bringer of rain' (L) (*pluvia*, 'rain')
Polieus	'protector of cities' (G) (*polis*, 'city')
Praedator	'plunderer', 'pillager' (L), i.e. bringer of booty in battle
Praestes	'presiding', 'protecting' (L) (compare same name for Athena)

Prodigialis	'dealing with portents' (L), as such was invoked when an evil portent or sign was noted
Pulverulentes	'dusty' (L) (*pulvis*, 'dust') (for story see Conius)
Regnator (Rex)	'king' (L)
Ruminus	'nourisher' (L) (*rumis*, 'breast')
Salaminius	worshipped at Salamis, Cyprus
Salutaris	'health-giving' (L) (*salus*, 'health')
Saotas	'preserver' (G) (*saos*, 'safe' or *saoteros*, 'safer')
Sator	'promoter', 'author' (L) (literally 'sower'; compare Saturn in Dictionary) i.e. as 'father of the universe'
Saturnigena } Saturnius }	'son of Saturn' (G, L)
Scotius	'dark', 'secret', 'mysterious' (G) (*scotios*)
Secretus	'apart', 'separate' (L). i.e. different from all other gods
Serenus	'clear', 'bright' (L)
Servator	'preserver', 'deliverer' (L)
Sosipolis	'saviour of the city' (G) (see this name in Dictionary)
Soter	'saviour', 'deliver' (G)
Sponsor	'bringer of security' (L) (*sponsor*, 'bondsman', 'surety')
Stabilitor	'supporter', 'bringer of stability' (L) (compare Centipeda)
Stator	'stayer' (L), i.e. one who stops soldiers fleeing in battle
Steropegeretes	'collector of lightning' (G) (compare Asteropetes and Nephelegeretes)
Sthenius	'strong', 'mighty' (G)
Stratius	'warlike' (G) (compare Athena's by-name, Stratea)
Summus	'highest', 'chief', 'supreme' (L)
Teleius	'perfect' (G) (*telos*, 'completion'), both as one who gives perfection and who is himself perfect
Terminalis	'guardian of boundaries' (L), so worshipped before introduction of worship of Terminus (see him in Dictionary)
Terpiceraunus	'delighting in thunder' (G) (*terpo*, 'to delight' and see Ceraunius)
Tigillus	'supporter' (L) (*tigillum*, 'beam', 'log of wood', diminutive of *tignum*) (compare Centipeda and Stabilitor)
Tonans	'thundering' (L)
Trioculus	'three-eyed' (L) (see Infernalis)
Triphthalmus	'three-eyed' (G) (see Infernalis)
Tropaeuchus	'presiding over trophies' (G) (*tropaion*, 'trophy', *echo*, 'to hold')
Tropaeus	'turner' (G) (*tropaios*, 'turning', 'rout'), i.e. as one who routs enemy in battle
Ultor	'avenger', 'punisher' (L)
Uranius	'heavenly' (G) (compare Uranus in Dictionary)
Urius	'sender of favourable winds' (G) (*oura*, 'tail', 'stern')
Valens	'strong' (L)
Victor	'bringer of victory' (L)
Xenius	'presiding over hospitality' (G) (*xenos*, 'common', 'public') (compare Hospes)
Zenogonos	'preserver of life' (G) (Zen, poetic form of Zeus, *gonos*, 'child', 'race', 'birth')
Zeuxippus	'yoker of horses' (G) (*zeugos*, 'yoke', *hippos*, 'horse') (compare Zeuxippe in Dictionary)
Zoogonos	'bearer of life' (G) (*zoos*, 'living', *gonos*, 'birth')

335

APPENDIX VI

The Hounds of Actaeon

Aello	'whirlwind' (*aella*)
Agre	'hunter' (*agre*, 'catching')
Agriodos	'wild track' (*agrios*, 'wild', *odos*, 'path', 'track')
Alce	'powerful' (*alce*, 'power')
Argus	'bright', 'swift' (see Argus in Dictionary)
Asbolus	'sooty' (*asbolos*, 'soot')
Canache	'barker' (*canache*, 'ringing sound') (compare Canace in Dictionary)
Doörga	'double angry' (*doia*, 'in two ways', *orge*, 'anger')
Dorceus	'antelope' (*dorcas*), i.e. 'leaper', 'bounder' (Liddell and Scott say the antelope is 'so called from its large bright eyes', from *dercomai*, 'to look', 'gleam', and this sense could also apply to the dog)
Dromas	'runner' (*dromas*, 'running')
Harpalus	'grasper' (*harpaleos*, 'grasping'; compare Harpies in Dictionary)
Harpyea	'snatcher' (*harpazo*, 'to snatch'; compare Harpies in Dictionary)
Hylactor	'barker' (*hylao*, 'to bark', 'bay')
Hyleus	'barker' or 'brushwood' (*hylao*, 'to bark' or *hyle*, 'wood')
Ichnobates	'bramble track' (*ichnos*, 'track', 'trace', *batos*, 'bramble')
Labros	'boisterous' (*labros*)
Lachne	'shaggy' (*lachne*, 'soft woolly hair', 'down')
Lacon	'strong and tough' (literally 'Laconian', 'Lacedaemonian', 'Spartan')
Ladon	'embracer' (like Ladon, whom see in Dictionary)
Lebros	'mangy' (*lepros*) (but this unlikely name may be error for Labros)
Lelaps	'tempest' (*lailaps*) (compare famous dog Laelaps in Dictionary)
Leucite	'white' (*leucites*, same as *leucos*, 'white')
Leucos	'white' (maybe same as Leucite)
Lycisa	'wolf-like' or 'light' (*lycos*, 'wolf' or *lyce*, 'light')
Melampus	'blackfoot' (*melas*, 'black', *pous*, 'foot' (compare Melampus in Dictionary)
Melanchaetus	'black hair' (*melas*, 'black', *chaite*, 'mane')
Melaneus	'inky' (*melan*, 'ink')
Molossus	'Molossian' (name of a type of wolf-hound, originally from people of Epirus known as Molossi; compare 'Alsatian', also named for race)
Nape	'glen' (*nape*, 'woody dell') (Ovid says he was offspring of a wolf)

Nebrophonos	'deerslayer' (*nebros*, 'fawn', *phone*, 'slaughter')
Oresitrophus	'mountain-bred' (*oros*, 'mountain', *trophe*, 'rearing', 'tending')
Oribasus	'mountain ranger' (*oros*, 'mountain', *basis*, 'stepping')
Pachytus	'thick-skinned' (*pachytes*, 'thickness')
Pamphagus	'all-devouring', 'omnivorous' (*pan*, 'all', *phagein*, 'to eat')
Poemenis	'shepherd' (*poimen*, 'herdsman')
Pterelas	'feather launcher' (*pteron*, 'feather', *elasis*, 'driving') (compare Pterelas in Dictionary)
Sticte	'spot' (*stictos*, 'spotted', 'dappled')
Theridamas	'tamer of beasts' (*therion*, 'wild beast', *damazo*, 'to tame')
Theron	'beast' or 'beast slayer' (*therion*, 'wild beast' or short for *therophonos*, 'beast slayer' ('beast' could refer either to fierceness of hound or to its prey)
Thous	'eager' (*thouros*)

APPENDIX VII

Corresponding Names of Characters

Greek	Roman	Greek	Roman
Aphrodite	Venus	Hecabe	Hecuba
Ares	Mars	Helios	Sol
Artemis	Diana	Hephaestus	Vulcan
Asclepius	Aesculapius	Hera	Juno
Athena	Minerva	Heracles	Hercules
Charites	Gratiae	Hermes	Mercury
	(=Graces)	Hesperus	Vesper
Cronos	Saturn	Hestia	Vesta
Demeter	Ceres	Hyades	Suculae
Dionysus	Liber	Hypnos	Somnus
(Bacchus)	(Bacchus)	Irene	Pax
Eileithyia	Lucina	Leto	Latona
Enyo	Bellona	Nike	Victoria
Eos	Aurora	Odysseus	Ulysses
Eosphorus	Lucifer	Pan	Faunus
Erinyes (Moirai)	Furiae	Persephone	Prosperine
	(= Furies)	Polydeuces	Pollux
	(Parcae)	Poseidon	Neptune
Eris	Discordia	Rhea	Ops
Eros	Amor (Cupid)	Selene	Luna
Hades (Pluto,	Dis (Orcus)*	Tyche	Fortuna
Tartarus)		Zeus	Jupiter (Jove)
Hebe	Juventas		

* The exact correspondences here are Pluto and Dis (see these names in Dictionary)

BIBLIOGRAPHY

Allen, Richard Hinckley, *Star Names: Their Lore and Meaning*, Dover Publications, New York, 1963 [1899].

Ashley, Leonard R.N. and Hanifin, Michael J.F., 'Onomasticon of Roman Anthroponyms', in *Names: Journal of the American Name Society*, vol. 26 no. 4, December 1978.

Asimov, Isaac, *Words from the Myths*, New American Library, New York, 1969.

Born, Mrs, *Classical Manual: A Commentary, Mythological, Historical, and Geographical, on Pope's Homer, and Dryden's Aeneid of Virgil*, John Murray, London, 1829.

Boswell, Fred and Jeanetta, *What Men or Gods Are These?: A Genealogical Approach to Classical Mythology*, Scarecrow Press, Metuchen, 1980.

Camden, William, *Remains Concerning Britain*, University of Toronto Press, Toronto, 1984.

Collignon, Maxime, *Mythologie figurée de la Grèce*, A. Quantin, Paris, n.d. (1883).

Corsar, P. Kenneth *et al.*, *Discovering Greek Mythology*, Edward Arnold, London, 1977.

Cotterell, Arthur, *A Dictionary of World Mythology*, Putnam, New York, 1982.

Dimock, George E., Jr., 'The Name of Odysseus', in *Homer: A Collection of Critical Essays*, Prentice-Hall, Englewood Cliffs, 1962.

Duthie, Alexander, *Greek Mythology: A Reader's Handbook*, Oliver & Boyd, Edinburgh, 1961.

Dunkling, Leslie, and Gosling, William, *Everyman's Dictionary of First Names*, Dent, London and Melbourne, 1983.

Evans, Ivor H., *Brewer's Dictionary of Phrase and Fable*, Harper & Row, New York, 1989.

Feder, Lillian, *Apollo Handbook of Classical Literature*, Crowell, New York, 1964.

Fox, William S., *Greek and Roman Mythology*, Cooper Publishers, New York, 1964.

Gayley, Charles Mills, *The Classic Myths in English Literature*, Ginn, Boston, 1968 [1900].

Grant, Michael, *Myths of the Greeks and Romans*, World, Cleveland, 1965.

Grant, M., and Hazel, J., *Who's Who in Classical Mythology*, Hodder & Stoughton, Sevenoaks, 1979.

Graves, Robert, *The Greek Myths*, Dell, New York, 1965.

Grigson, Geoffrey, *The Goddess of Love*, Quartet Books, London, 1978.

Grimal, Pierre, *The Dictionary of Classical Mythology*, translated by A.R. Maxwell-Hyslop, Basil Blackwell, Oxford, 1986.

Guerber, H.A., *The Myths of Greece and Rome: Their Stories, Signification and Origin*, Harrap, London, 1912.

Hamilton, Edith, *Mythology*, New American Library, New York, 1969.

Hammond, N.G.L., and Scullard, H.H. (eds), *The Oxford Classical Dictionary*, Clarendon Press, Oxford, 1979.

Harrison, Jane Ellen, *Themis: A Study of the Social Origins of Greek Religion*, Merlin Press, London, 1977 [1927].

Hathorn, Richmond Y., *Crowell's Handbook to Classical Drama*, Crowell, New York, 1967.

Hendricks, Rhoda, *Classical Gods and Heroes*, William Morrow, New York, 1974.

Howatson, M.C. (ed), *The Oxford Companion to Classical Literature*, 2nd ed, Oxford University Press, Oxford, 1989.

Johnson, Charles and Sleigh, Linwood, *The Harrap Book of Boys' and Girls' Names*, George Harrap, London, 1973.

Karpenko, Yu. A., *Nazvaniya zvyozdnogo neba* ['Names of the starry sky'], Nauka, Moscow, 1981.

Keightley, Thomas, *Classical Mythology: The Myths of Ancient Greece and Ancient Italy*, revised and edited by L. Schmitz, Ares Publishers, Chicago, 1976 [1902].

Kerényi, C., *The Gods of the Greeks*, Thames & Hudson, London, 1961.

Kerényi, C., *The Heroes of the Greeks*, Thames & Hudson, London, 1978.

Kirk, G.S., *The Nature of Greek Myths*, Penguin Books, Harmondsworth, 1974.

Kolatch, Alfred J., *The Name Dictionary: Modern English and Hebrew Names*, Jonathan David, New York, 1967.

Lemprière's Classical Dictionary of Proper Names mentioned in Ancient Authors revised with additions by F.A. Wright, Routledge & Kegan Paul, London, 1972.

Levith, Murray J., *What's in Shakespeare's Names*, George Allen & Unwin, London, 1978.

Liddell, H.G., and Scott, R., *A Greek-English Lexicon*, Oxford University Press, Oxford, 1977.

Long, Harry Alfred, *Personal and Family Names: A Popular Monograph on the Origin and History of the Nomenclature of the Present and Former Times*, Hamilton, Adams, London, 1883.

Meadows, Gilbert, *An Illustrated Dictionary of Classical Mythology*, Jupiter Books, London, 1978.

Meister, K., *Lateinisch-griechische Eigennamen* ['Latin and Greek proper names'], Verlag Dr. H.A. Gerstenberg, Hildesheim, 1975 [1916].

Morford, Mark P.O., and Lenardon, Robert J., *Classical Mythology*, McKay, New York, 1971.

Naumann, Horst, *et al.*, *Das Kleine Vornamenbuch* ['The little book of first names'], VEB Bibliographisches Institut, Leipzig, 1979.

Norton, Daniel S., and Rushton, Peters, *Classical Myths in English Literature*, Holt, New York, 1952.

Ogilvie, R.M., *The Romans and Their Gods*, W.W. Norton, New York, 1970.

Palmer, Leonard R., *The Greek Language*, Faber, London, 1980.

Partridge, Eric, *Origins: A Short Etymological Dictionary of Modern English*, Routledge & Kegan Paul, London, 1978.

Petrovsky, N.A., *Slovar' russkikh lichnykh imyon* ['Dictionary of Russian personal names'], Soviet Encylopedia, Moscow, 1966.

Radice, Betty, *Who's Who in the Ancient World*, Penguin Books, Harmondsworth, 1973.

Ridpath, Ian, *Star Tales*, Universe Books, New York, 1988.

Room, Adrian, *Dictionary of Astronomical Names*, Routledge, London, 1988.

Rose, H.J., *Gods and Heroes of the Greeks*, World, Cleveland, 1958.

Rose, H.J., *A Handbook of Greek Mythology*, Methuen, London, 1978.

Rosenberg, Donna, *World Mythology*, National Textbook Company, Lincolnwood (IL), 1986.

Rybakin, A.I., *Slovar' angliyskikh lichnykh imyon* ['Dictionary of English personal names'], Soviet Encylopedia, Moscow, 1973.

Smith, William (ed), *A Dictionary of Greek and Roman Biography and Mythology by Various Writers*, John Murray, London, 1876.

Smith, Sir William, *A Smaller Latin-English Dictionary*, revised by J.F. Lockwood, John Murray, London, 1959.

Stewart, George R., *American Given Names*, Oxford University Press, New York, 1979.

Tripp, Edward, *Crowell's Handbook of Classical Mythology*, Harper & Row, New York, 1970.

Warrington, John, *Everyman's Classical Dictionary*, Dent, London, 1978.

Webb, E.J., *The Names of the Stars*, Nisbet, London, 1952.

Weekley, Ernest, *Words and Names*, John Murray, London, 1932.

Withycombe, E.G., *The Oxford Dictionary of English Christian Names*, Clarendon Press, Oxford, 1977.

Yonge, C.D., *An English-Greek Lexicon*, Longmans, Green, London, 1887.

Zimmerman, J.E., *Dictionary of Classical Mythology*, Harper & Row, New York, 1964.